D0328589

TESTING FAITH
and
TRADITION

GLOBAL MENNONITE HISTORY SERIES

The Global Mennonite History Series was initiated by Mennonite World Conference at its thirteenth Assembly held in Calcutta, India, January 1997. In order to "tell the story of Mennonite and Brethren in Christ churches" and to promote "mutual understanding, and stimulate the renewal and extension of Anabaptist Christianity world wide," the Global Mennonite History organizers received a mandate to produce a five-volume history series, with the aim of telling the stories of Mennonite and Brethren in Christ churches from around the world. The volumes, one for each continent, were to be written by persons from their respective continents, and would reflect the experiences, perspectives and interpretations of the local churches.

The volume on Africa was published in 2003, and presented at the MWC Assembly in Bulawayo, Zimbabwe. The present volume will be presented at the Mennonite European Regional Conference (MERK), meeting at Barcelona, Spain, in May, 2006. Still under preparation are individual volumes on Asia, North America and Latin America. John A. Lapp is the project coordinator for the GMHS; C. Arnold Snyder is the general editor for the Series.

Global Mennonite History Organizing Committee Members

Premanand Bagh, Asia
Gerhard Ratzlaff, Latin America
Doris Dube, Africa
Pakisa Tshimika, Africa
Adolf Ens, North America
Walter Sawatsky, North America
Alle G. Hoekema, Europe
Aristarchus Sukharto, Asia
Hanspeter Jecker, Europe
Paul T. Toews, North America
Juan Francisco Martinez, Latin America
Takanobu Tojo, Asia
Larry Miller, MWC

TESTING FAITH
and
TRADITION

GLOBAL MENNONITE HISTORY SERIES: EUROPE

Authors
Claude Baecher, Neal Blough, James Jakob Fehr, Alle G. Hoekema,
Hanspeter Jecker, John N. Klassen, Diether Götz Lichdi,
Ed van Straten, Annelies Verbeek

General Editors
John A. Lapp, C. Arnold Snyder

Good Books

Intercourse, PA 17534
800/762-7171
www.GoodBks.com

co-published with

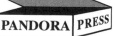

PANDORA PRESS

Kitchener, ON N2G 3R2
519/578-2381
www.pandorapress.com

Photography and Illustration Credits

Cover photograph, Taolmor; Cover photo scroll (left to right), drawing by Jan Mankes, courtesy of the Rijksprentenkabinet, Amsterdam; Mennonite Library and Archives, North Newton, KS; J. Robert Charles, Mennonite Mission Network; Claude Baecher; Rosedale Mennonite Missions; Daniel Widmer; Back cover photograph, *Road to Freedom: Mennonites Escape the Land of Suffering* (Kitchener, ON: Pandora Press, 2000).

Used by permission of the Zentralbibliothek Zürich, 4; courtesy Agape Verlag, 9, 10, 11, 17, 28, 29, 30, 100, 107, 112, 115, 117, 129, 131, 137, 143, 145, 148, 163, 205; courtesy of Mennonite Library, Amsterdam, 13, 23, 62; used by permission of Amsterdam Historical Museum, 21; Arno A. Thimm, 26, 111; used by permission Musée cantonal des Beaux-Arts de Lausanne, 31; courtesy of the University Library, University of Amsterdam, 34; Claude Baecher, 43, 171, 172, 173, 180; Bienenberg Theological Seminary collection, 45, 160, 162; *Leonhard Ragaz und der religiöse Sozialismus. Eine Biographie*, vol 1. (Zollikon: Evangelischer Verlag, 1957), 51; Alle G. Hoekema, 58, 60, 70, 76, 90, 92, 121, 274; portrait by W. B. van der Kooi, used by permission of the Fries Museum, Leeuwarden, 66; courtesy of Mennonite Library and Archives, North Newton, KS, 74, 132, 133, 134, 190, 195, 200, 202, 234; drawing by Jan Mankes, courtesy of the Rijksprentenkabinet, Amsterdam, 80; courtesy of Nationaal Archief, Netherlands, 83; courtesy of MCC archives, 86, 87, 134, 235, 270; Boudewijn Bach, 91, 102, 130; *Sie kamen als Fremde. Die Mennoniten in Krefeld von den Anfängen bis zur Gegenwart*, (Krefeld [Stadt Krefeld], 1995), 106; courtesy of Archives DZR (in Gemeentearchief, Amsterdam), 108; *Collection des costumes suisses des XXII cantons* (Bâle: Birmann et Huber, 1802/03), 153; courtesy of Schweizerischer Verein für Täufergeschichte, 154; private collections, 98, 156, 165, 227; courtesy Annie Yoder, Goshen, Indiana; photograph by Claude Baecher, 176; Raymond Eyer, 178; Claude Nardin, 179; wikipedia.com (Yekaterina II), 181; *Als ihre Zeit erfüllt war; 150 Jahre Bewährung in Russland* (Saskatoon, Sask., 1963), 188, top; *Heritage Remembered: A Pictorial Survey of Mennonites in Prussia and Russia*, 2nd ed., (CMBC Publications, 1977); 188, bottom, 205, middle; *Mennonite Encyclopedia I*, 191; courtesy of Centre for Mennonite Brethren Studies, Winnipeg, Manitoba, 197; *Lost Fatherland* (Scottdale, PA: Herald Press, 1967), 205, top; *Weltweite Bruderschaft* (Weierhof: Mennonitischer Geschichtsverein, 1995), 206; John N. Klassen, 214; *Festschrift zum 30-jährigen Gemeindejubiläum der Mennoniten-Brüdergemeinde Bielefeld* (Bielefeld), 223; *New Awakenings in an Ancient Land*, (1999), 238; courtesy Wood Green Mennonite Church, 239; courtesy the archives, Centre Mennonite de Paris, 240; Robert Witmer, 241; 249; Jeltje de Jong, 243; Rosedale Mennonite Missions, 244; Janie Blough, 253, top; Mennonite Mission Network, 253, bottom; Ed van Straten, 256, 273; courtesy of the Mennonite Congregation Haarlem/Noord-Hollands Archief, 259; *Wederdopers, menisten, doopsgezinden in Nederland* (Zutphen: Walburg, 1980), 262; *Doopsgezind Jaarboekje 1979*, 265; Fokke Fennema, 284.

Maps designed by Cliff Snyder

Design by Cliff Snyder

TESTING FAITH AND TRADITION
Copyright © 2006 by Good Books, Intercourse, Pennsylvania 17534
ISBN-10: 1-56148-550-0
ISBN-13: 978-1-56148-550-5

Table of Contents

Foreword

One of the special joys of the Global Mennonite History is the involvement of many people in organizing, researching, and writing a fresh history. This is especially evident in this volume on Mennonites in Europe with nine writers, including the editors. They have worked, even struggled, together in constructing a remarkable and engaging story. We are exceedingly grateful for the unique insights and contributions of each writer.

Although the oldest global Mennonite communities are in Europe, this is the first time representatives of these major church bodies on this continent have cooperated in producing a shared narrative. The editors of this volume—Alle G. Hoekema and Hanspeter Jecker, well-established historians in their own right—have nurtured and encouraged a team of researcher-writers to produce a fine book in a timely fashion. These editors represent in themselves two major streams of Anabaptist-Mennonite history in Europe from the sixteenth century to the present, namely the Dutch and the Swiss Mennonite traditions.

As the editors point out in their preface, this volume benefits from the historical work done by a much larger group of historians. We join in thanking all persons involved for participating in this highly communal project. We also thank the European Mennonite Conferences for underwriting this volume financially. While the writers and editors contributed their time to this effort, there were travel, translation, and publication costs that were met by conference bodies in France, Germany, the Netherlands, and Switzerland. A number of individuals and several foundations in Europe and North America who have contributed to the Global Mennonite History also assisted in publication and translation costs.

We are enthusiastic about the story recorded here. Like each of the volumes in this series, this makes an important contribution to understanding a significant part of the global Mennonite and Brethren in Christ movement. Loss and decline are conspicuous motifs, but visible too is the vision, faith, and hope that characterizes the church everywhere, and that leads to renewal and new life.

The preface notes the much lamented deaths of two writers enroute to the completion of this project. We conclude with the words of one of these, Sjouke Voolstra, who observed that Anabaptist and Mennonite history is significant to the degree that, like the biblical record, it points us to "God's promises which have not yet been fulfilled in the world." There will yet be more history to come through Mennonite participation in the revitalized Christian movement in Europe.

John A. Lapp and C. Arnold Snyder,
Global Mennonite History Series Editors

Preface

by Hanspeter Jecker and Alle G. Hoekema

Over the years Anabaptist-Mennonite history and theology has been a predominantly European and North American affair. Anabaptism had its beginnings in Europe in the sixteenth century, and in spite of all the affliction showered on its followers, it experienced its first blossoming in Europe. No later than the nineteenth century, however, its centre of balance shifted with the countless waves of emigrants from Europe who relocated to North America. Nevertheless, the Anabaptist-Mennonite landscape continued to be shaped by people who had their roots in European soil, and who continued to cultivate the memory of these roots.

Thus well into the twentieth century, the typical, dyed-in-the-wool Mennonite was Caucasian, spoke German (Swiss-, Palatinate- or Low-German—or "at least" some related form of Dutch or Pennsylvania Dutch) and possessed a genealogy connecting him or her with the context of an Anabaptist pioneer like a Conrad Grebel in Switzerland's Zürich, or that of a Menno Simons in the Netherlands' Friesland. These characteristics remained in force even when Anabaptist descendants had long been settled on the Asian-Siberian steppe or the South American Chaco in order to seek their livelihood.

But now the times have changed. At the beginning of the twenty-first century, the typical member of an Anabaptist-Mennonite congregation no longer lives predominantly in the northern hemisphere, but rather in the southern hemisphere; most Anabaptist-Mennonites no longer speak a German dialect, but a multitude of international languages.

Thus the pursuit of Anabaptist-Mennonite history and theology is no longer the exclusive domain of specialists from Europe and North America. Justifiably, the increasingly diverse members in the younger Anabaptist-Mennonite churches in Asia, Africa and Latin America are inquiring more and more about the specific historical, theological and spiritual accents of the tradition to which their congregations belong today. They would like to know the history of their own national, continental and worldwide Anabaptist-Mennonite congregations and conferences. And furthermore, they would like to hear more about the history of those Anabaptist-Mennonite churches in Europe and North America which for generations have sent missionaries and relief-workers to their countries and regions in the south.

The Mennonite World Conference has responded to this interest with the Global Mennonite History Project (GMHP). The purpose of this project is "to tell the story of Mennonite and Brethren in Christ churches in their regional and global relationships with the goal of nurturing a sense of belonging together, promoting mutual under-standing, and stimulating the renewal and extension of Anabaptist Christianity world wide."

This Europe volume marks the second publication of the Global Mennonite History Project. The first volume in this series told the story of Mennonite and Brethren in Christ churches on the African continent, and was published in 2003. In contrast to the volumes on Africa, Asia and Latin America, the Europe volume can draw, at least in part, upon a wealth of previously-researched materials. But this vol-ume additionally contains contributions to topics and themes which have—in recent years or until now—scarcely received attention, but are of great interest from the perspective of the global Mennonite community. Thus this volume weaves together into a new synthesis many well-known dates and facts, along with numerous freshly-won insights and current questions. The book is addressed not primarily to specialists in Anabaptist-Mennonite history, but rather to interested members and friends of the worldwide Anabaptist-Mennonite fellow-ship, and other interested readers. Yet it also contains information and portrayals which will be new and helpful for specialists, and which cannot be found in this form anywhere else.

Since 2000 we—Alle G. Hoekema (Haarlem, Netherlands) and Hanspeter Jecker (Bienenberg, Switzerland)—have been working as the designated editors of this volume. Our task was to develop an overall plan for this publication and to enlist various authors for the writing of individual chapters. At workshops of several days' duration in Strasbourg (2003) and Paris (2005), the project was discussed ex-tensively with contributing authors, anticipated articles were reviewed individually and new tasks assigned. With numerous telephone conver-sations, letters and e-mails as well as multiple regional meetings, this endeavour pressed ahead and moved toward completion. Significant problems arose with the unexpected deaths of two especially competent authors: Peter Foth (April 2004) and Sjouke Voolstra (October 2004). Beyond the sorrow and mourning related to the sudden loss of these two valued friends and companions, we had the additional problem of finding individuals who might take over responsibility for the corresponding sections of this volume. As editors we are extremely thankful to have found very competent contributors for the chapters on northern Germany and the Netherlands in the persons of James Jakob Fehr and Annelies Verbeek (the latter supported by the collaboration of Alle G. Hoekema). With their able help, we are very pleased to be able to present the completed Europe volume to an interested public. The following notes serve as a prefix for the book that follows.

The time-frame for the present project—from 1850 to the present—seemed to us to require first an introductory survey of the Anabaptist-Mennonite story from its beginnings to 1850. This introductory chapter was written by Diether Götz Lichdi (chapter I). In the second place, we thought it important to sketch the political, economic, social and religious contexts in Europe, so that readers might gain a better understanding of more recent Mennonite history. For this purpose it seemed necessary to begin with the profound upheavals of the French Revolution (1789) rather than with the year 1850. This introduction was written by Claude Baecher (chapter II).

Following these introductory chapters, the history of Anabaptist-Mennonite churches in Europe is presented in the main part of this volume, by country or by region. This approach has both strengths and weaknesses. It does justice to the fact that Anabaptist-Mennonite existence in Europe has always been intensely affected by different national and political contexts, and thus also has had to develop unique accents and responses to concrete historical challenges. However, it was also important not to lose sight of the solidarity of Anabaptist-Mennonite congregational conferences—in part stronger in earlier years than later—reaching beyond national borders. This dual concern led to some unavoidable overlap in the presentation. However it had the advantage of making explicit the international dimension of Anabaptist-Mennonite existence and theology.

The regional presentation begins with a longer chapter on the Netherlands, which was compiled by Annelies Verbeek and Alle G. Hoekema (chapter III), followed by a similarly extensive chapter on Germany. For the period extending to 1933, the text is divided into sub-sections on north Germany, West Prussia and south Germany. This geographical partitioning is dropped for the period after 1933 in order to better reflect the increasingly shared commonalities of all Germans and the growing sense of German-Mennonite together-ness. The authorship of this chapter is shared by Diether Götz Lichdi and James Jakob Fehr (chapter IV). Diether G. Lichdi also authored the shorter chapters on Switzerland and France (chapters V and VI) with the support of contributions from Hanspeter Jecker (V) and Claude Baecher (VI). John N. Klassen's recounting of the history of Mennonites in Russia and their migration back to Germany contains much material which has not been published previously, particularly on the recent migration and resettlement (chapter VII).

The pattern of regionally-divided narration of the historical development of European Mennonites is discontinued with the two concluding chapters of this volume. In the section on "Mission Ef-forts in Europe," Neal Blough presents the recent church-planting and missionary initiatives undertaken by Mennonite conferences and mission agencies (chapter VIII). The concluding chapter by Ed van Straten discusses a series of current issues with which all Anabaptist-Mennonite conferences have had to struggle in recent years—in part, regionally defined, but also as part of their shared, larger European context (chapter IX). Finally, this Europe-volume is rounded off with an Epilogue, a reflection by the editors on the way ahead, together with an appendix containing historical time-lines, a directory of Men-nonite conferences in Europe, a bibliography, and an index.

We wish to especially thank each of the authors for their valuable collaboration; this volume would not have come into being without them. The variety of perspectives, accents, and interpretative ap-proaches represented in their contributions impressively reflects the variety present in Anabaptist-Mennonite reality in Europe today. As editors, we were very careful not to level out differing emphases and interpretations, or to harmonize and sort out overlapping points. Edges and corners as well as intense controversies have always been noticeably present throughout the history of Mennonites in Europe, and they must not be swept under the table in a narration of this story. But it should also be appreciated that despite the many painful divisions (some of which reach into the present!) and beyond the fre-quent indifferent and self-righteous parallel existences of Anabaptist-Mennonite groups in Europe, there also are many hopeful signs and efforts pointing towards a growing sense of togetherness. One of these signs is the writing of this common Europe volume!

The present book would not have been possible without the multifaceted support of a large number of individuals and institutions. For financial contributions we would like to thank the Mennonite World Conference, the Oosterbaan Foundation, as well as a series of Mennonite conferences and historical societies in Europe. For longer and shorter proof-reading assignments and for valuable additions, corrections and suggestions, we thank Claude Baecher, Robert Baecher, Neal Blough, Frédéric de Coninck, Herbert Hege, Lydie Hege, Hans-Adolf Hertzler, Kurt Kerber, Andrea Lange, Piet Visser, Marie-Noëlle von der Recke-Faure, Johannes Reimer, and Michel Ummel. For the translation of the text from German and French into English, we thank Luci Driedger, Dennis Slabaugh, Janie Blough, James Jakob Fehr, Anita Lichdi, Dean Kunkle, Arnold Neufeldt-Fast, Walter Sawatsky, and Victor Duerksen.

We also wish to thank all who assisted us in the search for illustrations and in obtaining publishing rights, especially the Agape-Verlag, the Mennonite Central Committee, as well as Bethel College (Newton, KS). For producing maps and for attending to the many minute design and editorial details of publication we thank above all the team at Pandora Press in Kitchener, Ontario, especially Arnold and Clifford Snyder for their diligent work.

In the Preface to the Africa-volume the following statement by Roman Catholic missiologist Walbert Bühlmann was cited: "The 'Third Church' [= the church of the global South] needs the second [= the Euro-American church] for support and the second needs the third for renewal." The present Europe volume gives witness that in the course of its history, European Anabaptism was both an "exporter" of renewal and also often a recipient (or at least needy) of renewal in its history, and in the present as well. We hope that this volume will make a supportive contribution to the Anabaptist-Mennonite churches in the south—that with a knowledge of the strengths and weaknesses of European Anabaptism, their own witness may be strengthened, refined and deepened; and that the awareness of a common journey may grow. Furthermore, if this volume enables us in the northern hemisphere to become more clearly aware of the journey we have made and why we are where we are, then there is good reason to hope that with an enhanced knowledge of the past and a better understanding of the present we will also be inspired in our own struggles toward a more credible, more inviting and more united witness for Christ for the future.

Translation: Arnold Neufeldt-Fast

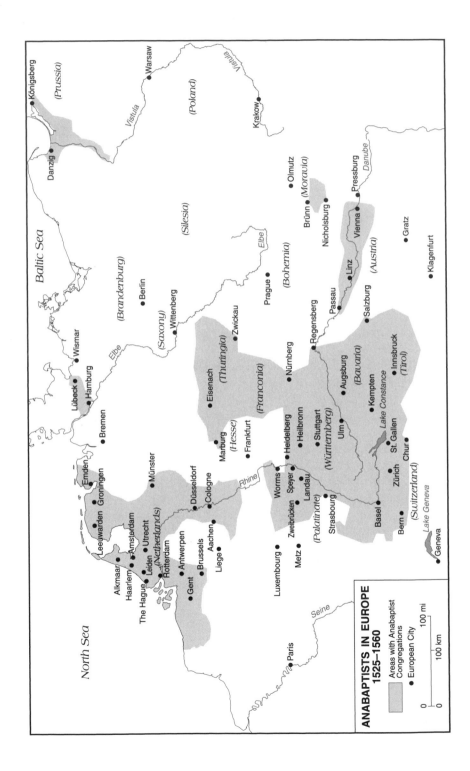

ANABAPTISTS IN EUROPE
1525–1560

Areas with Anabaptist
Congregations

• European City

0   100 mi
0   100 km

An Overview of Anabaptist-Mennonite History, 1525–1800

by Diether Götz Lichdi

New Beginnings and Survival—The Anabaptist Movement (1525–1618)

There are approximately 200 Mennonite and related conferences and groups among the spiritual descendants of the sixteenth-century Anabaptists. The Anabaptist movement arose after disagreements with the Reformation of Zwingli and Luther. The Anabaptist groups agreed in their rejection of the former churches and in their criticism of the emerging churches of the Reformation era; they agreed that churches should be formed by adults who were baptized on confession of faith. Nevertheless, they held a variety of convictions: some were biblicists, others awaited the return of Christ in the near future, while some had mystical roots and trusted deeply in the moving of the Holy Spirit. In addition, differing regional and political conditions played an important role in creating Anabaptist differences. Researchers have counted between thirty and forty different kinds of Anabaptist groups during the decade preceding the catastrophe of Münster.

In the last century and a half, historians have used the terms "Anabaptists" and the "Anabaptist movement" in the desire to use a neutral term. Contemporaries in the sixteenth century and thereafter labelled the deviants "Anabaptists"[1] and thus pinned an ancient ecclesiastical condemnation on them. Many of the afflicted, however, called themselves *Brüder in Christo* (Brothers in Christ), *Bondgenoten* (allies, confederates) or *Doopsgezinden/Taufgesinnte* (literally: baptism-minded). Others called them *Menisten*, from which the name Mennonites is derived. It took about 150 years for the term *Mennonites* to become the accepted name for this independent group, at which point the Mennonites in south Germany[2] also called themselves by this name.

All religious dissidents and critics were slandered and excluded from society by being labelled *Anabaptists*, during the Reformation and also thereafter. We come upon this term in many sources without being certain about the convictions that accompany it. This abusive word was used as a name tag for critics within the church as well as for some Pietists, in order to avoid having to converse with them.

Only a few Anabaptist groups survived persecution and expulsion. After the Thirty Years' War (1618–1648) there were three groups: the largest groups by far were (1) the *Doopsgezinden* and Mennonites in the Netherlands and West Prussia; (2) the Swiss Brethren in parts of Switzerland, Alsace and southwest Germany, who barely survived, as well as (3) the Hutterites, who were driven out of Slovakia to Transylvania. All the other groups disappeared.

Preconditions for the Reformation

The Environment and its General Conditions

The political and social scene in Europe changed around 1500. Spain, with its colonies in Latin America, the Netherlands, Austria, parts of south Germany, Hungary, Bohemia and Moravia, all belonged to the empire of Charles V of the Catholic house of Hapsburg. The German rulers built their territorial rule with a unified judicial and monetary system. The economic standard of living had recovered after the great plague epidemics of the fourteenth century; agricultural production grew with the population; craft production rose in the cities, and in some areas mining led to great prosperity. Many free imperial cities, which were responsible only to the Emperor, became centres of trade and culture. Because "city air makes one free," cities like Strasbourg, Augsburg, Nuremberg or Amsterdam attracted people who were eager for education and who were adventurous. The preachers who occupied positions founded and funded by the city councils, usually supported reforming endeavours.

Horizons were greatly broadened by the voyages of discovery of Columbus and Vasco da Gama. From the time the New World was discovered and the passage was found around Africa to the mysterious lands of the far East, the known world had grown. The supply of goods, knowledge and possibilities expanded within a few years and provided a new picture of the world, changing trading patterns and the economy of Europe. Prosperity such as had never been known before came to Europe.

The Intellectual Turning Point

Copernicus' discovery that the earth revolves around the sun questioned the church's geocentric view of the world, in which the earth was seen as a disc located between heaven and hell. With advances in astronomy, science began to develop, at first through experiments but also with the help of rational deduction.

During these years the legacy of ancient times was newly discovered. The precondition for this was the cultivation of the Greek language, which occurred through its dissemination by refugees from Constantinople, and renewed access to the Hebrew language. The publication of a Hebrew dictionary and grammar by Johannes Reuchlin (1506) and the publication of the New Testament in original Greek by Erasmus of Rotterdam (1516) were milestones. Without these aids, Bible translations into vernacular languages would not have been possible.

In addition, printed books replaced hand-copied texts. The new technique of printing with movable type made it possible to produce an uncountable number of books. As a result, texts and books circulated quickly in many languages. The knowledge of Latin, the language in which books had been published earlier, was no longer absolutely necessary. Thus, everyone could read about the new discoveries and ideas in their native languages. The quickly-swelling flood of books encountered a great eagerness to read among all social strata. The Reformation would not have been conceivable without the spread of printed books in the vernacular languages.

The wave of enlightenment called Humanism not only promoted the knowledge of the ancient languages, but also contributed to changing the self-consciousness of people. Old wisdom was no longer simply accepted but was now subjected to scrutiny; many convictions were publicly exposed as superstitions, and religious theories as well as traditional convictions were questioned.

The Roman church had long been criticized. Its many abuses had been denounced in literature and at numerous councils as early as the fifteenth century. A widespread anger was directed at the fiscal policy of the Pope, the Bishops, and the monasteries, and many chastised the moral lapses of the priests. A common complaint was that many pastorates were run only by administrators, while the pastor himself enjoyed his benefice or devoted his time to other tasks. Finally, the anger about the buying of indulgences[3] brought the anti-ecclesiastical mood to a climax.

"German Mysticism" had developed since the fourteenth century. It originated among the spiritually lively Dominicans along the upper Rhine Valley. The mystic felt a "spark within his soul" because God shared himself with that person's soul. If human beings would give themselves unconditionally to God in "serenity," then God would unite with them. The human being would experience God directly in the soul. Perhaps for this reason some mystics tended not to accept the authority of the church hierarchy. Influences of mysticism can be observed in various reformed movements. They also became visible later among the south German Anabaptists and the Hutterites.

In the Kingdom of Bohemia, the sermons of professor Jan Hus (ca. 1370–1415) from Prague, led to the Hussite and Taborite movements. Hus had accused the church of the accumulation of wealth and criticized its practice of the Mass. After a sensational trial in Constance, Hus was burned at the stake; his martyr's death led to uprisings in Bohemia. The Taborites, who wanted to establish God's kingdom with violence, were defeated; the congregations of the Bohemian Brethren, who strove for a renewal of life based on the New Testament and the re-establishment of the Early Church, survived.

Early Reformation pamphlet "Description of the divine mill" (1521): Christ pours the grain in the shape of the biblical evangelists into the funnel of the mill. The humanist Erasmus of Rotterdam fills the flour into the bag, from which the reformer Martin Luther bakes loaves of bread in the form of Bibles. Huldrych Zwingli passes these on to the clerics, who want to know nothing of it. In the background Karsthans, the embodiment of the "common man," swings his threshing instrument threateningly: the peasants are ready to support the reformation even with rebellion! A two-line title comments: Two Swiss farmers have made this (picture)—they indeed have had a good insight.

In the cities of the Netherlands, the lower Rhine Valley, and in east Friesland, that is, in the important areas in which Anabaptism later spread, a partly monastic lay movement under the name of *Devotio Moderna* (the "Modern Devotion") spread during the fifteenth century. These "brothers of the common life" preached a pious life in imitation of Christ. The influential devotional book, *The Imitation of Christ* (*Imitatio Christi*) by Thomas à Kempis, emerged from this setting and is recognized as the most-read Christian book before the Reformation. Also in the Netherlands the critique of the official teachings of the sacraments of the church strongly increased and led to protests before the Reformation; in retrospect, historians have called this the "Sacramentarian Movement."

The Reformation

The complex event called the Reformation was begun and furthered by many people in their own spheres of activity. From small beginnings a great movement soon arose in which people of all kinds came together, with a variety of motivations. They were influenced by the rediscovery of the Bible and resentment toward the Roman Church.

One of the most important standard-bearers was Martin Luther (1483–1546), professor at the new university in Wittenberg. This Augustinian monk was searching for a "gracious God" because he was tormented by the knowledge of his sins. One of the fundamental discoveries for him was one of Paul's sentences in Romans (1:17): In the Gospel "the righteousness of God is revealed through faith to faith, as is written, 'He who is righteous will live by faith.'" With this understanding he rejected the church's teaching of salvation, which expected sins to be forgiven through the cooperation of good works of penance by believers, or through the added merit of the saints. If the important thing was simply forgiveness by God's grace alone, then the church's role in communicating grace through the sacraments was brought into question. The famous Ninety-five Theses (1517), which initiated the public events of the Reformation, dealt with the saving power claimed for letters of indulgence, which technically were part of the sacrament of penance. Luther's most important concerns can be described by three slogans:

a) *solus Christus* (Christ alone): Salvation is granted directly by the death and resurrection of Jesus Christ. As Lord of the church, Christ needs no representative and no mediator. He alone is the foundation and the reason for faith.

b) *sola fide* (by faith alone): Before God's countenance, humanity recognizes its vanity and sinfulness. God turns to the person in grace and does not take one's sins into account. Through faith, human beings claim God's forgiveness. The important thing is faith first of all, faith which then will bear fruit.

c) *sola scriptura* (Scripture alone): God reveals His will in the Scriptures and nowhere else, neither in the traditions of the church nor in the spirit or the soul of man. Luther freed himself from traditional allegorical scriptural interpretations and sought the original and direct meaning of the biblical texts. Thus, the preached Word of God became central in Protestant worship, instead of sacraments administered by priests.

The Beginnings of Anabaptism in Zürich: The Grebel Circle

Zwingli and His Students

The beginning of the Reformation by the people's priest in Zürich, Huldrych Zwingli (1484–1531) differed from Luther's. As a preacher, Zwingli gathered a growing number of listeners around him at the Grossmünster in Zürich. He invited theologians and humanists, i.e. people with whom he could read both Testaments in their original languages, to attend Bible studies. Among them were the humanists Conrad Grebel, the son of a Zürich patrician, Felix Mantz, a sought-after classical scholar, the bookseller Andreas Castelberger, and the priest Ludwig Haetzer. Together with others these early students of Zwingli later initiated the Anabaptist movement.

In November, 1522, Zwingli resigned from the priesthood in order to become independent of the orders of church officials. The city council immediately called him to be the preacher of the Grossmünster: he was to preach the Word freely and without hindrance. The first Disputation of Zürich in March, 1523, publicly stated that Zwingli's preaching was to be in accordance with the Scriptures. The second Disputation of Zürich in October, 1523, came to the conclusion that the Mass should be reformed; it proclaimed that the Mass actually is not a sacrifice but a memorial of Christ's death and resurrection. However, Zwingli did not want to push for changes in practice without the confirmation of the conservative council. He felt that *mine Herren* ("My Lords") would recognize in which form and with what understanding the Mass should be celebrated in the future. This was the first obvious difference of opinion between Zwingli and some of his followers, for example, Conrad Grebel and Felix Mantz. Grebel and Mantz pushed to have a congregation of true believers and wanted to celebrate worship services strictly according to the Word as they understood it. But everything remained as it was. They knew that they agreed with Zwingli in principle, but they could not enforce their ideas. Zwingli shared the medieval idea that the citizenry and the church were identical and, therefore, he did everything possible in order to avoid breaking them apart. Grebel and his brethren did not want biblical reform to conform to political and social restrictions. They began to meet together privately to study the questions which concerned them, without direction from Zwingli.

The Creation of the Grebel Circle
After the Disputation in October, 1523, Grebel and his friends agreed that their newly-won knowledge should take visible form, but it remained unclear how this should happen. After difficult discussions, two tendencies became clear. One group, coming especially, but not exclusively, from rural communities and represented by their pastors and spiritual leaders (like Simon Stumpf, Wilhelm Reublin and Johannes Brötli), strove for a more populist, local, village-based solution. These rural communities sought to avoid the authority of the council and Grossmünster and attempted to control the reform of the churches in their own communities. A second group, with leaders like Conrad Grebel and Felix Mantz, living in the city of Zürich, proposed more separatist or "free church" solutions. Both interpretations depended on the preconditions and the people involved, but in the context of these on-going discussions, the lay groups associated with Grebel and Mantz re-thought their position. The results are seen in a letter written to Thomas Müntzer in September, 1524, which expresses a new understanding of communion, baptism and the structure of worship. Grebel complained about the Zürich preachers who were "stuck in their old ways." With his criticism of a church dominated by pastors, he advocated the opinion that lay people could achieve better results by reading the Bible than by listening to the theologians.

The Grebel circle understood itself as a minority, and wrote to Müntzer: "We are not even twenty people who believe God's word... if you have to suffer because of it, you certainly know that it cannot be otherwise. Christ has to suffer more in his members." These few people saw themselves called "to build up a Christian community with the help of Christ and his rule (Matt. 18:15–20)." This Christian community would not be identified with the city or the countryside; rather it would be a community of a few called-out people, who "truly believed and lived with virtue" and according to the ways of the Early Church. This community renounced spreading its convictions through anything other than evangelism: "he who doesn't want to believe…, shouldn't be … killed, but should rather be seen as a heathen or a tax collector and left like that." On the other hand, "one shouldn't protect the Gospel and its followers with a sword and they themselves shouldn't either." This was the first time that defencelessness showed itself as a Christian attitude. Grebel and his brothers knew that they were endangered as a minority because "truly believing Christians (are) sheep among wolves, also they use neither worldly swords nor war. For them, killing is totally abolished."

In the fall of 1524, the discussion about the correct form of baptism began. In December, Mantz presented a letter of justification to the Council in which he claimed infant baptism to be unbiblical, and challenged Zwingli to a disputation. The "purpose of baptism" is that "everyone who should be baptized, who becomes a better person, takes on new life, dies to sin, will be buried with Christ and be resurrected with Him to a renewed life through baptism." The Council set the date for a public disputation for January 17, 1525, at which time the biblical case for and against infant baptism would be presented. The result was pre-determined right from the start; the council and Zwingli had agreed among themselves that the troublemakers should be put in their place. The arguments of the Grebel Circle were rejected and the council ordered all infants to be baptized within eight days of their birth. Whoever did not follow this order was to be banished within eight days.

Baptism following Confession of Faith
and Communion among Brothers and Sisters
On the evening of the same day (January 21, 1525) the Grebel circle met in Felix Mantz' house in the Neustadtgasse to talk about how to proceed. After a long period of consultation and prayer, Georg Blaurock, a priest from Graubünden who had recently joined the group, asked Grebel to baptize him. He did, and then Blaurock baptized Mantz and about ten other people. Baptism was "a symbol that one had died to one's sins and would remain so, walking in a new life and spirit." Later on, it also meant that the baptized person became part of the church, which was seen as the visible body of Christ.

The next day, Conrad Grebel celebrated the first communion of the Anabaptist movement in Jakob Hottinger's house in Zollikon, together with a gathering of like-minded people. It was a simple communion:

Grebel read one text about communion and preached about it. The participants sat around one table; a plain loaf of bread was in the middle as well as a pitcher of wine. Both were passed around the circle. The participants took part in communion with the intention "that they henceforth would lead and keep living a Christian life." They wanted to "have God in their hearts at all times and think about Him." Others called the communion "a bread of love," a "symbol of peace." They really did not have a different interpretation of communion than did Zwingli. It was celebrated as a remembrance of salvation through Christ and as an incentive for preaching. Communion was a symbol of fellowship and emphasized the ties among brothers and sisters.

In the week after the first baptisms, the first Anabaptist congregation came into being in Zollikon. At the same time, the revival movement had reached the neighbouring communities. Soon there were arrests, and with them came the end of the new congregations.

Expansion through Exile

The Anabaptists were driven out of Zürich and its surroundings. They travelled through the country, evangelized, and talked with relatives and acquaintances, among whom they could expect to find listening ears and open hearts. The first men who were baptized did not long survive the baptismal event. Felix Mantz was drowned in the Limmat River, near Lake Zürich, on January 5, 1527. In 2004, a plaque was placed there as a public memorial of the martyrdom. Conrad Grebel apparently died because of the plague; Haetzer and Blaurock were publicly burned at the stake.

Place of the drowning of Felix Mantz in the Limmat river in Zürich.

After their expulsion, Wilhelm Reublin and Johannes Brötli left Zürich and travelled to the Klettgau, between Schaffhausen and Waldshut; together they started an Anabaptist church in Hallau.

Reublin made contact with the preacher from Waldshut, Dr. Balthasar Hubmaier, and was able to fire his interest in an Anabaptist Reformation. At Easter, 1525, Hubmaier and sixty citizens of Waldshut were baptized by Reublin, and soon after about 300 people from Waldshut were baptized, among them most of the council members. However, after the victory of the Swabian League (*Schwäbischer Bund*) over the army of the peasants, Waldshut also had to give up its Reformation and capitulate to the arrival of Hapsburg troops.

Portrait of Balthasar Hubmaier (1480?–1528), vice-chancellor of the University of Ingolstadt, preacher in Regensburg and pastor in Waldshut before he joined the Anabaptist movement to become one of its major theologians.

Hubmaier, who escaped Waldshut, travelled via Zürich and Augsburg, arriving in Nikolsburg (Mikulov), Moravia in April 1526, where Count Leonhart of Liechtenstein had offered a homeland to refugees of faith. They were to help rebuild the land which had been exhausted during the Turkish wars. With Liechtenstein's support, Hubmaier was able to establish an Anabaptist Reformation. Nikolsburg and Hubmaier became the focus for a large people's movement. Around 1527, some 12,000 Anabaptists, mostly refugees, lived in Nikolsburg. This surge in membership led to some public differences of opinion. Under the influence of the Swiss Brethren, a group formed in opposition to Hubmaier. They criticized his cooperation with the authorities and urged defenselessness. Along with the *Schwertlern* ("sword bearers") under Hubmaier's influence, more and more *Stäbler* ("staff bearers") could be found in Nikolsburg. In the late summer of 1527, Hubmaier was arrested by the "Anabaptist hunters" of the Archduke Ferdinand of Austria (the later King and Holy Roman Emperor). Hubmaier was burned at the stake in Vienna on March 10, 1528, charged with heresy and high treason.

The Swiss Brethren

Michael Sattler and the Schleitheim Articles

After Grebel's early death, the drowning of Mantz, Blaurock's retreat into the mountains, and Hubmaier's removal to Moravia, the existence of the "Brethren in Christ" in Switzerland was endangered. All attempts to establish an Anabaptist Reformation in Switzerland had failed. Many Anabaptists were unnerved and intimidated by the energetic action of the authorities. In this situation, Michael Sattler (ca. 1489–1527) took on a significant leadership role. He had been the prior of the Benedictine monastery of St. Peter's of the Black Forest and had joined Anabaptists in the course of the year 1525. He was active as a missionary in the Zürich lowlands, in Lahr, and in Strasbourg. Early in 1527, he summoned his fellow believers to an assembly at Schleitheim in the Randen mountain chain in the region of Schaffhausen. At Schleitheim, those present "united" in a confession that became constitutive for the Swiss Brethren. It describes the "path into separation" as the fate of a Christian congregation.

In the "brotherly union," the remnant of the persecuted came together, borne by the consciousness of election. This "tiny flock" consulted and agreed upon principles that became the constitution of a Free Church, as it would be called today. The consequence was the founding of congregations free from governmental and societal influence, and also free from ecclesiastical paternalism and clerical domination. In this sense, Schleitheim represents the first step from an unstructured, lay protest movement toward an organized "Free Church."[4] The Swiss Brethren organized themselves and grew stronger with the Schleitheim Articles. The "brotherly union" also meant a turning away from the attempt to impose an Anabaptist Reformation according to the model of the established church.

Sattler, his wife, and several other Anabaptists were arrested in Horb on the Neckar River several days after the Schleitheim meeting by henchmen of Archduke Ferdinand. After an imprisonment of two months, a brutal judgment was pronounced: "In the matter between the advocate of His Imperial Majesty

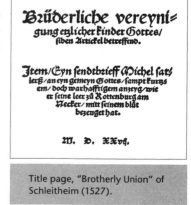

Title page, "Brotherly Union" of Schleitheim (1527).

and Michael Sattler, it has been found, and rightly so, that Michael Sattler should be given into the hands of the hangman. The latter shall lead him to the public square and there, first of all, cut off his tongue, then chain him to the wagon, tear his body twice with red-hot tongs, and do so again five more times on the way to the place of execution. Thereafter, he shall burn his body to powder, as is done with an arch-heretic." In his farewell letter to the congregation at Horb, Sattler expressed his conviction "that the day of the Lord might not be delayed any further." He died on the gallows in Rottenburg on May 20, 1527. His wife Margaretha, who also refused to recant, was drowned in the Neckar river two days later. On Pentecost Monday, 1997, on the 470th anniversary of this martyrdom, a monument was unveiled in Rottenburg. Mennonites, Baptists, Lutheran and Catholic Christians gathered together on this occasion for a memorial worship service in the St. Moriz Catholic Church to remember Michael Sattler as a father in the faith.

The Mennonites

In the Beginning were the Melchiorites
The Reformation in the Netherlands began with the "prophet" Melchior Hoffman (ca. 1495/1500–1543), who had begun his Reformation activities as a lay Lutheran preacher. He was the most successful lay preacher of the Reformation era and brought the Anabaptist movement to east Friesland and the Netherlands—of course, in a different form than it had existed previously. His preaching sparked a mass movement. Hoffman came to believe in the freedom of the human will against Luther's doctrine of justification and, as a consequence, advocated baptism upon confession of faith. Along with this, he developed his incarnational doctrine of the "celestial flesh of Christ" that passed through Mary like "water through a pipe," and thus received no "accursed Adam's flesh" from her.

Hoffman arrived in Emden, the commercial centre of the county of Frisia, in May, 1530. His preaching in the *Groote Kerk* (Great Church) in Emden triggered enthusiastic approval. He is said to have baptized more than three hundred persons as "comrades in the covenant with Jesus Christ." The congregation he left behind still exists today and can look back upon an unbroken tradition. From Emden, Hoffman sent out "apostolic messengers" to the Netherlands; the seed he sowed there fell upon fertile soil. In June, 1533, he was thrown into the tower in Strasbourg and died there after ten years of imprisonment, worn down, plagued by sickness, and abandoned by his followers.

The Anabaptist Kingdom of Münster

In 1534, some of Hoffman's followers used a political opportunity to oust the Bishop of Münster, in Westphalia, and established an Anabaptist Reformation in that city. The Bishop thereupon summoned aid and besieged Münster. The rule of the Anabaptists quickly degenerated under the external pressure, and turned increasingly repressive. Expropriations, polygamy, and a reign of terror took place in the besieged city which, after a year's time, fell by an act of betrayal to the besiegers, who then exacted a bloody judgment of their own upon the Anabaptists. The "Anabaptist Kingdom of Münster" defined the image of the Anabaptists for the next 250 years because all baptizing dissidents were identified with the terrible scenes that occurred in Münster.

Menno Simons becomes the Leading Figure

In spite of this catastrophe, however, the Anabaptist movement was not at an end. Many Melchiorite groups gathered anew in the following years. One of these groups was led by the brothers Obbe and Dirk Philips; a priest named Menno Simons (1496–1561), from Witmarsum in Friesland, joined them. He was baptized and installed as elder in 1537. As a point of departure for his further work, he chose Paul's confession in 1 Corinthians 3:11: "For no one can lay a foundation other than the one which is laid, which is Jesus Christ." He began with the gathering and renewal of the Melchiorites in east Frisia, where everything had started, and then worked in north Germany and in the Cologne area. He died in 1561 at Wüstenfelde, near Oldesloe, where he had operated a printing press in his last years. This house, the "Mennokate," can still be visited today. It commemorates the man whose name was given as early as 1544 to peaceful Anabaptists, the man who developed into the outstanding figure among

Menno Simons (1496–1561). At the occasion of the commemoration of Menno's 500th birth year, the Dutch artist Aizo Betten composed a new portrait of Menno, based upon the existing engraving of Christoffel van Sichem (1607; the first known portrait of Menno, done 45 years after his death) and a woodcarving by Warren Rohrer (1961).

the second generation of Anabaptists in the Netherlands and north Germany.

Menno's thought is recorded in his early major work *The Foundation of Christian Doctrine* (1539), the so-called "Foundation Book": "The entire matter and the whole of true Christianity is rebirth, or a new creation, true repentance, dying to sin, and a new walk in life, righteousness, obedience, blessedness, and eternal life in an upright, active faith." His doctrine was aimed primarily at the practical demonstration of faith in the life of the Christian. In this, he emphasized love for the neighbour, and especially the defencelessness growing out of it.

The End of the Persecution

Apart from Menno, there were many other peripatetic elders in the Netherlands, such as Lenaert Bouwens and Gillis van Aken, who disseminated Anabaptist ideas rapidly, even if they did so at great personal sacrifice and daily difficulties. From the beginning Dutch Anabaptism was also an urban phenomenon; it easily found resonance where trade routes crossed and the craft trades flourished. For this reason, it was also easy to establish at those locations.

The persecution of the Anabaptists after the incidents at Münster resulted in numerous martyrdoms. Many Anabaptists fled into the northern Netherlands, to England, and to West Prussia. Many of the congregations that were founded in rapid succession dispersed when their elders were arrested by the officials sent out by the Emperor to hunt them down. In this period, Calvinism took over the leading role in the Netherlands not only in the Reformation movement, but also in the political struggle for independence from Spain. By mid-century the Anabaptist movement had passed its high point. In the southern Netherlands, today's Belgium, persecution, emigration, and a militant Catholic revival led to the disappearance of the Anabaptists; they were able to survive only in the north, the present-day Netherlands. They remained an important minority force in the Reformation, alongside the dominant Reformed tradition.

The Refuge of West Prussia

The delta at the mouth of the Weichsel and Nogat rivers belonged to the Kingdom of Poland. Wars in the years before 1530 had depopulated and devastated the country. The delta of the Weichsel as far as Marienwerder was low-lying, swampy land and frequently stood under water. The political and economic situation offered many opportunities for refugees, most of whom came from the Netherlands. Dutch farmers who understood something about dike construction were highly welcome, even if they were Anabaptists. They were needed in the settlement and drainage of the *Werder* (boggy land between a river and a body of water) and in rebuilding destroyed villages. Mennonite artisans and merchants settled in the commercial centres of Danzig and Elbing.

The Anabaptist immigrants found it difficult to gather themselves into congregations. They came from quite different regions, such as Flanders, Limburg, Friesland, or the Lower Rhine area, and had different social and cultural backgrounds. As refugees persecuted for their faith, they also brought with them their different experiences and fears. Nevertheless, as a minority in West Prussia, they distinguished themselves through their cohesion and their industry. Although the urban Mennonites were forced into a limited number of professions, they quickly drew attention to themselves through outstanding achievements in these professions. Most Mennonites settled as farmers in the lowlands of the *Werder*, which they drained and made fertile by constructing dikes and canals.

The Controversy about the Pure Congregation
From the very beginning, the young movement experienced many tensions. These frequently could be attributed to contradictions present at the origins of Dutch Anabaptism. From the beginning, there were revolutionary and peaceful groups among the Melchiorites. The biblicist understanding of Scripture was represented among them, as was also a more spiritualist understanding. In addition, there was still Melchior's special view that Jesus had brought a "celestial flesh" from heaven, and the resulting conclusion that the congregation needed to be "without spot or wrinkle." This latter emphasis led in 1556 to a schism concerning the purity of the congregation when the controversy about the ban and avoidance of banned members (shunning) reached its climax. Some were worried about unity; others were worried about the purity of the Bride of Christ. In the end, the "Waterlanders" separated from the Mennonites. They called themselves henceforth the *Doopsgezinden* ("baptism-minded") and, at times, were more numerous than the Mennonites.

The Frisian-Flemish separation two years later once again divided the Mennonites in the Netherlands. This time the issue was the different attitudes of the Flemish and Frisians that quickly led to personal friction. The Flemings felt themselves discriminated against when they were passed over in regard to a local affair. Thereupon, the local Frisian and refugee Flemish Mennonites in many congregations gradually separated from each other and met in their own congregations.

The Beginning of Official Toleration

From 1550 on, Genevan Calvinism began to spread in the Netherlands and east Friesland. It offered a uniform and understandable theology. The five Calvinist principles of the irresistible grace of God, God's unconditional election, the human being's complete subjection and lack of will, "limited" reconciliation, and patient waiting on the part of the saints were not compatible with the Mennonites' belief in a God who daily says yes or no to the conduct of human beings. Above and beyond this, Calvinism permitted resistance to tyrannical governments. Dutch Calvinists considered it to be the duty of the Christian to overthrow a godless regime, such as the one they believed was clearly embodied by the Habsburg Philip II of Spain, in order to make "the progress of the Kingdom of God" possible.

In this situation both Mennonites and Waterlanders quickly lost importance as Reformation parties. Their belief in the defencelessness of the Christian did not permit a political statement, much less participation in the struggle for independence. They were not so much interested in freedom from the "Spanish yoke" as they were in a life of sanctification in a gathered congregation. To this were added the schisms and tensions within the movement. Thus the Anabaptist congregations lost their attraction and appeal, in comparison with the younger Calvinist movement.

The persecution of the Mennonites and Waterlanders ended when the "Staten Generaal" in the present-day Netherlands won independence from Spain. In 1579 the Union of Utrecht guaranteed the freedom of religious confession. The broad toleration and the economic development in the Netherlands resulted in the Mennonites and Waterlanders quickly assuming a role in public life and becoming good patriots. They did not lead lives in separation from broader society, as did their co-religionists in south Germany. They soon were active in all the professions and, in the course of time, produced outstanding ship owners and merchants, well-known engineers and artists, as well as prominent doctors and modern farmers.

The Hutterites

Jakob Hutter and the Community of Goods
In the course of his flight to Moravia in 1529, Jakob Hutter (ca. 1500–1536), an Anabaptist from South Tyrol, encountered Anabaptists who had introduced community of goods into their congregations. Impressed, he joined them and began to campaign for the emigration of his fellow countrymen to this community. Hutter assumed the leadership of the community in 1533. He was successful in sorting out the forces contending with each other and in uniting them in a brotherly and sisterly community. His model was the original Christian community in Jerusalem. Hutter did not originate the partnership of life and labour later named after him, but he gave this community a shape and form that extends into our own time. He encouraged his followers to hold fast to their faith, "to cultivate the garden," and imparted to them a great sense of mission. In November, 1535, Hutter was arrested and, in February, 1536, he was burned at the stake on the market square in Innsbruck.

An Overview of the History of the Hutterites
As the political pressure on the Anabaptists in Moravia receded after 1540, many Hutterite groups were successful in obtaining land from Moravian magnates for the erection of *Bruderhöfe*, tracts of land on which they could realize their ideals of the "commonality" of production and consumption. The high point of Hutterite history in Moravia was the "Golden Age" between the years 1560 and 1590. The Hutterite school system and their codes of regulations for the craft trades were considered exemplary, even after their expulsion. As a result of the tumult of the wars that engulfed Moravia after this period, and also because of the re-Catholicization of the territory, the Hutterites were required either to conform or to leave the country.

A Hutterite family dressed in traditional apparel.

A small group of Hutterites came to Siebenburgen in 1621-22 at the invitation of the Reformed prince Bethlen Gabor (1580–1622). Approximately two hundred settled in Alwinz. Here they abolished community of goods and gradually conformed themselves to their German-speaking, Protestant environment. In 1755, several religious refugees from Carinthia joined them. These Carinthian Lutherans read Hutterite literature and became convinced that Christians ought to live in community of goods. Together with the Hutterites from Alwinz they founded a new *Bruderhof,* but they soon were expelled by the Austrian government. The Hutterite remnant found refuge in the Ukraine for a time, but then all Hutterites emigrated after 1874, settling in North America, where they are still found today.

Tendencies and Factors

In the almost 300 years of Anabaptist and Mennonite history, one can detect several basic trends and patterns of behaviour that occurred repeatedly.

General Political and Social Conditions

Anabaptists were able to survive in locations where political circumstances were not firmly established, and where the larger confessions eyed each other suspiciously. This was the case in the imperial cities and smaller principalities and many ecclesiastical territories, but not in the Hapsburg lands (with the exception of the Netherlands), in Bavaria, or Saxony. In regions far from the centres of power, such as Frisia, the Emmental, West Prussia, or Moravia, various branches of the Anabaptist movement could feel quite at home for a longer period of time.

In the Netherlands, after independence from Spain, the situation was different. Here, the Anabaptist groups could develop without being oppressed by the emerging state authority. In a climate of freedom and economic competition, many of the baptist-minded became economically successful and influential in Dutch society. They thus found themselves in the position of being able to help their hard-pressed brothers and sisters in the faith in West Prussia, the Palatinate, Alsace, and Switzerland by providing money and wielding political influence.

With the exception of the Netherlands, the Thirty Years' War represented a turning point for the Anabaptists-Mennonites, leaving Anabaptist congregations in the Emmental, Alsace, east Friesland, and

West Prussia on the periphery. Since reconstruction after the War could be carried out only with the aid of all available forces, individual rulers tolerated the influx of Anabaptist immigrants in order to encourage trade and the crafts, and to reinvigorate agricultural production.

On the basis of this more practically-motivated toleration of people who had been persecuted earlier, under the diminishing influence of mainline churches, and as a result of the Enlightenment, toleration began to take shape as a basic right that guaranteed the equality of all citizens. With the adoption of constitutions in individual European countries, a process concluded by 1820, Mennonites became citizens with rights and duties equal to those of other citizens.

Theological Convergences and Divergences

Personal faith and the inviolability of an individual's conscience, which Grebel and his circle in Zürich emphasized as central Reformation teachings, were also decisive for many other dissidents. Although some of these dissidents shared certain convictions with others, they were not ready to compromise in questions of faith that they considered necessary. The lack of willingness to compromise and the tendency to transform individual themes into decisive community issues contributed to the numerous schisms among Anabaptists-Mennonites. Differences of opinion frequently led to schism; the schisms, however, endangered the credibility of the Anabaptists-Mennonites internally and externally. Their history could also be described as a succession of conferences and separations, of confessions of faith and appeals to reflect upon Anabaptist origins.

On the basis of respect for personal conscience, the Anabaptists-Mennonites drew two, apparently conflicting, conclusions: the Swiss Brethren sought the path of separation from society at large, while the Mennonites in the Netherlands and the northwestern German cities found their place in the societies surrounding them. Both started with individual, personal decisions for Anabaptist faith convictions. The one group believed it was possible to live out their faith only as "the quiet ones in the land"; the others, who understood themselves as "light" and "salt," attempted to live as Anabaptists-Mennonites "in the world," oriented not on separation, but rather on a fundamental openness.

The appeal to the individual conscience called congregations into being that were free from state intervention, free from hierarchical domination, and free from binding dogmas. Membership in these congregations was voluntary. The individual became a member of the congregation through a confession of faith, a confession that, in the beginning, was coupled with mortal danger. Baptism following confession of faith was the path into congregations of believers of like mind, believers who had confessed Jesus Christ and were ready to change their lives. In the process, they also accepted potential martyrdom for themselves.

The readiness to change one's life was the starting point for a major ethical claim that influenced Anabaptist-Mennonite congregations more than the formulation of theological principles: orthopraxis always was more important than orthodoxy, life more than doctrine, doing what was right more than believing the right things.

The congregation of confessing believers understood itself as the Body of Christ; it stood in contrast to the churches of the old and new confessions in which believers and non-believers were gathered together. In the Anabaptist congregations, only followers of Christ were to be members. The congregation was supposed to keep an eye on its members and exercise congregational discipline. The ideal image of the "congregation without spot or wrinkle," as advocated by the Melchiorites and then also by the Mennonites, quickly showed its negative side in divisions and painful separations. In retrospect, we can say that its effect was more destructive than constructive.

In contrast to the large state churches, the Anabaptists-Mennonites had neither a supreme leader nor a doctrinal office that could decide what was to be believed and what was to be done. These decisions had to be made by individuals and congregations for themselves. Because such decisions were difficult, things tended to remain the way they always had been.

In regard to the doctrine of Christ, the Anabaptists-Mennonites pursued two concepts: the Swiss Brethren advocated the Christological interpretation that emphasized two natures in one person, that is, Christ as the truly human and truly divine, while the successors to Melchior and Menno emphasized that Christ was in essence God who, during His sojourn upon earth, did not assume an essential human nature. From these divergent Christologies, there arose in each case a different doctrine of reconciliation. In the first case, the crucified and resurrected Lord is the Saviour from sin, death, and the Law; in the other, the earthly Jesus is the model which it is necessary to imitate, in order to enter the Kingdom of God. This latter interpretation tended towards works righteousness. Historically, Anabaptists-Mennonites found it difficult to keep the earthly Jesus and the resurrected Christ together.

Toleration and Adaptation in the Eighteenth and Nineteenth Centuries

Mennonites and Waterlanders in the Netherlands

The Mennonite/*Doopsgezinde* congregations in the Netherlands had to hold their ground in the midst of a developing confessional diversity and economic and cultural upheaval. The need for confessional formulations had become clear as early as the sixteenth century. In composing these confessions the Dutch Mennonites mirrored Reformation practice. The confessions had a two-fold purpose: they were intended to make clear the Mennonite point of view in contrast to other confessions, and they were intended to unite diverging opinions in their own group upon a common basis. These accents characterized the Waterlander Confession of 1610 and the Flemish "Olive Branch" Confession in the Netherlands. The Dordrecht Confession of 1632 represented a high point. In the course of time it achieved a broad dissemination and acceptance: it was acknowledged not only in West Prussia, but also was adopted by

Anabaptist Dirk Willems escaped from prison and crossed the thin ice of a pond. The guard who pursued him was stronger and heavier and did not make it across. Dirk Willems came back and rescued his captor, who took him back to prison. Later Dirk was burned at the stake in Asperen in 1569. Jan Luyken's preliminary sketch, shown here, became the well-known etching in the Martyrs Mirror.

the congregations in Alsace (1660), in the Palatinate, and in northern Germany. American Mennonites in Pennsylvania adopted it in 1725 and used it for many years afterward.

The *Martyrs Mirror*, published in 1660, also circulated widely. In the space of 1290 pages, Thieleman van Braght depicted a long series of the martyrs, beginning with Stephen (Acts 7:54) and continuing through the Waldensians of the Reformation period. There then follow 1396 Anabaptist martyrs, approximately half of them from the Netherlands, with an emphasis on the Flemish. About a third of the martyrs were women. One of the last blood witnesses was Hans Landis, who was beheaded in Zürich in 1614. The Anabaptist martyrs were thus placed within the context of witnesses to the faith from all periods of time, in a panorama of persecution and suffering throughout the centuries. The message was clear: the persecuted and slaughtered Christians are the true Christians. The true congregation of Christ is to be found among those who are persecuted for the sake of His name and His baptism. The *Martyrs Mirror* gave clarity to faith, inspired pious thoughts, and encouraged perseverance in a hostile world.

From an early time the Dutch Mennonites/*Doopsgezinden* saw themselves called to relief work outside of their own fellowship. They frequently came to the aid of the Swiss Brethren with petitions to the Zürich and Bern governments, and several times they provided money to Anabaptist groups for emigration and received individual groups into their own country. Deserving of special recognition are the major relief efforts in 1678 and 1696 for the brothers and sisters in the Palatinate, in 1672 for the Hutterites in Slovakia, in 1660 for the needy in Danzig, and in 1711-1713 for the West Prussians, who were struck hard by flooding. Significant contributions also were gathered for the settlement of Palatine Mennonites in Pennsylvania. In order better to co-ordinate these relief efforts, the *Fonds voor Buitenlandsche Nooden* (Fund for Foreign Needs) was established in 1710.

The general decline of the churches in the eighteenth century hit the Dutch Mennonites particularly hard. In this regard, it appears that the conservative churches in the countryside recorded fewer losses than did the liberal churches in the cities. Apart from the well-known causes such as spiritualism, rationalism, Enlightenment, and liberalism, under whose influence all confessions suffered, the Mennonites had to cope with the increasing number of confessionally-mixed marriages, the loosening of congregational discipline, and the noticeable lack of pastors, whose numbers steadily declined.

Nevertheless, Mennonites and Waterlanders, along with other groups such as the Remonstrants, assumed an outstanding position in the cultural and scientific life of the Netherlands in the eighteenth century, as well as being active as translators and publishers of religious and Enlightenment literature. They stood in the vanguard of social initiatives, such as the founding of fire departments and social welfare institutions, and also participated in the establishment and organization of adult education.

In 1735, the Lamist congregation in Amsterdam founded a seminary for the education of preachers. It was intended to help lead the Dutch Mennonites out of their crisis. One of the prominent founders and board members of the seminary was Jan Deknatel (1698–1759). He enjoyed a great reputation as a preacher and religious author. Deknatel was an early supporter of the pietist Moravian Brothers, and he had good contacts with his Zonist and more pietist colleague Hermannus Schijn. Count Zinzendorf arrived in February, 1736 in Amsterdam and visited with Deknatel, and several other Mennonites (coming from the circle of Collegiants) joined and financed the Moravian Brethren in Zeist. Deknatel also met John Wesley in Amsterdam in June, 1738. Deknatel's

Lord's Supper in the Singel Church (Bij 't Lam), Amsterdam, ca. 1750.

devotional writings breathed a Pietist spirit and emphasized personal piety. Deknatel's influence, however, was limited to only a few congregations, some northwest German and Palatine congregations among them.[5]

The City Congregations in Northwest Germany: Artisans and Merchants

The Mennonite congregations in Holstein were established in most cases by refugees from the Netherlands. These immigrants responded to invitations from local rulers, or moved to locations that were furnished with "freedoms" for the purpose of stimulating economic development. Regional rulers, to a greater extent than earlier, were in a position to enlarge their tax revenues by means of state-supported economic promotion (mercantilism). They sought groups that could stimulate trade and exchange (Danzig, Altona, Neuwied), or immigrants who were able to provide competition (as in Glücksburg and Altona) to economically dominant Hamburg, or to populate empty regions and make them fertile (as in the lowlands of the Weichsel, in the Palatinate, and in the Swiss Jura); or again immigrants able to introduce skills previously unknown in the country, such as dike construction, agriculture under difficult conditions, and textile production and trade. This princely "population policy" became important in the seventeenth century for the Mennonites of Krefeld, Neuwied, and Altona as well as for the Swiss Brethren of the Basel region, the Jura, Alsace, and the Palatinate. Toward the end of the eighteenth century the same policy was responsible for the settlement of Mennonites in southern Ukraine. Everywhere the *Taufgesinnte*, robbed of their homes and goods in one place, were invited to stimulate economic development and to lead the way for local populations elsewhere, through the good example desired of them by the inviting authorities.

The Mennonites remained aliens for a long time in their new environments. They spoke their original dialects, pursued their own forms of worship, restrained themselves in public, and were active in most cases only in modern professions outside of the guilds, where they did not have to be admitted on the basis of conformity to professional codes or be impeded by special conditions and traditions. They married only fellow members of the faith from the congregation, or brought their potential spouses from the old homeland.

The Mennonites in the cities enjoyed a minority status that was not rigidly controlled and that treated them rather preferentially in comparison with established citizens. Their conviction that they were required to provide an accounting to God for the entirety of their lives, including their professional activity, made it possible for them to accomplish outstanding achievements in collaboration with the sovereign's patronage. Because the Mennonites were allowed to be active in only a few professions, the competition that thereby ensued in these professions sparked their capacity for achievement. The congregations had a greater chance for survival when their members were economically successful for, with growing prosperity among individual families, the external pressures also slackened. Economic success, however, was accompanied by the danger that Anabaptist concerns would be suppressed or reduced to mere formalities.

In the seventeenth and eighteenth centuries, Mennonites made a name for themselves as producers of textiles and spirits, as traders in the retail, wholesale, and overseas trades, and as ship owners in the fishing industry. As prominent businessmen, they were for a time at the very top of their industries. Thus it is reported that in the last quarter of the seventeenth century, two Mennonite merchants in Hamburg-Altona dominated the fishing trade and the whaling industry in the grounds around Greenland, and that the von der Leyen family of Krefeld controlled the silk business in Prussia until the second half of the eighteenth century.

A dominant figure among the Mennonites in Altona in the seventeenth century was the elder Gerrit Roosen (1612–1711). In his long life, he distinguished himself not only as a versatile businessman and magnanimous donor, but also as a long-time preacher and elder of the congregation. Toward the end of his life he composed a catechism: *Christliches Gemüthsgespräch von dem geistlichen und seligmachenden Glauben* (Dialogue of the Christian Soul on Spiritual and Saving Faith). This small book went through twenty-two editions between 1702 and 1857, and was even translated into English. It breathed a mild, generous Christian spirit; traditional Mennonite concerns were mentioned only in passing. On the other hand, it emphasized the diligence and conformity displayed by the Mennonites.

The Mennonites in West Prussia

In spite of many setbacks, the Mennonites in West Prussia survived the political tumult as a firmly established group that distinguished itself from its neighbours through its faith, origins, language, cohesion, its agricultural ability, and its prosperity. A portion of their areas of settlement amid the *Werder* belonged to the crown estates of the King. The latter allowed the Mennonites to pay repeatedly for the privilege of an unhindered exercise of worship, especially when he was in urgent need of money. However, the ruler's favour had to be bought anew at every change on the throne. Since the Mennonites were forbidden to evangelize new converts, they grew in numbers only through having large families. Of course, there were always increases as well as losses through marriage with non-Mennonite partners. The number of Mennonites rose from about 3000 (ca. 1600) to 13,000 (ca. 1780). The Mennonite community was firmly established through its family ties and was easy to recognize as Mennonite through family names.

Mennonites in the West Prussian *Werder* formed a social/religious organism that embraced their lives completely and kept them apart from the society surrounding them. A religious party grew into a living community. The colonies in Russia and later, the Old Colony Mennonites in Mexico, Bolivia, and Paraguay have their roots here. Many common interests contributed to this cohesive Mennonite world: the shared faith convictions for which their ancestors had to flee, the Low German dialects they spoke, the settlement in loose neighbourly groups (they shared their villages with others), the same type of labour in agriculture, and the shared economic and social tasks in the community. This firmly established Mennonite world insulated these communities from the outside world, and prevented a decline such as the one their co-religionists experienced in north-western Germany.

The former Mennonite church in Elbing, probably the oldest Mennonite church building in Europe, built in 1590. It served the congregation until 1900 when a larger church was constructed. The congregation was destroyed in 1945.

The achievements of the West Prussian Mennonite farmers were impressive. They were successful in draining the swamps by using dikes and canals; as a result the yearly outbreak of swamp fever disappeared and the country became inhabitable once again. The low-lying land had long been considered barren because of the persistent floods; now, it was transformed into fertile farmland upon which the Mennonites successfully grew grain and cultivated pasture land.

The sense of community among the Mennonites led to an exemplary social welfare system: every congregation maintained an orphanage and a retirement home for the care of those who could not help themselves. Around 1620, a fire insurance plan based on mutual aid was established; this was the first fire insurance plan in modern economic history, without which house ownership today would be completely unthinkable. Up to this time, the Mennonites had helped each other in case of fire or accident. Through the establishment of fire insurance, this neighbourly aid became an institution upon which every member could call without having to ask for help again and again.

Congregational discipline was strictly applied; confessionally-mixed marriages were not tolerated. As a rule, a non-Mennonite partner had to be accepted into the congregation through baptism. Congregational discipline threatened in cases of dancing, drunkenness, and gambling, and in cases of indebtedness, tax offences, or an extravagant lifestyle; it intervened in cases of adultery and also in criminal cases. Those who did not escape punishment with a fine were excluded from communion. After a certain period of time, with an apology and a promise of improvement, the disciplined person was readmitted once again. A member seldom was excluded permanently. In view of the close social cohesion of the group, a permanently excluded person had no choice but to leave the area. The Mennonites as a rule refrained from making use of the courts in disputes among themselves (see 1 Cor. 6:1–11). Conflicts and property or inheritance disagreements were settled by the elder, or many times also by the village mayors. The Mennonites separated themselves from the world by means of this congregational discipline, and they thereby distinguished themselves also from other farmers in the *Werder*. A Mennonite world had arisen marked by faith and tied together by agriculture. An island mentality and familial loyalty complemented each other. These Mennonites were characterized by a pioneer spirit and congregational discipline, as well as a simple piety and trust in God's Word.

The acid test for the West Prussian Mennonites came when Prussia occupied the Weichsel delta (1772, 1793, 1795). The Prussian annexation was welcomed at first because it removed the previous political uncertainty. The new state, however, now meddled with the old ways of life by releasing a flood of new laws and decrees. Prussian militarism placed the Mennonites in the middle of a momentous confrontation. Payments for the support of military institutions were imposed upon them and then the purchase of additional land was made much more difficult, robbing the younger generation of its livelihood as farmers.

Thus many were confronted by the choice of taking up another profession, emigrating, or converting to the Lutheran faith. When the recruiters from the Russian Czarina Catherine II arrived and promoted settlement on the Ukrainian steppe, about 600 hundred families comprising roughly 4,000 persons (one third of the West Prussian Mennonites) decided to emigrate, a movement that began in 1789. By 1864 between 10,000–12,000 Mennonites had migrated to Russia. Those left behind came to terms with conditions as they were.

The Mennonites in Switzerland, Alsace, and the Palatinate

Persecution and Emigration

The persecution of the Anabaptists by the Zürich authorities did not diminish after the execution of Felix Mantz; reformed Zürich also was responsible for one of the last executions when it led the seventy-year-old elder Hans Landis, from Horgen, to the executioner's block in 1614 because he was the "ringleader of this sect." By 1700, Zürich was largely free of Anabaptists.

In spite of all the persecution, the Anabaptists in the more remote parts of the Bern region not only were able to survive but actually experienced a numerical increase for several decades. This development began around 1650 in the context of Pietism and came to an end only toward the middle of the eighteenth century. One of the main reasons for this increase was a growing dissatisfaction with the status quo in church and society. Many of those who were dissatisfied were longing for spiritual and ecclesiastical renewal. They felt attracted by the credible

The origins of the Swiss Brethren hymnal, the *Ausbund*, go back to a group of Anabaptists imprisoned in a castle dungeon in Passau during the years 1535–1536 where they composed 53 songs. These compositions were preserved and later became the core of the first known publication of the *Ausbund* (1583)—the oldest hymnal in continuous use in the world. The Old Order Amish of North America still regularly sing selections from the *Ausbund* in their worship services.

and convincing witness of Anabaptist neighbours and sympathized with their positions. Especially after 1670, a growing number of these sympathizers finally became members of the Anabaptist congregations; the majority of them, however, feared the consequences of turning fully Anabaptist and remained what was then called "half-Anabaptist" (*Halb-Täufer*). After 1700, these Anabaptist sympathizers often associated with the expanding movement of pietism, allowing more hidden or internalized forms of spiritual renewal.

A second reason for this increase of Anabaptists may also have been that the remote, broad valleys of the Bern region could not be kept under tight surveillance. In spite of the difficulties, however, the Bern Council wanted to restore confessional unity in its territory by every means available. Authorities and pastors attempted to persuade the Anabaptists to affiliate with local churches, in most cases in vain. Deportations and discrimination

Bernese Anabaptists were regularly exiled by their authorities. Here they leave their home country by boat on the Aare river.

were more successful. Professions in commerce and the trades were, as a rule, closed to the Anabaptists because citizens were forbidden to have business dealings with them. It was not permitted either to give lodging to the Anabaptists or to employ them. All that was left to them for survival was self-sufficient farming in remote areas. Since marriages among the Anabaptists were not solemnized by local pastors, Anabaptist couples were not considered to be legally married; their children, accordingly, were deemed illegitimate and so were not legitimate heirs. The parents' property was seized after their deaths and was released only when the heir converted to the established church. The Anabaptists were not permitted to bury their dead in the cemeteries; they were required to inter them behind the cemetery walls along with Jews and vagrants.

In response to these measures, many decided to emigrate. Among those who remained, some groups assimilated, but many others remained steadfast and accepted the discrimination. From time to time, the Bern Council tightened the measures against the *Wiedertäufer* (re-baptizers). The *Täuferkammer* (administrative department in charge of the Anabaptists) periodically arrested the known Anabaptist preachers, placed them in the pillories, whipped them and branded their foreheads with the sign of the Bern bear, so that they could be identified by this mark. Other unfortunates were sold to Venice as galley slaves. Many Anabaptists, above all the fathers of families, were expelled from the country. If any returned secretly, they ran the risk of languishing in prison for many years. The Council's measures led to a constant exodus of Anabaptists.

In addition, there were two major deportations: In 1671, approximately 700 Swiss Brethren Anabaptists (*Schweizer Brüder Taufgesinnte*) were rounded up and required to leave their homeland as a group; they moved to the Palatinate. In 1710, the deportation of fifty-six Anabaptists on a ship on the Rhine caused a sensation. The Anabaptists were to be transported far enough away so that they could no longer return. A year later, in 1711, the authorities allowed emigration with bag and baggage and everything the Anabaptists owned. The authorities thereby abstained—in contrast to earlier practice—from the seizure of property. A mass migration now ensued. Those who remained behind continued to be threatened and persecuted; they were able, however, to maintain their congregations in the areas around Langnau and Sumiswald in the Emmental up until the time of the establishment of equal rights for all citizens.

The Dutch Mennonite fellowship played a praiseworthy role in these events. It mobilized political and financial aid for the Swiss Brethren in a number of different campaigns. At the Mennonites' urging, the *Staten Generaal*, the government of the Netherlands, sent several appeals (*Intercessionen*) on behalf of the persecuted. They accepted a portion of those deported into the Netherlands, and helped with the settlement of others in the Palatinate and Alsace and then later also with their passage by ship to Pennsylvania and their settlement there.

An Attempt at Reformation—the Amish Split
In the last decade of the seventeenth century the Anabaptist elder Jacob Amman (1644–ca. 1730) was shocked by the increasing acculturation of many Swiss Brethren, especially in areas of growing toleration such as Alsace. He therefore demanded the revival of Anabaptist separation—against any forms of concessions for the "half-Anabaptists" and compromises with pietism—and the return to a stricter congregational discipline: he wanted "to rebuild the Temple of God on the old farmstead." Amman campaigned for his interpretation of congregations "without spot or wrinkle" in the Swiss and Alsatian congregations. Not

everyone approved of his radical ideas. Many congregations, above all in the Emmental, were not ready to practice strict banning and shunning as demanded by Amman. However, almost the entire large group of Anabaptists in the Bernese *Oberland* (upland region) supported Amman's view. Thus 1693 marked the separation and formation of Amish congregations in Switzerland and Alsace (centred in Markirch), and then later in Hesse, the Palatinate, and Bavaria, in the Montbéliard-Belfort area, and in the Neuenburg region (under Prussian rule from 1707), as well as in other locations. Beginning in 1720 most Amish, above all those from Alsace, emigrated to Pennsylvania. Many of the Mennonites in Alsace, along the Saar River, in the former Duchy of Zweibrücken, in Lorraine, and in Bavaria are descendants of the Amish.

Swiss Brethren Anabaptists (Taufgesinnte Schweizer Brüder) Settle in the Jura

A large part of the Jura belonged to the Bishop of Basel, who ruled his thinly-populated land from his seat at Pruntrut (Porrentruy). To be sure he, like his neighbours, was constrained to drive away the Anabaptists, but he gladly tolerated the miners, most of whom had their origins in the Bern area or came from Alsace. The immigrants were hard-working and experienced people who were happy when they found a home. They contributed to the economic development of this remote and desolate region and proved themselves to be models (not beloved by everyone) of diligence and solidity within a modest standard of living. The immigrants preserved their German language, in the midst of their French-speaking environment, well into the twentieth century. Most

Mennonite preacher visits a family in the Bernese Jura around 1850. Painting by Aurèle Robert.

of the Swiss Anabaptists today live in the region of the Jura.

In the seventeenth and eighteenth centuries, some Anabaptists emigrated to the Württemberg county of Mömpelgard (modern-day Montbéliard) and found an undisturbed refuge there.

Alsace

Some Swiss Anabaptists moved to Alsace before the Thirty Years' War, most of them however after the war. They were in demand as tenants because they earned enough from the land to justify a higher rent than did the resident farmers. When Amman demanded a tightening of congregational discipline and a stricter separation from their neighbours, most of the congregations in Alsace followed him. In 1712, the French King Louis XIV drove the Mennonites out of Alsace, which for the most part had become a part of France between 1648 and 1687. They moved on to Mömpelgard (Montbéliard), into the Duchy of Zweibrücken, the Palatinate, Bavaria, and Lorraine (which at that time belonged to the German Empire). A larger portion, most of them Amish, emigrated to Pennsylvania. The Mennonites re-entered the public eye only in the revolutionary year of 1793, when they petitioned the Paris government for exemption from military service. This request was complied with only in part, for which reason many emigrated to America after 1815.

The Palatinate

The Palatine *Kurfürst* (Elector) Karl Ludwig allowed Anabaptist farmers, whom he called *Menisten*, to enter his war-torn land by virtue of a *Privileg-Concession* issued in 1664. Several families had come to the area around Sinsheim and Kriegsheim already during the War. The Elector promised freedom of assembly in exchange for a recognition fee. At first he limited immigration to 200 families. Their freedom of assembly also was limited: only twenty persons were permitted to gather on any occasion at one location for worship and, of course, the Mennonites were forbidden to persuade others to embrace their faith. The influx of Mennonites began in 1671-72 as the persecution in Bern reached its high point. The Dutch helped to overcome initial difficulties by providing donations.

In the course of the eighteenth century, the Mennonites of the Palatinate acquired a reputation as excellent farmers because they were able to increase the yields from the barren soil. The Mennonite farmers began to replace the traditional three-field system with an intensive use of the land made possible by fertilizers. They thereby sparked an agricultural revolution. Through the maintenance of larger livestock herds, the fields could be fertilized more intensively. The Mennonites remained tenants for a long time because the purchase of land at first was denied to them, and then later allowed only under difficult circumstances.

These economic obstacles contributed to many emigrating in the eighteenth and nineteenth centuries, above all to America, but also to Bavaria. In the course of the French Revolution, they were recognized as citizens, and afterwards had to fear neither economic, political or religious discrimination.

Translation: Luci Driedger and Dennis Slabaugh

The Political, Economic, Social and Religious Context in Europe, 1789–2000

by Claude Baecher

An understanding of the evolution of Europe in the last two centuries of the second millennium—roughly since the French Revolution (1789)—will do much to enhance the reader's comprehension of this volume. It is a well-established fact that politics, economics, demography, social changes, and philosophical and religious currents are deeply intertwined. Highlighting the main traits of this period will offer a useful framework within which to situate the history of European Mennonites, given that the intention of this volume is to give a general panoramic view of a particular period in history. The broadest story can be told in one sentence: Christianity left its mark on European nations very early on, only to be succeeded by a secularized Europe today.

Outstanding Events after the Revolution of 1789

The Revolution and the Monarchies

In the Middle Ages, the Hussite Christians were the first to espouse the idea of establishing democracy in a "Christian" land and the first to bring it to fruition. The first revolutionary experiments sprang up in certain cities in Bohemia and Moravia. This was followed by the "glorious revolution" in England in 1688 which launched the movement that would lead to the end of the despotic European monarchies. Constitutional monarchies appeared in their place, and grew in popularity during the Enlightenment period. This idea was formulated in reaction to the abuse of power by monarchs and in defense of universal individual liberties. The claim to independence by the thirteen colonies

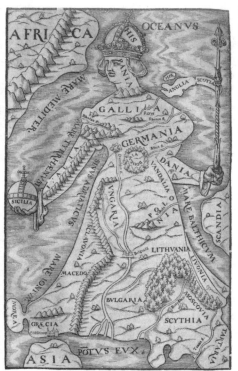

During the late sixteenth century, several map makers created map images, wherein countries and continents were given human or animal forms. This representation of *Europa Regina* or "Queen Europe" appeared in several editions of Sebastian Münster's *Cosmography* from 1580 onwards. West is shown at top with Spain forming the crown and head, France the neck and bust, Italy the left arm and Denmark the right arm holding a scepter with Britain as the flag. The remainder of the figure is a flowing robe with Greece and Russia at the feet.

in North America contributed to the European movement. The Americans adopted the Declaration of Independence on July 4, 1776, which led to their independence in 1783. A president replaced the king as head of the country, with presidential powers shared with two legislative bodies.

Five years later, beginning with the French Revolution (1789), the nation was generally no longer personified by the monarch and his laws, but rather constituted a territory with clearly-marked borders and a strong centralized state government. These political ideas spread from France throughout Europe, and along with them a "French European Enlightenment" also came into being in the eighteenth century. Enlightenment philosophers saw themselves as citizens of the world and formed a kind of European "intellectual community." The political reality, however, was not a "world community." At the end of the eighteenth and the beginning of the nineteenth century Europeans, notably from Italy, Spain, and Prussia, reacted vigorously against the intrusion of revolutionary troops, choosing rather to advance the idea of cultural nationalism. This would be an important element in the rise of nationalism in general.

Both the values of the French Revolution and the challenge of rising nationalisms confronted the Mennonite communities in Europe with difficult questions, as they now faced new political realities as full citizens of European nations. The ways they dealt with these issues and the decisions they took led to a broad variety of models of faith and church life, as will be seen in the chapters that follow.

After 1789, the equilibrium of the European monarchies was first disrupted by a revolutionary France, which was followed by the expansion of imperial France. Despite the defeat of Napoleon, who had wanted to promote liberal ideas in the lands he had conquered, what emerged instead was a new order. In spite of a noble philosophy that asserted the rights of European peoples, the revolutionary enterprise had quickly turned to annexation and looting. Revolutionary troops lived off of the countries they occupied. In response, these occupied countries fought for their liberation, which enhanced the development of nationalism.[1] From 1807 onwards, certain German-speaking regions came to view Napoleon as the Anti-Christ. Bonaparte abdicated in 1814, and the defeat of his troops at Waterloo in 1815 put a definite end to his imperialistic adventure. The European Powers, although they had a certain admiration for the political revolutionary model, nevertheless rejected it. Ideals pertaining to liberty and nations' rights had run their course. Still, in a good many places those ideals left a legacy of imperial legislation, in particular, the Code of Napoleon. In other places, however, as in the case of Prussia, revolutionary events and French domination led to the awakening of an aggressive form of nationalism.

Decree of December 15–17, 1792 (Parliamentary Archives of Paris)

"In the countries which are or will be occupied by the armies of the Republic, the generals will, in the name of the French Nation, immediately proclaim the sovereignty of the people, the suppression of all established authorities, of existing taxes or contributions, the abolition of tithing, feudalism, the rights of the nobility, of existing personal servitude ... duties, nobility, and of all privileges in general ... They will announce to the people that they are bringing peace, aid, fraternity, liberty and equality."

This form of nationalism, which so strongly shaped European political and social life in the nineteenth and twentieth centuries, turned out to be quite attractive for many European Mennonites—much more than one might have thought, given the Anabaptist heritage of these churches.

New Borders

In 1814–1815, the Congress of Vienna reconfigured the map of Europe on the principle of a monarchical dynasty's right to govern (Great Britain, Russia, Prussia and Austria), denying the principle of nationalities. The treaties that followed asserted the will of European rulers to oppose any future revolutionary ideas. Some of the territorial decisions taken at this time also affected the future of the Mennonites. Prussia acquired significant parts of Westphalia and territories along the Rhine;

Russia acquired total control over the new kingdom of Poland. However, revolutionary movements aspiring for unity also emerged in a variety of countries to contest the absolute monarchies in Germany and Italy.

During the second half of the nineteenth century, thinkers reshaped the intellectual landscape by contesting the existence of objective reason and objective foundations for personal ethics. Hegel, Marx, Engels and Nietzsche forced Europeans to take into account the struggle between the proletariat and the bourgeoisie. A quarter of a century later Freud introduced a new understanding of the human psyche.

The Bitterness of the Russian Peasantry

There was a significant shift in Russia in 1861 during the reign of Czar Nicolas II. Serfdom was abolished, and the *mujiks*, the Russian peasants, came into possession of part of the land. However, the terrible famine of 1901 left enormous bitterness among them, and the large landowners alone still possessed 60 percent of the land. Ideas of revolution were preceded by scenes of plundering. At the same time, waves of peasants with no visible means of support were swelling city ranks. All of this paved the way for the revolution in February 1917, and resulted in the abdication of Czar Nicolas II. This gave rise to a form of communism which abolished all private property. For the Mennonites in Russia—many of whom had become quite wealthy, and all of whom relied on imperial promises and exemptions—the Bolshevik revolution would present a wide array of difficult problems (see chapter VII).

The War of 1870

Prussian power increased from 1862 onwards. Bismarck became minister to Wilhelm I, and the German States in the south decided to side with Prussia in 1870. In that same year, Napoleon III declared war on Prussia over hereditary claims to the Spanish crown. The beginning of the following year saw the defeat of the French, and brought an end to the French Empire. Part of its territory, the regions of Alsace and Lorraine, passed over into German hands. The many Mennonite congregations in these regions were strongly affected, as these territories became contested lands in the continuing struggle between France and Germany (see chapters IV and VI).

The twentieth century began in peaceful optimism, but little by little anti-Semitism and a general xenophobia recaptured the hearts of the masses; Mennonites breathed this same cultural atmosphere. Technological discoveries rendered wars more destructive, and new forms of propaganda effectively manipulated the masses. These cultural, political and technological sea changes carried Mennonites along, just as they did other European people.

The First World War (1914–1918)

Tensions broke out in the second decade of the twentieth century between Germany and France, over a question of political expansion in Morocco. Because of political alliances already in place, France sided with Russia, an ally of Serbia. The assassination of the Archduke of Austria, engineered by Serbian nationalists, led the Austro-Hungarian Empire to declare war on Serbia's ally Russia, which, in turn, led Germany to declare war on France in 1914, and the First World War was underway.

In 1914, Lenin—the Russian Communist leader and most influential opponent of the Czar—called the European people to transform this war "between imperialists" into a "civil" war. The First World War was a disaster for the Russian Czarist army, which was forced to pull back and sign an armistice with Germany; the war continued in the west. In Russia, Lenin's companion Trotsky organized the Red Army to continue the battle against the Czarist regime; civil war did in fact break out between the Red Bolshevik army, the White Czarist army, and "Black" anarchist mobs. During the period of general chaos that followed, armies, anarchists and criminals spread fear and terror through random destruction, robbery, rape and murder. Among their victims were also many Mennonites, as will be seen in more detail in chapter VII. In 1920, the White Army, faithful to the Czar, was conquered and the Bolsheviks established their kind of order.

Under the Bolsheviks the Russian State became a one-party machine. Lenin became partially and momentarily open to a more liberal economy in order to fight against the 1921 famine. However, his successor Stalin tightened control in 1929, and imposed collectivization. The secret police—the NKDV, and later the KGB—became the instrument of Stalin's control. Its harsh and brutal policy against all kinds of "dissidents"—that is, persons perceived as not completely supporting revolutionary actions and values—affected millions of people and led to massive suffering and millions of deaths. Among the victims were descendants of the Mennonite immigrants from Prussia who had created prosperous colonies in the Ukraine and had already suffered through the Civil War and its aftermath.

After a long period of trench warfare on the western front, an internal revolution in Germany in 1918 led the emperor to abdicate.

Germany was forced to capitulate and sign a fourteen-point armistice which included the return of Alsace and Lorraine to France—regions in which Mennonites now found themselves under French rule again. Deaths in this first international war numbered close to nine million. In the Treaty of Versailles, Germany was forced to agree to reparation payments for damages caused by the war, and the League of Nations was created. Germany, now disarmed and humiliated, no longer was a powerful colonial empire; the country fell into economic crisis and already in 1923, Adolph Hitler had attempted an unsuccessful coup d'état with Ludendorff. Tensions between Germany and France resurfaced, and Mennonites in those countries were not untouched by these rising nationalist feelings.

The Second World War (1939–1945)

The National Socialist (Nazi) party in Germany made significant advances from 1930 onwards, and came to power in 1933, when the Third Reich was proclaimed. In the following year, the ruling Nazis passed racist laws with the intention of "purifying the German race" by sterilizing any persons exhibiting physical or psychological pathologies/abnormalities. When German troops annexed Austria in 1938 and occupied the Sudetenland and the city of Prague, England, followed by France, declared war on Germany. This was the beginning of the disastrous and horrendous Second World War. The Netherlands was occupied by German troops between 1940 and 1945, bringing German and Dutch Mennonites into directly conflictive and difficult situations. The attack on Pearl Harbor by Japan brought the United States into the conflict, a step which accelerated the triumph of the Allies. The Second World War revealed the horror of modern warfare: there were forty- to fifty-million deaths, with as many civilian casualties as military. With the exception of Mennonites in Switzerland, which remained neutral, Mennonites in all countries of Europe were devastated in many different ways by these events, as will be seen below in chapters III, IV, VI and VII.

A New Balance of Power

Roosevelt, Stalin and Churchill prepared the new world order at Yalta in February 1945. Germany surrendered unconditionally in May and was forced back to its 1937 borders. Europe rose ever so slowly from its ruins, and the wounds ran deep on all sides.

In June of 1945, fifty nation-states signed the United Nations (UN) charter in San Francisco, but optimism about peace on a global level soon evaporated with the emergence of the Cold War (1947–1962) between the West and the communist Eastern Bloc. As a first consequence of the war, Germany was divided in 1948. On an ecclesiastical level, the World Council of Churches was founded in the same year with the expressed intention of drawing Protestant and Orthodox Christians closer together. One of the most difficult questions of the post-war period was how to imagine the future of the surviving Jews after the Holocaust. Judaism rose up from the ashes following the Second World War. Nazi ideology had claimed the lives of more than six million Jews in concentration camps and elsewhere. Many saw in the proclamation of the independent state of Israel in 1948 the proper and adequate solution to the traumatic experiences of the Jews.

As part of the European economic recovery, treaties were signed at the end of the war which put into place the European Common Market, the economic union between France, Italy, Germany, and the Benelux countries (Belgium, the Netherlands, Luxembourg), foreshadowing the significant economic integration of Europe that occurred by the end of the twentieth century.

The End of the USSR and the Destruction of the Berlin Wall

Mikhail Gorbachev launched his policies of *Perestroika* (economic and administrative reforms) and *Glasnost* (political and cultural transparency) in 1982. This increasingly affected the lives of the Mennonite communities that had survived in the former Soviet Union (see chapter VII). However, the countries on the periphery of the USSR, and some of the *nomenklatura* (Soviet power elite) were opposed to Gorbachev's policies. New possibilities suddenly appeared, even though many western Christians had considered the USSR to be the embodiment of the Antichrist. In 1989 and under certain conditions, the *Stasi*, the secret police of the Republic of East Germany, tolerated meetings in churches where socio-political questions were discussed. During the same period, a massive European peace movement was born. The demolition of the Berlin wall in 1989, twenty-eight years after its construction, was the consequence of the collapse of the Communist regimes of eastern Europe. With the collapse of the "Soviet Bloc," the question of European unity would be considered once again, but now in a new context.

The union of Serbs, Croats, Slovenians, and Montenegrans had been proclaimed in 1918. After the Second World War, a "federalized" Yugoslavia was formed under the dictatorship of Tito, a Stalinist, but after Tito's death in 1980, and a failed presidential election in 1991, the "federal" solution came to an end. The collegial presidency was hampered by the Serbian refusal to allow an anticommunist Croat to take his turn as president. The ensuing failure of Yugoslavia brought with it years of civil war within Europe proper. European Mennonites undertook positive initiatives in response to this war.

After seventy years, the very heart of the Soviet system in the USSR was affected in 1991 when a failed coup d'état in the USSR ousted the communist leadership and accelerated the country's democratization. However, the new government had difficulty in coming to terms with food shortages during the transition, because supplies were at times either in the hands of the Mafia or former government officials. The welfare state was displaced by another economy. The Warsaw Pact, the former Eastern Bloc military union, was dissolved in 1991.

Another Balance of Power

Events in the former Soviet Union opened the borders, but brought into question the function of national borders in the old European Union, in effect rendering borders less and less significant. At the beginning of the 1990s, an agreement permitting free movement between the borders of Belgium, France, Luxembourg, the Netherlands, Germany, Spain and Portugal came into effect. In 2003, the European Union was composed of the fifteen European countries that had ratified the Treaty of Maastricht on February 7, 1992, but on April 2, 2003, the European Parliament welcomed an additional ten countries into the European Union, among them some countries from the former Communist Warsaw Pact. Movements toward political union were mirrored in the economic sphere: the "euro" zone, created in 1999, designates twelve countries of the European Union who have adopted the euro as their common currency.

Two conflicts in Iraq between 1991 and 2003 illustrated that the European nations did not always adopt a common political approach to political conflict, and that there still was no coherent European foreign or military policy. As of 1995, with world wars no longer needing to mobilize large numbers of soldiers, fewer and fewer European armies resorted to obligatory conscription. In the absence of conscription, but in the face of injustice, racism and violence, for most Mennonites the central peace issue no longer is a matter of being or not being a conscientious objector, but of articulating a prophetic witness of justice, peace and reconciliation in nations whose armies are involved in wars and whose societies and economies do not favour the poor and the powerless in society.

Religious and Philosophical Developments

Significant philosophical and religious developments accompanied the historical changes outlined above. The wars of religion at the beginning of the seventeenth century had a disastrous impact: Catholic troops attacked Protestant populations and armies, and Protestant troops fought against Catholic populations and armies. These wars and massacres were the prelude which led to the eighteenth-century Enlightenment, and finally to the disenchantment of European people with institutional Christianity. Religious toleration and acceptance of religious pluralism, as decrees of the state, seemed the "rational" way to organize European political life to Enlightenment thinkers. Groups such as the Mennonites, formerly considered religious dissidents and sanctioned as such, now found a new social acceptance and political freedom, but Christian faith as a whole was largely removed from European public life: one's "faith" was considered a personal matter. Intellectual critiques of religion also weakened the institutional church, whose power was reduced politically through revolution, emigration and the emergence of American colonies, and religiously, by efforts to live the Christian faith in new ways.

"Western man" was born into the eighteenth century with a pre-established set of fundamental rights based on reason. The Enlightenment was accompanied by a passion for discovery and explanation. At the same time, for European Christianity the Enlightenment signified a sad and difficult road to religious pluralism, opening the way to a multiplicity of beliefs or disbelief. The Enlightenment was the clear announcement of the "de-constantinianization" of the institutional church in Europe. The Christian church and faith no longer dictated social, political and intellectual life in Europe; rather, European culture and the Christian faith agreed to cohabitate in an atmosphere of toleration. In certain countries, the medieval relationship between the church and the secular power was a straightforward divorce, approved by some while deplored by others. By the end of the millennium, the Christian churches, including the Mennonite churches, were left looking for their place in society.

The Catholic Church lost more during the period of revolution than did the Protestant churches, notably its religious monopoly, for it was now forced to open itself to religious pluralism in countries where it had enjoyed exclusive political support. The Catholic Church in France, for example, no longer controlled the issuing of certificates of birth, marriage and death. The Roman Catholic Church strongly reacted against the Revolution for three reasons: 1) the confiscation of its land holdings (in the sixteenth century the Catholic church owned 20 percent of the land in France), 2) the order of the Civil Constitution of the Clergy, which made the clergy subordinate to the State, and 3) the persecution of priests who resisted this order. According to the Catholic Church, "human rights" were not in agreement with revelation or tradition. It was not until Vatican II (1962–1965) that the Roman Catholic Church got in step with modernity.

The Protestant churches adapted better to the Enlightenment. In France, the Revolution was experienced by Protestants as a liberation from the yoke of Catholicism. However, in certain regions occupied by Napoleon's revolutionary troops, resistance took place under the form of late Pietism, which fiercely rejected the French Revolution. Where Mennonites were influenced by this later Pietism, they often became more nationalistic, but other Mennonites were also susceptible to the pandemic nationalistic trend of nineteenth-century Europe.

"Enlightened" philosophy made inroads in both Catholic and Protestant circles, calling into question traditional methods of biblical interpretation with new "historico-critical" methods. These rational, empirical approaches to the study of Scripture called into question traditional orthodoxy and raised issues such as the historical reliability of the biblical texts. This was only the beginning of a long period of strained relations between "orthodox Protestants," later called evangelicals, and "liberal Protestants." Mennonites in different regions of Europe responded in their own ways to these theological currents. While generally the Mennonites in southern Germany, France and Switzerland were more influenced by the more conservative former group, those in northern Germany and the Netherlands had closer relationships with the more liberal tendency. This led to growing tensions between the two groups of European Mennonites, as will be noted in more detail in the chapters that follow.

The intellectual and artistic wave called Romanticism (from "romantic," originally designating picturesque landscape painting), emerged throughout Europe between 1789 and 1815. In reaction to the rationalism of the Enlightenment, romanticism brought intuition and feeling to the forefront, and reasserted the value of the individual who was in the process of rediscovering the meaning of mystery and the sacred. This movement took place after the failure of the Revolution, and emphasized that happiness would be found in the rediscovery of the self. This further encouraged the movement of Christian expression from the public sphere to the private sphere. In much the same way that Pietism appeared in response to the rigid orthodoxy of seventeenth-century state Protestantism and the corresponding wars of religion, nineteenth-century revivalism was a religious echo to the rationalism of the Enlightenment period, in which man had been considered an end in himself. The historian Karl Heussi asserts that in the official Protestant churches of the nineteenth century, a pietistic and revivalist wave followed a generation of theologians and pastors who had been, essentially, rationalists. The struggle against lukewarm religiosity was implicit. International missionary societies, Bible institutes and Christian social and diaconal organizations sprang up as part of the revivalist wave, as did Christian labour unions, deacon and deaconesses' homes, the Red Cross, the Blue Cross, etc.

German Postcard with the title *"Die Vision des verwundeten Kriegers"* (The Vision of the Wounded Soldier). The Postcard was sent in November 1915 from an Alsatian Mennonite soldier wounded in Milan, Italy, to another Mennonite soldier from Alsace in a hospital in Trier, Germany during the First World War. It was a time when nationalism eclipsed Christian nonresistance.

In order to understand the nineteenth-century revival, one must not lose sight of the fact that it was largely inspired by Pietism. The latter was a vast religious renewal movement within the confines of the "official" Protestant churches, but very profoundly touched Mennonite congregations as well, especially in southern Germany, France and Switzerland. Pietism was born in Germany in the seventeenth century. The Alsatian Lutheran pastor, Philip Jakob Spener (1635–1705), was one of the outstanding figures of this movement. Some of its aspects bore a resemblance to certain aspects of Anabaptism. Pietism was marked by an emphasis on the Bible and Bible study for the church and in the life of the believer; spiritual illumination by the Holy Spirit; a priesthood of believers; a "personal decision" of conversion following repentance for sin; individual sanctification and a holy life; pastors who had experienced conversion; and sermons focused on salvation and sanctification, rather than doctrine or scholarship.

Mennonites both in northern and southern Europe were influenced by earlier and later forms of Pietism, which always contributed to renewal and reshaped their theology and practice, but which, at the same time, also regularly led to internal tensions and splits.

After 1871, a new empire emerged in Germany, headed by a Protestant emperor. This empire contributed to nationalistic euphoria. Outside of Germany, however, this state of affairs was seen as equating the German empire with Protestantism.

In terms of philosophy, the Enlightenment's "rational individual" began to think in "universal" terms. Historical philosophers, such as Hegel (1770–1831), saw the contradictions and tensions between knowledge and faith, Enlightenment and Romanticism, mind and nature, as part of a comprehensive, evolving, rational unity that Hegel called "the absolute idea" or "absolute knowledge." Following and modifying Hegel, Karl Marx (1818–1883) maintained that the struggle between social classes was the driving force of history; all events needed to be understood as manifestations of the class struggle. Stalin concluded that such a universal interpretation of history necessarily implied a one-party system, and the need for isolating dissidents by sending them to the *Gulag* (state administration of prison camps). The *Gulag* used dissidents to exploit the resources found in such inhospitable regions as Siberia, or for digging canals. It is estimated that there were twelve million deaths in these Stalinist work camps between 1936 and 1950. This figure does not include the six million more deaths that resulted from collectivization. Some historians suggest even higher casualty numbers.

Christians from the USSR and its satellite countries were often imprisoned in these Gulags along with other opponents of the Soviet regime. Alexander Solzhenitsyn, the great Russian author born in 1918, was sent to a work camp in 1945 for having criticized Stalin. His books, such as *The Gulag Archipelago* (1973), criticized the dangers of the Soviet system. In exile in the West, he criticized in turn the decadent lifestyle of western society after 1990 as much as he did the weakening and break-up of the Soviet economic system. Chapter VII describes some of the Mennonite experience during these difficult years in the Soviet Union.

Protestant theology went through significant changes in the twentieth century. The horror of World War I gave birth to theological tendencies which no longer saw God and human civilization, nation and culture united in a harmonious relationship. Karl Barth, (1886–1968) a Swiss Reformed professor in Germany and one of the leaders of this theological reorientation, was dismissed from his job in 1935 by the Nazi regime. He was then called to teach at the University of Basel in Switzerland. He contributed enormously to a return to the Bible, introducing a dialectical hermeneutic, affirming that God, and not humankind, was at the centre of theology. He was in conflict with derivations of liberal theology which were represented most notably at that time by Rudolph Bultmann (1884–1976). Other important Protestant thinkers of this time include Emil Brunner of Switzerland and Dietrich Bonhoeffer of Germany.

Renowned Swiss Reformed theologian Karl Barth (right) visits the European Mennonite Bible School at Bienenberg/Liestal in Switzerland in 1967. He is pictured with Bienenberg director and Swiss Mennonite elder Samuel Gerber. Barth's theology had a significant impact on several generations of Mennonite scholars and pastors in the twentieth century, including Frits Kuiper and Johannes Oosterbaan of the Netherlands and John H. Yoder, who studied with Barth in Basel.

In the so-called "free" countries of Europe, however, individualism mixed with materialism gained ground. The unbridled search for personal happiness led to the desertion of the traditional mainline churches.

In the "free world," the idea of an ecumenical "common household" of all Christians appeared already in the middle of the nineteenth century. This idea was launched primarily by evangelical Christians from the revival movement.[2] Since 1948 and to the present, two movements seem to be in competition with each other: the World Council of Churches, better known in the English-speaking world, and the International Council of Christian Churches. Christians of differing convictions have found it difficult to recognize the positive contributions and limitations of other groups.

In 1974, evangelical representatives at a missionary convention produced the Lausanne Covenant, which was followed by the Manila Manifesto in 1989. These were significant events because for the first time in recent history, concerns voiced by evangelical theologians from the two-thirds world were heard. These ecumenical Christian texts expressed a clear emphasis on social concerns (see article 5 of the Lausanne Covenant). This emphasis on "faith and works" also recovered an important holistic dimension of the early Anabaptist understanding of salvation that had been somewhat obscured in the Mennonite traditions that developed after the sixteenth century, whether through an emphasis on rationalism, introverted spiritual renewal (Pietism), or traditional observances. It should be noted that some North American theologians from Anabaptist-Mennonite backgrounds, like John H. Yoder and Ronald Sider, played an important role in supporting theological developments that emphasized a holistic faith, embracing all dimensions of life. Again, while the majority of Mennonites in southern Germany, Switzerland, France and Russia had closer contacts with evangelical groups, those in northern Germany and the Netherlands traditionally put their emphasis more on ecumenical relationships. Nevertheless, in more recent years these clear-cut distinctions between Mennonites in the north and south have given way to a broader variety of contacts and cooperation for both groups.

Article 5 of the Lausanne Covenant

5. CHRISTIAN SOCIAL RESPONSIBILITY
... Because men and women are made in the image of God, every person, regardless of race, religion, colour, culture, class, sex or age, has an intrinsic dignity because of which he or she should be respected and served, not exploited. ... ... we affirm that evangelism and socio-political involvement are both part of our Christian duty. For both are necessary expressions of our doctrines of God and man, our love for our neighbour and our obedience to Jesus Christ. ... The salvation we claim should be transforming us in the totality of our personal and social responsibilities. Faith without works is dead.

Today

Pentecostalism was born in Los Angeles in 1906, and spread progressively throughout all of Europe and the world. Pentecostalism is an extension of John Wesley's distinctive doctrine of the second experience of sanctification, further interpreted as the baptism of the Holy

Spirit. Pentecostal churches originated out of a desire for more spiritual power in the life of Christians. Their understanding of the charismatic experience made a necessary connection between speaking in tongues and the baptism of the Holy Spirit. At present, they constitute a fourth tendency in world Christianity (Orthodox, Catholic, Protestant and Pentecostal). Currently Pentecostal Christianity has the greatest rate of growth of all Christian groups in Europe. All Protestants, however, compose less than one percent of the population in more than twenty countries in Europe.

Similarly, the charismatic movement, which began in the United States in the middle of the twentieth century and made its way to Europe and into all denominations, including some of the larger Roman Catholic parishes, accentuated this search for spiritual gifts (speaking in tongues, prophecy, healing) and more fervour. The accent is on praise and a search for spiritual power which will mobilize and engage Christians. Unlike Pentecostalism, the goal of charismatic Christians is not to create new churches. These Christians are often characterized by a strong capacity for compassion. They are also keenly aware of the necessity of Bible study, evangelization and the need to live out church unity on a larger scale.

Today's Europe is culturally pluralistic and represents a combination of many cultural and philosophical influences: Greek, Latin, Jewish, Christian, Muslim, rationalistic and agnostic. It is also marked by a permanent critique of religion known as secularization. Some observers see secularization positively, as designating the expectation of an "adult" form of Christianity; more negatively, some use the term to describe the religious crisis of a society which has marginalized Christianity.

The total population of Europe, including Russia and other East-European countries, is around 730,000,000 inhabitants. The countries which belong to the European Union (including the ten countries which became members in 2004) number some 455,000,000 people—more inhabitants than in the United States.

It is not easy to find proper statistics as to new immigrants into Europe, since several countries only have statistics about the nationality of persons and not about their countries of birth. Also, many countries do not keep statistics about religious affiliation (which belongs to the personal sphere and not to the public sphere!). Nevertheless it has been estimated that in the countries belonging to the EU there are ten- to twelve-million immigrants from outside the EU countries, among them a vast majority of probably more than nine million Muslims. There are also numerous Christians from Asia and Africa living in Europe. The latter belong mostly to international, independent or Pentecostal-type churches. Nobody knows how many "illegal" or undocumented immigrants can be found in the EU countries; there would be tens of thousands at least.

Today's Europe is made up of a variety of religious cultures, which have adopted different methods of treating the religious question.

Northern Europe remains principally Protestant, the south, Catholic, the east chiefly Orthodox, and the western fringe, moderately Anglican. Thus England has more Anglican leanings; Scotland, Presbyterian; Greece, Orthodox; Italy and Poland, Roman Catholic; Sweden and Denmark, Lutheran; Russia, Orthodox; Belgium and France secular or Catholic; Germany and Switzerland, Protestant and Catholic; Turkey, Muslim. Indeed, cultural and religious borders do exist in Europe, but today secularization and religious diversity remain at its collective core.

Although the media has promoted an impression that established churches in Germany and elsewhere were very influential during the years of the fall of the Berlin Wall, this cannot disguise these churches' loss of influence, nor the clear drop in attendance at worship services. This trend is also visible among Mennonites. The generally low number of students in the mainline seminaries is revealing. The difference is striking when compared to what is taking place in North America.

According to a study by Philip Jenkins in the year 2000, 44 percent of the British no longer claim any kind of religious affiliation, and half of young adults no longer believe that Jesus existed historically. Traditional Roman Catholic countries such as France and Italy reveal analogous tendencies: at the turn of the millennium in these countries, only eight percent of the population were regularly-practicing Catholics. A new generation is emerging whose only knowledge of Christianity will be what the mass media chooses to present.

In terms of religion, the end of the twentieth century bore witness to an increase in the number of mosques in Europe, with the expressed purpose of allowing Muslims, most of whom are immigrants, to live out their faith. With respect to Christians, with the exception of members in Believers' Churches and those of charismatic or Pentecostal tendencies, the decreasing number of people attending churches is inexorable. In spite of this, new forms of spirituality are emerging in the churches—including in many Mennonite congregations—such as the use of songs which facilitate contemplation, as for example those of the ecumenical community of Taizé.

Over the centuries, Europe has made the change from a civilization in which nature and history were seen to reflect God's purpose, to an understanding of nature as simply the space in which the laws for linking cause and effect are to be found. In secularized thought, whenever reference is still made to a divine being, it is often in terms of "deism." "God,"—or whatever name one wishes to attach to the divine being—is the great watchmaker who has completed his work and chooses to intervene no longer in his creation, abandoning it to natural law. Putting it generally, for the past several centuries, the western world has experienced an unprecedented cultural upheaval.

As the sociologist Hervieu-Léger has shown, modernity did not make religion disappear, but rather modified it, producing multi-forms.[3] Because of the political separation between church and state, membership in religious groups is now voluntary. Government institutions no longer intervene in the private sphere of individuals' lives, nor do they any longer define heresy or sacrilege, as long as society is not affected. Europe has moved away from "Constantinian" forms of religion in which belief was imposed on society, and where the institutional Christian church and the state mutually reinforced each other. From now on, Christian faith in the West will be lived and expressed in this new context, without seeking to restore the previous situation through coercive forms of evangelization.

Europe has progressively developed into a consumer society in which religious practices have opened up to free choice, something which has contributed to an ever further dislocation of Christianity. New media forms have provided access to very diverse spiritualities and convictions. Feeling threatened, the traditional (or official) churches have found it difficult to accept these new forms. In general, they are at present made up of small parishes whose members are more committed to the church than was the case in the past, since there are no longer any constraints or enticements to conform to a commonly shared religiosity.

The challenge for the European churches of the third millennium—including the Mennonite churches of Europe—will be in knowing how to retell the simple gospel story of Jesus Christ, and seeking to share it and exemplify its pertinence in a world that has become postmodern, multicultural and multi-religious. It will be necessary for the church to continue its struggle to remain faithful to the Lord, regardless of the number of people that are part of it, to find pertinent forms in this context and to seek to be in communion with those believers whose faith is centred on compatible principles; and finally, to continue to welcome and love others in need, thus weaving relationships with members of the universal Church which is now scattered across the surface of the known world. This is a challenge not only for all other churches and Christians, but certainly also for the European Mennonites!

Economy and Demography

The Rural Exodus and Industrialization

Industrial expansion began at the end of the eighteenth century as a result of new technology, and resulted in the appearance of a new social group: masses of workers and their families who moved from the countryside and concentrated in the cities that grew up in the industrial regions. The large European powers, headed up by Great Britain, France and Germany, quickly became the sources of manufactured goods and investment capital for the non-European countries. As the economic influence of these European countries increased, so too did their political predominance.

The churches had great difficulty coming to grips with the changes introduced by the industrial revolution, and also with the advent of socialism. Intellectuals and workers distanced themselves from the churches because of the close ties that had existed historically between the church and those exercising political power. This explains, in part, why socialism was so attractive to the working classes. There was a Christian response, however, especially in England, namely a vigorous revival movement called Methodism founded by John Wesley (1703–1791), an heir to German Pietism.

The difficult road to democracy up through the middle of the nineteenth century finally led to the end of slavery, but also inaugurated the beginning of what has sometimes been perceived as a new form of slavery: the emergence of a cheap labour force made up of the most destitute of society, exploited by the industrialists to run their factories. The arms industry also played an important role by furnishing tools for domination which allowed the exploitation of two-thirds of the world's countries and peoples.

Socialist leader August Bebel (1840–1913) wrote in 1874: "Christianity and Socialism are opposed like fire and water" ("Christentum und Sozialismus stehen sich gegenüber wie Feuer und Wasser").

Progress in technology and industry generated new problems at the beginning of the twentieth century. Four-fifths of the population lived in overpopulated rural areas, and among them, one person out of two was employed in agriculture. This was the case for all of the European nations. This resulted in the development of modern cities, first of all in England, then elsewhere in Europe, and contributed to the weakening of traditional village-based social structures, to an inevitable mixing of populations, and to the reinforcement of modern political structures.

The two World Wars contributed to the emptying of the countryside as much as industrialization had done earlier. In France, for example, the First World War caused the deaths of a million and a half people, essentially from the rural areas, and mostly males between the ages of nineteen to forty.

The Quest for Christian Economic Solutions

The social problems caused by technological and industrial progress required responses. There were attempts at solutions: the Christian Socialist movement (from the German *religiös sozial*) was founded in 1906 by the Swiss Reformed theologian and pastor Leonhard Ragaz. This movement spread into France and Germany. The American pastor, Walter Rauschenbusch, came to realize that the treatment granted to the proletariat in an industrial society should lead to a profound repentance in the church, and a turn to socialism which was considered a sign of the Kingdom against "Mammon," i.e. capitalism. Leonard Ragaz followed this logic and emphasized following the nonviolent teachings of Jesus.

Leonhard Ragaz (1868–1945): "In some respects the Anabaptists sought a more radical turning toward the gospel and toward the first-century church than the other Reformation. They took the priesthood of all believers seriously. They also took the moral demands and promises of the gospel seriously. They understood the Sermon on the Mount. They held the human Jesus in high regard. They drew out the social consequences of the gospel; they preached and practiced brotherhood and social justice. ... The spirit of a new age, and simultaneously a new display of Jesus' kingdom of God, was seen in them most purely." (1909).

After the Second World War, European countries faced economic chaos; the United States was an exception. The United States regained full employment just before the end of the war. American economic aid to Europe after 1945—called the Marshall Plan—poured colossal amounts of capital into Europe. By the 1950s, this infusion of capital brought about better living conditions. A new form of consumerism, coming from the other side of the Atlantic, also took root in Europe. America became the new hegemonic power, and Europe has imitated this model of civilization based on individual choice and economic consumerism—not without its own share of problems. It has had much more difficulty reproducing the religious model of the United States due to the European principle of pluralism.

In his famous book, *The Protestant Ethic and the Spirit of Capitalism*, Max Weber claimed that even though Protestantism helped contribute to the "spirit of capitalism," the pervasive western economic system subsequently moved away from the moral and ethical foundations of Protestantism.[4] Separated from its religious underpinning, the resulting "spirit of capitalism" has become something almost terrifying, lacking any form of periodic redistribution of wealth, as in the biblical spirit of jubilee. One may wonder if the "capitalist" model of traditionally Protestant countries such as the Netherlands, Germany, Switzerland and England can or should be exported, if original elements such as the fear of God, sobriety, and the reinvestment of profits no longer accompany it. New forms of fraternal life which will bear the torch of the Good News into a multicultural and multi-religious society—and at the same time into a globalized economy—have yet to be discovered. The various chapters of this volume illustrate and discuss to what extent European Mennonite churches have been affected by these developments and to what degree they have succeeded or failed to formulate and to practice attractive, authentic and reliable answers or alternatives to these challenges.

Emigration and Territorial Conquests

At the end of the eighteenth century, the wealth and power of a nation was calculated according to the number of inhabitants. In 1800, France, Germany and Austria each had 28 million people, Russia, 40 million, and Spain and Italy, 15 million each. In order to make this "wealth" available for the enforcement of national goals, these countries resorted to the introduction of obligatory military service. The result was the creation of huge national armies. Most nineteenth-century European nations dreamed of acquiring more land and more influence. Two options for achieving these goals were warfare against opposing neighbours and expansion of influence through colonization of territories beyond the oceans.

In the nineteenth century, a growing number of Europeans left their home countries not only as soldiers in their national armies or as representatives of a colonial power, but as political, religious and particularly economic refugees in search of a better future. Among them were also many European Mennonites who emigrated from Prussia to southern Russia and from central Europe to North America. Seen from the perspective of the local people, the coming of these settlers seemed to be linked to the armies and the colonial ambitions of their home countries or civilizations.

In Search of Better Land

Independent of religious status or affiliation, the French Revolution made everyone a full-fledged citizen of the nation. This fact constituted a revolution for all religious minorities, including the Mennonites and the Jews. This was "good news," but the "bad news" associated with this new situation was that it brought an assortment of new responsibilities to all citizens, in particular, military service. Depending on the region, there were some temporary exemptions from armed service granted for "defenseless Christians" (the name given to Mennonites), such as alternative service or payment for replacements. The precariousness of these exceptions pushed many Anabaptist descendants to seek more tolerant lands which offered "negotiated privileges," such as in Russia through the invitation of Catherine the Great, or in the "New World."

The increase in the European population of the nineteenth century helps to explain the massive waves of emigrants. European populations, including that of Russia, increased from around 190 million in 1800 to 420 million in 1900. The Irish population experienced famine and malnutrition, for example, because of the catastrophe of the potato harvest. People migrated to the cities and industrial centres. The persecution of the Jews in Russia in 1840 also drove them to emigrate to the United States. In the 1830s, some 10,000 Europeans emigrated each year, and there were approximately 1,500,000 emigrants per year by the end of the century.

Prussian settlers left for the east (Poland and the Ukraine) in the same period as the French Revolution, in order to acquire land, since legislation in Prussia had become less generous to "sectarians," and also because Mennonites still refused to participate in war. Between 1793 and 1794, the Reign of Terror which followed the Revolution claimed more than 20,000 victims in the Empire by the guillotine; even the most hesitant were convinced to take radical steps. Some Mennonites felt the push to emigrate to North America.

Colonialism

By the nineteenth century, the nations in Europe could no longer grow by political expansion, and therefore, territorial expansion outside of Europe was pursued. The Spanish, Portuguese, Dutch, English, French, Russians, Prussians, and Austrians made a dash for territories world wide. Colonial riches fed the rivalries between the European powers. Occupied territories served as extensions of the individual European states, but were not considered extensions of Europe.[5]

In 1885 the Berlin conference was organized by Germany, France, England and Belgium to establish the principles of colonization, and more specifically to negotiate the division of Africa among European powers. Colonization consisted of the occupation of territory on another continent, and the exploitation of its human and natural resources, for the profit of the colonizing nation. In distinction from the past, it was now a question of replacing the "infamous commerce" of slavery, in which several European nations had participated, with a "legitimate commerce" that included the active participation of African people. But the rivalry between western nations and their eagerness for profit turned these undertakings into plans of conquest. European missionaries often found themselves unwilling defenders of the "spirit of colonization." European Mennonites also were caught up in the new spirit of mission work—a welcome sign of spiritual revival in the sending churches on the one hand, and a troubling extension of European colonialism on the other, as the Africa volume of Global Mennonite History has already illustrated.[6] Ambivalence was evidenced by the fact that while European missionaries generally tried to contribute to de-colonization, they also benefited from the colonial infrastructure. On the positive side, one of the valuable contributions of Christian missions in colonized territories can be found in the participation of Christian churches in the education of the leaders of the future independent states.[7]

Between 1800 and 1945, people from Africa and Asia witnessed European nations compete for economic domination in their territories. They saw also that the Europeans accepted new technologies—usually without much reflection—guided primarily by profit.

Evaluating the period of colonialism which extended far into the second half of the twentieth century one could say that on the one hand, all forms of colonial exploitation like slavery, plunder, massacres and the enrollment of nationals in some of the colonial armies, must not be forgotten or down-played. These acts call for repentance. On the other hand, *some* elements have had positive effects, although too often they were intertwined with ambivalent consequences. Some of these positive effects have been literacy, and with it access and integration into worldwide (though "colonial") language families, the improvement of sanitary and hygienic conditions, some cases of agricultural self-sufficiency, and here and there the eradication of some diseases such as sleeping-sickness, smallpox, yellow fever, and the restriction of malaria. Many medical doctors and nurses, as well as missionaries resisted the more negative tendencies of colonialism noted above, although unfortunately not all of them did.

The period of European colonization in certain countries in Africa and Asia lasted from 1814 to 1968. National movements everywhere demanded independence, although some chose other alternatives, such as becoming protectorates of the Soviet Union or the United States. Rivalries for military and political influence seemed all the more intense in regions that possessed non-renewable sources of energy, most notably oil.

The Diversity of the Peoples of Europe

Although Europe is taking steps towards reunification today, it must be kept in mind that Europe is made up of diverse groups of people who gave birth to nations with distinct languages and peoples. Neither can it be forgotten that invasions in the past, world wars, and modern industrialization have made it possible for very diverse populations to mix and find refuge in different European countries. Much of the ur-ban landscape in Europe today is thus quite varied and cosmopolitan, a situation which offers a chance for the Church to find new ways to demonstrate that the Gospel of reconciliation transcends races and cultures. The various chapters of this book will illustrate how the European Mennonite churches have responded to the changing reali-ties of European history, and how they have sought and found new ways of making visible the Gospel of reconciliation.

Today modernity has reached fruition. The common language— also all over Europe—is coming from the United States, and many seem to be convinced of the universality of American culture: liberal capitalism, together with Coca Cola, McDonald's, CNN, Microsoft, Nike, and Hollywood stars. But, as in the past, most of the world's population has no access to the benefits (if benefits is what they are) of this civilization.

Conclusion

When considering the major events which took place in Europe in the past two centuries, it appears that the Enlightenment was as harm-ful to the church as was the earlier period when Christianity reigned supreme. At one time or another, the nations which make up Europe have tried to take the destiny of Europe in hand in order to "save the world," or to contribute to its salvation (Napoleon, Wilhelm I, Queen Victoria, Stalin, Hitler, Mussolini). A popular notion circulated that according to a divine plan, a particular nation was destined to save the world by conquering it—though a secularized version would not have expressed the idea in exactly these terms. This "reign of man" was recognizable by its mode of conquest, namely by crushing whoever chose to resist. All secular saviours believed that if they succeeded, a new era of peace would open up for all of humanity. If they failed, they were convinced that humanity would sink into despair. Their reigns have all been bloody and short-lived.

After struggling against Nazism, Communism, and unbridled capitalism, a democratic Europe views its present union as a guarantee of stability. As is often the case, common economic interest, more than common security, is seen as holding this entity together. Further steps toward unity will take time. Until now, the Franco-German axis has been the driving force behind the present European union. In certain countries, the monetary union of a common currency (the euro) was put into effect in 2002. The work to establish a European constitution was at its height in 2004, and is still an ongoing project.

Certain fundamental ideas have converged to shape today's Europe: the reaction of peoples to the usurpation of power by certain forms of Christianity, the development of autonomous human reason, the industrial revolution and the rural exodus, all have played a major role in the history of the peoples of Europe. The world wars have also played a part in this process. European nations fought each other ferociously before realizing they needed to show greater solidarity in the face of other hegemonies. The rule of law, the welfare state and urbanization have taken root in a relatively homogenous way in all of the European countries. An increase in the number of wage earners, and improvements in communication have accentuated individualism. Globally speaking, Europe has had to recognize the loss of hegemony, matched by a clearer awareness of the need to work in closer cooperation with the rest of the world. This process has been a difficult, yet indispensable part of learning what it means to share.

It sometimes happens that taking the gospel to the ends of the earth comes down to preaching it anew "at home," in a culture that has changed. It is one of the goals of this book not only to show to what extent the European Mennonites have (or have not) tried to do this, but also to encourage and to motivate the Mennonite church world wide—including Mennonites in Europe!—to reconsider this task and to learn lessons from the past—both the agreeable lessons and the more painful ones.

Translation: Janie Blough

Mennonites in the Netherlands

by Annelies Verbeek
and Alle G. Hoekema

Introduction and Terminology

The coming of the nineteenth century marked the beginning of an age of full freedom and emancipation for Dutch Mennonites. Not without reason this century has been called "the golden age of the Dutch *Doopsgezinden*." In 1795 the reign of the House of Orange ("stadtholders," not yet kings at that time) temporarily came to an end, due to the growing influence of the so-called Patriotic movement, inspired by the revolutions in North America and France. In fact, the eighteenth century had been a period of relative tolerance in the Netherlands. There were only a few instances when the government had interfered in conflicts between the dominant Reformed church and Mennonite pastors, when they suspected the Mennonites of being Socinians or otherwise heterodox. The most famous (and last) case was that of the Mennonite pastor Johannes Stinstra from Harlingen, who was suspended from 1742 to 1757. In 1796, the separation between church and state in the new republic came to be regulated by law. From that moment on every Christian and Jew had the same rights, at least in principle. All were free not only to exercise the religion of their choice, as they had done in the past, but also to do so in public. Churches could be built in plain sight and Calvinists, Mennonites, Lutherans and all other Christian churches could hold their services at the same time.

After the Napoleonic period, which came to an end in 1814, a time of political restoration took place. The House of Orange returned and within the new constitution their role was stronger than ever before: they were now sovereign kings. Freedom of religion and separation between church and state remained, however, as important pillars of Dutch society. This situation led also to a larger role for Catholics, one of the reasons for the secession of the predominantly Catholic Belgium from the Netherlands in 1830—the main reason being economic.[1] At the same time, the Netherlands enlarged its colonial influence in the Dutch Indies; in a few decades this colony became an important source of income. As in other European countries, the year 1848 marked important changes, as a new constitution restricted the power of the king—a move that signaled more democratization.

During the seventeenth and eighteenth centuries the Dutch Mennonites had been accepted in many realms of society; already in 1735 they had been able to found their own seminary to train their future ministers. During the nineteenth century this Mennonite

Singel church in Amsterdam, view from the Herengracht side, 1844.

seminary in Amsterdam became an even more important vehicle for the Dutch Mennonites than it had been already in the eighteenth century.

Nevertheless, at the beginning of the twentieth century, the Dutch Mennonites had to recover from a period that lacked initiatives and vision. At the end of the nineteenth century they had found few religious answers to the great political and social changes that affected society at large: the impact of the Franco-Prussian war; the colonization of Africa, the rising influence of organized labour, socialism, and industrialization. Fortunately, the Netherlands remained neutral during the First World War, and in the 1920s a time of spiritual renewal took place among the Mennonites. After the Second World War secularization took its toll, not only on the Mennonites, but also on almost all Christian churches, except among some orthodox and evangelical groups. Therefore, we will be concluding this chapter by noting a few aspects of reorientation and efforts at renewal.

Finally, in this introduction we have to say a few words about the terminology used. In 1980 a volume of historical essays was published under the title *Wederdopers, menisten, doopsgezinden*: "Anabaptists, Mennonites, *Doopsgezinden*." This volume took the position that the most prominent groups among the sixteenth century Dutch Anabaptists started to call themselves *Menisten*, "Mennonites." From around 1600 on, the moderates among these *Menisten* became known as *Doopsgezinden*, literally "baptism-minded." If we were following this line of thought consistently, we would only have to use the term *Doopsgezinde* to describe the Dutch brothers and sisters of the nineteenth and twentieth centuries, since most of them are spiritual descendants of these moderates. However, in international contacts (such as the Mennonite World Conference and the World Council of Churches) the Dutch *Doopsgezinden* identify themselves as "Mennonites." Therefore we will use "Mennonite/s" and "*Doopsgezinde/n*" interchangeably in this chapter.

The Nineteenth Century: Church and Seminary

Parties Unite

On the threshold of the nineteenth century the old differences between the various Mennonite parties started to fade away. These Mennonite groups had been named after their places of origin, although their churches were spread throughout the Netherlands. There were the *Friezen* (Frisians), Waterlanders and *Vlamingen* (Flemish), the Waterlanders and the Flemish traditionally being more liberal.

The confessions of faith of the sixteenth and seventeenth centuries, which had cemented differences, slowly lost their grip and Mennonite congregations grew more and more alike. Separation was often a matter of family, tradition and money. The money was lost to the tax collectors under French rule (1808–1813) and at the same time a unifying spirit, so heartily embraced by Napoleon, took hold of the Mennonites as well. Many congregations did unite into one local congregation: old churches were sold and the once bitterly-divided Mennonites gathered together in one local house of worship.

In 1811 the increasingly stringent demands of Napoleon virtually bankrupted the Dutch state. The Netherlands had become a sort of French province and had to pay heavily for the Napoleonic wars. The Mennonite congregation of Amsterdam, which traditionally had taken care of the training of new ministers, could no longer afford to carry the

Zon en Lam were symbols of the ADS until recently, and remain symbols of the Amsterdam congregation to the present. The "sun" and the "lamb" do not refer to biblical images; their origins are secular. In the seventeenth century the lamb was the gable sign of a brewery at the Singel near the present Amsterdam Mennonite church; likewise, the sun was the gable sign of a former brewery which had been turned into a chapel of the Zonists.

costs of a seminary on its own. In 1735 the Amsterdam "Lamist" party had started the seminary, whereas the "Zonist" group took care of private training for their future ministers. The "Lamists" represented the more liberal and worldly party; the "Zonists" the more "confessional" and conservative wing of the Dutch Mennonites in the eighteenth century—although currents of pietistic and liberal thinking were found in both parties.[2] In 1801 both Amsterdam groups united into one congregation and the "Zonists" became a part of the "Lamist" seminary.

Menno Simons and his ideas did not play a significant part in Mennonite theology in this period, although a few scholars redis-

covered Menno and his writings. Menno was "recovered" out of nationalist and romantic feelings—more for his unique Dutch participation in the Reformation than for his radical thoughts. The name "Mennonites" was rarely used in this period, as noted above. In 1879 a monument to Menno Simons was erected in Witmarsum (Friesland) at the spot where the old, simple meetinghouse had been and where, according to some traditions at least, Menno Simons had preached to his first followers. Outside the Netherlands Mennonites were less pleased with the monumental obelisk for the truly Dutch Reformer! However, such opinions apparently do change. At present hundreds of Mennonite "pilgrims" each year from all over the world come to Friesland to visit the monument and the old hidden church in nearby Pingjum. Plans are being made to establish a spiritual centre near the monument.

Picture of the Menno Simons Monument in Witmarsum, erected in 1879 on or near the site of the simple meetinghouse which stood there until 1877. Most probably, however, Menno himself never lived or preached at this site.

Growth

In the eighteenth century the number of Mennonites in the Netherlands declined. One of the reasons for this lay in the fact that Mennonites were not allowed to work in the public service. Nevertheless, the Mennonite population became more and more well-to-do and less satisfied with the restrictions. Some (we do not know how many) left Mennonite congregations to become Calvinists. They wanted complete equality, not only in wealth but also in social status. Their exodus was also a result of the churches abandoning Anabaptist exclusivity. Other Mennonites favoured a republic, modeled on the French, without the Calvinist Orange family, in which everyone would be equal. The nineteenth century, which started off with a republic, did indeed bring equality to the Mennonite congregations, as well as an increase in membership, more or less in line with the overall growth of the Dutch population. One estimate places the number of Dutch Mennonites in 1808 at 26,935 and in 1899 at 57,786 out of a total population of three to four million inhabitants.

The nineteenth century saw the founding of seventeen new congregations, while three existing ones disappeared. However, the new increase in numbers was not just a result of a new-found equality or the growth of the population as a whole, since membership had been declining previously. The Dutch seminary professor Samuel Muller played a significant role in reversing the downward spiral of the Mennonite congregations.

The Seminary of the ADS

The new seminary needed to be the responsibility of more, and preferably all, Dutch Mennonite congregations. Therefore in 1811 the General Mennonite Conference (*Algemene Doopsgezinde Sociëteit*, or ADS) came into being, replacing the regional or confessional associations ("societies") of an earlier time. The task of the ADS seminary was "to promote preaching." ADS members contributed money for the support of the seminary, subsidized poorer congregations to pay a full minister's salary, and made sure that the church buildings and ministers' houses were in good order. As the nineteenth century progressed a growing number of congregations became members of the ADS; by 1923 all Dutch Mennonite congregations were members. In a later development, administering pensions for pastors became a responsibility of the ADS as well.

The ADS did not, however, become the "head" of all congregations. It never received synodal authority and did not adopt a creed or confession to which member congregations had to subscribe. Not before the second half of the twentieth century did the Dutch Mennonites begin even to discuss the merits of such a document. Therefore local churches remained autonomous in doctrine (theology) and practice. The ADS primarily managed the finances and, from the twentieth century on, represented the body of Mennonites in interdenominational organizations and in contacts with the government.

Already in the eighteenth century more and more congregations asked for professionally trained ministers instead of the lay-preachers to which they had been accustomed. The *Doopsgezinden* gradually had become increasingly educated themselves and yearned for more learned teaching in their worship services as well. Of course, this can also be interpreted as a reflection of a general trend of assimilation and emancipation. Some congregations lost members to the Calvinist churches because of the higher quality of the preaching. Therefore, many concluded that qualified, well-trained preachers were essential for the continued existence of Dutch Mennonitism. This widespread sentiment formed the solid base of support for the ADS.

Samuel Muller and the Mennonite Seminary in Amsterdam

Samuel Muller (1785–1875) was born and raised in the rather pietistic congregation of Krefeld (Germany), just across the Dutch border. The Krefeld congregation was served by Dutch ministers trained at the Amsterdam seminary until 1834. When Muller was sixteen years old

he received a scholarship to study at the seminary in Amsterdam. Within five years he had learned to speak Dutch like a native, received his degree and became acquainted with Mennonite life in the Netherlands. The difference between his Krefeld upbringing and Dutch congregational life was significant. Muller had not absorbed the Mennonite liberalist tradition of the eighteenth century through every pore—as had most students at the seminary in Amsterdam—and hence he questioned the prevalent liberalist theology of that time. He adapted to his new surroundings, though, and became pastor of the liberal congregations of Zutphen (1801), Zaandam-Oost (1807) and Amsterdam (1814). In the eyes of Muller (and others of his time) the Bible remained the only authoritative source.

Portrait of Samuel Muller, co-founder of the ADS (1811), the Dutch branch of the Baptist Missionary Society (1820) and the Dutch Mennonite Mission Association (1847). He was an influential seminary professor from 1827 until 1856.

The "liberalism" of that time meant emphasizing that the believer's role within church and society was to give an example of living the faith, rather than emphasizing verbal or written confessions. Muller's inaugural address in Zutphen was based upon Titus 2:7: "Show yourself in all respects a model of good works, and in your teaching show integrity, gravity, and sound speech that cannot be censured."[3]

As a minister in the influential Zaandam congregation (Zaandam being an important center of industry) he was one of the founders and board-members of the new General Mennonite Conference (ADS). In 1827 he became one of the two professors at the Mennonite seminary; he left office in 1856 when he reached the age of retirement.

Before Samuel Muller became a seminary professor, he already was deeply involved in seminary matters as a member of the ADS board. He had a strong conviction that the seminary had an important role to play in the renewal of Dutch Mennonitism. He emphasized that the seminary had to teach practical theology as well as academic subjects: homiletics, Christian education, speaking ability and also Mennonite history. When he had finished his own seminary training and started to work as a minister he had not felt adequately equipped for the task, and he wanted to remedy this defect in his education. When Muller became a professor at the seminary his ideas became reality. He made sure his students were skilled preachers, able teachers of the young, and clear and articulate public speakers. He also put Mennonite history on the seminary schedule in the hope of strengthening Dutch Mennonite identity, not so much by studying old confessions, but more by looking at typically Mennonite ways of living and contributing to society. For Muller, Mennonitism was the only truly Dutch reformed church, brought to birth by a real Dutch reformer (Menno Simons) and therefore superior to the Calvinist Reformed church, which in fact was a faith tradition imported into the Netherlands.

Theology

With the Enlightenment and its so-called "physico-theology" of the eighteenth century, physics and mathematics became important subjects in the seminary curriculum. In that century this kind of theology became very popular among Mennonites in the Netherlands. It was thought that by studying nature and its laws one learned to know God, who had so beautifully created the world. Therefore subjects like physics and mathematics were considered important for future ministers;

they had to tell the people about God, after all. Under Muller's influence, the seminary programs were reorganized; he made sure that Bible study received more emphasis in the curriculum.

Muller and others were proud of the non-dogmatic *Doopsgezinde* approach to the Bible, the traditional rejection of dogmatism and the independent, individualist approach to religion. He was happy that the Dutch Mennonites had come out of their seclusion and had become a modern church, like the still dominant Calvinist Dutch Reformed Church. He taught his students that theological developments outside their own denomination could benefit Mennonites as well, and he made sure that new English and German ideas in the fields of theology and philosophy were incorporated into seminary lessons.

Many ministers were trained under Muller's long professorate, and became pastors throughout the whole of the Netherlands. In this way almost all congregations got acquainted with Muller's ideas. He shaped Dutch Mennonite identity in the first half of the nineteenth century. His pupils carried on the good work, became his successors at the seminary and also introduced "modern theology" to the Mennonites—a development that the more biblically-oriented Muller greeted with worry in his heart. One of his former students, Jan Hartog, wrote a well-known *History of Homiletics* (1861, revised edition 1887) and received an honorary degree from the theological faculty of the Utrecht University in 1878 because of his critical, scholarly work.

Samuel Muller's view on the new Mennonite theology in the 1820s:

An ardent desire arose to re-examine the foundations of Christian faith and make it resistant to all shocks. Piety of the heart was no longer separated from knowledge of the unseen. Science was given breath as if by a higher spirit and Religion and Theology from then on entered more and more into the most intimate association with man's awareness of God.

In the 1860s and 70s, at the end of Muller's life, the so-called "modern theology" came on the scene. This new theological approach, developed at Groningen University and influenced by philosophical idealism and cultural and political liberalism, attempted to answer modern questions about revelation. Miracles and the laws of nature did not go together; incomprehensible matters like the resurrection, the atonement for sin and miraculous healings could not be taken literally anymore. The modernists sought rational explanations and more or less denied revelation altogether. Reason and human experience gave direction to their theology. For Muller and his generation, the modernists denied the core of Christianity (to be found in the life and death of Christ), but some of his pupils favoured modern theology. In most congregations, and particularly in those where the heritage of eighteenth century Enlightenment was still alive, these modern ideas were very welcome.

Muller's successor, professor Sytze Hoekstra (1822–1898), became one of the most distinguished modern theologians of his time, well known among colleagues from other denominations. From 1856 to 1892 he taught generations of future Mennonite ministers. He was less rationalistic than some of his Calvinist colleagues and rather a religious-ethicist, but still a modernist. With the modernists he believed that faith should not be based on authority—not that of the church, the Bible or dogma. He did not base faith in human reason or human experience as others did, but sought the foundations for faith in the idealistic human spirit that contemplates the world.

Sytze Hoekstra:

We believe in God, because life in a world without God would not be an essential life. All religious belief is therefore belief of man in himself, i.e. in the truth of his own spiritual being.

Modern theology had a large impact on developments in the twentieth-century Dutch Mennonite church; a majority of the Mennonites felt at home within the mainstream of the so-called *vrijzinnig-protestantisme* (literally: free-thinking Protestantism), characterized by tolerance towards other religious currents, an emphasis on individual spirituality and human autonomy, a longing for moral and religious renewal and emancipation from ecclesial patronage. This theological movement exerted much influence in Dutch society, especially in the period before World War II.

Yearbooks and Religious Literature

One way the Dutch Mennonites attempted to strengthen the bond between congregations and to enhance interest in theology and history, was to publish periodicals. Beginning in 1731, an occasional *Naamlijst* (name list) was published, which later also included information about the congregations in Prussia, France and Switzerland; however, it ceased publication in 1829. Between 1837 and 1850 Muller published a more extensive *Jaarboekje voor Doopsgezinde Gemeenten in de Nederlanden* (Yearbook); three editions appeared. Another popular periodical was Douwe Simon Gorter's *Godsdienstige Lectuur*, published between 1854 and 1858. In 1861 it was succeeded by the *Doopsgezinde Bijdragen* (1861–1919) which soon became an influential yearly scholarly periodical; it still is a valuable source of information about the history of Dutch Mennonites. However, its readership was restricted to the clergy. Therefore in 1901 A. Binnerts, minister in Meppel and Assen, launched a new initiative by publishing another yearbook, the *Doopsgezind Jaarboekje*, which contained edifying and novelistic prose and poetry directed to a wide audience. The *Jaarboekje* has proven its relevance to this very day, though in contrast with its original purpose its primary aim now is to be a directory of *Doopsgezinde* pastors, congregations and institutions. The former *Bijdragen* was revived in 1975; currently the *Doopsgezinde Bijdragen* is published yearly by the Mennonite Historical Society of the Netherlands.

In 1887 a Mennonite weekly called *De Zondagsbode* began publication. H. Koekebakker was its first editor. In its early years it also was read by many Baptists, since it included news from Baptist congregations in the Netherlands. In 1926 it became the official publication of the ADS. It was published until the German occupation forces suppressed it in 1942. Finally, the *Doopsgezinde Zendings Vereeniging* (Dutch Mennonite Mission Society) began publication of a monthly periodical *De kleine medearbeider* (The little co-worker) in 1899; in 1911 it was continued as the *Doopsgezind Maandblad voor in- en uitwendige zending* (Mennonite Monthly for Home and Foreign Mission), which ceased publication in 1917, at the end of the First World War.

Left Wing and Right Wing

Despite Muller's influence, he was not favoured by all Mennonites in the Netherlands. Halfway through his career as a professional theologian he found himself caught, so to speak, between Scylla and Charibdis, between the cliffs of neo-orthodoxy on the one side and hardcore liberalism on the other. First he was sharply criticized by the liberal minister and man of letters Joost Hiddes Halbertsma (1789–1869), who did not approve of Muller's emphasis on biblical preaching. He considered professor Muller a great danger to the Mennonite heritage because he trained the young ministers, and therefore he had a great influence on all Mennonite congregations in the Netherlands. For Halbertsma, real Mennonitism was a reasonable liberalism.

Halbertsma wrote why he favored rationalism (philosophy) above orthodox theology:

For philosophy and orthodoxy resemble the iron and earthen pots that together float down the river undisturbed, until a whirling current's pull bashes the pots together, causing the earthen one to break and sink to the bottom in shards, whilst its iron companion floats on gently on the waves.

Halbertsma's book on the history of the Mennonites (1843) attempted to prove—in line with a much earlier hypothesis—that the roots of the Mennonites were to be found with the Waldensians. The book caused great upheaval and was countered by polemical writings, but nevertheless, Halbertsma really did succeed in discrediting Muller, as he had hoped. Halbertsma's book mentioned a few of Muller's pupils who had become "orthodox" Mennonites—something he considered a sign of danger.

One of these pupils was Jan de Liefde (1814–1869), pastor in the town of Zutphen. De Liefde answered Halbertsma's accusations one year later. His book, titled *Danger, Danger! And no Peace!*[4] actually was a reaction to Muller's politics of appeasement, more than a defense of his own theological position. De Liefde did not receive support within the Dutch Mennonite community. He criticized Muller for his attempts to please both the liberal and the more orthodox Mennonites. In De Liefde's opinion, his teacher Muller had come halfway, not daring to fully embrace the gospel. But Muller was a community-builder, ready to compromise if necessary, and cast in a totally different mould than was De Liefde. After his Baptist and Darbyist sympathies became more and more evident, De Liefde resigned as a pastor in 1845, left the Mennonites, went briefly to Barmen, Germany as a director of the *Rheinische Mission*, and then founded an evangelization movement of his own in Amsterdam in 1849, supported by followers of the *Réveil* (Revival movement). He spent the rest of his life searching for a church community where his beliefs would be fully embraced. In some evangelical circles his name is still held in high regard.

Jan de Liefde's book, in which he analyzes the Dutch Mennonite brotherhood, begins with a comparison that contains his views in a few playful words:

There once was a fishing barge, run aground by the carelessness of its crew. The passengers, gladdened by the silent calm after so many rolls on the deep sea, lay themselves to a peaceful sleep and worried not about any rising tide. Then all of a sudden, an old helmsman raised his head from sleep and cried: Danger! Danger! seeing the approaching flood and storm. He proposed to pull the barge farther onto the beach and spend the winter there. [J.H. Halbertsma] *The passengers arose in alarm but another helmsman reassured them, saying they would merely bob gently along the coast.* [S. Muller] *Then a third helmsman stood up and said that staying the winter they would starve and hugging the coast they would never reach home.* [J. de Liefde] *He called upon all to get the barge afloat with might and main and return to the deep. Therefore he grabbed hooks and poles to drive the vessel out to sea. "Leave off," yelled many, "leave off, you are pushing it too far." "Ah well," he replied, "had you not drifted off, I would not be pushing it." Thereafter, he was called Pusher.*

The Nineteenth Century: Integration and Assimilation

During most of the nineteenth century questions relating to modernity dominated Mennonite thinking. Samuel Muller and several of his colleagues tried to connect the non-dogmatic autonomous spirit of the liberal Mennonites with biblical values. With reason and clear thinking they sought to explain the miracles of the Bible, but at the point where reason could no longer understand or explain, revelation prevailed. People just could not understand everything, but were able to believe anyhow. For modernists this compromise between reason and the biblical accounts no longer was convincing. They tried to find other ways to explain the Christian faith. In Muller's generation the search by the modern theologians succeeded in shedding many of the core beliefs common to the Christian tradition.

Assimilation

The growing nationalist spirit of the first half of the nineteenth century, after Napoleon's reign in the so called Restoration-period (1815–1847), was deliberately promoted by the Mennonites as well. Several examples can be given. For instance, Mennonites wholeheartedly participated in special prayer meetings organized by the state, in which Christians prayed for the prosperity and peace of the Dutch nation. Only a few congregations preserved the ways of their faith parents and did not assimilate nineteenth century values. One of these was the congregation of Balk in Friesland. In 1853 a good part of the Mennonite community in Balk emigrated to the United States because they could not maintain their old values in the Netherlands. Economic reasons also played a part in their leaving. Several families from Ouddorp migrated to the USA as well. Some other congregations, such as Aalsmeer, Ameland and Giethoorn (partly), maintained their original identity during a greater part of the nineteenth century. These congregations continued to use, for instance, the old seventeenth century hymnbooks. It is worth noting that by 1800, more than a hundred and fifty Mennonite hymnbooks had been published in the Netherlands.

The motive underlying the Mennonite attempt to assimilate fully in Dutch society was their weariness at being different, and being looked upon as sectarians. The Mennonites did not feel different from other Dutch citizens, and they wanted to gain the same respect due to the "non-dissenters." Little by little they became more like the Dutch Reformed Church—of course, without the hierarchy, the dogmas or confessions of the Reformed. Mennonites did, however, take on more important roles in society, accepting high offices in public service and even a few in the military, although that continued to be a profession frowned upon by Mennonites.

A few striking Mennonite values were kept alive: adult baptism was retained—although the baptism of new members coming from other denominations was intensively discussed in the 1850s and 60s— as was also the traditional custom of "affirming" (promising) instead of swearing oaths. The traditional Mennonite plainness and a sort of "smell of home" were still thought of nostalgically, although they were not always visible to the eye.

Church Services and Church Buildings

The liturgy of the worship services remained sober, although in their efforts to assimilate, most congregations now used a pipe organ to accompany congregational singing. Utrecht was the first Mennonite church to install such a novelty, in 1765. Pastors also began to wear robes and followed the current rules of rhetoric in their sermons.

A new era also required new hymnbooks, but here we see a limit to the attempts to assimilate. The old hymn books represented "the smell of home" and embodied something distinctly Mennonite. Several congregations, such as Haarlem, Amsterdam, and Leiden, composed and published their own hymnals. All in all at least fifteen different hymnals were in use during the nineteenth century. Though most of the hymns were not written by Mennonites, their content reflected the spirit of the time. In the so-called *Groote Bundel,* published by the Zonist congregation in Amsterdam in 1796, the influence of the Enlightenment is visible in the fact, for instance, that the word *Christ,* used as a title to describe the divinity of Jesus Christ, is used only seven times. In spite of an apparent emphasis on the humanity of Jesus, he is called Saviour, Guide or Ruler in these hymns.[5]

The church buildings changed as well, both outside and inside. Several old churches, hidden behind private houses in earlier times, became visible when these houses were torn down. Other churches were built. Former dissenter churches were entitled to receive a government subsidy when building a new church; however, in that case government architects had to provide the design, and mostly they used a rather simple uniform classical model. Therefore several Mennonite

Postcard of nineteenth century church building: IJlst in Friesland, dedicated in 1857. Between 1551–1557 Leenaart Bouwens baptized forty-nine persons here. Later two congregations existed in IJlst, until 1819. The present church was built at a time of growth and relative prosperity.

church buildings today have a rather dull façade. More wealthy congregations, often in the bigger cities, were able to construct more stylish buildings.[6] Often the interior of the Mennonite churches now changed as well. Pulpits replaced the traditional benches where elders and deacons sat; the new organs also required adaptations.

The Peace Tradition

From the 1780s on, the peace tradition among Dutch Mennonites became virtually extinct, at least among the dominant liberalist party. Exemptions from military conscription for Mennonites were dropped by the government during the period of French rule. In 1811 seven boys, orphans in the Mennonite orphanage "De Oranjeappel" in Amsterdam, were summoned to serve in the French army in Versailles, in spite of fierce protests by the trustees of the orphanage. However, most Mennonites supported the French Revolution (1787) and more than a few were prepared to take up arms in their own country to promote the revolution in Holland as well. In the ten-day Dutch-Belgian war that resulted in the independence of Belgium (1831), many Dutch students fought for their country. Among them were even a few Mennonite seminary students. The seminary board did not oppose this, although the subject was strongly discussed, both there and at the board of the ADS, which finally decided not to act as a synod: individual consciences had to decide the question of military service. It is not a surprise that at this time of pro-French sympathy, the formerly close relationships with the German and Prussian congregations were lost.

Participation in Public Service, Trade and Commerce, Science and Arts

In the second half of the nineteenth century Mennonites began to participate in the national government as members of parliament, and even as chairmen of the Senate and cabinet ministers. More than thirty parliamentary or Senate members can be counted in this century; no less than nine of them served as cabinet ministers; one even served as minister of Naval Affairs. Many of these Mennonite politicians belonged to the guild of traders, bankers and factory owners in Amsterdam, Zaandam, Rotterdam or the eastern region of Twente, but even a former pastor became a Member of Parliament. Mostly they were members of a (conservative) liberal party, though with a concern to meet social needs. A few were noted for being anti-militarists. One of the famous MPs of Mennonite descent was Samuel van Houten, still well-known for his law banning child labour, passed in 1874.

At the local level, Mennonites played a significant role in trade, commerce and industry, or as mayors of cities like Amsterdam. Often they had important international networks. Here contacts with fellow Mennonites in Hamburg, for instance, could be fruitful. Often these merchants and traders, with a broad view of the world, served as deacons in congregations such as Amsterdam, Zaandam, Rotterdam and Enschede. As an example we can mention the pious Van Eeghen family, who owned a trading house and a shipping company (shipping both to the Dutch Indies and to North America), with banking activities as well. Until recently they served as deacons of the Amsterdam congregation,

The faithful Deventer Mennonite, Mr. Albert van Delden, was Minister of Finance in a liberal cabinet between 1872 and 1874. Though he was proud of his appointment, nevertheless he soon realized that this office did not fit his character very well, and in a letter to his sister, 1872, he quoted a prayer by their grandmother: "may we be saved from the extremes of human suffering and human celebrity." "And," he added, "if being a cabinet minister may be reckoned as belonging to the extreme of human celebrity," then "it is really worth a prayer to remain free or be saved from this grandeur!"

or as members of the Mennonite Mission Board. Such people took initiatives to establish public bath houses, public housing, savings banks, municipal parks and museums.

Muller gave the Dutch Mennonites a firm place among other denominations in the Netherlands. He taught Mennonites that they were as good as members of other churches, and in fact, even better: Mennonites were the truly Dutch reformed church. He led the Mennonites to look beyond their own walls, and made sure that they were visible to everyone. As a result, Mennonites wrote in newspapers and magazines, participated in public debate and contributed to science.

Quite a few Dutch Mennonites were active as academic scholars in many areas: linguistics and literature (Matthijs Siegenbeek and Matthias de Vries), international law, education, biology (Jan Kops

The nineteenth century (Calvinist) Dutch church had a strong tradition of the dichter-dominee, the minister who was also a poet or writer of prose. Popular magazines, meant for a general public, describing progress in philosophy, sciences and medicine were also full of poems and short stories. Many of these articles were written anonymously by clergymen. Mennonite pastors also participated in this tradition. The Mennonite Loosjes family of Haarlem published one of the most popular, non orthodox magazines, the Vaderlandsche Letteroefeningen. Besides publishing they occupied themselves with writing and preaching.

and in the Dutch Indies, Pieter Bleeker), medicine (Matthias van Geuns) and church history (Christian Sepp) were disciplines in which several Doopsgezinden excelled, beginning in the late eighteenth century. A famous contributor to Dutch culture and learning was the Mennonite pastor Anthony Winkler Prins (1817–1908) in Veendam who, along with many other literary works, composed the Winkler Prins Encyclopedia (1870–1882, 16 volumes). This Encyclopedia is still the best-known Dutch Encyclopedia (now available on CD Rom as well).

Mennonites also were active in learned and charitable societies. The Maatschappij tot Nut van 't Algemeen (Society for the Propagation of Public Well-Being) was founded in the eighteenth century by the Mennonite pastor Jan Nieuwenhuijzen; many Mennonites were active members of this educational institution, which still exists. Among them, at least until he went to the Dutch Indies, was Eduard Douwes Dekker, later known by his pen name Multatuli—without question the most important writer of novels and critical essays of this century. It is true that he did leave the Mennonites, first to become Roman Catholic and later, an agnostic. One of his brothers served as a Mennonite pastor.

Finally, Mennonites were represented in the fine arts as well. Hendrik Willem Mesdag (1831–1915), for example, was a gifted painter, belonging to the so-called "Hague school of painting," as was his spouse, Sientje Mesdag-van Houten. His large "Panorama of Scheveningen," displayed in a special Mesdag museum at The Hague, is still considered "one of the world's miracles." Another Mennonite painter, Anton Mauve, son of a Mennonite pastor in Zaandam and later Haarlem, influenced the young Vincent van Gogh, who was his wife's cousin. When Mauve died in 1888,

GEÏLLUSTREERDE
ENCYCLOPÆDIE.

WOORDENBOEK

VOOR

WETENSCHAP EN KUNST, BESCHAVING EN NIJVERHEID.

Onder hoofdredactie van

A. WINKLER PRINS,

MET MEDEWERKING VAN VELE VADERLANDSCHE GELEERDEN.

Eerste Deel.

A ANGOSTURA.

AMSTERDAM,
C. L. BRINKMAN.
1870.

Title page of the first volume of the first edition of Winkler Prins encyclopedia.

Van Gogh dedicated a painting to his memory ("Blossoming Peach Tree: Souvenir de Mauve").

Mission

The early nineteenth century saw the beginning of many missionary initiatives in Protestant Europe, among them the English Baptist Missionary Society (BMS), founded in London in 1792. In 1820 two English Baptists, William Ward, a noted missionary in Bengal, India, and the shipowner William Henry Angas, came to Holland to raise funds among the Mennonites on behalf of their mission work in Bengal. They felt Baptists and Mennonites shared common roots and adult baptism. Ward soon returned to India; Angas later became a fervent propagator of the BMS and even travelled to Hamburg, Danzig, the German Palatinate and Switzerland to meet and convince Mennonites there. Two of the Mennonite ministers these Baptist fundraisers visited in the Netherlands, were the seminary professors Samuel Muller and Rinse Koopmans in Amsterdam. Inspired by a new missionary spirit, Muller and Koopmans called upon colleagues and friends to establish a Dutch branch of the English BMS. Until 1847 the Dutch Mennonites contributed to the English Baptist society, and then became convinced that the time had come to begin their own Dutch Mennonite Mission Society, the *Doopsgezinde Zendings Vereeniging* (founded in 1847). Civilization and conversion were the main aims of this DZV, led by some of the same pious members of the Amsterdam congregation who also were active in the field of social welfare.

The Mennonites had different reasons for thinking that they needed their own missionary society. One reason was their nationalistic perspective: why support missions to "foreign heathen" when the Dutch had their own colonies full of "heathen" ready to be converted? The Dutch Indies (now Indonesia) should receive their support instead of the British Indies. Furthermore, since the English had not supported the Dutch in the war with the Belgians, the English should not count on the unreserved support of the Dutch anymore. Theologically it was also time to take matters into their own hands. Joining the Dutch Reformed Mission was a problem, since the Reformed practiced child baptism. The Baptists themselves did practice adult baptism, but the Dutch Mennonites had other problems with the Baptists. In north Germany, Baptist missionaries were baptizing publicly and—in the eyes of the moderate Dutch—baptizing aggressively, and at the same time affiliating themselves with the good "Mennonite" name. Even worse: they insisted on the word "immersion" instead of "baptism" in their translation of the New Testament. The Dutch Bible Society did not agree with this translation, and the Baptists withdrew their membership. The Dutch Mennonites fully supported the Bible Society and disapproved of these stubborn Baptists.

In 1851 Pieter Jansz (1820–1904), the first Mennonite missionary of the modern era, was sent to the Dutch Indies. Others would follow him. Jansz and one of his co-workers, Hillebrandus Klinkert (1829–1913), became well-known linguists, experts in the Javanese and Malay languages, respectively. They composed dictionaries and translated the Bible into those languages. A few years later even donations from Germany (East Prussia) and Russia were received by the Dutch Mennonite Mission. The

old differences were temporarily forgotten in the fire of missionary spirit. Financial donations were even overshadowed by individual efforts in these communities: young men with missionary zeal asked to be trained by the Dutch to be sent abroad. For some time Mennonites from the North Sea to southern Russia worked side by side in the Mission among the "heathen" of the Dutch Indies.

Heinrich Dirks (1842–1915) from the Gnadenfeld congregation in the Molotschna area was the first of a rather large group of German-Russian missionaries to work in the Dutch Indies; he opened a new mission field in South Tapanuli, Sumatra. Thanks to his work, no less than thirteen Russian Mennonite missionaries and their families joined the mission work in Indonesia. Back in Europe, Dirks became a prominent promoter of the mission at many conferences and mission festivals.

Picture of Heinrich Dirks and his wife, Agnetha Schröder. From 1862 to 1866 Dirks received his training in the *Missionshaus* in Barmen, Germany. From 1870 to 1881 he worked as a missionary in Pakanten, South Tapanuli, Sumatra; he then returned to Russia to become a travelling evangelist (*Missionsreiseprediger*).

International Contacts

Already in the seventeenth century the Dutch Mennonites had maintained relationships with brothers and sisters elsewhere in Europe, and even in Pennsylvania, through the *Fonds voor Buitenlandsche Nooden*, the "Relief Fund for Foreign Needs." This fund functioned for almost a hundred years; it finally ceased to operate in 1758. Certain Dutch Mennonite groups, like the Old Flemish, maintained regular contacts with brothers and sisters in the faith in Danzig and the surrounding area; shipping and trade links made this possible.

The Dutch language was used in the church services in Danzig until around 1750; then ties with Holland loosened. In the congregation of Hamburg, served by several pastors who had received their training at the Amsterdam seminary, the Dutch language was used until 1839. The situation in other German congregations near the Dutch border, such as at Krefeld and Emden was similar, and demonstrates the economic and intellectual hegemony of the Dutch Mennonites at that time. This is also apparent from the many nineteenth century translations of older Dutch Mennonite sources into German and English, both in Europe and North America, such as the collected works of Menno Simons and Dirk Philips, the confessions of Dordrecht (1632) and of Cornelis Ris (1776), the *Martyrs Mirror*; and especially Jan Philips Schabaelje's often-reprinted prose texts.

International contacts intensified during the nineteenth century through the increasing role of secular newspapers, trade, and banking. Samuel Muller had a network of scholarly relations, not only with Mennonites but also with others. His opponents Jan de Liefde and Joost Halbertsma also had an international network, and others did as well. As noted above, addresses and other facts about Mennonite congregations in Germany, Alsace and Switzerland were included in the *Naamlijst*. The work of the DZV made use of existing contacts and enlarged such networks. For instance, in 1875 the DZV dearly wanted Samuel S. Haury (1847–1927) from Ingolstadt, Bavaria, to work with the mission in the Dutch Indies. He chose to work among the Native Americans instead because North American Mennonites had sponsored his studies in Barmen. This led to correspondence between the Netherlands and the USA. The mission board also maintained good relationships with fraternal missions such as the *Rheinische Mission* in Barmen. It is true, of course, that all these contacts were limited to western Christians. Although the DZV had many contacts with its missionaries and with others in the Dutch Indies, unfortunately letters or other written statements by Javanese or Sumatran believers during this century are lacking.

The First Half of the Twentieth Century

At the end of the nineteenth century, the spiritual growth of Dutch Mennonites stagnated, much as happened in other Protestant denominations. At the beginning of the twentieth century Dutch Mennonites needed new enthusiasm. As mentioned above, in 1902 the mid-nineteenth century yearbooks (*Jaarboekje*) were published again, a sign of a growing common interest of which the *Zondagsbode* was evidence. Nevertheless, the main motivation for renewal came from an external source.

Congregational Renewal

In 1903 George Cadbury, a wealthy Quaker chocolate manufacturer, put his large country house called "Woodbrooke" at Selly Oak, near Birmingham, UK, at the disposal of an "Adult School Movement," a religious renewal movement. Woodbrooke became a retreat and conference center where Quaker spirituality formed the driving force. Young theology students from the Netherlands felt attracted to this work. Among them were several Mennonites, notably Tjeerd Oeds Hylkema who wrote his seminary paper on that subject in 1911. Back home, those who had attended meetings in Woodbrooke continued to come together and founded a still-existing inter-confessional retreat center in the village of Barchem, in the eastern part of the country.

Ten Mennonite participants went one step further. They wanted to transmit their pietistic experiences of religious renewal to the wider church. Hence they founded the so-called *Gemeentedagbeweging*

Postcard of main building of "Broederschapshuis Schoorl."

(literally: Congregations' Day Movement), a movement on behalf of yearly spiritual meetings of all Mennonites. In a non-dogmatic, Bible-oriented way this new movement encouraged congregational and individual faith, and became a stimulus for Bible study and mission. The first national Congregations' day was held in 1917, in Utrecht. The movement clearly wanted to counterbalance the self-complacent mentality of bourgeois Mennonitism.

Soon the organizers realized that they needed conference centres of their own to meet their goals. The first *Broederschapshuis* (home of/for the Mennonite brotherhood) to be built, as a simple barracks, was near the village of Elspeet (1925); now it is called *Mennorode*. Soon other homes followed: *Fredeshiem* ("Grounds of Peace," in the Frisian language) near Steenwijk in 1931; Schoorl in 1933; and finally Bilthoven. Mennonites from all over the country gathered at these retreat centres for study, retreat and holidays. Though they have been extended and modernized since, the first three centres still function well. The fact that these projects came into being at a time of serious economic recession (from 1929 on) demonstrates both the need for a commitment to spiritual renewal and community building during these years as well as the optimistic mood and inner strength of the Dutch Mennonites at that time.

The *Gemeentedagbeweging* founded a number of task forces: on behalf of mission, Bible study, total abstinence from alcohol, promotion of church music and against military service.

According to the architect of the Schoorl home, G. Knuttel, who also designed the Elspeet buildings, the many glass doors and windows, opening on all directions, "express the hospitality of this Brotherhood house, but also its being open to the impressions of God's Creation which surrounds us on all sides. The ascending contour of the building, resulting in a slender peak, symbolizes how the brotherly community is aiming at God above." The opening of the home was accompanied by a small incident. The "Working Group against Military Service" had offered a flag, portraying a peace dove on a blue field. However, not all Dutch Mennonites were pacifists. The flag therefore had to be taken down. Later on the Board of Schoorl decided that the flag was not to be seen as the symbol of a particular working group, but as expressing "Here peace is reigning, here God's voice is being heard." Therefore it was used again.

Contacts with Mennonites, Quakers and others abroad were stimulated. Several pamphlets were published, many conferences organized and a monthly periodical, *Brieven* (Letters) served as a communication channel between 1917 and 1941.

In 1928 the Mennonite Youth Association (*Doopsgezinde Jongeren Bond*) was founded. This organization joined the already existing *Vrijzinnige Christelijke Jeugd Centrale*. Both associations organized summer camps, scouting groups and discussion groups. Youth homes were built in Giethoorn and elsewhere.

Peace Issues

The *Arbeidsgroep tegen den Krijgsdienst* (Task Force against Military Service), founded in 1923, became the most active group within the renewal movement. From the end of the nineteenth century there had been pacifist and anti-militaristic groups in Europe, often connected with (Christian-)anarchism and socialism. Tolstoy's idealism provided one example. These movements also had followers in the Netherlands. One important event was the publication of a manifesto in 1915, in the middle of the First World War, during which the Netherlands remained neutral; the signatories expressed support to those who refused to serve in the army. A number of signers were brought into court because of "agitation"; among those who were sentenced to two weeks in prison were two Dutch Mennonites, Jan Gleysteen and Lodewijk van Nierop.

In prison, Cor Inja had many deep discussions with the schoolteacher, the guards and others. On Monday, July 6 he had a fierce debate with the religious teacher, a staunch Calvinist who accepted violence by Christians when it was supported by the church. Cor Inja's reaction: "So, a Mennonite in Germany has to take his sword against Mennonites from other countries? A Christian from England has to fight in the name of England and God against German Christians, who in their turn fight in the name of their nation and God?"

From 1947 to 1973 Inja (1903–1989) worked as secretary of the Doopsgezinde Vredesgroep (Mennonite Peace Group) and—paid by the State Department of Defense—as an adviser and spiritual coach of conscientious objectors.

The first conscientious objector in the Netherlands was jailed in 1895, even before a law on military conscription had been passed (1898); the first conscientious objector from a Mennonite background was Jan Terweij, in 1904. The best known among a limited group of Mennonite conscientious objectors who were jailed was Cor Inja from Zaandam, who wrote a diary during the eight months he spent in prison in 1925 in The Hague—the same prison where the Serbian ex-president Milosevic was detained. Inja received good support from many pastors and members of Mennonite congregations, and even got a visit by the North American Henry J. Krehbiel, who a month earlier had attended the first Mennonite World Conference in Basel.

The Task Force against Military Service remained active until 1940; in 1928 it formulated a statement of principles. Together with other organizations, such as *Kerk en Vrede* (Church and Peace) a number of conferences and actions were organized, and brochures written. The group represented a minority opinion among the Dutch Mennonites of those years.

The Role of the ADS

The *Gemeentedagbeweging* took the lead as a grass roots renewal movement and also as a tool for the growing involvement of women. Women participated and even took the lead in many task forces and committees and were the ones who assisted impoverished families during the years of economic crisis after 1929. For some years the Haarlem congregation even promoted a kind of voluntary social service year for women, called *dienende arbeidsters* or "serving labourers." However, the ADS enlarged its role as well. Next to its responsibility to maintain a seminary and to safeguard the old age pensions of ministers, the ADS represented Mennonites in inter-denominational organizations, such as the Dutch Bible Society, and beginning in 1923 on the Central Committee of Liberal Protestantism (though expressly "on behalf of a majority within the ADS"). When an *Oecumenische Raad* (Ecumenical Council) was created in 1935, the ADS was among the seven founding churches. In practice, this council became active only after World War II.

The increasing mobility of the population, mainly caused by industrialization, led to church members living in places where no Mennonite congregation was to be found. Some 10 percent of all *Doopsgezinden* belonged to this group. They held mainly white collar jobs in factories and mining companies, worked for the railway system or were public servants. On behalf of these "diaspora" *Doopsgezinden* a new series of edifying pamphlets was published, the *Geschriftjes ten Behoeve van de Doopsgezinden in de Verstrooiing* ("Small writings on behalf of *Doopsgezinden* living in dispersion") not only about church history and the present life of the church, but also about the problems of Mennonites in Russia (by Cornelius Krahn) and Brazil (by Z. Kamerling). Sixty-one issues were published between 1897 and 1941. There even were a number of Dutch Mennonites living in the Dutch Indies who asked the ADS to "come here and help us." Several new congregations came into being from this diaspora situation

Up to the present time one of the most popular hymns from the Liederenbundel ten dienste van de Doopsgezinde Broederschap *is number 289. It expresses the optimistic and active mood of the Dutch Mennonites between the two world wars:*

Ik voel de winden Gods vandaag;
I feel the winds of God today,

vandaag hijsch ik het zeil.
today I hoist my sails.

Gehavend is 't en zwaar van schuim,
Though battered and too heavy with foam,

maar 'k hijsch 't en hoop op heil!
I hope at being saved.

Want Christus zelf, als stille gast,
When Christ himself, a quiet guest,

reist in mijn scheepje mee
Will board my tiny craft,

Op Zijn bevel durf 'k uit te gaan
I dare set out at his command

op wilde, hooge zee!
However wild the waves.

in cities like Apeldoorn, Heerlen, Eindhoven and 's Hertogenbosch. Finally the ADS founded a *Commissie ter Uitdeling*, a committee which still exists and deals with financial subsidies to poor congregations. In the field of liturgy, the ADS participated in preparing and publishing a new hymnal along with several smaller, liberal churches (1943); some fifty Mennonite hymns were included in this collection.

Seminary and Theology

In 1876 a new law governing higher education established a clear distinction between "general" theological disciplines, for which the state was responsible at the universities, and "church-bound" disciplines (such as dogmatics and practical theology), to be taught and financed by the churches themselves. This so-called *duplex ordo* system still exists at state universities. From this point on, some Mennonite professors taught as university professors; others were appointed by the seminary only. At the municipal University of Amsterdam the Mennonite seminary worked together with the Reformed Church (except during the period between 1893–1945) and with the Lutherans.

The changing social and cultural mood in society at large also influenced the Mennonite seminary. After serious discussions in the seminary board and within the ADS, female students were welcomed from 1906 onwards, though in the beginning they were not entitled to receive scholarships. The Dutch Mennonites were the leading Protestant church in this respect.[7] The first woman to finish her seminary studies was Annie Mankes-Zernike (1911). She became the first female minister in the Netherlands and served the congregation of Bovenknijpe (near Heerenveen, Friesland) from 1911–1915. Then she married a painter, Jan Mankes, and resigned her ministry. Between 1925 and 1940, 97 students were admitted to the Seminary; 33 of them were women. In 1939 twelve female ministers (out of a total of 102) were working in Mennonite congregations.

Annie Mankes-Zernike (1886–1971) was appointed a minister because "the attractive, modest and true attitude of this pioneer had strengthened the conviction of many people, that merely ecclesial conservatism so far had prevented women from developing their gifts and strength in the pulpit" (De Zondagsbode, November 12, 1911). Many members of her congregation De Knipe (near Heerenveen, Friesland) were Christian-socialists, and female members had been allowed to vote in the congregation since 1887. Annie Mankes-Zernike got her PhD in 1918, having done a study of the ethics of Marxism. After her husband died in 1920, she became pastor of the (liberal) Protestantenbond congregation in Rotterdam. She wrote several devotional books. Her sister was a well-known novelist, and her brother a physicist who was awarded the Nobel Prize in 1953. The drawing is by her husband.

Though seminary professors like I. J. de Bussy and later W. Leendertz were respected in the field of ethics and philosophy of religion—the latter was the first to promote Kierkegaard's philosophy in the Netherlands—the most influential person of this period was Wilhelmus Johannes Kühler (1874–1946). He revived interest in the history of the Dutch Mennonites and played an important role in the ADS itself. His hypothesis, that there was an historical continuity between the Modern Devotion of the late Middle Ages (Geert Groote and others) and the early Dutch Anabaptists and the modern *Doopsgezinde*, has been contested recently by Sjouke Voolstra.

Between the wars, Mennonite theology was partly influenced by the stream of liberal, rationalistic theology, but several theologians and pastors were attracted by Karl Barth's dialectical theology. Frits Kuiper (1898–1974) even debated with Barth concerning infant baptism, when the latter visited the Netherlands, and he wrote a report on Barth's refusal of infant baptism (1939). Kuiper was an active socialist and anti-militarist; between 1922–1924 he stayed eighteen months in the Soviet Union. In 1938 he vigorously rejected any totalitarian regime and stood up in defense of the Jews.[8] As a pastor, he took part in the resistance movement during the war, and later became an influential Old Testament scholar with special emphasis on Jewish thought; as a Christian with Messianic expectations, he called himself a Zionist.

International Contacts, Relief, Mission

The former *Fonds voor Buitenlandsche Nooden* (Dutch Relief Fund for Foreign Needs) had ended its activities in 1758, due to the fact that the persecution of brothers and sisters in the faith had ceased, but it got a successor in 1920. Dutch Mennonites had been well informed about the fate of Russian Mennonites through the letters of Benjamin H. Unruh in 1920 and by a booklet written by T. O. Hylkema in this same year. Within four years, some 240,000 Dutch guilders were collected; some Dutch Mennonites were sent to Russia to organize the relief, and food and clothing were shipped to Sebastopol.

In 1924 another phase began, as many Russian Mennonites tried to escape. In June 1924 a *Hollandsch Doopsgezind Emigranten Bureau* (Dutch Mennonite Office of Migration) was founded in Rotterdam.[9] The work of this Office was carried out only because of the good relations between the local congregation, especially its minister S. H. N. Gorter, and the local government and the harbour authorities. Of course, this relief work was done in close cooperation with the Mennonite Central

Committee. By 1930, over 1,000 Russian refugees had passed through Rotterdam; later the numbers decreased and the activities of the Office came almost to a standstill in 1936. The early groups migrated to Canada; later they went to Mexico, Brazil and Paraguay.

From a letter by the Mennonite emigrant Abram Bärg, Rotterdam, June 16, 1924:

It was a great joy to us, that we got acquainted here with Mennonites, who welcomed us very friendly. There are some 700 Mennonites in Rotterdam. Even though we cannot understand their language, nevertheless they feel a deep relationship with us, and when one sees the old women with their cap, one really gets the impression that the origins of our forefathers are to be found in Holland. Since Mrs. Sawatski was unable to pay the costs of the hospital, the Rotterdam Mennonites offered to pay everything for this widow, even though we didn't ask for it. They also wanted to collect clothes and money on our behalf, but we thanked them for their good intentions and asked them to save their abundance on behalf of later passing poor Mennonites.

In April 1937, the Dutch Mennonites briefly supported a group of thirty-one anti-militarist Hutterites, who had been expelled by Germany; it led to protests by German Mennonites, who denied that these Hutterites had ties to the Mennonites.[10]

Dutch Mennonites took an active part in the international Mennonite World Conferences of Basel (1925) and Danzig (1930), the latter meant to coordinate the international relief to Russian Mennonites. And of course, the Mennonite World Conference of 1936 in Elspeet and Witmarsum, primarily organized by the Dutch Mennonites, provided an excellent opportunity to broaden international ties, though the shadows of the Nazi regime in Germany were already falling over Europe.

In the meantime, the work of the mission in the Dutch Indies continued. In several respects it was enlarged, partly because the colonial government provided financial means for educational and medical programs. Therefore a number of nurses (also from Russia), medical doctors (mostly Dutch non-Mennonites), administrators and teachers could be sent. The missionary work proper, both on Java and in South Tapanuli (North Sumatra), was carried out and financed predominantly by Russian, and later German, missionaries. Unfortunately the mission work seemed to lack real vision during these decades, though the German missionaries Schmitt and Stauffer, and also the Dutch medical doctor Karl Gramberg, had an open eye for the need of renewal.

Public Life and Culture

From 1900 until the outbreak of the Second World War, twelve Dutch Mennonites served as members of Parliament or the Senate during one or more terms. Five of them were cabinet ministers, and one even was

Minister of Defense. An important parliamentarian was the lawyer Dirk Fock (1858–1941), minister of Colonial Affairs and Governor of the Dutch East Indies between 1921 and 1926. Fock was a conservative politician; nevertheless during the years of his governorship the nationalist movement in the Indies grew. By far the most prominent *Doopsgezinde* politician was the engineer Cornelis Lely (1854–1929), minister of Public Works and Trade in three cabinets (1891–1894, 1897–1901, 1913–1918), and in between Governor of Suriname (Dutch Guyana). He can be called the spiritual father of the thirty-kilometer-long *Afsluitdijk*, the dyke which connects Friesland with the Province of North Holland, and which is an important means of controlling the devastating forces of the sea.

Cornelis Lely, a man of great honesty, was a faithful member of the Mennonite congregation in The Hague, where he also served as deacon. At his funeral service Romans 12:18 was quoted from his farewell letter to his children, and the pastor mentioned the fact that on Sundays, Lely "walked to church together with a streetcar driver," a sign of his plain lifestyle. His biographers called Lely "a pious, red liberal." In 1954, on the occasion of his 100th birth year, a statue of Cornelis Lely was placed at the North Holland end of the Afsluitdijk. Later even the capital of the twelfth Dutch province, the completely reclaimed Flevoland, was named after him: Lelystad.

The role of Dutch Mennonites in the culture of the Netherlands was less conspicuous in these years compared to the nineteenth century, although Dutch Mennonites occasionally turned up in novels by non-Mennonites. The renowned historian Johan Huizinga (1874–1945), author of, among other works, *The Waning of the Middle Ages* (1919) and a descendant of a well-known Dutch Mennonite family, was baptized in 1890 and though not active in congregational life, remained a member until his death.[11]

National Socialism and the Second World War

The chapter on Germany in this book provides an extensive report concerning the impact of National Socialism on German Mennonites from 1933 on. Of course, Dutch Mennonites experienced this period in a completely different way. Germany remained a "befriended nation" until 1940, even though the majority of the Dutch population strongly disliked its policies. This national stance hampered clear statements by Mennonites. Anti-Nazi voices could be heard most clearly within the *Arbeidsgroep tegen den Krijgsdienst* (Task Force against Military Service), where contacts with other peace groups existed, as well as in Barth's ideas as expressed in the *Theological Declaration of Barmen* by the so-called Confessing Church in Germany, in May of 1934. Within the ADS things were more complicated. Could followers of the NSB, the *Nationaal-Socialistische Beweging* (National Socialist Movement), which supported the Nazi ideology, be shunned or kept out of Mennonite congregations? The Reformed churches in the Netherlands (*Gereformeerde Kerken in Nederland*) gave an affirmative answer to this question in their synod meeting of 1936; unfortunately in the same sentence they also condemned anti-militarism.

The Mennonites, however, wanted to keep politics out of their religious convictions, so deeply were they marked by tolerance and a liberal attitude. In 1937 one member of the Executive Board of the ADS phrased this general view in the following words: "In our congregations the Kingdom of God is preached, which is not of this world; therefore all political persuasions may feel at home in our midst" (including adherents of the NSB).[12] Furthermore, there was a genuine fear that a rupture would be caused between European Mennonites. In preparing for the World Conference of 1936, held in Amsterdam, Elspeet and Witmarsum, proposals for presentations that were deemed "too political" were turned down. Nevertheless, many Dutch *Doopsgezinden* felt disappointed by the attitude of German Mennonites towards the new regime. For similar reasons Dutch aid to Brazilian and Paraguayan Mennonites ceased during the late thirties. Groups of Dutch Mennonites were able to host fleeing German Jews in the Schoorl center and, together with Quakers, helped Christian Jews before and during the war. Others were active in several resistance movements after 1940.

Once the war began in 1940, things changed rapidly. Mennonite churches in Rotterdam and Wageningen were destroyed in May 1940, the one in Vlissingen in 1942 during Allied bombings on this harbour city. Some other churches were heavily damaged, and the church building of Nijmegen was destroyed in June 1944 during the military offensive of the Allied forces, known as *Market Garden*. The *Zondagsbode* was suppressed in 1942, and the conference centres in Schoorl and Elspeet were commandeered by the German army in 1943. Travelling became difficult and communication between congregations was often impossible. The board of the ADS tried to continue its meetings, and the ADS cooperated closely with other churches in an Inter Church Consultative Body (*Inter Kerkelijk Overleg*) in resisting the occupiers. They sent protest letters, composed messages to be read from the Sunday

morning pulpits, assisted those who suffered or who had to go underground, and discussed ways to continue theological training after the
universities and the Mennonite seminary had been closed. Since the
ADS secretary was a pro-German brother (until 1942), an Advisory
Committee of Spiritual Concerns (*Commissie voor Geestelijke Belangen*)
was created which consisted of "good" brothers and functioned as a
parallel body next to the official ADS Board. This committee took over
several tasks from the ADS board during these dark years. In the last
year of the war and immediately after the war, when the food situation
in the large cities of the western part of the country had become very
critical, sometimes northern congregations (Friesland, Groningen)
were able to send some relief (potatoes,
grain) or to host children and others who
had to flee from these exhausted cities, or
who needed a time of rest.

A number of Mennonites died as a result of the war. A few joined the German
army or supported Nazi ideology, and died
for that reason. Many more were killed
for belonging to resistance groups, were
attacked during bombings or perished
because of the forced labour they had to
do in German factories. According to one
estimate, some one hundred Mennonites
were among those imprisoned in German
concentration camps, and lost their lives
there. A commemoration volume of a
large, predominantly Christian resistance
movement mentions nineteen names
of Mennonites in its obituary list. Several Dutch Mennonites lost their lives in
Japanese prison camps in Indonesia or because their ship was torpedoed or bombed,
as happened to the German missionaries
Hermann Schmitt and Otto Stauffer near
Sibolga, North Sumatra (chapter IV).

In the last chapter of the present book
a moving example is given of reconciliation between Dutch and German individuals in the last days of the atrocious

*A good number of pastors and lay people
were involved in hiding Jews and others during the war. Below is part of a story told by
the late pastor Nine Treffers-Mesdag, whose
father was a pastor in Sneek, Friesland. His
parsonage was one of the centres from
which Jews, and especially Jewish children,
escaped the persecution of the Nazis and
were brought to private shelter homes.*

*"Jaapje van der Meer (now Jaakov Agmon
and living in Israel) came to our house in
1942. With an Amsterdam tram ticket in
his hand, he was brought by one of the
many female students from Amsterdam
who served as couriers. They belonged to a
resistance group [...]. We didn't know the
names of the people involved in it. The couriers took ration cards along and had forged
legal papers for the children. In 1943 it was
necessary to look for a different address for
Jaapje. That was organized by pastor Hans
Sipkema [in Terhorne, also Friesland]. My
mother would call him in such cases, saying
that she needed a birthday present. "Do
you have something for me for a boy/girl
aged ... years?" This way it worked, through
colleagues; in a way similar to what my
parents did, he found a place in the home of
trustworthy members of his congregation.
After a year, it became too dangerous there
as well, and Jaapje moved to Drachtster
Compagnie."*

war. Directly after the war, several pastors in a truly reconciling way asked for a fair trial of those who had collaborated with the German enemy (including a few pastors); they visited these traitors in prison and declared themselves opponents of the death penalty.[13]

After 1945: Renewal and Decline

The first decades after 1945 can be characterized by the themes of renewal of congregational life, a spirit of ecumenism, continuation of an attitude of peace and service, and the desire to define the central issues of Mennonite belief. At the same time secularization and individualism became important values in Dutch society. The role of all churches, including the Mennonite church, became more marginal.

Peace, Relief Work, and Mission

Immediately after World War II two aspects of church life received priority: peace and relief. The *Doopsgezinde Vredes Groep* (Dutch Mennonite Peace Group, DVG) was founded in 1946. It functioned initially as a meeting place for scores of conscientious objectors who refused to be sent to the Dutch Indies (now, Indonesia) to fight there against the Republican army of president Sukarno between 1945 and 1948.

Somewhat later the focus changed to protests against the Vietnam war, cruise missiles ("no cruise missiles in my back yard"), and opposing taxes for armed defense. In many of these endeavours the DVG cooperated with other interchurch or interreligious peace groups, such as *Eirene, Church and Peace*, the *International Fellowship of Reconciliation*, the MCC Peace Section and especially the *Interkerkelijk Vredesberaad* (Interchurch Peace Platform, IKV). After the latter organization left its basic anti-militarist principle the Quakers, belonging to the same

Right after World War II MCC started its relief work in Europe, including in the Netherlands. Here clothing is distributed in the Mennonite Church of Den Burg, (island of Texel), spring, 1946.

Peace Church tradition as the Mennonites, terminated their membership; the Mennonites suspended their participation. Recently the

Peace Group (DVG) has been promoting conflict mediation in schools, offices, at home and in churches. For many people, the peace summer camps in a simple barn called *The Promised Land* on the island of Texel, have been very important. The barn has now been replaced by a better building called *Bloem en Bos* (Flower and Woods) which still continues the same work.

Relief was a second point of focus immediately following World War II.[14] Many people in the Netherlands remember the work of MCC at that time with gratitude. Young men from MCC and PAX assisted in rebuilding churches (as in Buitenpost and Warga, both in Friesland) and provided assistance in 1953, after the flood disaster which took 1800 lives. Dutch Mennonites also were confronted with the arrival of 500 Mennonite refugees from Russia and—at the request of the WCC—a small group of old Eastern-Orthodox refugees from eastern Europe, all of whom needed attention and care.

In order to provide efficient assistance to those groups and other people, in March 1947 the ADS and two other partners founded

MCC Relief workers and Dutch church leaders in front of Heerewegen, Zeist, which functioned as the centre for the Peace Office in the years after World War II. Front row from left to right: Rev. Carl Brüsewitz, three MCC workers and Irvin Horst, then MCC director in the Netherlands. Second row from left to right: Rev. T. O. Hylkema, Rev. W. Mesdag (then pastor in Zeist), Paula Thijssen, secretary of the Peace Office, and two unidentified persons.

Bijzondere Noden (BN, Special Needs)—a kind of successor of the eighteenth-century Fund for Foreign Needs. From 1947 to the present, BN has been an institution which has received much support from the Mennonite constituency. Until 1965, its emphasis lay in providing assistance to European refugees. Some Dutch Mennonites worked, for instance, in the Berlin *Mennoheim*, a meeting point between east and west, and a place where a congregation was being built. After that time, *Rückwanderer* (returnees) from Paraguay came into the picture, and consequently, assistance to Mennonites in the Chaco of Paraguay became important. Several Dutch voluntary workers assisted there and BN still has many contacts with Latin American and Central American Mennonite groups. Several Dutch volunteers worked overseas in MCC or MCC related projects.

For all these tasks, cooperation with MCC and other European Mennonite relief agencies was important; it was coordinated in 1956 by the *Internationale Mennonitische Hilfswerke*, replaced in 1967 by the *Internationale Mennonitische Organisation für Hilfswerk und andere christlichen Aufgaben* (IMO). Since most other European Mennonite conferences had no ties with the WCC, BN also joined ecumenical efforts such as SOH (*Stichting Oecumenische Hulp*, Foundation of Ecumenical Assistance to refugees) and Christian development agencies such as ICCO. In the 1960s a shift took place from an emphasis on refugees, to development projects and assistance in situations of disaster. Along with BN, a small organization was founded in 1968 as a consequence of the call at the Uppsala assembly of the WCC to place two percent of the income of congregations and individuals into a development fund, from which the churches from poor countries themselves could draw, having made their own spending decisions.

Ecumenical theology in the late 1950s regarded *koinonia* (unity), *diakonia* (service) and *kerygma* (mission) as constituent aspects of the nature of the church. Dutch Mennonites went along with this line of thought, but added *peace* to these three aspects. Hence, cooperation began between the DVG (peace group), BN and the *Doopsgezinde Zendings Raad* (DZR, Dutch Mennonite Mission), and in many respects this cooperation has functioned well since that time. Recently, BN and DVG have even decided to merge into one organization (2005).

Political and military circumstances in Indonesia made it impossible for the Dutch Mennonite mission to renew its work immediately after World War II. Furthermore, all Protestant churches in Indonesia had become fully independent in the meantime. Therefore, a new way of cooperating became necessary, on the basis of equality. In 1949–1950 the Swiss missionary Daniel Amstutz temporarily represented the Dutch mission on Java. A genuinely new beginning, however, was made when Jan and Mary Matthijssen-Berkman began working in Pati, in 1951. Their cooperation with Suhadiweko Djojodihardjo and other church leaders on Java was intense and profound. Unfortunately, at the end of the 1950s, political tensions between the Netherlands and Indonesia made a Dutch missionary presence impossible again, for a period of some five years.

In 1951 missionary equality at another level became reality, when Dutch, Swiss, German and French Mennonite mission boards joined hands and formed the *Europäisches Mennonitisches Evangelisations Komitee* (European Mennonite Evangelization Committee, EMEK);[15] this also was an early sign of reconciliation between Dutch and German Mennonites after the tensions of the Second World War. Even though theological differences and even some suspicion between the Dutch and French Mennonites continued to exist, their cooperation allowed them to face new missionary challenges. In 1950 the Dutch had already taken over the responsibility for mission work on the Birds' Head, West Papua (Indonesia). This work lasted until West Papua officially became a province of Indonesia in 1962, and all Dutch people had to leave the area. By that time more than twenty missionaries had worked there, partly as government-salaried teachers. Fortunately the Swiss nurses Ruth and Lydia Bähler were able to continue their work in the leprosy hospital "Sele be Solu." In the meantime French brothers and sisters initiated a work in Chad, the Swiss began work in Ecuador, and from 1962–1969 Roelf Kuitse and his family worked in Ghana, initiating a dialogue between Christians and Muslims there. Finally, the DZR maintained ties with the work of Foppe and Aaltje Brouwer in Australia.

Fraternal contacts with Indonesian churches have continued until the present day, but in the 1970s and 80s it became clear that the Netherlands itself had become a mission field as well. "Mission on six continents" was the slogan in these years. With a new focus on home mission, the DZR initiated an *Inloophuis* (an Open House) in the new city of Almere near Amsterdam; other mission activities that focused on the Netherlands would follow. During the most recent decade, the DZR initiated fresh contacts with Mennonites in Africa, in Zambia and Tanzania, although not with the aim of establishing a long-lasting missionary presence in these countries.

Congregational Life: More Open to the Outside World

After the Second World War, the earlier Congregations' Day Movement was restructured as *Gemeenschap voor Doopsgezind Broederschapswerk* (Community of Mennonite Brotherhood Work, or GDB), which co-ordinated the reconstruction of the earlier-mentioned conference centres, and organized conferences on behalf of church board members and others. Lay training, emphasizing both theological content and educational methods, became an increasingly important function of the GDB. Around 1950 the GDB organized a distance-learning course: a two-year theological training course consisting of forty lessons taught by theologians and lay persons. Later emphases included church music, Bible study groups, retreat weeks for men and women, as well as a task force studying the relationship between homosexuals and heterosexuals in the 1980s. The latter task force certainly has contributed to a better understanding of this issue.

In the meantime the many women's circles in the congregations organized themselves in 1952 as a "Federation of Mennonite Sisters' Circles." At present some 140 such circles exist; they form the backbone of many congregations. Later, during the 1980s, a more radical group of active women formed a feminist task force.

Baptism in the old meeting house (Vermaning) of Zaandam, 1960s. Baptism by aspersion is the usual practice in the Netherlands; from time to time baptism by immersion also takes place. The church building (Het Nieuwe Huys) dates from 1687. The wooden floor is still covered by fine white sand, as was the practice in several church buildings from that period.

Organizations focused on the youth also began after World War II. In 1946 a *Doopsgezinde Jeugd Raad,* later called *Doopsgezinde Jeugd Centrale* was founded as an umbrella organization to include separate youth groups such as the *Doopsgezinde Jongeren Bond* (founded in 1926), the so-called *Menniste Bouwers* (Mennonite builders), scouting groups (*Elfregi*), local students' groups and children's Sunday school groups. The *Algemene Kamp Centrale* organized summer camps. These organizations still function well, though on a smaller scale than they did fifty years ago. Young people have continued to participate in the international *Mennonite Voluntary Service* work camps, and in exchange visitors' programs with Canada and the USA (Intermenno).

There have been recent changes within the congregations themselves: more open forms of worship; a more democratic way of governing the congregations; different kinds of discussion groups and activities. Homes for the elderly were founded beginning in the 1930s; several of these still exist in modernized buildings, subsidized by the government.

Finally, congregations themselves began to make lasting contacts with groups abroad, and Dutch Mennonites began forming tour groups to visit Mennonites and others elsewhere. Several groups, including a youth group from Haarlem, have visited West Prussia (Danzig/Gdansk); other groups have gone to Switzerland, Russia, Indonesia, Israel, and South Africa; a large "Menno-choir" visited North America. This activity reflects not only the increasing mobility of most European people, but also a growing interest in the life and faith of Christians elsewhere. In 1993 a Mennonite Foundation Netherlands-Poland was founded. Its purpose is to increase understanding of the history of the (Dutch) Mennonites in the land that is now Poland. This aim has been pursued by personal contacts, publications, study meetings and restoration of Mennonite graveyards in the former Prussia.

The graveyard of Heubuden, like other Mennonite graveyards in Prussia, is maintained at present by members of Mennonite-Polish Associations in the Netherlands and Germany.

At the organizational level, the ADS board has been restructured several times. In 1979 Jo van Ingen Schenau became chairperson of the ADS board, the first time a woman had held this post, and the rules and bylaws of the ADS show clear signs of the same democratization process which has so strongly influenced European society from 1968 onwards. Contacts between congregations are maintained by way of the weekly *Algemeen Doopsgezind Weekblad*, successor to the pre-war *Zondagsbode* and other periodicals.

All these congregational and organizational changes, however, have not prevented a dramatic decrease of membership, from around 40,000 baptized members in 1940 to 10,000 members currently. This decrease, which is mirrored in other denominations, had begun already in the period between the wars, when for the first time in Dutch history socialism and atheism seriously challenged the religiously-structured society. The decline in membership has led to the closing of Mennonite schools (as in Haarlem), orphanages and even a few churches.

Seminary and Theology

Immediately following the Second World War the Mennonite seminary experienced a large influx of students. They studied at the (state) University of Amsterdam, and the seminary provided additional courses in theology, Mennonite history and practical theology. Whenever possible, seminary professors (such as J. A. Oosterbaan, W. F. Golterman and N. van der Zijpp) also were appointed by (and paid by) the university. Since Dutch Mennonites still were rather influential during the first decades after 1945, this situation lasted through the 1970s, when the situation changed. In the late 1960s, Lutherans, Reformed (*Hervormde*) and Mennonites began to cooperate in the field of practical theology. From the 1970s on, the seminary also provided special courses for those who were unable to study at the university level; in the 1980s it became responsible for lay-training courses as well.

The seminary library and a part of the archives has now become part of the University library; both church and university profit from this relationship. Unfortunately the faculty of theology at the University of Amsterdam was closed down at the end of the twentieth century; the seminary found a new home at the (Christian) Vrije Universiteit, also in Amsterdam.

In the 1950s there was a renewed emphasis on studying the Bible (and later, a focus on Jewish exegetical methods), and a new attempt to define once again the central issues of Dutch Mennonite faith. Hence, in 1954 a group of eleven younger pastors wrote an original, non-dogmatic confession of faith in a booklet called *Doopsgezind belijden nu* (Confessing in a Mennonite Way Now). It was followed by other efforts to define a common Mennonite belief, such as in a broad discussion about the so-called "narrow way" in 1989. Questions were

By far the best known and loved confessional statement is the brief one, composed by pastor S. S. Smeding, some fifty years ago:

Dopen wat mondig is: (Baptize those who have come of age)
Spreken wat bondig is: (Speak briefly and to the point)
Vrij in't christelijk geloven: (Feel free in your Christian belief)
Daden gaan woorden te boven: (Deeds surpass words)

This text, either in Frisian or in Dutch, painted on tiles made of typically Makkum (Friesland) pottery and produced by a centuries' old Mennonite company, can be found hanging on the wall in many Mennonite homes.

posed: Should Dutch Mennonites merge with other Protestant churches, at a time of decline of membership and influence of all churches, or should they continue to distinguish themselves from these other churches and follow their own, more radical track? Similar efforts to describe our Anabaptist faith can be found in the booklets *Geloven vragenderwijs* (Believing by Questioning, 1989) and *Aangeraakt door de Eeuwige* (Touched by the Eternal One, 2001). Such study material has been used widely in congregational discussion groups. None of these confessional statements ever received official status, but some of them are widely respected.

In the meantime church historians and theologians, encouraged by Sjouke Voolstra and others, founded the *Doopsgezinde Historische Kring* (Mennonite Historical Society) in 1974 with its scholarly yearbook, *Doopsgezinde Bijdragen*, which has a current circulation of over 600 readers. In the past decades, great questions of objective historiography and their implications for Mennonite theology have been a point of focus (initially using history as a tool to redefine *Doopsgezinde* identity), but also local church history, the publishing of biographies, the inventory of archives, and the study of culture in relation to the *Doopsgezinden* have received attention.

In the field of practical theology, liturgy received the most attention. In 1948 a *Kanselboek* (literally: Pulpit Book) was written by a church committee, in order to establish more unity in matters such as the questions asked of baptismal candidates. Though it is a sober and simple book which is still useful, half a century later a new church service manual was written by a seminary committee. The new manual provides more opportunity for lay participation in worship services, and shows some evidence of Alan and Eleanor Kreider's insights.

Inter-Church Relations

From the very beginning, the Dutch Mennonites were members of the National Council of Churches and the World Council of Churches (1948). Mennonite theologians such as Willem F. Golterman and Henk B. Kossen held important positions in the national ecumenical discourse. A serious debate about the necessity of this membership did not seem necessary, except for the theological question of the necessity and authority of ecumenical creeds and confessional statements. Since all churches in the Netherlands have become minority churches, free from the state, cooperation between them, both theologically and practically at the local level, is regarded as normal. A number of

Mennonite congregations cooperate closely with other, non-confessional congregations such as the *Remonstranten* (Unitarians).

Dutch Mennonites and Baptists, as representatives of faith-baptism traditions, had official theological discussions with Presbyterians and Calvinists only in the 1970s. As a result of these discussions, the main Reformed Church and the Mennonite Church recognized each others' ministries. Such a discussion never took place with the small Lutheran church, perhaps because the Lutheran and Mennonite seminaries had cooperated closely already for more than a century. Only a minority of the Dutch Mennonites have contacts with evangelical organizations, such as the Dutch Baptists, whose roots are found in J. G. Oncken's German Baptism. At present a few Mennonite pastors have a Baptist background.

Most church members appreciate these interdenominational relations, even with Roman Catholics, yet at the same time they cherish being Mennonites. In fact, they are constantly balancing between having an ecumenical attitude and retaining a Mennonite identity. The latter feeling is visible in the enthusiasm the Mennonite World Conferences and European MERK conferences create. The MWC conferences of Karlsruhe (1957) and Kitchener (1962) already included many participants from the Netherlands. The Amsterdam conference of 1967 was a highlight in the post-war life of Dutch Mennonites; it even led to a movement of anonymous members who pledged themselves to tithing. The MWC conferences that followed were again attended by hundreds of Dutch participants and Johannes Oosterbaan for many years played a significant role in the MWC leadership. Though the MWC study material has not been translated very often, several hymns from the MWC hymnals have been widely accepted, and regular contacts with Mennonites from abroad (choirs, visiting congregations, tour groups) are welcomed. Several Dutch congregations have made contacts with evangelical congregations in the former German Democratic Republic; others with immigrant (*Aussiedler*) congregations in Germany, and a few congregations have visited Mennonites and others in Russia and the Ukraine for missionary or fraternal reasons.

A Limited Role in Society

In the most recent decades, the public role of the Dutch Mennonites has diminished, but not disappeared. Several Mennonites are noted scientists. The Dutch nuclear scientist Dr. Jacob Klinkhamer was born in a Mennonite family in the northern part of Holland, although he himself never became a member. Others Mennonites served or serve as university professors in a variety of disciplines, such as medicine, psychiatry, law and technology. Most family industrial companies, such as Honig, have become part of larger conglomerates. A number of Mennonites have held prominent positions in public service, although the number of Mennonite members of parliament has decreased. However, most Mennonites involved in politics no longer belong to the liberal or conservative parties: several of them are social-democrats or representatives of smaller leftist groups. In recent years, three Mennonites have been appointed (junior) cabinet ministers; several have become mayors of smaller towns.

As to the recent Mennonite contribution to culture, here again many poets, novelists or musicians whose parents were Mennonites could be mentioned, more than those who are still practicing members of a congregation. All in all, this decreasing role reflects the shrinking position of Christianity as a whole and of the Mennonite community in particular within Dutch society.

The Dutch Mennonites: Some Closing Remarks

A well-known Dutch historian, Geert Mak, some years ago described the influence of secularization in a Frisian village in a book titled *How God Disappeared from the Village Jorwerd*: first the farm hands died out; then the bakeries and groceries were closed, and finally the church was unable to pay a pastor and closed its doors entirely. Several rural Mennonite congregations have experienced this fate, and the formerly large urban congregations have become rather small. These realities have influenced the general attitude of believers in the Netherlands.

The nineteenth century has been characterized as the Golden Age of Dutch Mennonites. During the first part of the twentieth century the Mennonites still exerted a self-confident presence as a non-confessional free church, allied with several liberal thinking groups and churches, and yet aware of their own Anabaptist roots and historic ties. The numerical decline after the Second World War has made them insecure about their identity and about the road into the future. Partly, of course, this decline is due to the type of Enlightenment belief the majority of Dutch Mennonites hold which is shared by many other Christians in the Netherlands. The cultural ethos makes institutional churches, and to a certain degree Christianity itself, superfluous.

On the other hand, it would be unfair to blame the many faithful members and pastors for this situation of decline. Unfortunately much of their energy is spent in the struggle for life which dominates many congregations. The decline across the board for all Christian denominations, and for the Mennonites in particular, has led to debate on the following question: should Mennonites continue to be a radical type of believers' community—even though we risk remaining very small or even risk dying out—or should Mennonites look for renewal by engaging the culture and the social context, leading to new communities of seeking believers—if necessary by joining hands with other denominations?

At this moment it does not seem realistic to expect the return of a new golden age. Nevertheless, there are also signs of hope. A few congregations are growing. The most spectacular example is the congregation of Ouddorp, which twenty-five years ago had eighteen members left and now numbers almost 200 members. Several other congregations have shown a remarkable renewal as well. Charismatic leadership, combined with trust and a daring willingness to take risks in heading into the future are factors in this renewal movement. Just as several young pastors were influenced by the Quaker spirituality of Woodbrooke, UK at the beginning of the twentieth century, we now see the renewal influences of the Celtic spirituality of Iona and the ecumenical impulses of Taizé. Young pastors are beginning to lead the churches, and different kinds of believers are becoming members. The circle of those belonging to the household of Christ, who refrain from full membership, is increasing whereas baptized membership is too big a step for most people. This fact brings Dutch Mennonites closer to the small group situation of the new missionary congregations, described elsewhere in this volume. Yet, to be honest, for several small congregations it may be too late; much as happened in the eighteenth century, several of these congregations may disappear in the coming decades.

Mennonites in Germany

by James Jakob Fehr
and Diether Götz Lichdi

Mennonites in Northern Germany to 1933
(West and East Prussia, Danzig, Königsberg, and Polish Lithuania)

The history of Mennonite life in northern German-speaking regions is a collection of different histories. Some of these communities have maintained a continuous witness for over 450 years. But some communities which were among the largest and most vibrant of all Mennonite congregations seventy years ago no longer exist, having been destroyed at the end of World War II. Consequently, Mennonite history in some regions of northern Germany has strong traditions, while in other regions it has been completely erased, marked only by a few gravestones in lands where German is no longer spoken.

There are also many north German congregations which are young and have only tenuous links to these historical roots.

North German Mennonites in the Nineteenth Century

There were two major groups of Mennonite congregations in northern Germany at the beginning of the nineteenth century: the rural West Prussians (about 10,000 members) and the urban Mennonites in Krefeld, Goch, Kleve, Emmerich, Neustadtgödens, Neuwied, Emden, Norden, Leer, Hamburg-Altona, Friedrichstadt, Danzig and Königsberg (under 3,000 members).

By the Napoleonic era most of the long-standing Mennonite communities in the northern half of German-speaking lands had developed quite separate histories. Although there was no organizational unity, the autonomous congregations communicated freely with each other. Whether the communities fully acknowledged one another depended for the most part on the recognition of the authority of their respective elders, preachers and, in later times, their full-time pastors. Since Mennonites had no dogmatic criteria for determining orthodoxy of faith, this recognition depended in large part on having a standing in one's own congregation and having this recognized by other congregational leaders. In this way Mennonites could move from Hamburg to Königsberg and gain full acceptance, even being admitted to the celebration of the Lord's Supper. But where personal animosity or mistrust existed, as between the Frisian and Flemish branches of Mennonites in Prussia, marriage between Frisians and Flemish, or even just regular visits in another congregation could, and often did, lead to excommunication.

In the nineteenth century, the life of north German Mennonites progressed along two different paths: rural and urban. On the one hand, many members of the city congregations, such as those in

Krefeld, Hamburg and Danzig were recognized as part of the urban, progressive, economic elite of the bourgeoisie. These Mennonites sent their children to public schools and universities, adopted various professions, joined social clubs and took on public offices. At the same time, there also were urban workers and day-labourers among them who did not enjoy these advantages. The rural Mennonites, on the other hand, tended to restrict their social connections to the Mennonite community; they did not place as much emphasis on education and avoided public office, and most were involved in farming or farm-related occupations.

The liberalization of social life in the nineteenth century led to a decline in the influence of churches in society in general; the congregations in the larger cities

Interior of the Krefeld church before 1940.

like Hamburg-Altona and Krefeld (the origin of the first settlers in Germantown, Pennsylvania, in the 1680s and 1690s) were especially affected by this loss of kinship. On a positive note, these fading traditions also led to the disappearance of conflicts between Frisian and Flemish groups.

In earlier times, Hamburg-Altona and West Prussia had been intimately connected through commercial and familial links, but the life of the Hamburg congregation in the period 1850–1933 bore hardly any resemblance to that of the West Prussian congregations of that time, and relations became increasingly distant.

These congregations perhaps shared the consciousness that they were the descendants of Dutch and Frisian foreigners, that they had "overcome" this past and had built up a stable milieu for family, work and faith, but the differences between them had become substantial. The Hamburg Mennonites were involved in textile production, trading, ship-owning, whaling and insurance. Most young men were sent to study; young women were sent to finishing schools. In West Prussia, on the other hand, young persons who did not work in farming served apprenticeships and learned trades. Another difference was social integration. West Prussian Mennonites thrived in part because they were culturally and socially distinct from their neighbours. Their identity as Mennonites was as much social and familial as it was theological. In Hamburg-Altona, by contrast, worship services after 1839 no longer used the Dutch language, and the congregation adopted the regional Lutheran hymnal. Marriage with non-Mennonites became common. Families lived much farther away from their "home town" of Altona. As a result, church membership in Hamburg-Altona declined from 320 members in 1780, to 125 in 1840, to 65 in 1887. How then did they maintain their unity? The confessional family as a whole had no "internal" forms of socio-religious control, since Mennonite teachings had no concrete dogmatic form that could serve as a unifying factor. Each congregation was thoroughly independent and the religious leaders did not attempt to establish a centralized (synodal) authority over the congregations.

Congregational independence led Mennonite communities in each region to develop in reaction to the social, economic and legal conditions of the specific part of Germany which dictated its political status. Where the Mennonite community was led by extremely wealthy businessmen, as in Krefeld, Emden and Leer, Mennonites exerted considerable authority in society, although this influence gradually declined over time.

Since these congregations possess no single, shared historical continuity, no one story will serve to describe them all. Nevertheless, there are at least three common themes within the histories of north German Mennonites after 1800: military service, a history as an ethnic and religious minority, and congregational autonomy.

First, these Mennonite churches resembled each other because of their persistent, but ultimately unsuccessful struggle against military service. The question of military service was a central political issue in this era of growing nationalism. It also was the predominant issue for determining the social, economic and theological survival of the Mennonites. The questions were these:

- Did Mennonites regard themselves as part of the German "nation"?
- Could Mennonites obtain all the rights and privileges of citizenship and ownership within this nation?
- Should they attempt to do so?
- What kind of status should the Mennonite church adopt in a European culture where Christendom and militarism were seen as thoroughly compatible?

We can illustrate the differences of opinion and divergent approaches with two examples. A wealthy Krefeld Mennonite, Hermann von Beckerath, was an important banker and political figure in western Germany. For a brief time he was Prussian Minister of Finance and later

a member of the Frankfurt Parliament, where he argued for the complete assimilation of Mennonites; he opposed any exemption from military service. Beckerath gave voice to views of the wealthiest and most privileged of his class, who advanced their own position by adopting the values and mores of public German life, while at the same time remaining members of Mennonite congregations. Beckerath stood in the tradition of the Krefeld Mennonites, who had given up their pacifist stance at the beginning of the nineteenth century. However, his opinion did not represent the views of the majority

Hermann von Beckerath

of Mennonite religious leaders, a fact made all the more poignant by Beckerath's highly visible and influential political position. He was a representative who did not represent all of his people.

More characteristic of West Prussian attitudes was the fate of a new congregation that had been established by Mennonites on the Memel River. In 1711 Mennonites were granted permission to settle in this region (now Lithuania). In the course of the nineteenth century successful farming and large families led to a rapid expansion of their numbers. But since the community was only allotted sixty-four plots of land that were *kantonfrei*, that is, free of standard duties such as military service, they soon ran out of land. Many younger Mennonites made the decision to move onto other lands where military service was obligatory. As a consequence they were excommunicated from the church. In 1855 this group attempted to start its own Mennonite congregation, but since it had no outside support, the effort eventually failed. Members of this group then joined the state church and were "lost to the Mennonite faith."

What united all of these German Mennonites, in spite of their divergent views and decisions, was their reflection on the meaning of belonging at the same time to both the Mennonite church and the increasingly assertive German state, with its growing militarist obligations.

A second similarity among all these churches was the fact that the great majority of north German Mennonites were descended from refugees from the Netherlands, and remained a linguistic, ethnic and religious minority. Indeed, the traditional distinction between "northern" and "southern" German Mennonites is a reflection of the difference between Swiss and Dutch lines of influence. The common basis of north German Mennonites was their special connection to Dutch Mennonite origins. Most, but certainly not all, northern Mennonite congregations of the early nineteenth century were still working to overcome the earlier disputes between the Frisian and the Flemish Dutch traditions; by the middle of the same century these distinctions had completely disappeared, because the ties to the Dutch tradition had largely disappeared.

From a united linguistic, ethnic, and religious starting point in the north, urban and rural congregations now went different ways. The urban churches were strongly influenced by their theologically-educated preachers and pastors, who in turn were influenced by groups outside of their own communities (whether Lutheran, Pietist or Methodist). The attempt to preserve older traditions and social exemptions held on much longer in the farming regions to the northeast.

A third similarity has its source in the congregational autonomy that also divided them. All Mennonites in Germany were conscious of the fact that they had a special history where the themes of adult baptism, refusal of oaths and congregational independence were dominant. They knew that they belonged to a unique religious minority with hardly any political support. In making this generalization, we must note the exception: Krefeld marks a special case, because Mennonites formed a minority of unusual political influence. In 1716 one quarter of the entire city population (395 households) was Mennonite, and although their percentage of the population declined as the city rapidly grew, their political and economic influence persisted through the nineteenth century. But in general, given Mennonite minority status and the reality of congregational autonomy, any efforts at maintaining a united character remained unorganized and ineffectual. There was no unified Mennonite voice, and so it is not surprising that external conditions had a great influence on the development of congregations.

In this respect they were all alike: all north German Mennonites found themselves struggling to retain a morally and religiously worthy tradition while at the same time adapting to society. Surprisingly, perhaps, most of them did not seek to organize themselves as a formal ecclesiastical body. Rather, they tried to strengthen personal contacts between preachers and elders, coordinating their interests informally. But in the end, each individual community had to face the challenge of

The Danzig church building. After 1945 there was no longer a congregation in Danzig. Recently the church building has been renovated. It is now used by a Pentecostal congregation.

adapting to the extreme changes forced upon German society through political upheaval and economic change. So, for example, the Danzig congregation suffered greatly during the wars that raged between France, Prussia and Russia between 1807 and 1814. The church building and the "Hospital" (the institute for the poor and elderly) both were burned down, and many Mennonites lost property and assets. They appealed for financial assistance and received aid from the Netherlands and Hamburg, and a new church building was erected in 1819.

In spite of the great differences between rural and urban Mennonites, they shared two features of German political life that would both revolutionize their social behaviour and transform their self-conception as Christian communities: nationalism and religious toleration. In the aftermath of Napoleon's defeat, nationalist fervour swept German lands and religious toleration became a widespread reality. Most importantly, toleration ended the centuries-long sanctions imposed on them and brought Mennonites greater legal rights, and consequently afforded them far greater acceptance in society in general. (Again the exception to this is Krefeld, where the government had established religious freedom in the previous century.) Soon after the arrival of religious toleration, Mennonites began to adopt the social behaviours of other Germans in clothing, family life and work. Their congregations also were afforded legal rights and soon gained recognition as corporate bodies (*Körperschaftsrecht*). This freedom and acceptance as full citizens, however, also meant that now Mennonites were confronted with the obligations of citizenship, as will be seen below.

Although the Mennonites formed socially distinct groups in their respective societies (cultural Anabaptism) and attempted to regulate their congregations internally, they became less and less isolated from each other or from the "outside." The increasing acceptance of Mennonites in civil society also led to their involvement in "non-Mennonite" activities, such as literary circles dealing with Enlightenment issues concerning education, aesthetics and morality. Until the establishment of the Weimar Republic after World War I, Mennonites in Emden, Hamburg and especially Krefeld were able to exercise direct influence on the political, economic and artistic life of their cities as political leaders (mayors), musicians, teachers, bankers, businessmen and industrialists. Pietist influences were relatively weak in most urban and West Prussian congregations, although some persons were strongly affected by Pietist literature.

In spite of all the differences, the sense of belonging together as Mennonites was so strong that the well-to-do groups assisted those in financial difficulty, even if they differed widely in theological outlook. There were irregular, but frequent visits between Mennonites in different regions. It is true that the political authority of the independent German states restricted the movement of citizens, but there was still a great deal of interaction between Mennonite communities.

We can illustrate this movement and change with two examples. First of all, it was a regular experience in the Mennonite churches that individuals joined or left the membership. South German and Swiss Mennonites were welcomed into their ranks. Marriage was the greatest source of social movement, even in the most self-isolated groups. In this way, north German Mennonites maintained a strong sense of identity with south German, Dutch, Russian and North American Mennonites. Among north German Mennonites there was close contact with non-Mennonites and frequent marriages outside the Mennonite church. Although some church members left to join the Lutheran or Reformed churches, in every generation some non-Mennonite persons (usually Lutherans or Reformed) were accepted into the congregations.

The second form of movement was emigration, one of the greatest problems faced by the rural congregations in Prussia. Beginning in 1789, large numbers of Prussian Mennonites sold their few possessions and moved to the expanding Mennonite colonies in Russia. Since family unity had always been important in these congregations—most Mennonites being related in some way to each other—families were torn apart and church unity was lost because of the eastward trek.

In 1816 Ferdinand von Baczko, a First Lieutenant in the Prussian army, travelled through parts of Prussia, Poland and Russia, where he met groups of Mennonites in southern Russia in the Chortitza and Molotschna colonies. In his travel journals he praised the rapid economic development of these gifted and industrious German immigrants. But then he directed a remark at those Prussian Mennonites who might be contemplating joining them. In West and East Prussia they had enjoyed nearly a century without military invasion. And in the event of fire or cattle diseases, the Prussian Mennonites could rely on a well-developed system of support and insurance. In Russia, he argued, they would not have access to reliable markets or means of transport for their produce and wares. Indeed,

the only point of complaint they have is this: because they refuse military service, they are restricted in acquiring property and may not purchase farms that were not formerly owned by a Mennonite. Formerly, it may have been the case that buying such land was an urgent concern, but now that so many have emigrated, with the result that the number of all Mennonites in Prussia is between 14 and 15 thousand, acquiring land plots can no longer be so difficult, inasmuch as it is extraordinarily rare that a Mennonite would sell his property to someone of another confession.

Von Baczko's comments show how the Mennonites of Prussia were regarded as a separate people with a distinctive social and religious character. We should remember, however, that among their number were educated, rich Danzig businessmen with top hats and fine livery, as well as impoverished, illiterate day labourers. Von Baczko's remarks also show that in 1816, Mennonites no longer were treated as a threat to the religio-political integrity of Prussia. And yet the situation was about to change significantly.

At the beginning of the nineteenth century, Dutch was still the language used in most church services, strict church discipline was practiced and respected, and most persons accepted the disadvantageous legal restrictions imposed by their continuing refusal of military service. Before the end of the century, however, new congregations would appear in East Prussia, Memel and Königsberg. The Dutch language died out, discipline became more lax, and conscientious objection was given up entirely. The spread of Mennonite congregations at this time should not, however, be thought of as missionary activity. The new communities in East Prussia, in southern Russia, Siberia, Turkistan, Canada, Mexico, etc. were extended family groups seeking better living conditions. In the nineteenth century Mennonites perceived their "faith witness" as exemplary conduct in the sense of high moral standards, harmonious living in family and congregation and honest economic dealings with non-Mennonites.

Interestingly, there was an early ecumenical interest in the city congregations—a long-standing trait of Mennonites in Emden and Hamburg. During the French occupation of Krefeld, the congregation was examined by the new authorities in 1810 and explained that they held anyone who believed in Christ and who was committed to the duties and virtues of an honest man to be a "brother" (there is no mention of "sister"). All such persons were welcome to participate in the Lord's Supper. The Krefeld Mennonites distinguished their own undogmatic and ecumenical theology from "fanatics" with conservative or Pietist beliefs. This was clearly a reference to the exclusionist Anabaptists of Alsace and the Palatinate, who refused to work hand-in-hand with the political authorities.

North Germans were the first to concern themselves with the organizational unity of Mennonites. The first Mennonite periodical in Germany was undertaken by Jakob Mannhardt in Danzig. In January 1854 he began the *Mennonitische Blätter* to help consolidate and revive the fellowship of Mennonites. The chief focus of the *Blätter* was not current news, but rather historical reports.

Enlightenment views of religion were influential in the urban Mennonite congregations. Before his baptism in 1797, Peter van der Herberg from Krefeld wrote in his answer to the question of the "duty of man" that in addition to our duties toward God (obedience, humility, thankfulness and faith), we have duties to ourselves and our neighbours, "that we seek to develop, increase and purify all the powers and faculties of our nature in accordance with our divine purpose, by perfecting our reason, will, memory and conscience, as well as attending to our life, health, livelihood and pleasures."

The conviction among German Mennonites, that their history is an essential part of their communion of faith, has persisted to this day.

The Napoleonic wars and the Franco-Prussian War of 1870–1871 were "wars of liberation" for Germans. They had a galvanizing effect on many Mennonites of northern Germany, especially in the city congregations, inspiring many to patriotism. Mennonites now became politically active and volunteered for military service. How divisive this could be may be illustrated by several examples. In 1818 (five years after

Prussian governments continually applied pressure on the West Prussian Mennonites to do more than make financial contributions to the military. The elder Johann Donner wrote in his *Orlofferfelde Chronik* about how Mennonites used diplomacy to assuage the authorities during the Napoleonic wars:

In this manner—God be thanked and praised—we were saved from this affliction of joining the military reserve. And so this year, 1813, was one of the most unusual and distressing we Mennonites in Prussia have ever experienced. Never before was the hostility against our faith and freedom of conscience greater or more ubiquitous. The hostility was caused in part by the mustering of all able-bodied men, whether married or single, for the military reserve on account of this horrible war, [...] as well as by the understandable hatred and jealousy of our Lutheran neighbours, who observe the disreputable morals and self-indulgent lifestyle of certain Mennonites, which is the chief cause of it. May God lead all these dissipated people to repentance and improvement.

Donner's remarks in the *Orlofferfelde Chronik*) Lieutenant Jansen, a Hamburg Mennonite, complained to the military authorities because he had been excommunicated by his congregation for joining the war effort. By the second half of the century such opposition was no longer present in the Hamburg congregation, or in many other congregations either. Hinrich van der Smissen served as a medical orderly in the Franco-Prussian War and was awarded the Iron Cross for his services in combat. He was later elected pastor in Ibersheim and then in Hamburg-Altona from 1885 to 1928, where he was a leading figure in the *Vereinigung* (Union of Mennonite Churches).

In West Prussia change was slower. From 1874 to 1876 the Lord's Supper was not celebrated in the Heubuden congregation, because of ongoing controversies and splits. The source of dispute was the loss of conscientious objection in Prussia in 1867, when laws were passed that obliged all male citizens to perform military service. Some parts of the leadership thought it best to accept the status quo; others disagreed. This dispute caused many years of bitter animosity in the church.

The role of women in Mennonite churches of this period was largely restricted to care-giving activities. The most liberal development occurred in Krefeld, where the statutes were revised to give women voting rights for the election of the new pastor in 1835. Even in Krefeld, however, it was considered obvious by most Mennonites that no woman could take on a leadership role. The only leadership position open to women in Krefeld was the directorship of the home for orphans and the poor. In the 1840s the wealthy sisters Charlotte and Susanne von Beckerath were the first women to take a dominant role in this part of the church's life.

Charlotte and Susanne von Beckerath

In earlier times an official church office of "deaconess" (*Diakonisse*) was open to women, but the last north German deaconess to serve in supporting poor, sick and aged members was Magdalena van Kampen of Danzig, who died in 1810.

North German Mennonites from Bismarck to 1933

Defining the limits of "German" Mennonites in this period is not easy. The present-day French congregations of Alsace were German-speaking in the nineteenth century and became part of the German Reich from 1871 to 1918. After the Franco-Prussian war, different parts of the Heubuden congregation stood under the political jurisdiction of Prussia, Russia and Poland. Russia invaded East Prussia during World War I, which meant that the Mennonites living in the region east of Danzig were officially living in Russia. Then after 1918 there were Mennonites who fled Russia after the Revolution who found refuge in German congregations like Gronau, where the wealthy industrialists in the congregation offered them jobs in their factories. And finally, Krefeld and Neuwied (until 1926), as well as the congregations in the Palatinate (until 1930), were occupied by French troops in the post-war years.

Church building in Neuwied, built in 1768, commissioned by Count Alexander zu Wied. In the nineteenth century the membership of this large and influential congregation declined. After World War II, Neuwied once again became an important Mennonite centre due to the arrival of West Prussian and later Russian refugees (including Mennonite Brethren). Today some 3,000 members live in and around Neuwied, and belong to eight congregations.

These were politically unstable times. Mennonites had long become upright citizens in good standing who were just as frustrated by political disruption as were other citizens. In some regions they were counted among the most industrious and flourishing inhabitants. In West Prussia they owned large estates where Poles were hired by the dozens for menial labour. In Ostfriesland and Münsterland, it was a generally-held opinion that "only rich folks belong to the Mennonites." In this northern part of Germany, traditional Mennonites were extraordinarily wealthy and "kept to themselves." An example can be seen in the school tax in Emden in 1892, which was based on income: Reformed persons paid on average 7.40 Marks, Lutherans 7.20, Catholics 8.40 and Mennonites 73.70! Of course, there were many Mennonites who were no more affluent than other citizens.

As noted above, all German Mennonites were confronted with the question about their relationship to their "nation" and the implications of this nationhood for their confession, particularly after the establishment of a united German nation in 1871. Persecution for reasons of faith had entirely ceased and Mennonites were accepted as a Christian group. North German Mennonites in this period saw themselves as a socially distinct group with very intimate cultural and family ties, but having adopted the traits and manners of their Lutheran, Reformed and Catholic neighbours, Mennonites still had to face historical Lutheran polemics which damned Anabaptists as seditious Münsterites. Especially in the latter part of the nineteenth century many Mennonites were proud of their tradition and yet suffered from a sense of inferiority. They were greatly comforted by historical-theological books that rejuvenated their sense of purpose as Mennonites.

The three most significant authors of this period were Ludwig Keller, Anna Brons and Wilhelm Mannhardt. Keller, who was not a Mennonite, examined many archival sources that led him to the opinion that the smaller Christian groups of the Reformation had been falsely denigrated in most scholarly work. He emphasized a third tradition in western

The interior of the church in Heubuden, at the end of nineteenth century. At that time Heubuden, near Danzig, was a large and active congregation with 1100 to 1500 members. In 1890 the first organ was installed. Heubuden belonged to the very first congregations to show interest in missions; William Henry Angas visited Heubuden in 1823. Together with other Protestants a branch of the *Danziger Missionsgesellschaft* was founded. Mission festivals were organized from 1830 onwards and beginning in 1892 this festival was held in the Mennonite church.

Christianity alongside Catholicism and mainstream Protestantism that placed the life of the community of faith at its centre. Brons wrote the very first history of Mennonites in the German language; she was the daughter of a very wealthy politician and businessman from Emden. Mannhardt's writings documented the long history of resistance to military service among Anabaptists.

With the establishment of the German Reich in 1871, concerned leaders like Ernst Weydmann of Krefeld and Samuel Cramer of Emden worked toward uniting the disparate groups of Mennonites throughout the Reich. In their view, more than a mere historical consciousness was necessary for unity. The city congregations of Emden, Krefeld and Danzig played leading roles in establishing a national conference of Mennonites, the *Vereinigung der Mennoniten-Gemeinden im Deutschen Reich* (Union of Mennonite Churches in the German Reich); the constituting assembly was held in Berlin on April 28–29, 1886. Eight congregations from the Palatinate were present; of the north German congregations only urban congregations joined the union: Krefeld, Neuwied, Emden, Leer, Norden, Hamburg-Altona, Friedrichstadt, Danzig, Elbing, Königsberg and Berlin, the latter a newly-formed congregation. Modelled on the *Algemeene Doopsgezinde Societeit* (ADS) in the Netherlands, plans were made for a church publication, an educational institute and financial assistance for young men studying theology.

As distinct from the *Verband* in the southeast, which will be described below, the *Vereinigung* was intended to be a forum for congregations, each of which maintained its financial and organizational independence and its own spiritual emphases. The ranks of the *Vereinigung* increased gradually over the years, as individual congregations in West Prussia and southern Germany decided to join. One of its most important activities was financial support for pastors' widows and for retired pastors without financial means. Financial assistance also went to the *Mennonitische Blätter* and other historical publication projects. The Union officially supported the publication of an encyclopedia of Mennonite history and established an historical society, about which more will be said below. Finally, the *Vereinigung* coordinated German involvement in the Mennonite World Conferences and was active in ecumenical groups, working toward dialogue and cooperation with other Protestant confessions. After Hitler came to power, a conference of West Prussian Mennonites in August 1933 heatedly discussed the question of whether they should support the Nazis. In the end a statement of greeting and loyalty was issued. The *Vereinigung* itself did not issue an official statement.

In general most congregations within the German Reich maintained themselves in these decades, although no real outreach to non-Mennonites was practiced, because of the desire to preserve friendly relations with the Roman Catholic and Protestant Churches. But there also were places where old congregations died out (Goch and Kleve) and at least three new congregations were established: Berlin (1887), Gronau (1888), and Hannover (1891). Church plantings usually took place in cities where a larger number of Mennonites had already settled and not as a result of missionary activity. The *Vereinigung* helped coordinate preaching assistance in the new churches. In this period many of the older congregations gradually declined in numbers and importance in their communities. Adolf Ellenberger, for example, who was pastor in Friedrichstadt until 1922, emigrated to the United States in part because he could see no future for his congregation. Many others did the same. This sense of decline was in large measure due to the loss of cultural and economic influence experienced by German Mennonites in the first decades of the century.

> **In April 1933, three months after Hitler was elected Chancellor, the** curatorium **of the** Vereinigung **discussed the question of military duty:**
>
> *The question as to which position our community would adopt if universal military service were reintroduced was discussed energetically and with great unanimity. We emphasized our duty to submit and to serve in the greater interest of the state, while at the same time on the basis of the gospel distancing ourselves from any deification of the state. The Word of God remains our guiding principle. ... We also emphasized that he who cannot bear arms on account of his conscience must be willing to sacrifice himself for the greater good, for example by being prepared to serve in the medical corps on the front lines of battle. The* curatorium *takes the position "that in the case of reintroduction of military service the German Mennonites no longer claim any special rights."*

At the same time, there was a remarkable development in Emden, where the congregation experienced an unusual boom thanks to the personality of its pastor, Abraham Fast. He caught the imagination of many non-Mennonites in the city through his presentation of biblical faith together with teaching on scientific and philosophical advances, as well as cultural and artistic progress. In a time when other Mennonites focused on their exclusivity, he promoted the Mennonite faith publicly and brought many non-Mennonites into the congregation.

The issue of assimilation to the culture of the majority has been a long-standing issue of concern for Mennonites in Germany. In 1821 Ferdinand von Baczko made an observation that has been repeated in virtually every generation since the eighteenth century, namely that the Mennonites were gradually being fully assimilated into German culture and were about to die out. Von Baczko assured his non-Mennonite readership that this group would lose its religious distinctiveness and cease to exist. He observed that they had divided into factions and had come into friendly contact with other religious groups. Consequently, they would no longer live in sequestered communities, and would lose their "current strictness." A similar remark had also been made in 1722 by the Prussian Minister of State, Johann Friedrich von Lesgewang, as a justification for not banning Mennonites from the city of Königsberg. They would certainly become an insignificant, dying community, he claimed.

This question has of course also played a role in Mennonite discussions. In 1863 Wilhelm Mannhardt reported that from 1816 to 1858 the number of Mennonites in Prussia had declined from 13,175 to 12,515. He concluded, "If we look carefully at the reasons for this decline (namely, emigration, mixed marriages, lack of new membership coming from other confessions), ... [there is good reason to believe] that this tendency will persist in the future." At a national *Mennonitentag* in Gronau in 1936 Christian Neff, the Mennonite pastor in Weierhof, posed the same question in a talk titled "Do our Congregations have a Future?" Most recently Christoph Wiebe, pastor in the Krefeld congregation, who cited Mannhardt's remark in a recent essay, has voiced similar concerns.[1]

The remote farm of the family of Johannes Ferdinand Thimm (1905-1945) and Liesbeth Thimm Regier (1908-1995) in Reimerswalde near Danzig. Thimm was vehemently opposed to the Nazi regime; he was drafted into the German army and died in Russia, probably in April 1945. His widow and 7 children came to West Germany after having been detained for more than two years in a Danish camp. From this refugee camp many Mennonites migrated to Latin America; others went to Germany. Peter Dyck and others visited the camp on behalf of the MCC. The farm, still existing in 1973, has since been demolished.

Mennonites in Southern Germany to 1933

Mennonite Acculturation

At the beginning of the nineteenth century approximately 2,000 Mennonites were living west of the Rhine River in the Palatinate (Pfalz); some 1,500 Mennonites were living east of the Rhine in the states of Baden and Württemberg. The former group formed about twelve congregations; the latter group thought of themselves as having only one congregation, concentrated at various locations. These groups traced their historical origins back to the "Swiss Brethren," most of whom had been expelled from Switzerland by the eighteenth century. They formed a largely homogeneous group, united by kinship and their shared history of survival. Some observers called them a family church, and these traits united them with Mennonites in Switzerland and Alsace.

The French Revolution and the wars that followed thoroughly transformed the south German Mennonites. Formerly they had been treated as suspect outsiders; now they took part in the transformation of German society. The principle of legal equality of all citizens, independent of race, class, origin or religion, now found its way into the constitutions of Bavaria, Württemberg and Baden. The old injustices ceased: Mennonites were permitted to live where they wished, their worship services were no longer kept under surveillance, they could purchase land without restrictions and needed only to pay those taxes that were required of other citizens. Indeed, Mennonites became full

Mennonite family in the Palatinate, with Bible, around 1920.

citizens, and on account of their diligence and ability many of them— especially the more affluent—gained social acceptance and respect. As the external pressures on them lifted, they began to widen their horizons and take on new views. This was true for many inherited Anabaptist convictions such as conscientious objection and church discipline, which no longer played such dominant roles.

The Organization of Conferences

Mennonite Organization in the Southeast: the Verband

The part of the Palatinate that lay east of the Rhine was incorporated into the Grand Duchy of Baden in 1815. In this region, called the Kraichgau, Mennonites lived on isolated rural estates. Their situation was different from that of the other Palatinate Mennonites, who mostly lived as minorities in villages. The Kraichgau Mennonites were descended from war refugees, partly coming directly from Switzerland after the

Thirty Years War, partly having fled from other parts of the Palatinate that had been ravaged by the wars at the end of the eighteenth and beginning of the nineteenth centuries. The Mennonites in this part of Baden were largely tenants on landed estates. A few of them still are to this day, their leases extending over several generations. Since there were only a limited number of leases, some of the Mennonites of the Kraichgau gradually moved farther away to Württemberg, Bavaria and Franconia. They kept their close relationships by visiting regularly, and in this manner they developed a consciousness of their unity, of belonging to one large congregation that assembled at various geographical locations.

The Kraichgau Mennonites maintained friendly and familial relations with the Palatinate Mennonites farther to the west, but the two groups clearly developed in different directions. The Palatinate Mennonites developed local congregations in villages like Weierhof and Ibersheim. Farther to the east, village congregations did not develop; for the most part, members had to travel long distances to assemble for worship. As a consequence, they made the compromise of holding services once a month at various locations. A number of lay elders and preachers took turns preaching; an intellectually demanding sermon such as was common in other confessions of the time was considered to be affectation or arrogance. The elders, preachers and deacons met regularly (probably as early as the eighteenth century) to consult on issues of common concern, especially on matters of church discipline. Election to the offices of preacher and deacon took place when worship services were assembled. Elders, on the other hand, were elected from among the preachers by the whole community and were consecrated in assemblies where the entire community was represented. These practices led to the formation of the *Verband deutscher Mennonitengemeinden* (Association of German Mennonite Churches), which is usually just called the *Verband*. The earliest minutes of the meetings of elders and preachers date from 1854. The activity of the *Verband* gained a public face in 1870, when Ulrich Hege began publishing the *Gemeindeblatt*. In the following year the Association hired its first itinerant preacher, Christian Herrmann. His task was to travel

Johann Michael Hahn wrote many hundreds of hymns. Two, later three of these got a place in the *Gesangbuch zum gottesdienstlichen und häuslichen Gebrauche in Evangelischen Mennoniten-Gemeinden* (1854, 1876, revised edition 1910, 1950). An example is the first of seven lines of hymn 381 (347 in the revised edition)—in the section "about sanctification and devotion":

Lord, may I receive your sanctification
Through your Spirit.
You, you yourself have made a start
With the change of mind within me;
Your Spirit brings about sanctification,
Your strength alone purifies hearts,
Since you have gone to God.

regularly to the scattered families, to preach where his services were needed, to instruct baptismal candidates and to assist in baptisms, communion services, marriages and funerals. Two groups of Mennonites (Ursenbacherhof and Haimbronnerhof) left the *Verband* in 1858 after being influenced by Johann Michael Hahn (1758–1819), one of the Pietist leaders in Swabia. Hahn strongly emphasized holiness, separation from the world and preparation for Christ's return. During World War II these so-called "Hahnische" Mennonites re-entered the *Verband*.

Mennonite Organization in the Southwest
Various forms of organization took place in southwestern Germany. The Conference of Palatinate-Hessian Mennonites began with a meeting of regional church leaders at Branchweilerhof in 1824; the purpose of the meeting was to organize support for Baptist missionaries from England. Sporadic meetings followed until 1871, when meetings took on a regular form. The cooperation in the Conference increased gradually among the Palatinate and Hessian congregations, excluding Deutschhof and Branchweilerhof, which were members in the *Verband*. The preachers of the Conference met several times a year for consultations. In 1887 an association of south German Mennonites, the *Konferenz Süddeutscher Mennonitengemeinden* (Conference of South German Mennonite Churches, or KSM) was established to unify all the descendants of the Swiss Brethren throughout southern Germany. At first it was a loose alliance of interested persons; in 1967 it became a union of congregations. It met practical needs, for example, producing a *Christlicher Gemeinde-Kalender* (Congregational Calendar, since 1971 a yearbook called *Mennonitisches Jahrbuch*) and a hymnal that were widely used by German-speaking Mennonites in Germany, Switzerland and Alsace. Nowadays the only one of these

Chriſtlicher Gemeinde=Kalender

für das Jahr

1·9·2·7

herausgegeben von der Konferenz
:-: der :-:
Süddeutſchen Mennoniten

36. Jahrgang

In Kommiſſion von
A. Hirſchler, Kaiſerslautern (Pfalz)

Title page of *Christlicher Gemeinde-Kalender* 1927, published between 1892 and 1941. From 1934 on the *Konferenz der Ost- und Westpreussischen Mennonitengemeinden* (Conference of East and West Prussian Mennonite Congregations) also supported this publication. In 1951 the *Gemeinde-Kalender* was published again; however, the congregations in East and West Prussia had ceased to exist by that time.

tasks performed by the KSM is youth work. In 2004 the name of the KSM was changed to *Jugendwerk der Süddeutschen Mennonitengemeinden* (Youth Work of South German Mennonite Congregations: JSM) to reflect this altered situation.

For over forty years, beginning in 1903, Christian Neff (1863–1946) served as chairman of the KSM. He was the minister of the Weierhof congregation for fifty-five years, beginning his work in 1887. He came out of retirement during World War II because his successor had been recruited into the army. Neff also led the preachers' meetings in the Conference for many decades and was an exemplary role model for his colleagues; he also was one of the initiators of the Mennonite World Conference. In 1925, on the occasion of the 400th anniversary of the first believer's baptism in the Mantz house in Zürich, he invited Mennonites from around the world to

Neff's successor at the Weierhof, Paul Schowalter, wrote about him:

The spiritual centre of the congregation was its preacher Christian Neff, assisted by several church board members. Usually the members were appointed for life, which at times led to some of them being too old for office. The chairman and secretary of the church board was Christian Neff himself; in his work he had the trusting support of both board and congregation. Central to the spiritual life of the congregations was the Sunday worship service, nearly always run as a "one-man-show." And yet the worship service was always well attended... Neff's sermons were biblically well founded, as he had learned from his teachers during his studies. He took present realities into account, and especially the history he loved so much. He was able to picture and express things through his eloquence and his picturesque language.

a conference at Basel and Zürich, and edited an important commemorative text for the occasion (*Gedenkschrift zum 400 jährigen Jubiläum der Mennoniten*). He also chaired the next two Mennonite World Conferences in Danzig (1930) and Amsterdam/Elspeet (1936). He published more essays and sermons than any other Mennonite preacher of his day. And finally, together with Christian Hege he co-edited the *Mennonitisches Lexikon* (1913–1967). This monumental work—an indispensable source of detailed information about the origins and development of Mennonite life—provided thousands of articles detailing 400 years of Mennonite life and history. The *Mennonite Encyclopedia* published in the United States (1957–1991) relied heavily on this earlier German-language work.

The Peace Witness in Germany to 1933

The Controversy over Conscientious Objection in the early Nineteenth Century

The process of Mennonite integration into German society can be measured by the diminishing role played by the peace witness during the course of the nineteenth and twentieth centuries. The wars of revolution between 1792 and 1815 gave birth to an extraordinary patriotic enthusiasm for the "Fatherland." With the ideas of "equality, freedom and brotherhood" the state now came to be understood as a nation to which every person belonged and for whose ideals everyone was obliged to fight. Even the conservative and reclusive Mennonites of southern Germany were caught up in the enthusiasm, and some of them went to war for their country. In reaction to this, a large convention of preachers and deacons met twice in 1803 and 1805 in Ibersheim to pray and deliberate on the changed situation. Their decisions were then communicated to the south German congregations, and have come to be known as the "Ibersheimer Resolutions" (*Ibersheimer Beschlüsse*). The resolutions sought to establish guiding principles for these challenging new times: military service was to be rejected and the principle of non-retaliation emphasised. The Ibersheim document concludes: "On account of the widespread distress and misery of military conscription, a general day of repentance, fasting and prayer should be observed in all congregations on this side of the Rhine and on the Neckar, so that this general evil may be averted." And yet the repeated emphasis on conscientious objection did not stop many from participating in the next Napoleonic War of 1813–1815. After this war the military participation of these church members was ignored or covered up in the community, instead of resulting in expulsion from their congregations.

Article 14 of the Ibersheimer Beschlüsse of 1803 (from the copy belonging to the Weierhof congregation):

Bearing arms is contrary to the teachings of Jesus and the confession of our faith, because according to these teachings the faithful ought to confront one another in love, abstain from revenge and leave vengeance to God, to whom it belongs. Consequently, military service is forbidden among us and will remain so, and all who choose to take up arms fall under our church discipline and have no further spiritual communion with us, but are to be expelled until they repent and seek reconciliation with the church.

When peace returned, church discipline was much more relaxed than it had been before, in spite of the Ibersheimer Resolutions. Marriage with non-Mennonites was now tolerated, many persons took on other occupations rather than traditional farming jobs and frequently they also strove for advanced education, which earlier had been rejected by Mennonites and had also been legally forbidden to them. The traditional lay preacher in southern Germany and West Prussia was gradually replaced by an educated pastor, who took on numerous other tasks and was paid for his work. Ibersheim in 1813 and Monsheim in 1819 were the first congregations in southern Germany with professional pastors. The pastors were trained at several German Universities (such as Bonn, Halle, Berlin), or at pietistic schools like Sankt Chrischona in Beuggen (Baden, near the Swiss border), and sometimes at the Amsterdam seminary. In Hamburg, Gerrit Karsdorp was the full-time pastor in the early eighteenth century; in Krefeld two professional pastors were appointed in 1770.

In many respects the Mennonites reversed their behaviour of the last 150 years, adapting to the dominant culture and seeking acceptance in society. Their neighbours stopped treating them as untrustworthy foreigners, and Mennonites began to take pride in their achievements. In this way, the dominant conception of their ancestors, namely that we are "strangers and pilgrims" in this world (1 Peter 2:11), was no longer taken literally but was spiritualised. Mennonites were now intent on fulfilling the obligations of citizenship, and this showed itself most clearly in their altered stance on military service.

The Mennonite Church of Ibersheim, built in 1836, was the first and only Mennonite church in Germany with a bell tower. It is the only church in Worms-Ibersheim and therefore also hosts the Evangelische (Protestant) church services.

And yet the obligation to military service remained a controversial issue. When the National Assembly met in St. Paul's Church in Frankfurt in 1848, the question of rights and duties was a key political issue. Mennonite preachers, elders and deacons (forty-five persons representing twelve congregations) convened at Rappenau in September to deliberate these issues and formulated the following response that was sent to the National Assembly.

> The rule of universal military service demands of our sons and brothers the same civic duty of bearing weapons that all other citizens have. However, this civic duty collides with our religious obligation. Our religious principles, which strive to preserve the purity and simplicity of the early apostolic church, oblige us as defenceless Christians to suffer in patience and not to defend ourselves.

Pacifism as a religious observation is also a consequence of adult baptism, the document maintained: "since it is a matter of conscience for us to believe that holy baptism is a real consecration into Christianity, its blessings and duties, we feel that our conscience is being wronged [...] and plead that our freedom of belief be preserved." They offered to pay a supplementary tax in lieu of conscription, as this was practiced in other countries. This justification was not strictly theological; it was an argument from tradition and from baptismal vows and made no reference to Christ's death, creation theology or God's commandments.

It is also worthy of notice that during the constitutional talks in Frankfurt in 1848, a representative from Danzig who knew the position of the Mennonites in his region put forward the motion to allow persons to refuse military service on the grounds of religious conviction. As already noted above, the liberal Mennonite representative from Krefeld, Hermann von Beckerath contradicted him, claiming that this would injure the essential principle of balancing rights and duties!

The Consent to Military Service
The north German Alliance decreed in 1867 that Mennonites would no longer be excused from military service by paying a special fee. The West Prussian Mennonites who were immediately affected petitioned the government in Berlin unsuccessfully to have their former status restored. In the end they agreed to follow the standing order of March 3, 1868, which ruled that Mennonites were obliged to serve in the army, but not with weapons. Henceforth, Mennonite recruits were to serve as medical orderlies and in supply and transport. There were similar regulations in the Netherlands, Switzerland and France. The fundamental obligation to perform these duties was never doubted. But no one suggested an approach such as the one adopted in Russia, namely a forestry service entirely independent of the military. Nevertheless, not all Mennonites were satisfied with the situation and some individuals and small West Prussian groups chose to emigrate to North America as a result.

Most young men in the congregations did not want to suffer the insult of being called cowards by their fellows, and so they did not take the non-combatant option, but rather served as combatants in the armed forces. The congregation in Danzig reacted by altering its congregational rule to permit individual freedom on the issue: "When our fatherland demands the duty of military service, we leave it open to everyone's conscience to decide which form of national service he adopts."

After the initial reluctance toward military service first began to weaken during the Wars of Freedom at the beginning of the nineteenth century, it gradually became more and more common for Mennonites to bear arms and participate in war. During the Franco-Prussian War of 1870–1871, Mennonite farms near Weissenburg were the site of a battle where the commanding general of the French forces, Abel Douay, died of his injuries in a Mennonite house at Schafbusch. During the First World War, south German Mennonites not only were medical orderlies, but in many cases also military men. Numerous different Mennonite publications, during and after the war, published obituaries and memorials of fallen Mennonite soldiers. In form and content these did not differ from the obituaries of non-Mennonites.

> A Mennonite writer in the *Gemeinde-Kalender* of 1920 displayed the characteristic viewpoint of his day when looking back at the end of the First World War:
>
> *... after we had established peace in the east and the glorious battles of our brave troops in the west were penetrating far into enemy terrain, I was full of hope that we would soon achieve a victorious peace accord with our chief adversaries. But now I observe that not only are our hopes dashed, but also our greatest fears are being realised. We have collapsed—collapsed not so much under the external pressures of a greater power ..., but under the internal pressures of attrition from long-term privation ... The spirit [of revolution] has swept everything away. Bravery, the truest virtue of German manhood, no longer has room on account of the spirit of world brotherhood. Those who are proud of what we have achieved and who believe in the future of our nation are suspected of militarism.*

The defeat of the German army only led to calls for revenge and did not provoke anyone to call for reconciliation or to renew the peace witness. Nor did Mennonites noticeably contradict the predominant opinion in society that the Treaty of Versailles ought to be rescinded.

Missionary Activity and Social Service

The Beginnings and Motivations of Missionary Activity

The early Anabaptists had been energetic missionaries and communicated their beliefs in many parts of Europe, but the persecutions and expulsions they suffered soon made this impossible; soon thereafter they became known as the *Stillen im Lande* (the quiet in the land, Ps. 35:20). They withheld their faith from their neighbours, because they wanted to live their faith without suffering persecution. The revival movements of the early nineteenth century motivated the Mennonites to revise their thinking about mission work. Revivalism served as a corrective to the moralising and individualistic conception of faith expounded in the eighteenth century; revivalism challenged entire congregations, emphasizing a personal experience of faith and the fellowship of believers. The movement was supported by inter-confessional Bible societies that were dedicated to the promulgation of Christian literature and the support of missions within and beyond Europe. These societies, usually established and organized by lay believers, prepared the groundwork for mission activity in Asia (especially in India) and Africa.

The Baptist Missionary Society was responsible for refocusing European Mennonites on missions. The BMS was begun by the Baptist preacher, William Carey, whose writings focused on the universal scope of the Great Commission of Matthew 28, understood as the duty of all Christians. His co-worker William Ward and an independent Baptist missionary from London, William Henry Angas, visited the Dutch Mennonites, as noted in the preceding chapter. A pamphlet written in Dutch by Samuel Muller and others was translated into German by the pastor of the Mennonite congregation in Monsheim, Leonhard Weydmann, in 1823 and subsequently shared with others in the Palatinate. The congregations showed great interest and Angas, who was travelling among Mennonites in Poland and northern Germany, was invited to present a talk on missions at Branchweilerhof on July 13, 1824. His talk was enthusiastically received. All those present agreed that once a month, news from the mission field should be read aloud during worship services, that a prayer should be offered for the poor heathens and the power and outpouring of the Holy Spirit upon them, and that each congregation should gather funds regularly for this cause.

After this first "missions conference" Angas visited the congregations on both sides of the Rhine, promoting missions and leaving a strong impression. Collection boxes were set up in the congregations, and modest sums were raised to support the Baptist Missionary Society and the *Basler Missionsgesellschaft*.

With the establishment of the Dutch Mennonite Mission Association (*Doopsgezinde Zendings Vereniging*) in 1847 financial support for missions was redirected to the Netherlands. It was accepted practice to direct missionary activity toward the lands of the southern hemisphere and not toward Germany itself. The meeting at Branchweilerhof led to further missions conventions. These forums also aided the development of the internal organization of German Mennonites in the Palatinate, an organization now known as the ASM. Missions remained an abiding concern. Reports concerning the missionary activity on the island of Java beginning in 1851, for example, aroused great interest and motivated generous donations. Beginning around 1890 the south German Mennonites met annually for missionary conferences (for example: Langnau/Emmental 1890, Giebelstadt/Würzburg 1892, Monsheim/Kaiserslautern 1913, Heilbronn 1915, Deutschhof 1924), and in this way kept alive an interest in mission work. Also noteworthy is the missionary convention in Würzburg in 1911, where the German, Russian-born missionaries Peter Nachtigall and Peter Löwen were consecrated and sent into their mission field of Sumatra in Indonesia.

The KSM (Conference of South German Mennonite Churches) also supported mission work from the time of its foundation in 1887, and established a German Mennonite Missionary Committee (*Deutsches Mennonitisches Missions Komitee*, DMMK). Initially it promoted backing for the Dutch Missionary Union in southern Germany, but it also began to attract support from Mennonites in northern and western Germany, so that it gradually took on a national role.

Part of the Registration form of the Waisen- und Missions-Anstalt in Neukirchen (Orphans- and Mission-Institution Neukirchen, Germany), 1904, at which Peter Löwen is registered as "Hospitant" (student). Löwen (1882-1955) was born in Muntau near Halbstadt (Molotschna); in 1914 he returned to Europe due to the ill health of his wife and became a Missionsreiseprediger (travelling missionary preacher) among the south German Mennonites.

Since the First World War the annual Thanksgiving celebrations of the *Verband* have focused on mission work. Mennonites from many congregations assembled at Heilbronn to hear a Thanksgiving sermon and reports from missionaries and mission workers. In this way the fellowship with Mennonites in Java and later in Sumatra was kept alive. The offerings collected on these occasions also were designated specifically for mission work, over and above the regular financial contributions of the congregations.

In spite of this enthusiasm, it was a long time until the first missionary was commissioned from southern Germany. Hermann Schmitt from Deutschhof was sent to Java in 1926 by the Dutch Missionary Union. He led the youth work and supervised the twenty-three schools that had been set up by missionaries there. He was joined by his brother-in-law Otto Stauffer from Obersülzen in 1934, who also was engaged in youth work. When German troops invaded the Netherlands in May 1940 both Schmitt and Stauffer were arrested by colonial Dutch troops in Java. They lost their lives at sea while being transported from Sumatra to India with other German prisoners when the Japanese navy torpedoed their ship on January 18, 1942.

The School at the Weierhof
As a minority in Germany, Mennonites were naturally very concerned with educational issues, and made significant efforts to instruct their youth. In 1867 the teacher and preacher Michael Löwenberg established the *Gymnasium* (high school) in the northern Palatinate. It was intended to be a Christian boarding school for secondary education, with additional instruction and training in practical skills such as bookkeeping and farming. Löwenberg was supported by a group of about fifty Mennonites, who set up a financial support group for the so-called "Anstalt am Donnersberg." It was Löwenberg's idea to develop this school further into a theological seminary like the one in Amsterdam, but the German Mennonites could not agree to support this idea. After about twenty years of difficulties, the school finally attained governmental recognition as a six-year *Realschule* and gradually became more attractive to students of all confessions in the rural area of the north Palatinate.

Against the will of the organizers and financial supporters the school was nationalised during the Hitler regime, during which time it became one of the elite Nazi schools. During this period religious instruction at the school was forbidden. In the aftermath of the war, the *Gymnasium* was reopened only in 1959. In the following decades the number of students rose to about 800. As the number of boarders decreased and the day-students significantly increased, the facilities needed were restructured and expanded. In 1980 the financial support group was taken over by an external organization, and the original Mennonite conception disappeared. Mennonites are no longer prominent in its membership, or among the teachers or students.

The Beginnings of German Social Relief
The Mennonites in Germany have always been willing to support relief needs. In the nineteenth century they gave aid to the needy in their own or other congregations, and assisted one another with church-building. The *Vereinigung* established a relief committee in 1888 to assist West Prussian farmers who had suffered from a severe flood. More commonly they helped neighbours or the poor of their congregations out of pure Christian charity, without organizing their services. The West Prussian and south Russian Mennonite farmers were particularly well-known for their generosity.

Charitable trusts were first organized by the *Verband* in 1922 with the establishment of the Mennonite Relief Agency "Christian Duty" (MHC). The immediate focus was the general food shortage in

Germany and the deportation, pillaging and starvation among Russian Mennonites occasioned by the civil war in revolutionary Russia. The second Mennonite World Conference held in Danzig and West Prussia in 1930 concentrated on aiding these Russian Mennonite refugees; from Danzig a general plea was issued to the Mennonite world to assist these "brothers in need." MHC was modelled on the Mennonite Central Committee that had been founded two years earlier in the United States. Because of widespread food shortages in the country, these first German efforts were relatively small-scale, and yet they were serious attempts to help needy and displaced persons. The MHC set up a refugee camp for Russians in Lechfeld in the winter of 1922–1923.

German Mennonites and National Socialism, 1933–1945

One consequence of World War I was that it separated German Mennonites into different countries. The redrawn political borders partitioned West Prussia into three different states, and the German-speaking Alsatian Mennonites, who had been part of the south German Mennonite conference and had close contact to the *Verband*, were now once again part of France. Furthermore, 400 Mennonite soldiers lost their lives in the war (about four percent of all German Mennonite men). Nevertheless, losing the Great War did not provoke the Germans to rethink their values. They still were convinced that it had been right to go to war, and their losses were attributed to manipulative and dark powers. Nor did Mennonites question their participation or recall their Anabaptist anti-militarist heritage, in spite of the unspeakable horrors of trench warfare, gas attacks and the millions of war dead on both sides. Much rather, the political division of West Prussia and the loss of Alsace only increased the patriotism and chauvinism in the congregations. This was especially true in West Prussia, where the partition led the Mennonite leadership in later years to approve of the reintroduction of military duty under the National Socialists.

In addition to the general political disruption and frustration, the destruction of German-speaking Mennonite colonies in Communist Russia caused great dismay. After the Russian revolution some 30,000 Mennonite refugees entered Germany, where they were given temporary shelter until they could emigrate to other lands such as Canada or Paraguay, since it was the general opinion in Germany that there was "no room" for them to stay. The dreadful situation of the *Russländer* only increased the virulent anti-communist, nationalist opinions of most rural Mennonites.

Another source of discontent was the erratic economic situation of the Weimar Republic, which caused many large and successful Mennonite farm businesses to fail or go heavily into debt. These Mennonites distrusted the new parliamentary democracy and yearned for a return to the stability of the monarchy. Germany's subservient role in international politics after the Treaty of Versailles in 1919 and the extremely high unemployment rate after the worldwide economic collapse (1929–1932) were also humiliating, and prepared the way for National Socialism.

These disruptive transitional years brought much soul-searching and adjustment to new living conditions, but it was during this time that Mennonites rediscovered their history and genealogy. Many began to study their past and this resulted in numerous articles in *Der Mennonit* and other publications. The pastors Christian Neff and Christian Hege established a German Mennonite Historical Society in 1936 and soon began publishing the *Mennonitische Geschichtsblätter*, which has remained an annual journal for Mennonite history until the present day. Many others participated in another project initiated by Neff, an exhaustive encyclopedia of history, social life and theology titled *Mennonitisches Lexikon* (first volume published 1913), under the auspices of the *Vereinigung*. Nevertheless, this interest in Mennonite history, including the study of the early Anabaptists with their protest against political and religious authority, had little effect on the perception of the relationship of Mennonites to National Socialism and its authoritarian philosophy of life.

When Hitler was elected chancellor in 1933, his call to revive Germany's international power impressed many people. They were excited by the National Socialist appeal to great ideals and the challenge to participate personally in attaining its goals. Henceforth, public interest was to precede personal interest, a claim that sounded to the hearer like a Christian principle. It sounded like a return to the "good old days" and the end of frivolity and permissiveness. Individual congregations and both of the general conferences of Mennonites freely volunteered their support to the new regime. They joined the masses of the "German race" in celebrating the new political leadership, hoping that it would fulfill its promise to rebuild the economy and re-invigorate society. Mennonite farmers were also among those who profited financially from "blood and earth" politics. The majority of citizens soon stood united behind Hitler, not recognizing the criminal energy that motivated him.

Emil Händiges, at that time pastor in Ibersheim, was the editor of the journal the *Mennonitische Blätter* in 1924, and from 1927 on he exercised a growing influence on Mennonite life. His approval of National Socialism was supported by most Mennonites. The statutes of the newly reconstituted *Vereinigung* dating from July 1934 took a clear position that reflected Nazi vocabulary:

> Honouring the temporal authorities and the social order in accordance with the apostolic witness, we hold it to be the duty of Christians to serve our nation and state (*Volk und Staat*) conscientiously.[2]

A communiqué also was sent to the new government: "Should mandatory military service be re-introduced, we German Mennonites will no longer claim any special rights." This affirmation encouraged hesitant Mennonites to accept the duty of military service when this became German law in the following year. The *Verband* held a somewhat bolder position, stating that "The *Verband* holds to the principle of conscientious objection, without thereby restricting the free decision of each individual." This position tacitly allowed military service without the express sanction of the church leadership. Most, though not all, Mennonites willingly accepted the duty to serve in the military, without demur. When conscription was introduced in 1935, all accepted it and some Mennonites also served willingly in various paramilitary organizations.

Even so, Mennonites were not unanimous on this issue: the remilitarization of Germany and the enthusiasm for the Nazi regime with its belief in a national rebirth was an object of controversial discussion for years. After the initial enthusiasm many soon became indifferent; they concerned themselves with their personal lives. But others, especially among the youth, saw the growing totalitarian claims of the Third Reich as standing in competition with their faith in Jesus Christ. When the Nazis tried to involve Mennonites in their new ideological church structure, the *Deutsche Christen*, the Mennonite church rejected its claims of enforced conformity (*Gleichschaltung*). Mennonite church structures were not reformed in accordance with the *Führer* principle, but at the same time Mennonites avoided conveying a sense of rebellion.

Seldom did the participants in the *Rundbriefe* take such a strong anti-National Socialist stance as Hilde Funk, who wrote in June of 1932:

Can a Christian be a Nazi? There are various answers. Some say yes, and argue that we must protect our nation from anti-Christianity, and they say that the National Socialists are our bastion against Bolshevism. Those who refute this claim ask: Is Communism the only anti-Christianity? It is in fact the lesser danger for the people of God, because it has always openly claimed to oppose religion! It is not the 'angel of light' who deceives the holy. The Nazis claim to stand for a Christian culture, but only insofar as it corresponds to their interests. The Nazis have only one purpose, to which everything else is subordinate: race! Christianity is cut down to size and only that part of 'positive Christianity' is retained that satisfies [their idea of] Germanic race. That is idolatry and godlessness.

Participants in a congregational meeting in Emden several months after the Nazis seized power in 1933 stood decisively on Hitler's side:

When in these weeks of national and social self-reflection the great will of our people seeks to overcome all the paltry obstacles between the various confessions and theologies and establish the divinely planned ethnic unity [Volksgemeinschaft] of our state, so also we desire the breakthrough of this spirit and progress in religious development here ... Our hope is that the reorganization of ecclesiastical structures will be borne by a rebirth of the German spirit in a consciousness of God's presence and with respect for the physical and spiritual inheritance of our people.

Debate among Mennonites was carried out in publications, meetings and especially in the so-called *Rundbrief* (Circular). The *Rundbrief* was a forum in which the relationship between Christianity and the political system was discussed. The minority of those in favour of pacifism argued on the basis of the fifth commandment, the Sermon on the Mount, the call to discipleship and Peter's avowal that we obey God and not man (Acts 5:29). These theological claims remained generalized and were not applied to the concrete situation, as in one of the *Rundbriefe* where it was in fact claimed that "war is sin," and so consequently politicians should take steps to outlaw war. The proponents of military service, on the other hand, claimed that Jesus' command to love one another need not lead to pacifism. Love is to be shown to neighbour, family and nation, but not necessarily toward foreigners. Thus, it could be an expression of love to make war against other nations, in order to protect home and family, even if it led to the death of foreigners.

Some Mennonites also adopted the very un-Mennonite just war theology. A defensive war is a just war, some argued, and even a pre-emptive (aggressive) war in the service of self-protection is acceptable. This was especially true for Germany, which had long borders with many enemies and was in bitter need of *Lebensraum* (more room to live) in order to secure its survival. Reference was made to Romans 13 and Matthew 22 to prove that loyalty to the state was absolutely necessary, especially when this state propagated great ideals. The government was after all part of God's creation "for our good" and had the right to command its subjects.

Disputes took place nonetheless over the question whether citizens should obey everything that the state considered to be right and just. In 1935 the German state took a more critical position toward the independent churches and Mennonites occasionally were faced with difficulties. From this point forward, political articles disappeared from Mennonite publications and were replaced by purely biblical themes which seldom reflected the actual political situation. In general believers assumed a quietist position, holding church services and continuing traditional baptismal and other practices in the usual manner. Whereas urban church services were attended by very few persons, in rural areas attendance seems not to have declined. In spite of the general hatred of foreigners in society, Mennonites maintained their interest in the mission field and collected money for mission work.

On the other hand, when Dutch Mennonites established a Peace Committee in 1934 and sought support in the Palatinate, they were received with suspicion and scepticism. When a "Peace Conference" was held at the conclusion of the Third Mennonite World Conference in Elspeet (Netherlands) in 1936, most German Mennonites refused to take part, hinting at the problems they would face from Nazis.

As war loomed, some raised their voices. Christian Neff in Weierhof also published a criticism of the war in the *Gemeindeblatt der Mennoniten* in January 1941:

> What this war is doing ... belongs to the earthly realm with its sins and deathly misery. How ... disgracefully the honour of God is being insulted in this present war! How much injustice! How much deception of peoples! ... How many great and small lies are being told! Everything that self-sacrificial love in the service of peace has accomplished is being destroyed by the hatred and rage of Christian peoples. ... Whoever knows Jesus, has peace and brings peace... God cannot be pleased, when peoples fight to the bitter death, when they strive only to destroy each other in unbelievable hatred.[3]

Following this publication, the *Gemeindeblatt* was banned and the author was forbidden to publish anything further. It should not go unmentioned here that by the late 1930s everyone in society was conscious of the aggressive reprisals suffered by all those who uttered public criticism of Nazi politics. Such persons and their families faced immediate danger from their neighbours and were likely to experience hostile police action.

No German Mennonite refused military service after its re-introduction in 1935. There are, however, several reports of Mennonite soldiers who attempted to be transferred from battle units to technical divisions. But in any case, after August of 1939 Mennonite men accepted their conscription into army, navy and air force, serving willingly and without appealing to the standing order of 1868—it remained in force until 1956—which had provided a noncombatant option for Mennonites. At the same time, many of them (there is no precise estimate of their number) sought transfers to non-fighting divisions, in order to avoid the duty to kill.

> **Emil Händiges, pastor in Elbing and chairman of the *Vereinigung*, wrote in the *Mennonitische Blätter* in 1936:**
>
> *How thankful we are to our heavenly Father who has sustained us individually and collectively, as a congregation and as a people, as on the wings of an eagle! ... Our newly established Reich is a protective barrier against Bolshevism. We have been spared the horrors that our brothers in faith and ethnicity are suffering in the Soviet Union. ... The Lord has done this and it is a miracle. May God protect our nation and our fatherland, may He bless our Führer and Chancellor and our government. May the Lord God build his kingdom [Reich] in us and through us, both at home and abroad.*

Another situation where Mennonites might be seen to have "failed" in this period was in their reaction to the difficulties faced by the Society of Brothers (*Bruderhof*). A group of believers established a community with a communal lifestyle at Rhönbruderhof in the 1920s, having been inspired in part by the Hutterites. They established loose contact with some Mennonite circles at that time, since they practiced the Anabaptist principles of nonviolence and took a critical stance concerning church-state relations. When the Gestapo acted against the Society of Brothers in 1937, the *Vereinigung* stated that these people were not Mennonites (which was formally true) and did not attempt to help them, because they did not want to endanger their own good reputation. In their desperate situation the Society of Brothers was aided by Dutch Mennonites, who helped them get to England. Bruderhof Communities still exist in the UK and the USA to this day.

> **Gerhard Thiessen in Ladekopp criticized the regime in a sermon in 1937. The government authorities, led by a former Mennonite, proscribed the sermon and censured Thiessen.**
>
> *Among all the teachings of Jesus, hatred is one of the most reprehensible sins, ... it is something that can and must lead to the death of a person, to the death of a congregation, indeed to the death of an entire people.*

It is perhaps not surprising that German Mennonites of those days did not assume a stronger critique of National Socialism. They were the heirs of groups who after long centuries of being disadvantaged had now made tremendous gains and had flourished quickly after adapting to German society. They had long since lost any connection to the critical stance of the first Anabaptists, and their understanding of their own history was revisionist. They adopted the predominant Protestant theology of Lutheranism, according to which the head of state is acting as God's instrument although there also was some dissent. In general, however, German Mennonites of this time separated their personal religious beliefs from their political opinions.

After the euphoria of the successful Blitzkrieg in 1939 and 1940 and the "reunification" with Mennonite congregations in Alsace and Lorraine, the war years became very stressful. Like other Germans,

Mennonite pastor Otto Schowalter in the uniform of the German army.

Mennonites gradually suffered more and more under the war economy. They also were fearful of being persecuted by the Gestapo and worried about their men fighting on the front lines. In the last year of war the danger of being strafed by fighter planes or being bombed in the air raids was very great. Church services and youth meetings stood under the shadow of this anxiety and concern.

For many years after the war Mennonites had trouble examining their relationship to the Nazi state. At first they were shocked by the collapse of Germany and had enough to do, simply trying to exist in the horrible and difficult post-war years. A predominant sense was "we've managed to survive." Nevertheless, some began to think through the situation. At the Fourth Mennonite World Conference in 1948, held in Goshen, Indiana, Dirk Cattepoel, pastor in Krefeld, pleaded for forgiveness from the Mennonites present:

> As a Christian from Germany I would confess with all my heart how deeply it burdens us that so much distress, so much cruelty, and so much destruction has come over others through men of our nation, and I would like to appeal particularly to you, my Dutch and French brothers

and sisters: during the years since 1940, terrible things have happened to your people through representatives of mine, so much, that from the human angle forgiveness seems impossible. And yet, for Christ's sake I ask you: Forgive us! And thus grant us—in the name of Christ—a new beginning of Christian brotherliness.[4]

It took thirty years before writings addressing the Nazi past came to be written by German Mennonites; for many this was a very painful process. In 1995 the AMG published a statement marking the fiftieth anniversary of the end of the war in Europe and confessed:

Most Mennonites in Germany gave in to the temptation of National Socialism and sacrificed the peace witness. Very often they valued their commitment to the state higher than their duties to Mennonite brothers and sisters in the Netherlands and France. ... Nearly all Mennonites remained silent in the face of Nazi crimes against Jews and others. ... We can only plead for forgiveness with the words of the Lord's Prayer.[5]

One of the Nazi concentration camps (Konzentrationslager, KZ), Stutthof, was located east of Danzig, in the midst of Mennonite farmhouses. A large number of smaller camps belonged to this "KZ" also, and the inhabitants of the area often saw starving prisoners in their striped dress on their way to the places of their forced labour.

The Revival of German Mennonite Faith after 1945

The Aftermath of the War and the Rebuilding Effort

In early 1945 the Mennonites of the former West Prussia were the hapless victims of the advancing Russian army. A general fear of being caught by the invaders led many to flee to the west; those who remained or waited too long to escape—usually the sick, the young and the elderly—suffered mightily at the hands of the Russian army: starvation, rape, bodily injury, torture, deportation to Russia and loss of life were among the many horrific events of those days. In the general rush to save what they could, congregations and families were torn apart. After the land route from the Danzig region to the west was cut off, many fled in boats, some of which were torpedoed. The survivors were held in refugee camps in Denmark in the last months of the war in Europe. After the cessation of hostilities even more joined their ranks. Most of them would never see their homeland again. The vibrant communities of Mennonites in West Prussia were utterly destroyed.

For those refugees from the east who had no relatives in post-war Germany, it was a difficult process to gain admission to the country. For several years church services in the refugee camps were organized by the West Prussian elders Bruno Ewert and Bruno Enß. Assistance came from MCC, the North American churches, as well as from the Netherlands and France. Some congregations in West Germany like Hamburg-Altona were strengthened by the influx of Prussian members; some new congregations were founded by war refugees: Göttingen (1945), Frankfurt, Espelkamp and Bechterdissen (1948), as well as Kiel, Lübeck, Bremen,

The rebuilt Krefeld Mennonite Church in the midst of the post-war ruins.

Oldenburg, Hannover and in Bergisches Land. But in general, the German church was seriously weakened by the loss of life and the destruction of church buildings in the west, to say nothing of the dispersal of German-speaking Mennonites to all other parts of the world.

About 9,000 German Mennonites were allowed to transfer from East to West Germany. MCC assisted the emigration of 7,000 German and Russian Mennonites to Canada, 1,000 to Uruguay and 2,500 to Paraguay. This refugee work was led by C. F. Klassen, himself a refugee from Russia during the 1920s.

In the midst of rebuilding the country, the remnants of the Mennonite church needed to be rebuilt as well. The city congregations in particular suffered from Allied air bombing, and many Mennonite soldiers had lost their lives. Another disaster was that many of the German-speaking Mennonites of Russia who had fled to the British, American and French sectors of post-war Germany were sent back to the Soviet Union. In addition to the complete destruction of economic life in Germany, the division of the country into East and West Germany and the isolation of West Berlin were sources of great suffering and disorientation. The Cold War led to further emigrations, but also to soul-searching as to the proper understanding of the gospel and of the Mennonite pacifist tradition.

The Mennonite Central Committee played a central role in the post-war recovery. Not only was MCC's material aid essential for survival, MCC also assisted spiritually in word and deed. Some 800 volunteers came to Europe to help people of all confessions and nationalities in the name of Christ. In the first five difficult years, 28,000 tons of goods, 170,000 Christmas packages and two million dollars in cash were distributed to the needy.

Mennonites on the trek from Ukraine to Germany, fall 1943

Germans had already experienced the ravages of war early in the twentieth century. After losing the First World War the economy in Germany had been in a catastrophic state and food shortages lasted several years in some regions. Bavarian Mennonites organized and transported food collections for these regions. In this way some 12,000 persons were helped in the three years after 1918. But now, large parts of Europe suffered massive devastation as a result of the Second World War, with the exception of Switzerland. Living quarters and industrial buildings had been bombed, so that millions of people had no place to live or work. In Germany, as in other lands, administration and transport were ruined. The roads were blocked by 20 million refugees; millions of women travelled daily across the region in a desperate search for food.

During the last months of the war, the North American MCC began organizing the transport of essential goods, at first for the French and the Dutch, then later for West Germany and Berlin. These goods were dispensed at the local level by national and local relief agencies. By 1949, 8,000 tons of food stuffs and 110 tons of textiles had been distributed. In addition to their Akron office, MCC set up a regional office in Germany in 1947, where the North American staff could direct the distribution of relief. They also readily accepted the assistance of German Mennonites. The Germans relied heavily on the recommendations and support of MCC. Many of their own initiatives were modelled on MCC's example, which suggested ideas and generously aided in the

Displaced Mennonites from Russia arrive in the ruins of Berlin.

In the West Prussian village of Heubuden, a Driedger family lived and worked their land for several centuries until 1945. The older sons fought in the German army and were either killed in action or wounded; the parents, their many servants and a 15-year-old son took care of the homestead. But when on March 10, 1945 they heard the approaching Russian guns and tanks, the Driedgers harnessed nine wagons and their private carriage and escaped. In Pomerania, German soldiers were preparing to detonate a charge on a river crossing and ordered them to stop. The young son driving the light carriage immediately took out his whip and hurried the horses across the bridge. Seconds later, the bridge exploded and debris flew around their ears. They and the Mennonites on the slower moving wagons behind them eventually managed to board a ship to the West, where they languished for several years in a refugee camp in Denmark. Some relatives emigrated to Uruguay; the young man, Eckbert Driedger, managed to establish a new farm and a family in the Palatinate. For many years he made active contributions to the music, preaching and leadership of the congregation at Weierhof.

In 1975 he contacted the Polish family now living in his ancestral home. The two families, one Catholic, one Mennonite, now visit each other often in a spirit of friendship and reconciliation.

Refugees in Backnang in December 1947. Powdered milk, sent over by the American Mennonites, provides lunch pails for the children.

organization and financing of these new projects. After World War II the relief agencies of the *Vereinigung* (HVDM) and the *Verband* (MHC) worked together with MCC.

The German *Vereinigung* lost all of its West Prussian congregations in the war and its other congregations in the west all suffered serious losses. For this reason, the *Vereinigung* established a relief agency (HVDM) in 1946 among the ruins of Hamburg. Workers were given the task of distributing food and tending to the needs of the West Prussians who were living in refugee camps in Denmark and northern Germany. A full-time worker set up an office in 1948 in Weierhof. Later the HVDM organized a permanent clothing collection service which was later taken over by the *Internationale Mennonitische Organisation* (IMO) and sent textiles and clothing to Brazil.

A settlement agency (*Siedlungshilfe*) was also set up in 1951 to direct homeless and destitute farmers and families, mostly from the former West Prussia, to settlements and farms. The settlement agency finished its work in the 1960s.

Because of these movements new Mennonite settlements came into existence in Backnang, Enkenbach, Neuwied, Bechterdissen,

A "PAX boy" in Dudelange, Luxembourg, renovating a window of a building to be used for church activities.

Espelkamp and Wedel. Houses also were set up in Heilbronn, Kaiserslautern and Berlin for needy families. The construction work was largely carried out by so-called "PAX boys," young conscientious objectors from North America, who worked under the auspices and with the financial assistance of MCC. Finally, beginning in 1972 the HVDM also saw to the needs of families in Paraguay who wished to return to Germany and who settled in the vicinity of the congregations of Neuwied, Bechterdissen and Espelkamp.

MCC also offered assistance in spiritual matters, for example in re-establishing the Mennonite position in military questions. It aided the establishment of the Bible school at Bienenberg, Switzerland, which since its beginnings in 1950 has served German Mennonites as well. It helped establish the magazine *Der Mennonit* and the Agape publishing house. And MCC began a volunteer service, the forerunner of *Christliche Dienste*, about which more will be said below. Finally, it initiated an inter-confessional network for peace theology, later called "Church and Peace" and the service and relief agency *Eirene*.

> **Hans Hübert recalls:**
>
> *During the years 1947 to 1949, several larger and smaller groups migrated from the terribly devastated Germany to Latin America, looking for a new homeland there. During the first years of settling there, conditions of life were extremely primitive and hard. I can hardly imagine how we could have kept alive during this time without the help of MCC and other North American Mennonite organizations. On the other hand, without any hindrance we were able to build our houses, villages, schools, churches and congregations.*
>
> *However, for many people the positive aspects did not make up for the negative and hard ones. ... Around the mid-fifties people started to go back to Germany as well. ... When it became known that the German government was offering favourable start-up help, that private homes could be built and congregations founded, even more wished to return.*

The Peace Witness

With the growing consciousness of the extent to which German society had collaborated with the Nazi regime, or passively stood by while the Nazis perpetrated crimes against Jews, minorities and other nations, German Mennonites felt the need to repent and take steps toward peace and justice in society. The renewal of the peace witness stands in this context. In contrast to individuals refusing military service on the basis of "conscience" in the nineteenth and early twentieth centuries, the concept of peace was taken up now as a theological and biblical issue of following Christ in discipleship. The role of North American Mennonites in this revival was crucial. Their witness helped in the transformation which then took clearer form in the so-called "Thomashof Declaration" of 1949.

In June of 1949 Mennonites from all parts of Germany assembled at Thomashof for three days to discuss the principles of pacifism and nonviolence. twenty-five persons signed the Thomashof Declaration.

We have become conscious of the significance of our [Anabaptist] heritage and view it as a renewed duty to give witness to the biblical truth of nonviolence. When we consider the indescribable suffering and demonic outcome of the last wars, we regard it to be a special duty for Mennonites to stand up for the idea of peace and its practical realisation in all parts of our lives and to commend it in private, congregational and governmental life. When our brothers and fellow church members object to being conscripted into military service for reasons of conscience, we regard it as our duty to assist them in every possible way to perform a non-military service.

The emotional devastation of the war and the shame over the atrocities performed in the name of the state united Mennonites with other Germans in the conviction that a new path needed to be opened and followed. More than mere nonviolence needed to be practiced. German soldiers returning after 1945 spoke with conviction: "Never again war, never again weapons and the destruction of defenceless cities." The remilitarization of West Germany in the 1950s, one of the consequences of the Cold War, aroused numerous opponents and led in the 1970s to the energizing of the peace movement. In this movement Mennonites stood with great masses of people who opposed forming a new standing army. Nevertheless, on account of the threats posed by the Cold War and the special concerns faced by Germans—their nation being divided into West and East—not everyone and not all Mennonites opposed the concept of a protective army.

During the discussion over remilitarization, elders, pastors and deacons from the *Verband* issued a joint statement on August 22, 1950, in Heilbronn: "The word of God obliges us to serve our fellow man in the spirit of the Sermon on the Mount and in the tradition of our ancestors, in such a manner that life be preserved and not destroyed." The *Verband* and the *Vereinigung* together presented this declaration to the West German government, focussing on the "command of Christ" and calling for "peace in spirit and in deed." The declaration appealed to the new German constitution, which guaranteed the right to refuse military service. Although the constitution had not been influenced by Mennonites, they were instrumental in the formulation of the law regulating conscientious objectors in 1956.

The German Mennonite Peace Committee (DMFK) helped to spread a pacifist conviction in the congregations, offering seminars and representing the rights of conscientious objectors and war resisters. There are no reliable statistics on this point, but at least half of all young Mennonite men who were drafted availed themselves of the opportunity to perform an alternative service between 1956 and 1975. DMFK also provided a useful service through a series of publications called "The Way to Peace" (*Der Weg des Friedens*). Sermons on peace issues or theological writings remained rare until stationing atomic missiles on American bases in West Germany became a hot political issue in the late 1970s. At this time, many Mennonites participated in political demonstrations in the Palatinate and in Baden-Württemberg, and the Mennonite leadership began to support conscientious objection publicly. Since 1984 DMFK has maintained a regularly staffed office. However, since military service is becoming less and less common in Germany as a whole, and the opportunities for alternative service correspondingly greater, the focus of the Peace Committee has turned toward many other activities that help raise the church's consciousness of the centrality of peace theology to the message of Jesus Christ, for example by teaching and training in nonviolence and mediation.

A general meeting of the *Vereinigung* (including southwestern Mennonites) presented a declaration in 1985, following discussions in the congregations: "We believe in the reconciling power of the gospel." It claimed that "the nonviolent way of Jesus is a valid and binding gospel for us." The congregations were encouraged to practice and teach peace and to avoid military service. But at the same time, the statement said, "we also respect and tolerate those who decide to perform military service." In the *Verband* a lengthy dialogue in the congregations led to the declaration "Our Peace Witness" in 1987. Strongly christological in its accents, this declaration also sup-

German Mennonites participate in demonstrations around the US Army air base in Sembach, 1987.

ported peace theology. An earlier declaration on its self-identity of the church also focused on nonviolence and the peace witness. During the war in Kosovo in 1999, the three major conferences also issued a declaration criticising the first use of German military personnel on foreign soil since World War II. In taking this stand, the Mennonite church stood in opposition to the general approval of the larger churches in Germany to the sending of German soldiers to Kosovo.

With these developments there has also been much reflection among Mennonites as to what exactly their peace witness should entail. Earlier, Mennonites concentrated their energies on not participating in war and performing only social duties for the state. At the same time, they paid taxes that were used in part to finance the military and military actions. Mennonites became aware of the fact that their actions were pacifying their consciences without doing anything to alter the reason for wars. The German peace witness emphasizes the need to seek and prevent the causes of "peacelessness," that is, not simply repudiating war but also working for harmony between peoples and standing up for justice. This involves going to regions of conflict, protesting against unjust regimes and structures of evil, which tend to dominate people and disadvantage the weak.

The Modern Organization of the Mennonite Church

In the aftermath of the war it quickly became obvious that German Mennonites needed to reappraise their situation and reorganize their church. Roughly speaking, there had been three large regional associations before the war, each with a different character. The *Vereinigung* was mostly in the north (although including many congregations of the southwest, as well as Munich and Regensburg) and the *Verband* was located in the southeast.

At the same time, the southwestern Mennonites (chiefly in the Palatinate) had also developed a similar regional structure, which after its reorganization is now named the ASM (*Arbeitsgemeinschaft Südwestdeutscher Mennonitengemeinden*) or Association of Southwest German Mennonite Congregations. These groups—the *Vereinigung, Verband* and ASM—are called the "three pillars" that support a national coalition of German Mennonites, namely the AMG or *Arbeitsgemeinschaft Mennonitischer Gemeinden in Deutschland*: the Association of German Mennonite Congregations. The creation of the AMG was the result of a vision of uniting Mennonites in Germany for which leaders struggled for over a century. Through the establishment of the AMG it finally became possible to address theological or political issues with a united voice. The AMG concerns itself with liturgical issues (the new hymnal of 2004 is one result) and with training young people for offices of ministry.

Since 1990 the *Vereinigung* has become a regional entity for eleven northern German communities. In its present-day form, the *Vereinigung* serves communities of greatly differing size, from the largest city congregation with several pastors (Krefeld) to the smallest, where five congregations share a single pastor: Emden, Gronau, Leer, Norden and Oldenburg. Some congregations have their own buildings, while others are guests in the church buildings of other confessions. The north German congregations sense a certain nearness to the Reformed and Lutheran (*Evangelische*) churches in their forms of worship and socializing, and in theology they tend toward a liberal and ecumenical position.

A special role played by the *Vereinigung* is the representation of Mennonites in the World Council of Churches, where it is a founding member. Through its representative there, Fernando Enns, the *Vereinigung* was instrumental in initiating the WCC's "Decade to Overcome Violence" in 2001, which united all Christian churches in an effort to promote reconciliation and peace. As a further step a Peace Centre has been established recently in the national capital, Berlin. The *Vereinigung*'s youth work also has a full-time staff person who works with the church youth, who are spread out across all of northern Germany.

The *Verband* is currently made up of twenty-six congregations with over 1,500 baptized members. The largest congregation in Backnang has 190 members, the smallest are in Freiburg and Kehl, with thirteen and twelve members respectively. The board of the *Verband* is especially active in counselling and advising its congregations, training pastors and coordinating the work of travelling preachers. It also has produced a guidebook for liturgical purposes and has begun a regular news publication. The *Verband* is committed to planting new churches: congregations have been formed over the last few years in Meßkirch, Pfullendorf and Landau. A special inherited mark of the *Verband* is that it historically focused on lay preachers, but in the last few decades it has gradually changed its structure. More than half of the congregations now have full- or part-time pastors, most of whom have been trained at Bible schools. Only the smallest congregations are now served exclusively by lay preachers.

Fernando Enns reflects on the divergent opinions among German Mennonites with regard to ecumenical involvement:

"*I observe two fundamental tendencies that seem to contradict one another. On the one hand we experience the growth of ecumenical fellowship in various churches and we as German Mennonites participate in and help to shape it. On the other hand we question ourselves as to what our Anabaptist-Mennonite identity actually is in the modern age. ... Many of our members who are spread throughout the diaspora seek contact with other confessions in their immediate vicinity, without wanting to give up their Mennonite-ness. But our congregations are also the new spiritual home for many who are no longer at home in their old traditions. In many ways the peaceful coexistence of the various traditions has become commonplace. This is in large measure due to our growing number of inter-confessional families. ... At the same time, there is a certain scepticism about anything "ecumenical," out of a fear of being swallowed up or losing one's own identity. The result is that Mennonites in the AMG have very divergent attitudes about whether we should be involved in ecumenical institutions.*"

The ASM, founded under another name in 1974, has had regular meetings since 1871. It is the youngest association of congregations and is concentrated geographically in the southwest. It formulated a mission statement in 1998 for its congregations, emphasizing that "missions" is not an isolated activity, but needs to be understood in a holistic manner, involving peace issues, relief work and proclamation of the gospel.

The statutes of the ASM accentuate baptism on confession of faith, the call for all believers to work for the gospel, the peace witness and the independence of each congregation. It is made up of sixteen congregations with about 2,000 members. Many of these congregations have historical roots back to the seventeenth century, but were rejuvenated by the influx of West Prussians after World War II; others, such as Enkenbach, were formed after 1945. All congregations have full-time pastors, with some sharing a single pastor. An important date in the ASM calendar is the *Forum der Werke* in autumn, when the various agencies present the latest developments in their activity.

Each of these three associations has its own managing board where pastors and lay members, both men and women, direct the work. Each year, they hold assemblies of delegates to deliberate and vote on decisions of concern for the congregations. However, since the associations are voluntary in nature, no congregation is bound by the resolutions of these assemblies. Consequently, the delegate assemblies and boards strive to attain consensus in their decisions. The financial costs of the associations are covered by contributions of the congregations as set out in their respective statutes.

German Mennonite journal *Die Brücke*

This description of organizational and financial structure is also true for the AMG, which was established in 1990 under its first chairman, Peter Foth, pastor in Hamburg. After initial meetings were held in 1982, a long-standing vision for a national representative umbrella organization to coordinate shared Mennonite activities finally came to fruition. The AMG includes the regional conferences as its three pillars. Its representation involves the three member groups as equal partners. The AMG is also the managing editor of *Die Brücke*, the Mennonite journal which is now published every two months. *Die Brücke* (The Bridge) was established in 1986 as the successor to the *Mennonitische Blätter*.

At first it was hoped that all Mennonite groups in Germany would join the AMG, but this did not prove feasible. Several thousand German-speaking persons of Mennonite descent had emigrated from Russia over the past few decades and formed large congregations in various regions of Germany, a story that will be told in more detail below, in chapter VII. With the reunification of Germany in 1990, the easing of east-west tensions and the liberalization of travel restrictions in the former Soviet Union, even more Russian-born Mennonites moved to Germany. Initially, efforts were made to integrate all of the new arrivals into the already-existing Mennonite congregations and into the AMG. However, the cultural and theological differences proved to be so great that most of the new arrivals, numerically far greater than the members of the "older" congregations, opted to develop their own organizations. Coming shortly after the fall of the Berlin Wall with its hopes for a revival of German society, this failure to form a united Mennonite organization was felt as a bitter disappointment by many in the AMG, and is still a lingering regret. Contact and dialogue with these other Mennonite organizations in Germany takes place at informal and personal levels.

> An example of a concise contemporary statement of distinctively Mennonite views is the following declaration from the ASM, dated March 1998:
>
> *The present-day Anabaptist-Mennonite understanding of faith and church includes the following points:*
>
> - *baptism upon confession of faith in Jesus Christ,*
> - *the Lord's Supper as a practice of remembrance [of Christ's death], celebrating community and hoping [for the Lord's return],*
> - *the summoning of all members of the congregation to participate in all aspects of church work,*
> - *the witness of peace through the rejection of military service and working for peace,*
> - *the rejection of swearing oaths as an expression of truthfulness ... and*
> - *the independence of church affairs from state intervention.*

We began the history of German Mennonites by mentioning that they have no common history. The collection of different stories of the congregations in the AMG are, however, increasingly growing together. The AMG attempts to assist congregations in acknowledging and strengthening their commonality. Indeed, the mere fact that modern Mennonites are very mobile means that many church members are now first-generation members of their congregations—a fact that would have been considered inconceivable in rural congregations a few generations ago. Traditions no longer play the immensely central role that they used to do, and so the various traditions of the different groups of Mennonites are slowly merging together.

Some Aspects of Modern Mennonite Life in the AMG

Congregational Worship

Most church services in AMG congregations take place on Sunday mornings. Although the great majority of congregations have full-time pastors, it is also common for lay members to take active roles in greeting visitors, reading the Bible, playing music and preaching. The liturgical forms are extremely varied. Some churches use the Evangelical Lutheran liturgical readings and sermon text recommendations, while others have free liturgical forms similar to younger non-denominational churches. Pastors in Hamburg and Krefeld wear formal cassocks or robes like Lutheran pastors, but in general, worship services have become much more informal since the liberalisation of society in the post-war years. No longer is Luther's Bible translation (which used to enjoy a role very similar to the KJV in English) predominant; song writers have written hymns and praise songs that are used not only in youth services but also sung by congregations. And whereas in earlier generations, non-Mennonite visitors were rare, nowadays it is very common to have Christians from other confessions worshipping our common God. The education of pastors (and some lay leaders) is also extremely various: some have been trained at Bible schools, some have gone to the Bienenberg, others still have studied Protestant theology at universities.

The Role of Women in the Church

One development in the AMG over the last few decades has been the expanding involvement of women in church life; this reflects a strong break with past traditions. This development is one of the major factors that distinguishes AMG congregations from other Mennonite groups in Germany. The most obvious example is the ordination of female pastors. Again, the Krefeld congregation paved this new path by electing the first female *Pastorin* in Germany, Dorothea Franzen (later Dorothea Ruthsatz), who served from 1981 to 1992. But women had begun preaching in church services much earlier. In 2004 there were at least seven female pastors serving in AMG congregations; if we add lay church members, then at least twenty women preach regularly in Mennonite services.

Another important transformation that has revived the life of German congregations since 1945 has been the expanding involvement of the general membership in various church activities. This move away from "holding an office" to "serving with one's gifts" in the congregation also empowers women and has helped to edify members and renew belief in our witness as the body of Christ in the world. This includes the involvement of women in ecumenical leadership, house and prayer groups, choirs, Sunday school teaching, youth group leadership and various other forms of service.

Youth Work

The KSM, the conference of south German Mennonites established in 1887, transferred most of its remaining duties (especially publications) to the AMG in 1990. Its chief task is now administering youth work in southern Germany. The so-called JuWe with four employees and a yearly budget of nearly 200,000 euros is now organized from its offices in Thomashof, caring for youth and young adult activities for 33 southern congregations. In the *Vereinigung* similar work is performed by the MJN. Each year MJN and JuWe plan camps and retreats, working together with many Mennonite volunteers who learn leadership skills and share their faith. MJN and JuWe coordinate activities for children as well.

JuWe Youth Camp Summer 2001

The youth work of individual congregations is directed by the vision of motivating young people to follow Jesus. Most congregations have their own youth groups, which often involve the participation of non-Mennonite friends, provide opportunities for youth to discuss issues and talk about the gospel. Many youth groups also organize youth services, in which the message of Christ is presented in praise, singing, dance and skits. The most successful large-scale event of recent years has been the monthly youth worship service at Sinsheim, which has often attracted over 200 young people from the entire south German region. It has become the model for similar large events in other churches. These services take place in a relaxed and vibrant atmosphere, using contemporary music and sound equipment. This makes it possible for youth to invite their friends to join them in worship in a context in which the youth culture feels more at home.

Nursing Care and Homes for the Aged

At the beginning of the twentieth century, and after many years of deliberation, the *Verband* established a nursing station (*Diakonissensta-tion*), based on the model of a famous German nursing institute. Two needs were met with this new project: job opportunities for young women (who had been leaving the Mennonite church to join nursing institutes run by other confessions), and the need for intensive care for family members within the *Verband*. The first nurse began in 1905. Over the next sixty years, twenty-five nurses, chiefly from within the *Verband,* were trained and served in this station. At first their work was directed toward individual nursing in private homes. Later they provided the complete nursing staff for two public hospitals. Gradually they also took on additional duties as nurses for the aged, for isolated villages and in missions. In the 1960s this profession gradually died out, because young women were no longer attracted to nursing. The last of these nurses died at an advanced age in 1987.

A home for the aged was first established near Neuwied in 1948 for elderly refugees. The responsibility for this work was taken on by a new organization (*Mennonitischer Heimeverein*, MHV) established the next year. Two further homes were established in 1950 at Enkenbach and Oldesloe; these facilities were gradually expanded until they each offered room for over 100 persons. The homes were then given over to another organization in 2003. Other independent homes for the aged were run by the MHC in Burgweinting and Thomashof. The "Bible House" at Thomashof which was later run by the *Verband* was converted to a conference centre in 1992.

Interconfessional Dialogues

In 1980 the Lutheran church in Germany celebrated the 450th anniversary of the Augsburg Confession, one of the central documents of the Reformation. In an ecumenical spirit the Mennonites were invited to join in these celebrations, but the Mennonites politely reminded the Lutherans that the Augsburg Confession contains six anathemas against the Anabaptists, and that these anathemas were used to persecute our Mennonite forebears—a fact of which most Lutherans were not aware. This reminder provided the impetus for further deliberation and consultation with the Association of Lutheran Churches in Germany (VELKD). A dialogue with official representatives of both churches, including five German Mennonites and five Lutheran, took place from 1989 to 1992. Both sides explained the major themes of their respective theologies; the central subjects of discussion were Scripture, Christology, ecclesiology, baptism and the state. In spite of much agreement, differences remained of course, but many misunderstandings also were overcome. So for example, differences remain in the theological significance of baptism (whether it is a confessional sign of following Christ or a sacrament) and the Lord's Supper.

Concluding the Lutheran-Mennonite Dialogue, a combined church service was held in the Regensburg Mennonite church on March 24, 1996. From left to right: Rainer W. Burkart, Oberkirchenrat Dr. Klaus Jürgen Roepke, Michael Martin, Diether Götz Lichdi, Lutheran Bishop Hermann von Loewenich and Andrea Lange.

The final document included three elements: recommendations for members of both churches for future cooperation, a Lutheran statement exempting Mennonites from past reproaches, and a joint statement of convergences and divergences in seven major theological points. In concluding worship services in Hamburg and Regensburg in March of 1996, a new beginning was made public.

Recently, a German Mennonite participated in an international dialogue between the Roman Catholic church and the Mennonite World Conference. Andrea Lange, pastor at Weierhof, was one of the members of an international group of seven Mennonites (among whom also were Neal Blough from Paris, France and Larry Miller, Strasbourg) and seven Catholics (among whom was the Dutch church historian Peter Nissen) which met from 1998 to 2003. They reported together on these discussions in the report "Called Together to be Peacemakers" in 2004. Both sides acknowledged each other in a spirit of repentance. Both sides urged a deeper mutual understanding and acknowledged that "we hold in common many basic aspects of the Christian faith and heritage."

In the dialogue report "Called Together to be Peacemakers" § 202, the Catholic side stated:

"Catholics ... can apply this spirit of repentance to the conflicts between Catholics and Mennonites in the sixteenth century, and can express a penitential spirit, asking forgiveness for any sins which were committed against Mennonites, asking God's mercy for that, and God's blessing for a new relationship with Mennonites today."

Missions and Relief Work

A further factor in the renewal of church life after the war was the revival of missions. In southern Germany a mission board was established in 1951, the so-called DMMK, which was then later supported by other congregations in the north and the west. At the same time, mission boards were also formed in neighbouring countries. Together with Swiss, French and Dutch Mennonites a united mission effort was brought into being. More than twenty-five missionaries, teachers, doctors and nurses have been sent out by this united effort, chiefly to Chad, but also to Indonesia, Ecuador and other countries. German Mennonites frequently are sent out by other mission organizations as well. At present, there are preachers, doctors and Bible translators working in this way. Among them are Roland Horsch, Ethiopia; Hermann Schirrmacher, Ecuador; Helene and Werner Heidebrecht in Bethlehem, Palestine.

Changing Mission Patterns
Mission work has altered in conception since the 1940s. Formerly, trained theologians were sent into the mission field; nowadays theological work is largely performed by local Christians, but the number of teachers, translators, medical personnel and other technical workers has increased steadily. Missions into the two-thirds World have taken on a different form, requiring special training and organizational skills. This is of course an attempt to address the specific needs in the mission field, but it is also a reaction caused by social structures in Germany itself, where persons are more often prepared to spend a specific period of time in an overseas service. And at the same time, passport regulations in these countries is often tied to the condition that one must have some special skills and training in order to work there.

It is a new fact of life that Germany is becoming de-christianized, and so it is itself becoming a field for mission work. Many contemporary Germans know little if anything about the Bible or the good news of Jesus Christ. The DMMK seeks to address this need at its own door step. Some activities of the last few decades include: a year-long effort to establish a mission-station at Neumühle in the Palatinate, the Agape mission together with the Eastern Mennonite Board of Missions (since 1969), the work of the Mennoniten-Brüdergemeinden (MB) in Bavaria and in Neustadt (seven new churches), two new churches established by the Überlingen congregation in the 1980s, a second MB congregation in Neustadt, an unusual new effort in the formerly Communist East Germany with the planting of a new church in Halle and a missions team in Kaiserslautern (since 2003). These new congregations bring faith to young Christians and so are quite different from the traditional, family-based churches that have been typical of German Mennonite life through the centuries.

Mennonite Relief Work and Organizations

In the year 2000, the various relief agencies of the three pillars were amalgamated in a central office as a unified agency, the *Mennonitisches Hilfswerk* (MH). This was a consequence of the harmonization of the three overarching regional church organizations into the AMG. The new united relief agency of the AMG promotes three annual fund raising actions in all the member congregations at Pentecost, Thanksgiving and Christmas. With these financial gifts the MH seeks to help asylum seekers and refugees in Karlsruhe, Niedergörsdorf, Berlin and Munich, placing trained workers where they are needed as well. In addition, children's homes in Romania and St. Petersburg are being supported. The work of *Christliche Dienste* (Christian Service, or CD) is also being supported, about which more will be said below.

The International Mennonite Organization (IMO, *Internationale Mennonitische Organisation)* for relief work was called into being around 1967–1968 by Dutch Mennonites in cooperation with the two German agencies HVDM and MHC, in an effort to coordinate their shared concerns. Numerous relief projects had already been set up by the MHC, for example on behalf of the Christian Bopkri schools and the Mennonite hospital in Tayu, Central Java. Together with other organizations a children's home in Chad was supplied regularly with medications and other supplies. But an international coordination offered more possibilities.

Setting up an international relief office enabled the Mennonites to professionalize their work and limited financial resources at a central office, at first in Frankfurt, then in Weierhof, now in Neuwied, where MCC-Europe had its offices. IMO identified four chief goals:

a) choosing places for volunteers to engage in social work,
b) supporting Paraguayan and Brazilian relief, which concentrated on helping indigenous peoples in the Chaco · with housing, hygiene and farming,
c) sponsoring youth and students to serve where MCC is active, and
d) since 1974, supporting Russian immigrants to Germany.

When funding became scarce, a professional manager could no longer be retained. Thereafter the various activities were coordinated voluntarily by members of the IMO advisory board. At present, IMO is active in various programs aiding indigenous people in the Paraguayan Chaco and providing financial assistance for students in Paraguay, Brazil and Bangladesh.

The horrors of war returned to Europe from 1991–1996 in the lands of the former Yugoslavia, arousing great empathy and willingness in Germany to offer relief and social assistance. At first, aid was intermittent but as the gravity of the situation became clearer, German Mennonites set up an agency for Bosnia. Three support stations were set

up in the Bosnian towns of Konjic, Kakanj and Jajce, where refugees or the homeless could find assistance. Transport trucks regularly conveyed food stuffs, clothing and medication to the support stations (often weekly). Volunteers assisted in the rebuilding effort or supervised children and youth who had suffered from the war. Various Mennonite relief agencies provided humanitarian assistance in the context of IMO. From the autumn of 1992 to

Trucks transported relief material from Mennonite churches in Germany, Switzerland and France to former Yugoslavia on a regular basis in the 1990s.

2001 around 4,300 tons of relief materials worth around 1.8 million euros were sent to Bosnia. Around 300 German Mennonites were involved in collecting, sorting, packing, transporting and distributing materials, supervising young persons or working in construction. This work has attracted more committed and active workers than has any other project of the last few decades.

An outgrowth of this work is the second-hand store called "Hand-in-Hand" begun in 1998 in Neustadt, in rooms belonging to the local Mennonite Brethren congregation. Profits from this enterprise are used for relief work such as that in Bosnia, or more recently in Ethiopia. Hand-in-Hand is run by fifteen female volunteers from the region.

Mention should also be made of the Mennonite Economic Development Agency (MEDA), which is modelled on a similar American programme. MEDA was set up in 1978 by some twenty German Mennonites with the goal of helping to establish industrial machinery in the Paraguayan Chaco for the traditional Mennonites and the native population. Tractors, machines and tools for preparing and working the land were to be lent out. Technical training for indigenous youth followed as a next step. Training personnel was sent from Europe for both of these programs. In 1984 leadership was transferred to the Consultation Board for Indigenous Peoples [in Latin America] (*Indianer Beratungs Behörde*, IBB). As well, MEDA aided the establishment of a machinery station in eastern Paraguay in 1979. In 1982 the first halting attempts were made to establish a bakery; some years later under other circumstances this idea came to fruition. Tax considerations led to the closure of MEDA in Germany in 1986. Up to that point, the supporters of the program had brought in a total of more than 500,000 euros (converted into modern currency), including donations and other financing. In addition to its two directors, MEDA also hired fifteen indigenous Paraguayans and two Mennonites of German descent.

Finally, the work of *Christliche Dienste* (CD, "Christian Service") needs to be recognized. CD is the name of the agency that mediates volunteers for various social services within Germany and internationally. It was organized in 1986 by MHC, DMMK, MHV and the Peace Committee, but also cooperates closely with international partner organizations, especially with MCC. It seeks out volunteers in Germany for Mennonite projects in other countries, and also accepts international volunteers for social services within Germany. This work requires a great deal of tact and discernment in order to bring volunteers into situations where their gifts can be best utilized; volunteers also need to be thoroughly prepared and guided in their new situations. Volunteers usually pledge to serve for one year, but many remain for two years. German men can perform their alternative service to the military in conjunction with CD. They do relief work or are occupied in childcare, social work (for example working with drug addicts or in orphanages) or in mediation work.

Since 1989 CD has enjoyed governmental recognition for its professional work and is authorized to send German conscientious objectors into other countries. Through the years a network has been built up of partners, local agencies and former volunteers. CD focuses on sending young people with a Christian motivation into socially needy situations. Its work is inspired by the conviction that missions, social service and peace work belong together. Between 1986 and 1998 more than 350 persons had been placed in service. At present, eighty young men and women (the majority of whom are Mennonite) are actively serving, mostly in Paraguay, Brazil and North America.

The various humanitarian and social services of German Mennonites are extraordinarily diverse; such work is often spontaneous or even eccentric because it usually is initiated by concerned individuals. Whether the various agencies persist over time depends on whether other persons can be motivated to take up the work of its initiators and whether the projects can be adapted to changing circumstances and obtain financing. Most relief agencies therefore have been short-lived. It is an interesting fact that many more German Mennonites have been actively engaged in these social services than in missionary work.

Nowadays the social and relief work is largely dependent on the technical support of international agencies, usually MCC. Relatively few social projects are directed solely by German Mennonites working alone. This is because most of the targeted needs are in foreign lands, where the Germans lack qualified management and sufficient funding. In the early days of these services, the initiators and workers explicitly distinguished between relief work and missionary work. However, there is a growing conviction that relief work and missions need to work together in the name of Christ. Cooperative ventures have sporadically taken place, albeit not always with the abiding determination to combine these two activities. Looking beyond our borders, we can observe that the Dutch and Swiss Mennonites have shown greater resolve in the manner in which they have unified mission and service agencies.

Looking Ahead

The number of church members in the congregations of the AMG has shrunk by two-thirds in the last fifty years (from 18,000 in 1953 to 5,700 in 2005), although this reduction is not representative of all regions. A number of reasons can be given for this upsetting fact. First, the Second World War destroyed many traditions and family groupings, and left deep wounds in Mennonite life. Many refugees eventually found new livelihoods in places where there were no congregations and soon joined other denominations. In a related manner, in the last few decades many young Mennonites seeking education and employment have gone to cities where there are no congregations. Some of these find other communities of faith, others lose all connection to Christian groups. Just how drastic this social change has been can best be illustrated by reference to the rural congregations. In the cities, Mennonites churches have always had to face rapid change, but in the countryside, Mennonite traditions changed very slowly over the centuries. However, since the Second World War, the rural churches have utterly lost their identity as farming communities: where before, 80 percent of south German Mennonites were active in agriculture, now 90 percent are not. Even young people who grow up on farms are no longer adopting this traditional occupation. This social uprooting has also led to the loss of a "Mennonite self-understanding" among the young.

Another factor is that more and more Mennonites marry non-Mennonites. Of course this has always been the case, but whereas in earlier days the partner often joined the Mennonite church, now this is no longer customary. As a consequence, the children of these couples often do not follow Mennonite baptismal practice. Youth activities that were formerly sponsored by our congregations have been taken over by parents, schools and clubs; or else Mennonite youth attend the local groups of other denominations instead of travelling to Mennonite churches.

A third factor is the low birth rate in Germany, with the consequence that society in general and Mennonite communities as well are becoming older. The elderly are often unable to attend services. A final significant factor is the cultural and religious transformation of German society since the war. Germans no longer see their nation as predominantly Christian. Where most people used to hold at least a tenuous connection to some church or another, there are now many faiths and personal options. The loss of religious and social traditions in a pluralistic, post-industrial society is seen by some as a "loss of values" and "indifference," but one does not need to adopt this pessimistic view to see that modern culture offers Europeans many religious, ethical and philosophical alternatives. The choices for entertainment and communication in one's free time are manifold. And so, where people used to believe that German society spoke with a united "Christian" ethical voice, this conviction no longer exists. It may well be argued that our congregations are only now slowly learning to deal with this changed world. The question of how we can articulate our present-day Anabaptist vision of the Kingdom of God in this altered society—and motivate people to join us—has not yet been fully answered.

There have been various attempts in the last few years to react to these structural and social changes and to present our faith in ways that will attract people to the Good News of Jesus Christ. Especially important is our work in the peace witness and in relief for war- and grief-stricken regions of the world like Bosnia. This work—both through financial assistance and volunteer work—has received broad acceptance in all our communities. In a related field, the volunteer mission of CD has been well-received, attracting growing interest from persons outside our congregations. Another new development is the involvement of our German congregations in helping to reform the Bible school training at Bienenberg, instituting the new Theological Seminary and making it more attractive to young people looking for qualified theological training with an Anabaptist accent. A special new emphasis of the *Verband* has been an intensive commitment to church-building and evangelisation. The monthly youth service in Sinsheim can also be seen in this light: the focus is on revival and conversion.

This is an unusual approach for German Mennonites, and it can be disturbing to traditionalists. Here it is important to offer room for the working of the Holy Spirit, while at the same time not losing the values of our Anabaptist heritage which challenge political, social and authoritarian structures. The ideal is to build a community where faith and discipleship can be expressed in ways that are challenging and appealing to all generations in the church. It is to be hoped that the various Mennonite "denominations" in Germany will eventually build bridges and work together on common projects in the fields of mission, social service and peace witness, to the greater glory of our Lord.

Translation: James Jakob Fehr

Mennonites in Switzerland

by Diether Götz Lichdi

Politics and Society

Mennonites in Switzerland have suffered persecution and discrimination by civil and ecclesiastical authorities longer than in any other European country. This caused many to leave their homes and flee already in the sixteenth century. Not only did religious minorities experience oppression in Switzerland, but the general population also increasingly longed for greater freedom, justice and equality in a state dominated by a small group of privileged families. The hopes of many Swiss citizens were raised by the political developments in revolutionary France, from where they expected initiatives for the overthrow of their own *Ancien Régime*. And in fact, due to pressure from the French, the old Swiss Confederation fell apart in the late 1790s. Many parts of the Basel bishopric—a popular place of refuge for many Mennonites from Bern—had been under French occupation since 1792, much to the pleasure of large segments of the population. The French invasion in the rest of Switzerland took place at the end of 1797, and the "Helvetic" Constitution was introduced under French influence in 1798. This constitution stated that "freedom of conscience is unrestricted ... every type of worship is allowed" and granted the Mennonites and the

Anabaptist couple from the Basel area (ca. 1800), by Joseph Reinhard.

Amish the same rights as other citizens, at least on a legal basis. The so-called "Toleration Act" granted them federal Swiss civil rights. This, however, did not significantly change their actual living situation.

As a result of the Congress of Vienna in 1815, many parts of the Jura were transferred from the Basel bishopric to the jurisdiction of the Canton of Bern. Many Mennonites in the Jura, who formerly had fled Bernese territory and found asylum and toleration in the Jura, were now again under Bernese authority and feared the return of oppression. To their great joy, the unification agreement contained assurances that the Bernese authorities would grant these numerous Mennonites in the Jura their existing rights. Nevertheless, the Mennonites from within the original boundaries of Bern were explicitly excluded from these concessions.

In the spirit of the Restoration Period (1815ff.), which was critical of the Revolution, the Bernese Reformed Church did its best to contain Mennonite growth. Mennonite marriages either were not legally recognized or the authorities used bureaucratic delaying tactics in registering them in the local registry, which was maintained by Reformed clergy. Thus Mennonites continued to live secluded lives in the Emmental, with its centre in Langnau, in the Bernese and Neuenburger Jura, with centres in Kleintal-Moron and Sonnenberg, and around La Chaux-de-Fonds, and increasingly in the region of Basel. In the Neuenburger Jura and the Basel area there also were strong Amish congregations. The majority of Mennonites and Amish were farmers; a few were craftsmen. Throughout the latter half of the century, many emigrated to North America and neighbouring France. As Swiss citizens, they were

Swiss Mennonite Family with Amish background in the Jura neuchâtelois, oil painting by Fritz Huguenin-Lassauquette.

exempt from military service and they were not extradited. The few Amish remaining in Switzerland gradually joined Mennonite groups.

The social climate in the Swiss cities of Basel, Zürich and Geneva became more liberal after 1848. As a result, many political refugees from Austria, the German states and France found refuge there. The living conditions of the Mennonites also improved in the second half of the nineteenth century. After the constitutional revision of 1874, local marriage registries were placed under the authority of state officials instead of the state church clergy. This brought about a more real constitutional equality. Economic conditions improved for the farmers as well, and the growing watch industry in the Jura provided many with an alternative source of income. The emigration of younger people ceased, even though obligatory military service for all men was also instituted in 1874. This military obligation, which had long been a reason for emigration to North America, was gradually accepted by the Mennonites who remained in Switzerland.

Theology and Faith

The continuous emigration of Swiss Anabaptists and later Mennonites led to a growing leadership and spiritual vacuum in Mennonite congregations throughout the nineteenth century. Those who remained behind were poorly equipped to take over leadership responsibilities and therefore they tended to maintain already-existing forms. Some Anabaptist convictions, such as baptism following confession of faith, the renunciation of violence, and the refusal to swear oaths, degenerated into mere traditions rigorously applied, but their original theological and spiritual meanings were not taught convincingly. From the perspective of the early nineteenth-century revival movements, the Mennonites projected a dim spiritual image. The south German Mennonite preacher Christian Schmutz from Rappenau, who was seized by the spirit of renewal, wrote in 1858, "During our visit among the Mennonites in Switzerland (in 1839) we were unable to detect true spiritual life. There was more concern with formalities and rules than with the spirit and power of Christianity."[1] This assessment cannot be generalized, but other sources confirm this tendency of a certain "spiritual aridity" for this period of time. In places where the revival movement gained a following, difficult and painful disputes often resulted. In the Bernese Emmental a split occurred among the Mennonites in the 1830s. Samuel Fröhlich led a number of active Anabaptists to form the *Neutäufer* movement, which is today called the *Evangelische Täufer-Gemeinden* (ETG), literally translated as the "Evangelical (Ana)baptist Church." This group is known in North America as the Apostolic Christian Church (Nazarene).

The south German itinerant preacher Jakob Hege was greatly affected by the influential Holiness Movement of the late 1870s. In 1879 he mourned the dramatic decline of the Mennonite congregations with the following words:

> I have met preachers in our congregations who are unclear about the way of salvation. They don't know what the soul needs, but rather they always preach about works and keeping God's commandments. But they don't mention what must happen first so that man can keep God's commandments and walk in the ways of the Lord, that is, a new birth and the renewal of the heart, which the Lord alone can accomplish through His Word and Spirit.[2]

The Holiness Movement found fertile ground, especially in the Mennonite congregations in the Jura. Many members of Mennonite congregations found a revivalist faith through the regular messages of itinerant preachers from southern Germany and other (mostly state-church based) representatives of this renewal movement such as Elias Schrenk, Carl Rappard and other graduates of the "Pilgrim Mission"

The Jeanguisboden chapel (left, constructed in 1900) belonging to the Mennonite Sonnenberg congregation.

St. Chrischona, located near Basel. As a result of this revival movement, church membership in the Jura grew considerably and resulted in the construction of several new meeting houses and chapels.

The Holiness Movement brought forward theological issues such as perfectionism, sinlessness and the healing of the sick, and these left their mark on Swiss Mennonite congregations. Conversions often took place in a charged atmosphere, as Emil Kocher, an evangelist from the Evangelical Society of St. Imier, clearly notes in a 1904 report: "In the (Mennonite) chapel in Moron, some awoke from their slumber of sin and, not able to bear it anymore, went outside and rolled in the snow in penance."[3]

The revival movements of the nineteenth and early twentieth centuries were more than transitory events; they brought enduring changes to the spiritual life of Swiss Mennonite congregations. Training centres such as St. Chrischona near Basel not only played a key role in shaping generations of Mennonite preachers and elders from Switzerland, Alsace, southern Germany, and south Russia, but also led to a certain harmony in theological orientation. Nevertheless, this indisputable spiritual upswing carried a price: some traditional Anabaptist convictions, such as nonresistance and maintaining a certain critical distance from the state, were often seen as signs of old-fashioned and separatist denominationalism and as hindrances for spiritual renewal. These aspects were therefore neglected, rejected and lost. Closer cooperation with revivalistic or evangelical partners within the state church or other free churches led not only to a growing mutual respect but sometimes also to a tendency for Mennonites to abandon their own Anabaptist-Mennonite identity. However, when the Emmental congregation published its own confession of faith in 1937 without an explicit article on nonresistance and with an article on baptism showing high respect for state church infant baptism (and dissociating itself from its own historical practice of re-baptism), the majority of the Swiss Conference voiced disapproval.[4]

Contact with North American Mennonites after World War I through the first assemblies of Mennonite World Conference, the relief work of Mennonite Central Committee and the occasional appearance of both church-oriented and secular peace movements in the second half of the twentieth century caused the Swiss Mennonites to re-examine their Anabaptist heritage and to discuss its value and significance.

Acceptance of its Anabaptist heritage grew gradually among Swiss Mennonites between 1940 and 1980, although the North American

Mennonite "rediscovery of the Anabaptist Vision" was not infrequently criticized and rejected as a form of theological neo-colonialism. This rejection occurred not only within traditionalist neo-pietistic and revivalist circles, but also among a growing number of active younger church members who wanted to seek their own theological answers to the burning questions of faith and life—independent of the patronage of their own congregational traditions and North American Mennonite tutelage. Heard frequently in such debates among Swiss Mennonites in those years was the phrase: "Not back to the forefathers, but back to the Scriptures!" Only with time did it become clear to some critics that a rediscovery of the Anabaptist Vision and a rediscovery of the centrality of the Bible were by no means contradictions.

During the last quarter of the twentieth century, the theological and liturgical tendencies among Swiss Mennonites became even broader, developing a variety of different styles and emphases. This was due both to general developments in society as well as to the full autonomy of Swiss Mennonite congregations. One of the great challenges in future years will be to continue to find sufficient common ground for the various theological and liturgical tendencies among Swiss Mennonites—whether they be traditional or progressive, conservative or liberal, liturgical or charismatic, evangelical or ecumenical, peace-church- or mainstream-oriented.

Church Life and Mennonite Schools

The Anabaptists met initially in forests and caves, and later in farmhouses and barns. As the nineteenth century progressed, there was no longer any reason to hide. The Swiss Mennonites were no longer persecuted; they became accepted in their communities and began to integrate into society. Evidence of this development was the appearance of meeting houses, which were built or acquired according to need and opportunity. The oldest meeting house was erected in Basel-Holee in 1847. This was the first non-state-church building erected in Switzerland with official permission. Additional meeting houses were built in Kehr near Langnau (1888), Lucelle/Grosslützel (1891), Moron (1892), Les Bulles (1894), Jeanguisboden/Sonnenberg (1900), Muttenz-Schänzli (1903) and La Chaux-d'Abel (1905).

Mennonite farms and meetings were islands of German language and the Bernese dialect in the French-speaking Jura. In order to educate their children in the faith of their ancestors and in the German language, the Mennonites had traditionally maintained their own schools. Mandatory school attendance was first introduced in Switzerland in the nineteenth century. Up until that time it was difficult to get a formal education for people in rural areas, and in the isolated mountain communities of the Jura it was nearly impossible. Since the Mennonites placed such a high value on the Bible, it was essential that their children learn to read and write. Children often learned from their parents after working the fields.

After compulsory education was introduced in Bern in 1835, Mennonites began to establish schools and hire teachers from within their own ranks. The first schools were founded in 1836 in Jeanguisboden and La Chaux d'Abel. An additional seven Mennonite schools were established in the Jura by 1900. These schools influenced the development of the Jura congregations well into the 1960s. The congregations financed the construction and maintenance of the buildings, paid teachers' salaries and purchased the teaching materials. The local cantons took over part of the financing in the latter half of the twentieth century and French increasingly became the official language of instruction. Many teachers, who often worked as preachers as well, spent their entire careers in these Mennonite schools and were highly respected throughout the entire Jura region.

The shift to the French language and the transfer of Mennonite schools to the public system, open to all, could not prevent the closings in La Pâturatte (1977) and Montbautier (1998). These schools, which consisted of only one room, were closed when long-term enrollment fell below twenty pupils. This development reflected the reality that Mennonites of the Jura now lived not only on isolated mountain farms, but also in the valleys where they had found jobs and sought an education for their children. Only Mont-Tramelan would provisionally maintain a bilingual school into the future.

Today the pupils from the mountains take the bus to attend the public schools in the valleys. The relinquishing of Mennonite schools was abetted by the change of language and by new communications technology, which rendered traditional separation obsolete. The physical isolation of Mennonites on mountain farms disappeared with increased mobility. Modern media opened the door to influences from popular culture and also made Mennonites receptive to thinking that originated no longer exclusively from pietistic or revivalist seminaries and Bible schools but also from university faculties of theology.

Swiss Mennonites in Transition

By no later than the last quarter of the nineteenth century Swiss Mennonite congregations found themselves uniting to form the *Konferenz der Altevangelischen Taufgesinnten-Gemeinden (Mennoniten)* (Conference of Old Evangelical (Ana)Baptist-Minded Churches [Mennonites]). Minutes exist from deliberations in 1889.[5] The scattered church members were kept informed by the magazine *Zionspilger* (Pilgrims of Zion), which was established in 1882. Interest in missions also grew during this time. Rodolphe Petter was commissioned in 1890 to Cheyenne, USA, as the first overseas missionary. In 1934 Daniel Amstutz was the first Swiss Mennonite Missionary sent to Java together with his wife, Wera Amstutz-Nachtigall. The Swiss Mennonite Evangelization Committee (SMEK) was founded in 1950. This organization sent out a number of missionaries, especially to Chad and Indonesia.

The Swiss Mennonites felt connected to Mennonites in France and southern Germany through historical and familial ties. These ties were maintained and strengthened through visits and preaching exchanges. This led to Switzerland hosting the first (1925) and fifth (1952) assemblies of the Mennonite World Conference and the European Mennonite Regional Conference assemblies in Liestal/Bienenberg (1975) and Tramelan (1988).

Mennonite World Conference 1952 in Basel

In 1983 the Swiss Mennonites approved new statutes and revised their Confession of Faith in order to define their position in a changing world. Compared to shorter confessional texts from the earlier twentieth century, this confession accentuated a stronger Mennonite identity as a believer's church and as a peace church. This led to a stronger differentiation from the neighbouring state and free churches, while showing a growing willingness for dialogue and cooperation. To identify themselves better with the worldwide community of Mennonites, they changed their name respectively to the *Konferenz der Mennoniten der Schweiz (Alttäufer)* (KMS) in German and *Conférence mennonite suisse (Anabaptistes)* [CMS] in French (Conference of Mennonites of Switzerland).

The last quarter of the twentieth century also brought occupational changes, as many Mennonites switched from agriculture to work in industry, trade, and service oriented professions. Mennonites also began attending universities and other institutions of higher learning on a more frequent basis. The French language became increasingly more prevalent in the Jura, and new church members were added from non-Mennonite and un-churched backgrounds, above all in urban settings. Today a growing majority of Swiss Mennonites live in French-speaking Switzerland. Of the eight congregations in the Jura, five are considered French speaking. One conducts half of the service in German and two are predominantly German speaking. In the near future it is likely that French will become as predominant in conference activities as German has been.

Public attention was focussed on Mennonites in 1988 when it became known that a rural Mennonite family had been illegally harbouring a family from Zaire (today Congo) threatened with deportation, allowing them to hide on their secluded farmyard in the Jura. When asked to give an explanation for their illegal and punishable conduct, the family referred to the story of their own Anabaptist forebears, who often survived only because there were people who, without asking too many questions, had granted them shelter. Where there are fellow human-beings who fear for their lives, God's command to love the neighbour takes precedence over any and all earthly laws.

The witness of this family left a deep impression on a wide range of people. Yet the event also polarized Mennonite congregations: some voiced strong approval of this family's moral courage and boldness of faith, while others criticized their illegal conduct.

Since the 1990s conference proceedings are held in both German and French, and all discussion and debate is simultaneously translated. Occasionally all participants or delegates in certain subcommittees are fully bilingual, and translation is not necessary.

German- and French-speaking Mennonites are now confronted with the new reality of not knowing and singing the same songs and not using the same hymnals. The recently published Mennonite hymnal for German-speaking congregations (2004) takes this into account and has incorporated a certain number of French songs and well-known German songs with French stanzas.

Swiss Mennonites both in German- and in French-speaking areas are generally known for their powerful four-part singing, either accompanied on piano or organ or sung a cappella. More recently, a growing number of congregations have also introduced "praise bands" and are working to find a good mix of more traditional and more recent music and liturgy. This search for a good balance between continuity and change, which respects and values the various expressions of spirituality among all generations is—as is true always and everywhere—not an easy task.

As part of the structural transformation, some rural congregations, such as Les Près-de-Cortébert and Lucelle, needed to be closed. Nevertheless, new congregations were established in Liestal, Vallon de St. Imier, Tavannes, and Unteres Birstal. Today there are over 2,300 members in fourteen congregations, which is a decline of nearly ten percent in the last twenty years. Sixty percent of all Swiss Mennonites gather in the four largest congregations: Emmental/Langnau, Les Bulles, Muttenz-Schänzli and Sonnenberg. Preaching and congregational leadership are no longer the exclusive domain of male lay people, as was the practice for more than four centuries. The majority of the fourteen Mennonite congregations have pastors employed on a part-time or full-time basis. Some congregations employ several pastors, most of whom have attended seminary (the majority of the older leaders at St. Chrischona) or who were trained at free-church-based, often Mennonite, theological seminaries.

A bird's eye view of the Bienenberg Theological Seminary

The European Mennonite Bible School, founded in 1950 in Basel, close to the German and the French border and with French- and German-speaking departments, is playing an increasingly important role—not only for Swiss Mennonites, but also for Mennonites in France and Germany. The school moved to Bienenberg in Liestal in 1957 and was later re-named *Ausbildungs- und Tagungszentrum Bienenberg / Centre de Formation et de Rencontre* (Study and Conference Centre Bienenberg) of which the "Bienenberg Theological Seminary" is a part. Offerings at the seminary include multi-year programs on Bachelor and Master's levels, a Discipleship Training School, a wide variety of thematic courses lasting from one day to several weeks, and multi-year part-time theological programs in French and German. Various Anabaptist-Mennonite conferences and institutions in Europe own and direct the Bienenberg Theological Seminary. Today hundreds of Bienenberg graduates from Mennonite and non-Mennonite backgrounds serve worldwide on a voluntary or full-time basis, as social workers, missionaries, evangelists, mediators, Bible translators, nurses, teachers, therapists, church planters and in many other fields as well.

Group of students and some faculty members from the Bienenberg Theological Seminary (2002).

The Conference of Mennonites of Switzerland (KMS/CMS)

The work of the KMS/CMS was initially shared by volunteer leaders. The conference eventually hired a part-time staff person in 1995 to oversee the increased activities. He or she not only administers and provides resources to the various service groups and ministries within the congregations and the conference, but also plans activities to keep the congregations in touch with one another. Since 1994 several multi-congregational gatherings have taken place in different regions to promote fellowship among the congregations. The conference is involved in the following ministries:

a) Two part-time staff involved in children and youth ministries organize camps and weekend encounters and provide resources to the congregational youth programs as well.

b) Working groups focus on issues related to aging.

c) A publications committee is responsible for publishing the *Perspektive/Perspective* (earlier known as *Zionspilger*), a bi-weekly, bi-lingual periodical.

d) The Swiss Mennonite Peace Committee, along with other groups in the 1980s and 1990s, advocates the introduction of community service as a legal alternative to military service. A popular referendum resulted in the ratification of the Civil Service Bill in 1996. In the early 1970s several young Mennonites had refused military service and were incarcerated. They were a public witness and incited the conscience of the Mennonite congregations to become a peace witness. The peace committee also promotes conflict resolution and mediation in congregations and families.

e) The two organizations responsible for relief work (Swiss Mennonite Organization for Relief—SMO) and missions (Swiss Mennonite Evangelization Committee) merged in 1998 to form the Swiss Mennonite Mission agency (SMM). This merger helped to overcome the old distinction between physical *or* spiritual care. SMM follows the Christian ideal of addressing all of a person's needs. Limited personnel and financial resources also played a major role in the merger.

f) The Archival Commission collects and preserves documents, maintains the conference archives and organizes visits. The Commission works together with the independent *Schweizerischer Verein für Täufergeschichte/ Société Suisse d'Histoire Mennonite* (Swiss Society for Anabaptist History), which publishes the annual journal *Mennonitica Helvetica*.

Swiss Mennonites were always aware that important roots of the Anabaptist movement lay in Switzerland, and that a considerable number of French, German, and North American Mennonites have ancestors who were once Swiss refugees or emigrants. One hundred years ago nearly half of all Mennonites in the world were of Swiss descent. As a result, Swiss Mennonites enjoyed a certain prestige in the Mennonite world. Swiss emigrants are recognizable everywhere by their family names. It was therefore natural that Swiss Mennonites sponsored several international Mennonite conferences, as already noted.

In 1994 and 1997 the *Evangelische Täufergemeinden* (ETG) from south Germany and Switzerland and the Swiss Mennonites conducted joint meetings at Bienenberg to explore commonalities and possibilities for future cooperation. Since then the Swiss Baptists have joined these regular meetings to enable an on-going inter-(ana)baptist dialogue and to present a coordinated believers' church presence in the Swiss ecumenical context.

Parallel to the expansion of this dialogue, an intensifying dialogue with the Reformed Church began in the 1980s. These conversations arose in part as a way to deal with the difficult history the Reformed and Mennonites share. Another goal was to discuss common projects and the struggle to become a credible Christian witness in the present and future—a common challenge shared by all Christian churches in Europe.

Swiss Mennonite congregations are to a degree still clan-dominated, to which the surnames on the membership rolls attest: Gerber, Geiser, Amstutz, Zürcher, Widmer, Schmutz, Sprunger, Gyger. In recent years new members from non-Mennonite backgrounds have entered the Swiss Mennonite churches, and are changing the traditional picture. Many congregations are open to such growth and new ideas, which challenge them to reflect on their own strengths and weaknesses, and to creatively reshape their Anabaptist identity.

Between 1970 and the 1990s, several young Swiss Mennonites were imprisoned because they refused to do military service. When one of them began his prison term in the mid-70s, he wanted to take along some study literature but his request was refused. To his great surprise he was told that the only book he was allowed to take into his cell was the Bible. "How strange!" he said to the guard. "This is precisely the book that brought me into prison! Rather than forbidding me to read further in this obviously dangerous and subversive book, you're eliminating all reading alternatives and helping me to concentrate on this book … !" Discovering that the Bible was not simply harmless and irrelevant for the status quo of both church and society, but that it often called for radical change, conversion, transformation or non-cooperation, led not only to a fresh discussion among Swiss Mennonites about the biblical basis of conscientious objection, but more generally to deeper reflections about the relationship of church and society.

Baptismal service at the Birs River near Basel (Schänzli Mennonite Church, 2004). Increasingly many Swiss Mennonite congregations celebrate their baptismal services at a river or a lake. A greater openness in congregations to varying forms of baptism has been developing for some time. Today baptism by immersion is the most frequently requested form—people appreciate its greater symbolic power as compared to the more traditional Swiss Mennonite form of baptism by affusion (sprinkling).

"Evangelische Täufergemeinden" (ETG)

In 1832 the Reformed pastoral candidate Samuel Fröhlich brought his message of revival to the Mennonites of the Emmental. His call to repentance and renewal fell upon fertile ground. Fröhlich was against infant baptism, and his encounter with Mennonites confirmed his conviction. He also adopted the Anabaptist practice of nonresistance, which the ETG maintains today. Fröhlich wanted to establish the pure church through rigorous membership requirements, a perfectionist understanding of sanctification, a firm regime of church discipline and a strict separation from other churches. Given these principles, integration with the "Old Anabaptists" became impossible.

Fröhlich's separatist behavior sometimes led the *Fröhlichianer* into legalism and isolationism, which defined this group until the second half of the twentieth century. Members of the "New Anabaptist" (*Neutäufer*) church came from the State churches in Switzerland, Alsace, Baden and Württemberg, as well as from Mennonite congregations in Switzerland and Baden. Today we still find typical Mennonite surnames among Fröhlich's followers. In Germany the *Fröhlichianer* also called themselves "Old Mennonites" in order to be included under the federal Cabinet order of 1868. Their official name today is *Evangelische Täufergemeinden* (ETG); in other places they call themselves "Nazarenes."

The ETG eventually divided into progressive and conservative groups. Their congregational structure is similar to that of the Swiss, south German and Alsatian Mennonites. Differences in confession and piety are barely distinguishable any more, and the ETG has always considered itself to be part of the Anabaptist movement.

In their early years the *Neutäufer* conducted large evangelistic activities, and congregations emerged in Hungary, Romania and Yugoslavia. The "New Anabaptists" were in North America by the nineteenth century, where they are known as the "Apostolic Christian Church." In 1956 the western European congregations founded the *Evangelischer Missions-Dienst* (Evangelical Mission Service) through which missionaries work in many countries of the world.

Today the Union of *Evangelische Täufergemeinden* (ETG) consists of 2,600 members in 34 congregations in Germany, Switzerland and France, with an additional 15 European congregations not affiliated with the ETG Union. There are also congregations in eastern Europe, North and South America, and Australia.

New relationships were forged between the ETG and the Mennonites after World War II. North American MCC volunteers helped *Neutäufer* refugees fleeing eastern Europe to build new settlements in Austria, and also helped construct the *Lindenwiese* retreat centre at Lake Constance. The ETG Union has been an official supporter of the Bienenberg Theological Seminary since 1999, collaborating with other European Mennonite Conferences. The ETG and Swiss Mennonites have had various consultations and joint efforts since 1974. Emmental congregations and the Bienenberg Theological Seminary have played important roles in this inter-church dialogue.

Conclusion

Swiss Mennonites no longer have a large membership nor are they theologically influential, but as heirs to a long and fascinating history, living in areas where important parts of this story took place, they are continually and uniquely involved in a process of reflecting upon and evaluating their heritage. Swiss Mennonites are often challenged to answer questions from a growing number of persons outside their own ranks, some of whom are simply interested in the Anabaptist-Mennonite story, and others who, such as fellow Christians in the state-sponsored church, are ashamed of their denomination's role in the story. In this regard representatives of the relatively small flock of Swiss Mennonites are often invited to tell their story by other denominations or by secular institutions who wish to know more about Mennonite congregational life, faith and practice—past and present.

It is both a challenge and an opportunity to inquire together about the lessons which this often painful and difficult story teaches us for the present and future, seeking not only more inviting and authentic ways of witnessing to Christ, but also greater harmony with fellow Christians and denominations in articulating this witness.

Indeed, truth is immortal, as the Anabaptist reformer Balthasar Hubmaier once said—but the Anabaptist descendants have also contributed to a darkening of this truth by neglecting to strive for Christian unity, as Jesus requested. Swiss Mennonites must also deal with this reality.

Translation: Dean Kunkle / Arnold Neufeldt-Fast

Mennonite Churches in Western Europe, 2006

* Not all churches shown

Mennonites in France

by Diether Götz Lichdi

Mennonites in France today number around 2,100 members, paralleling the number of baptised Mennonite members in Switzerland. French Mennonites trace their origins back to Swiss Anabaptist families who came in successive waves to settle in France. These migrations came as a result of persecution and economic difficulties.

The first immigrants found themselves face to face with an "indigenous" Anabaptism, already in place since the beginnings of the Reformation, particularly in the province of Alsace (northeastern France). This migratory movement was especially evident after the end of the Thirty Years' War (seventeenth century). Swiss Mennonites began to arrive, first from the region of Zürich (1653ff.), followed by the arrival of about sixty families from the Bernese Highlands (1671ff.). They settled in the valley of Sainte-Marie-Aux-Mines—one of the cradles of the Amish, which witnessed the birth of the "Jacob Amman Party" in 1693.

Further migrations also took place under the expulsion orders of the King of France in 1712. The immigrants moved to the regions of Montbéliard, Lorraine in the Duchy of Zweibrücken, or the county of Salm, smaller principalities where the feudal lords were more tolerant. Some returned later to the valleys they had left. In 1709, other Anabaptists from the Swiss Jura went to the Burgundy region, in the vicinity of Montbéliard.

Despite great diversity today, the most common Mennonite names still attest to Swiss origins, names such as Muller, Nussbaumer, Kauffmann, Goldschmidt, Widmer, Peterschmitt, Hege, Graber, Rich, Hirschler, Klopfenstein, Yoder, etc. Thanks to the citizenship which was granted during the French Revolution, these families were able, once again, to invest in property. The last Mennonite immigrants from Switzerland came into Upper Alsace, especially into the areas of Pfastatt and Altkirch, toward the end of the nineteenth century.

Political Development

The story of Mennonites in French territory in Europe is one of two separate paths. In slightly more than two generations, between 1870 (the Franco-Prussian War) and 1945 (the end of the Second World War), people in the Province of Alsace and a part of Lorraine changed their nationality four times. After 1870, the Alsatian congregations, somewhat more agrarian in character, joined the South German Conference at its founding in 1887, and sometimes had close contacts with individual congregations of the *Verband deutscher Mennonitengemeinden*, the Association of German Mennonite churches from southeast Germany and Mennonites in the Palatinate. Connections between families led to much visiting back and forth and frequent pulpit exchanges. Following World War I, after Alsace once again became French, these Alsatian congregations were cut off from the south German congregations and had to manage on their own. In 1925 they founded their own conference, *L'Association des Eglises Evangéliques Mennonites (Anabaptistes)* (Conference of Evangelical Mennonite [Anabaptist] Congregations).

A second group of Mennonites had settled earlier in the area of Belfort/Montbéliard and in parts of Lorraine. The territory in which they lived was French, and they did not have to change their nationality. These Mennonites had urban as well as agrarian professions and had begun to accept and adopt the French language already in the nineteenth century. Those who had come into the country after 1815 from the Swiss side of the Jura retained their Swiss citizenship, and some do so even today, which proved to be useful during times of war.

Because of the new national borders in 1870, the French-speaking congregations became quite isolated from each other. This isolation was broken when they formed a conference in order to hire itinerant evangelists. Some Mennonites who had gathered in the town of Belfort founded a French speaking conference in 1908; it was renewed once again after the First World War, in 1929.

After both Mennonite conferences in France had developed alongside each other for one generation, each with its linguistic particularities, they found they were able to share many tasks in mission and relief work. The two conferences finally united in 1979-1980 to form the Conference of Evangelical Mennonite Churches in France (l'*Association des Eglises Evangéliques mennonites de France*, AEEMF). This union was strengthened by the task of organizing the eleventh assembly of the Mennonite World Conference in Strasbourg in 1984, and by the natural transition by the majority of Lorraine and Alsatian Mennonites to the French language. Today the AEEMF works through various commissions for youth, mission, social welfare, peace, faith and life and ministries. Elders, deacons and preachers as well as delegates from each church in the conference continue to meet twice a year in their respective committees.

Migrations

Though there had been different indigenous Anabaptist groups in Alsace since the time of the Reformation, most of them either died out, chose to join other confessions or moved away. The last representatives of these original Alsatian Anabaptist families were the Mangolds, Schmitts and Habischs.

Many Anabaptists-Mennonites did not stay in Alsace. The majority were Amish, and an important percentage of them emigrated to North America between 1720 and 1850. Many other Mennonites also emigrated to the New World or sought new homes and land west of the Vosges mountains even before the "Amish" split at the end of the seventeenth century. This constant migration not only reduced the number of Mennonites but also weakened their ability to survive. As always, the young and the efficient emigrated, while the older and more established remained. The number of Mennonites in France decreased between 1820 and

Alsatian Anabaptist Couple

1950 from 5,000 persons to approximately 2,500 persons. This halving was only partially due to emigration, which was largely completed by 1870. The drop in numbers continued for a time, but around 1970 it began to increase again, so that in 2006 the conference (AEEMF) counts approximately 2,100 baptized members in thirty-one congregations.

Spiritual Causes and Consequences

Emigration was only one of the reasons for the decline observed in the second half of the nineteenth century; other reasons included legalism, loss of theological identity, diminishing church discipline, increase in denominationally mixed-marriages, destruction resulting from war, transfer of membership to other evangelical churches, occasional poor sermons and inadequate training for lay ministers. Many traditional practices had lost their meaning and could not be imparted convincingly to the young people. Though Christian norms were preached, they were not adapted to the relevant necessities of the time. The practice of foot washing according to John 13, which had been taken over from the Amish, disappeared in most of the congregations during the course of the nineteenth century. When France instituted military conscription in 1829 it was accepted by the Mennonites, at first only partially, and then increasingly without objection; those who had the strongest objections emigrated to America.

Language also was a problem in the nineteenth century, even if some could speak two or three languages: sermons were preached in the Bernese German dialect, the catechism was learned in High German, but in everyday life with neighbours and friends, French was spoken. Finally a French translation of the catechism was made. This discrepancy was first evident in Lorraine and in the area of Montbéliard. In addition, Anabaptist convictions were lost because the few preachers who did attempt to get theological training went

Hans Baecher/Bächer (Elder of the Hang Mennonite congregation from 1880 to 1887) and Madeleine Hung (1822–1893). They belonged to the last generation in Alsace who wore clothes without buttons and required the men not to wear moustaches (like the soldiers). Their children changed these traditions as can be seen in the family photograph albums.

to Bible Schools like St. Chrischona near Basel, Nogent-sur-Marne near Paris or later Emmaüs in the French part of Switzerland or to schools which, even if they were Evangelical, did not teach important Anabaptist principles, nor did they support a peace witness. Nationalism, accepted without much criticism by everyone in the nineteenth century, was not deeply questioned until the end of World War II.

Sociologist Jean Séguy is of the opinion that, because of the disbanding of congregations and the dispersal of their many members, by 1900 the French Mennonites suffered from a minority complex and considered themselves a sect: they were not at ease any more with their Mennonite identity. With such a limited self-image and without an identity rooted strongly in the teachings of Christ, many slid into materialism and worldliness: why continue carrying the burden of being a sectarian minority within a Protestant minority in a land in which the majority were Catholic or increasingly secular?

Between Anabaptist and Pentecostal Revival

Two important factors helped French Mennonites respond to the late nineteenth-century crisis:

a)   a revival movement between 1890 and 1940 and
b)   the influence of an American-led recovery of the Anabaptist heritage, which started in 1919 and was much more evident after 1945.

At the turn to the twentieth century, one of the last waves of the revival movement reached the French Mennonites. It pushed back the last remaining Amish influence and made individual renewal possible. Many congregations experienced revival. Up until this time congregations had withered away and had lost many members through indifference and exodus to the cities. After revival took root, one became Mennonite not by birth but by conversion to Jesus Christ. In the past nearly all children from Mennonite families had been baptized at the age of twelve to fourteen, as a matter of course; this is not the case anymore. Today the average age of baptismal candidates is between seventeen and twenty years.

Between the World Wars, some congregations in the Alsace experienced a Pentecostal revival, which led to self-examination in a number of churches but also continued to blur Anabaptist self-understanding.

Emile Krémer (1895–1990) was converted through contact with Swiss Pentecostals around 1927 and wholly endorsed their practical and theological ideals; he also was leader of the congregation in Colmar (1924) and Sarrebourg (1927). He desired baptism through the Holy Spirit and the resulting signs (speaking in tongues, prophecies, miracles and healing through laying on of hands). He also was convinced that there would be a revival before Christ's return in connection with a literally understood rapture. Later he recognized that he had gone too far in some of his convictions about healings.

One century earlier Anabaptists-Mennonites had been known for their agricultural expertise. They also were known for their prayer, care and healing of the sick—both people and animals. This activity occasionally led to uncontrolled, magical ways of thinking and was denounced by revivalist preachers influenced by the Holiness movement. A middle road, suggested by Pierre Sommer, editor of the church paper *Christ Seul*, emphasized conversion to Jesus Christ (the fruit of justification) and the role of the Holy Spirit in the everyday life of the individual Christian and in the life of the church. Sommer also was interested in Mennonite history and included aspects of Mennonite theology in his re-reading of the revival movement. This middle road had to be rediscovered constantly and adapted to current situations throughout the entire century. The middle way wasn't always satisfactory for those who left their congregations. They wanted to go further than the majority of the other members, even if some of these members had been touched by "revivals" too.

After 1950 the Pentecostal movement spread to eastern France; the result was the founding of many new Pentecostal or charismatic congregations. Many Mennonites found a new spiritual home in these congregations and served there in leading roles. Even today especially younger church members feel drawn to the spirituality of these congregations and, as a result, the Pentecostal as well as the charismatic movement continues to attract members away from Mennonite congregations.

But a more specifically Anabaptist theology also experienced a renewal among French Mennonites. In 1950, Harold Bender's "The Anabaptist Vision" was translated into French, and people such as Pierre Widmer made a constant effort to introduce Mennonite theology into the more recent Evangelical/revivalist theology that had found its way into the French Mennonite congregations. Between 1980 and 2005 the publishing house *Les Editions Mennonites* published approximately eighty books in the series *Cahiers de Christ Seul* and *Dossiers de Christ Seul*. These publications give expression to the Anabaptist-Mennonite interpretation of the Bible. Many evangelicals in France are also interested in Mennonite Anabaptism. A book series called "Anabaptist Perspectives" contains translations of sixteenth century Anabaptist documents and offers theological and historical books in a Mennonite perspective. The series is currently being published by an Evangelical publishing house. In 1980 an association for Mennonite Anabaptist history (AFHAM) was founded, independent from the conference. Since 1982 it has published a regular yearbook (*Souvenance Anabaptiste/Mennonitisches Gedächtnis*) with original research articles on the history and the theology of Mennonites/Anabaptists. For French Mennonites, the recovery and popularization of Mennonite history, theology and practice have reinforced the sense of belonging to a particular brother and sisterhood.

Renewal Through Social Welfare Work and Missions

The first concrete manifestation of Mennonite *oikoumenè* was a French financial contribution in 1922 to help the Russian Mennonites who suffered famine. They also helped, even if modestly, the Russians who found refuge in Germany. When Russian Mennonites came to the harbour of Marseille from the USSR via China in 1931, they had to go next to Le Havre, where French Mennonite elder Pierre Sommer waited for them. And in 1934 when they had to go from Marseille to Bordeaux, Pierre Sommer was again there in order to give help. Sommer also represented the Mennonites of France at the Mennonite World Conference of Danzig in 1930 and in Amsterdam in 1936.

The revival of French Mennonites was due to the untiring commitment of evangelically-minded Mennonite church leaders. Some of these leaders were Pierre Sommer (1874–1952), itinerant preacher within the French conference after 1927; Valentin Pelsy (1870–1925), elder in Sarrebourg; Joseph Muller (1889–1984) of Toul and Pierre Widmer of Montbéliard (1912–1999). Also worthy of mention is the impetus given to French Mennonite churches by the work of MCC in post-war times (after 1944). The church publication *Christ Seul* (Christ Alone) also played an important role after 1901.

After the war, notable historians and theologians of the Anabaptist tradition were no longer found in Germany, but North American Mennonite historians and theologians such as Harold Bender,

John H. Yoder and Marlin Miller, probably because they respected the evangelical heritage they already knew in their own home congregations, exercised a positive influence on the French Mennonite churches. The North American influence resulted in renewed reflection on the Anabaptist peace witness, as well as a new emphasis on mission and social welfare work. All three elements, combined with the lasting impression the North American "PAX boys" left in the country, contributed to the creation of a new identity, and a return to some of the values inherited from the Anabaptist tradition, of which small traces may have been in existence, but which needed to be rediscovered in their theological roots and reclaimed.

After World War II, MCC gathered orphaned children into several homes. It introduced the French Mennonites to this type of service, although hospitality was traditionally one of the better signs of true faith. Today the French Mennonites operate a children's and seniors' home in Valdoie-Belfort and a home for mentally-handicapped children on the *Mont des Oiseaux* near Wissembourg, as well as several similar institutions in Paris.

As a result of mission work done by American Mennonites after World War II, new congregations were founded in Longwy (on the border with Luxembourg) and in Châtenay-Malabry (near Paris). These congregations also came into being with the help of individual Mennonites from northeastern France, who were joined by new converts to Christ and Christians of other denominations. These churches were open to all, without the traditional and quite closed family-church character of some of the older and more traditional Mennonite churches of the west of France. *Foyer Grebel* in St. Maurice near Paris also originated with these mission efforts. Originally African students in Paris were cared for and some became acquainted with God's Word at this place. Today the *Foyer* is a study and conference centre, known as the Paris Mennonite Centre, open to interested persons from many countries.

The Children's Home Valdoie (Territoire de Belfort). In 1950, the French Mennonites bought this house in Valdoie with the help of North American Mennonites. It was the first of many Mennonite social institutions in France for helping the needy. Painting by Fritz Mosimann.

With renewal came also the founding of a missions committee in 1950. French Mennonites had related to Mennonite missions in Java before World War II, through the German and Swiss missionaries who worked there. Marthe Ropp (born in 1923), who began medical studies in 1940, was also interested in missionary service. After the war, churches in Java requested help, and MCC began a medical service to help the Mennonite church in Muria. Dr. Marthe Ropp left for Pati on Java in 1951, together with Sister Liesel Hege, a German-Mennonite nurse. The French Mennonites used their departure as an opportunity to found a missions committee, which later worked together with the EMEK (European Mennonite Missions Committee). After their three-year contract with MCC had run out, Dr. Marthe Ropp and Liesel Hege were asked by the Javanese Church (GITD, now GITJ) to work as missionaries with the *Jajasan Kesehatan Kristen* (Christian Health Foundation). They continued working there, along with theological teachers from the Netherlands and doctors, nurses and teachers sent out by MCC. While on an extended holiday in Europe, Marthe Ropp answered a call from missionaries of World Evangelism for Christ, and worked in medical emergency service in Gambia from 1971 to 1984, always in connection with the French Mennonite Church and its missions committee.

Among European Mennonites, the French Mennonites are known to be conservative. For this reason cooperation with more liberal European Mennonites in missions could sometimes be difficult. This was demonstrated clearly in the case of mission work in Chad. The Evangelical school of N'Djaména in Chad probably wouldn't have come into being in 1964 without the support of the EMEK. For a while French Mennonites supplied most of the missionaries, and considerable sums of money came from other Mennonite conferences of EMEK in Europe. Michel Widmer from France was the first director of this school (1964–1965). Answering a search for a new director, Albert Westerbaan, a Mennonite from the Netherlands applied in 1969, but hesitated signing TEAM's (the Evangelical Alliance Mission, interdenominational evangelical mission) somewhat narrow confession of faith. M. Gabel, who was a member of a Belgian Pentecostal church and who was supported by the French Mennonite Missions Committee, was accepted instead. As a result, relations between the French and the Dutch churches experienced some tension over the next few years. But there also were happy times of cooperation. In 1972 this school was given over to the Evangelical Church of Chad. To this day

Gilbert Klopfenstein, one of the French Mennonite well-diggers in Chad.

the school has maintained its course; it is being managed well and continues to grow, currently with 1032 pupils and an entirely Chadian administration and staff.

Furthermore, directors Michel Widmer and Daniel Muller and a dozen young people from the churches served in this school, each spending two years there as teachers and service volunteers. Charles Gabel and Gilbert Klopfenstein worked as well-diggers and Daniel Oberli helped build the first Evangelical/Protestant school. Besides, Raymond Eyer served in N'Djamena, translating the Bible into Chad-Arabic, and for many years after his return to France, he served as secretary of EMEK, thus contributing to better understanding of the EMEK partner organization.

With developments in the Tchadian town of Abéché and the orphanage in Bakan Assalam, a new level had been reached, since the missions committee was now working together with the Franco-Swiss Protestant Mission of Chad (the French-speaking arm of Sudan United Mission) and sending out young Mennonite workers. In consequence the missions committee added new areas of service, primarily in humanitarian work as was the case with Dr. Philippe Klopfenstein who worked in Laos.

Church Life

Sunday worship in French Mennonite churches is held in the French language. In a few congregations along the French-German border simultaneous translation into German is still offered, mainly for a few elderly persons who still speak only German or for German-speaking guests. Young people take an active part in worship and most congregations have more people attending worship than their number of baptized members. For example the Geisberg congregation has 140 members but 200 persons regularly attend worship services. Two congregations in northern France seem to go their own way with regard to the conference. They both grew out of an American Mennonite missionary effort and find their identity in a charismatic circle; they show relatively little interest in the activities of the AEEMF. On the other hand, more recently some unaffiliated local congregations whose confession of faith is close to that of Mennonites, have asked to join the French Mennonite conference. Three congregations in the Paris area, farther away from the churches in eastern France, participate in the life of the conference as well. Several new churches have appeared in the last years.

Although most of the congregations are served by lay ministers, in the last years ten trained pastors or evangelists have been employed on a part-time or full-time basis. For the first time in a long time there are again French Mennonite teachers with PhD degrees in theology. Nevertheless, the tradition of lay ministry continues to be held in very high esteem. Weekend seminars—such as those held at the Bienenberg Theological Seminary or organized by the Seminary—serve to further the education of lay ministers. The seminars help improve the quality of preaching and pastoral care. For several years now five or six congregations also accepted women preachers occasionally, and in three congrega-

Every few years, French Mennonites gather for a three-day conference. In March 2005, 1300 people from thirty-one member churches gathered in Blotzheim.

tions (Châtenay-Malabry, Lamorlaye and Strasbourg) women have been ordained for service as elders or preachers. Work with the youth has been fostered since the Second World War. Young people now meet regularly at "Youth Commission weekends," and retreats are held regularly for young people. The largest congregations of French Mennonites are Belfort and Montbéliard in the Franche Comté, and in Alsace the congregations of Basel-Holeestrasse (the latter is a member of both the Swiss and the French conference), Pfastatt, Colmar and Geisberg.

When German troops occupied Alsace during World War II, many Mennonites were forced into the German army against their will. Exactions of the German occupation forces and the ambiguous attitude of the majority of German Mennonites toward Nazism and "German cultural nationalism" (*Deutschtum*) during the Second World War, strained the formerly good relationships between Mennonites in France and Germany. There was the added difficulty of communication due to the evolution toward the French language in Alsace. Some

What a symbolic image! Two former Mennonite military officers during the Second World War, one from the German, the other from the French Army: Adolf Schnebele (1922–2005) and Pierre Widmer (1912–1999). Both were taken as prisoners of war, both were elders in their congregations and leaders of Mennonite conferences, and both were teachers at the European Mennonite Bible School at Bienenberg near Basel in Switzerland. During a moving moment in 1996—again at the Bienenberg during an alumni reunion—they recognized the necessity of repentance and reconciliation.

Germans considered Alsatian Mennonites to be less liberal on theological and ethical issues than their south German relatives. In spite of this, contacts between the Mennonites of German- and French-speaking Switzerland continue to be cultivated and could be fostered.

Slowly the French Mennonites have begun reaching out to other people of faith. Between 1981 and 1984, they entered into dialogue with Lutherans who hold to the Augsburg Confession. Points of agreement and differences between both groups were recorded and in 1984 a mutual policy document was published.[1] The year 1984 also was significant because the eleventh assembly of the MWC was held in Strasbourg with over 7,000 participants. A few years later, the MWC office came to be located in this historic city. All this has contributed to a larger degree of participation of the French Mennonites in the global Mennonite family and the wider Christian family.

Translation: Anita Lichti

Mennonites in Russia and their Migrations

CHAPTER
VII

by John N. Klassen

The Immigration to Russia

The settlement of several thousand Mennonites in the great Russian empire in the late eighteenth and early nineteenth century occurred through a fortuitous combination of events and political factors. The program of settlement undertaken by the Russian government did not involve only the Mennonites, but also the settlement of many other people from German territories in search of land. The early history of this Mennonite migration from Prussia to Russia and the Ukraine, has been described in chapter I of the present volume.

The Developments Leading to Immigration to Russia

In the two centuries following the discovery of America many people were attracted to the New World. At the same time others sought happiness or refuge in eastern Europe. Soon after the Reformation, churches and cultural centres were built for the growing German population in Russia, but the ambitious settlement programme of Czarina Catherine II (1729–1796), laid down in a manifesto in the year of her coronation (1762–1763) went far beyond earlier efforts of this kind.[1]

Her first invitation to settlement (1761) had produced no results. In order to promote the offer of settlement, persuasive advocates were sent out. In the case of the Mennonites the Russian contact was Georg von Trappe, a Swabian who claimed to

Portrait of Czarina Catherine II

speak Low German. His efforts were not in vain: he succeeded first with the Lutherans and then with the Mennonites.[2]

Most of the settlers willing to come to Russia came from German lands. The first settlers, some 30,000 mostly poor and landless people, came from the Palatinate and Hesse via the Baltic Sea. Between 1763 and 1765 they established 104 villages east of Moscow on both sides of the Volga River. It is possible that there were some Mennonite families among them—probably from the Palatinate. At the same time a settlement of the Herrnhut Community with missionary intentions was built adjacent to the Volga colony. The activity of the Herrnhut group would later influence the "Awakening" among the Mennonites in Russia.[3]

The First Mennonite Colony: Chortitza (the Old Colony)

In 1786 the aforementioned von Trappe was sent to Danzig to attract settlers, to the displeasure of the Prussian authorities. In a few months two-hundred families, most of them poor Lutherans from the city of Danzig, had applied for emigration. The first group left for South Russia (today the Ukraine) in October, 1786. They founded the colony of Josephstal and the village of Alt-Danzig west of the later Chortitza Colony. This small village would become one of the sources of the German Baptist movement in Russia.[4]

Two Mennonite representatives also travelled with these first settlers, Bernhard Bartsch and Johann Hoeppner. They travelled even further with von Trappe, along the Dnieper River, to find suitable agricultural land for the Mennonites. They were promised a large area at Berislaw, on the west side of the Dnieper across from the Molotschnaia River. The twenty-point settlement plan worked out by Bartsch and Hoeppner was approved by Potemkin and by the

Part of the pamphlet in which Georg von Trappe invites Mennonites to answer the call of Catherine II, issued on December 29, 1787, in Danzig.

To the highly esteemed and respected Members of the two Mennonite congregations in Danzig, especially those who may be interested and who signed the authorization of the representatives who have been sent to Russia, it is announced that these representatives, after having selected very fertile lands at the river Dnieper according to their instruction, have returned safely and happily, and that on May 13 of this year (new calendar), that is, on May 2 old calendar, have received the special honour, through His Highness Lord Potemkin-Tavrischeskoi, to be introduced in the city of Krementschuk to Her Royal Highness the Czarina, in the presence of Her cabinet minister Count Von Bresborodko, the Royal Ambassador in Rome, the envoys of England and France and many other dignitaries, and to receive from her Majesty's own mouth in the most gracious and benign manner the assurance of the most special Royal protection and grace for themselves and all Mennonite families in Danzig who wish to migrate to Russia.

authorities in St. Petersburg. It included the offer of 65 desjatin of land (71 hectares or 175 acres) to each settler family.

When the two emissaries returned on January 19, 1788, to West Prussia with von Trappe and the signed twenty-point plan, there was great rejoicing. By February 23, 1788, the first four Mennonite families had left Danzig, and by the end of 1788, 228 Mennonite families had made their way from Riga to Dubrovna. In a winter interlude they rested from the difficult journey. They then continued in a long column along the Dnieper River, which would be so important to them later. By late summer they had reached the bend of the river where the Great Oak stood, venerated by the Zaporozhian Cossacks who had lived on these lands until Catherine abruptly resettled them to the Caucasian border regions in 1775.

At this point the tired, wandering Mennonites discovered that they would be settled on the Dnieper, where the little Chortitza brook joined the river. Disappointment and discouragement were added to their weariness. The government confirmed what they had heard and the direction was given to settle here. Written records tell of helpless disappointment.[5] Built of earthen huts, the first eight villages arose before the icy winter.

In spite of the disappointment and the corresponding bad news which reached their old homeland, new settlers set out for the new home. By 1796, the year the Czarina died, 118 additional families had arrived in the Chortitza colony, which at that time was still struggling for its very existence. Nevertheless, still more families continued to arrive in the Old Colony from West Prussia. With the surveying of three further villages in 1824 the settlement process in Chortitza came to an end. According to careful research, 400 families with 1,200 persons (almost 2,000 according to Diedrich)[6] found a new home here, settling in eighteen villages.

The Second Mennonite Mother Colony: Molotschna

In the one hundred years of settlement of German farmers and craftsmen in the Russian empire there were times of aggressive settlement policy and then again periods of hesitation. With the death of Potemkin in 1791 and Czarina Catherine II in 1796, Mennonite immigration slowed during the reign of Paul I (1796–1801).

Czar Paul I created an improved legal basis for the administration of a third wave of immigration. Czar Paul I signed the so-called Grace Privilege (an improved version of the Manifest of Catherine II)

Europe: Testing Faith and Tradition

for the Mennonites. In his manifest of February 20, 1804, Alexander I (1801–1825) confirmed the Privilege for the Mennonites. In spite of all the problems experienced in the earlier settlements, the Russian government wanted to continue the settlement of foreign applicants. The settlers were expected not only to establish themselves, but also to become model farmers for the Russian inhabitants.

Elder Cornelius Warkentin, after his inspection of the Molotschna area, had strongly recommended a further resettlement there. The Grace Privilege in the hands of elder David Epp and teacher Gerhard Wilms on their return to West Prussia after a twenty-six-month stay in St. Petersburg did the rest. Opposition voices among their own people could not reverse the preparedness for emigration.

By the end of 1803, 163 families bound for the new settlement had reached the Chortitza settlement, and in 1804 the total numbered 342 families with 2,052 persons.[7] The new arrivals rented space with the earlier settlers—often old friends or relatives—in houses or barns, until their farmsteads in the Molotschna could be made habitable. In two to three years they had established eighteen villages there. By 1809 another 114 families joined them. By the time the immigration from Prussia stopped in 1836 the immigrants had established forty-four villages.

One of these villages will receive special mention here, because it played an important role in the history of the second mother colony, and beyond, in terms of its spiritual renewal. This group of immigrants had originally (ca. 1540) found refuge in Prussian Brandenburg, having fled the Low Countries. They became known as the Brenkenhoffswalde-congregation. A number of Pietist Lutherans joined them. Due to the issues of war-service and availability of land, most of the members decided in 1833 to emigrate to the Molotschna colony under the leadership of elder Wilhelm Lange. Here they founded the village which they prophetically, as it turned out, called Gnadenfeld (field of grace).[8]

The final thirteen settlements in Molotschna after 1836 were founded by children of the pioneers up until 1863. The available sources do not give a unified picture of the number of settlers, but there were an estimated 2,000 families with more than 8,000 persons who had immigrated from West Prussia and other German lands. Fifty-seven villages constituted the Molotschna Colony.

In addition, the two most important exemplary estates, Johann Cornies' *Juschanlee* (1811), and Claas Wiens' *Steinbach* (1812), were begun early in the settlement period. Both became very important for the economic growth of the Mennonite and German colonies in general.[9] Furthermore, many Württemberg immigrants also settled south of the colony, in addition to which the government also settled other peoples in this area.

The Third Mennonite Mother Colony: Am Trakt

Around 1840 the settlement projects supported by the Russian state—Mennonite and otherwise—came to a halt. Further settlement activities had to be self-supporting, but this did not stop further immigration by Mennonites. The last settlements in Russia were two Mennonite mother colonies. In 1850, after some twenty years of peace, the West Prussian Mennonites once again felt the need to emigrate. Adding to the impetus for establishing the new settlement Am Trakt—although not the only reason—was a new defense law, introduced in 1848 in Prussia, which "rejected freedom from military service on the basis of religious confession."[10]

On the basis of a request by the Mennonites, the Russian government permitted the immigration of 100 families. Claas Epp, a well-to-do farmer in Prussia, looked for, and found, suitable settlement land north of the Volga Colony. Together with Johann Wall he led the first twenty-two families, leaving Prussia in 1853. The other families, mostly well-to-do, followed soon after. In three to five years these one thousand persons had established ten villages. This was soon followed by economic prosperity.

The subsequent history of this colony was determined by a strong expectation of Christ's imminent return, based on the writings of Jung-Stilling. Initiated and led by Claas Epp, a part of the settlement moved on in 1880, toward Asia, looking for the place of Christ's return. If this "look eastward" played a role already in their immigration to Russia, this would be evidence that Mennonites (as also some of the Swabians) had emigrated also for religious reasons.

The Fourth and Last Mother Colony: Alt Samara

Only six years later (1859) the Alexandertal area, northeast of the Volga Colony and west of the Ural Mountains, was settled by Mennonites from West Prussia. The first settlers, once again led by Claas Epp, arrived on August 20, 1859. By 1870, more than 100 families established ten villages in the Samara area, a plain of no less than 10,000 hectares of land. This was the last closed settlement in Russia, although individual emigrations continued until 1880. Additions to the Mennonite colonies came also from small groups seeking land from East Prussia,

Lithuania, Neumark and Poland. There also were Swiss Anabaptists among the immigrants to Russia. These settlers, some 1,000 persons, brought their own culture and tradition into the new Mennonite society. This long, continuing settlement project was not unified in its goals. It was a case of the expansionary policy of the Russian government coinciding with the need for land of German farmers.

Russia understandably sought benefits from this undertaking. The government wanted a great and powerful Russia, and that required guarded and settled borders and an agriculturally productive land. Russia did not offer land to the poor primarily in a humanitarian spirit, but sought intact, experienced, capable families. Russia wanted to join the western countries and to be competitive. Following the wishes of both settlers and the authorities, settlements were located at some distance from Russian villages and separated by confession. According to the social and religious culture of the time, people of diverse faith and customs should not live in proximity. But this social isolation of the German peoples, including Mennonites, had negative results later. Unintentionally it gave the indigenous population cause for suspicion of the "foreign" Germans.

All of the immigrants who came on the basis of state-sponsored settlement projects had to become Russian citizens, regardless whether they were German or Dutch. The Mennonites mostly understood that to mean loyalty to the Crown, rather than to the country. Somewhat critically Harry Loewen writes: "the majority of the Russian Mennonites (around 1870) were patriotic and loyal to the Czar, but they did not identify with the Russian people and did not accommodate themselves to the culture."[11]

Claas Epp Jr., the seventh of eleven children of Claas Epp Sr. and Margaretha (Klaassen), had a definite gift of leadership. In the 1870s, influenced by pietistic writings from southern Germany, he began to stress the imminent end of the age and the return of Christ. Epp described personal visions of an open door in the East, through which to escape the impending tribulation. When the Russian government cancelled special privileges, and many Mennonites emigrated to America, Epp promised a special deliverance for those who would follow him to Central Asia. Epp finally led a group of families on a trek eastward, to the unknown land of Turkestan into the middle of a Muslim population. Before reaching the hoped-for goal they were met by another group of Mennonites from the Molotschna led by Elder Peters who had set out at the same time for the same reason. The weary sojourners established a Mennonite settlement at Aulie Ata in Turkestan, where the group divided, most staying with Elder Peters. Epp continued with a smaller group, finally reaching Ak-Mechet, close to Khiva, where they settled. On the date Claas Epp had determined that he was going to be lifted up to heaven, nothing happened except for the disillusionment of his followers. Some left, others were excommunicated, and finally the remnant excommunicated Epp. Claas Epp died February 3, 1913, in Ak-Mechet.

The settlers in Russia mostly belonged to the middle class. The first settlers in Russia were the poorest and the last settlers the wealthiest. Of the 228 families that reached Chortitza in 1789 Gerlach writes: "The emigrants were in the truest sense abandoned, poor in body and soul."[12] The second group of 118 families that settled in the Old Colony in 1793–96 brought with them, among other things, 400 horses and cows. Those who chose the Molotschna after 1804 were even better off.

The settlement projects planned and carried out by the Russian state were not unique. Austria and Prussia had carried out similar policies before Russia did. Since Peter the Great the Russian rulers had learned from the West. The goal of exploiting newly-won and largely unsettled and unprotected lands in order to make them fruitful was too great for the small number of land-seeking, free-church Protestants, but the Mennonite settlers were favoured for good reason—for the good of the Russian Empire.

Nevertheless, Mennonite settlers were a small minority among the total number of German immigrants. Between 1788 and 1864 between 10,000 and 12,000 Mennonites moved to the Ukraine, to the Volga and Samara regions out of a total of more than 100,000 persons who had relocated and founded some 370 villages in about ten colonies. In terms of the faith of these German settlers, 55 percent were Protestant, 35 percent were Roman Catholic, and 10 percent were Mennonite.

Accommodation to their New Home: Russia

The immigration of Mennonites took place over the span of eighty years. When the last arrived the pioneers had been in the country for two generations. They already had children and grandchildren. The early settlers were integrated and comfortable, while many of the new arrivals brought their West Prussian culture with them. Since all had not come from West Prussia there were few common traditions among the four colonies before the first emigration to America in 1874. The first need was survival, but it did not remain so; things got better.

Economic Life

The southern part of Ukraine, which at the time of colonization was known as New Russia or Little Russia, is for the most part a plain. This land profile strongly influenced the development of agriculture and

The "Kröger clock," wide spread and indestructible, made by Johann David Kröger in Rosental near Chortitza.

of the colonies in general. Both settlements learned to adapt to the land conditions and the climate.

Ordinarily a group of people cannot prosper on agriculture alone. In the German settlements, including those of the Mennonites, it was not otherwise. They began to raise horses, cattle and sheep, along with growing fruits and vegetables. But there were repeated setbacks. In the summer there could be drought and a total loss of the harvest (1833). In the winters of 1811 and 1824 unrelenting snow storms destroyed the larger part of the cattle herd. In 1824 the prosperous Johann Cornies (about whom more will be said below) lost 800 sheep and 200 horses because of cold and snow. The settlers also had to deal with dangerous floods, and learned how to cope with them. Apart from that their progress was hindered by illnesses, plagues of grasshoppers, and other disasters. Still they advanced.

The crafts also developed slowly by their own initiative. In 1819 in Chortitza colony there were: 1 dyer, 2 clockmakers, 9 turners, 10 barrel makers, 16 smithies, 20 shoemakers, 25 tailors, 26 carpenters, 49 weavers, and 88 carpenters.

In Chortitza the agricultural implement firm of Lepp und Wallmann was established. Already in 1881 the firm employed 200 workers. In 1889 the company built 1,200 grain swathers, and by 1900 it produced 50,000. In 1908 in the progressive town of Chortitza alone there were 151 Mennonite firms. According to Gerlach, the Mennonites made a great contribution to industrial progress in the country and in fact provided six percent of the agricultural equipment for the whole of Russia.[13]

Plow and seeder invented and manufactured by the Mennonites of Russia.

Success in agriculture, industry, and other endeavours only makes sense if there is also a profit. In the early years there was none: there were not enough customers for the products of the German colonies.

With the growth of the population and the opening of trading ports the possibilities for selling their products further afield grew, and by 1815, the worst years had passed.

Self-Government

The settlement manifest of 1763 made it clear that the colonies would be given the right to self-government. The right to administer their own affairs, which had been offered to all foreign settlers from the beginning, was for the Mennonites a new, highly-valued privilege that contained great promise for their development. At the same time it led to lasting problems.

Administration—secular or religious—calls for leadership. All of the sources dealing with the immigration into Russia by the Mennonites testify to the lack of church and civil leaders. Unfortunately, the first election of a minister for the settlers in 1788 did not succeed. Tensions arose and even quarreling between the ethically more liberal Flemish majority and the stricter Frisian minority. In response to a renewed request, the Prussian brothers in the faith sent two experienced men, Cornelius Regier and Cornelius Warkentin, who were able to offer long-term assistance. In the Molotschna there already were experienced and educated men among the first settlers, but the life of the congregation had to be ordered for their new situation.

For the first time in their history, these Mennonites were not immediately subject to the government of their country; the civil administrators of their colonies were drawn from their own ranks. They had had no experience of this kind and also no civil leaders. Bartsch and Hoeppner, who had scouted the territory, became the first political leaders, but they soon lost the confidence of the Mennonite people. They not only were released from their posts, but also charged and jailed, and this by the church leadership. There was no separation of civil and church powers. If there were differences of opinion between church and civil leaders, it was usually the church council that ruled, and this was supported by the civil arm.

Thus the Russian Mennonites constituted a kind of "state within a state." In doing so they relinquished a number of insights of the Early Church and of the first Anabaptists. Instead of just electing preachers and elders, they now also elected aldermen (*Schulzen*) and mayors (*Oberschulzen*), teachers and school boards, and even police officers. "In the beginning it seemed very strange to the individual that one 'brother' would be placed above another 'brother.'"[14]

Schools and Education

The immigrants arrived with the conviction that it was the duty of parents to look after the basic schooling of their children. The school and the church represented the two pillars of German culture and Christian life in the history of the colonies.

The infrastructure supporting education had remained in Prussia. In keeping with the independence of the colonies it was incumbent upon them to do something about this. At the outset there would be "a school in any room, with any and all equipment and any available 'schoolmaster' ... in every village, from the first or second year onward."[15] Improvement came only slowly. Since the move from Low to High German was still in progress in Prussia when the emigration to Russia began, the teacher often spoke Low German, even if the textbooks (the Bible, Catechism and a few other texts) were in High German. The Molotschna settlers, who immigrated twenty-five years later, had an advantage at the outset, since they had experienced the linguistic and educational development in Prussia for a generation longer. These new immigrants raised the reputation of the schools.

Girls' school in Chortitza.

Beginning in the Molotschna, model schools for all the Mennonite colonies were established based on Johann Cornies' educational reforms, schools which also became examples for other German settlers. In 1820 Cornies founded the Christian School Society, which set up the first secondary school, a kind of middle school. Here the model was created for the Central Schools (*Zentralschulen*), which later appeared in all the colonies. At first the church leaders were responsible for the schools, but later the School Society and School Counselors administered the schools. The schools were supported financially by the colonies. The first trained teachers were called from Prussia, and were in part influenced by Pietism. Later, teacher training schools were founded, which looked after the supply of teachers. There also were some schools which led to preparation for university study. All the costs were covered by the community.

The foundation of the progressive education system of the German Russian Mennonites was laid by Johann Cornies in his reforms of 1843. In that year he was given authority in the areas of education and agriculture by the state, and from that time on valid curricula and time-tables were worked out and the teaching tested. Shortly before his death in 1848 Cornies finalized his reform with a regulation requiring school attendance for all children from six to fourteen years of age. Gerlach notes that "This measure was welcomed by the teachers, but strongly criticized by the parents, but nonetheless put into force."[16] The trend to better education survived russification attempts, was held back by the First World War,

Johann Cornies (1789–1848) was born near Danzig, moving at the age of fifteen with his parents to south Russia. The family settled in the Molotschna colony where they took over a homestead in the newly established village of Ohrloff. Johann, the oldest of four sons, worked first as a labourer for a miller, and then marketed farm produce in the nearby cities. Soon after his marriage to Agnes Klassen in 1811 he bought and leased more than 10,000 acres of land from the government. A gifted entrepreneur, he started cattle, horse and sheep breeding operations. From his large nurseries he provided the colonists with tree seedlings, and his own brick factories provided bricks and tiles for a growing economy. The government soon took note of Cornies' large-scale activities, and by 1817 the twenty-eight-year-old Cornies was made lifelong chairman of the Agricultural Association. In this position he had almost unlimited power to motivate—sometimes by force—the Molotschna and the Chortitza colonies to improve agriculture, forestry and industry. Perhaps Cornies' most important contribution was improving and reforming the entire educational system, the benefits of which reached far beyond the limits of the Mennonite settlements. Cornies was loved—and opposed. In dealing with the opposition of religious leaders and conservative farmers he could be ruthless. But he was upright in his dealings, a pious man who, "in spite of his great wealth and influence ... remained a plain Mennonite farmer."

and finally destroyed by the laws of the USSR. Hildebrandt does write that in various places there still were "Mennonite" schools that remained intact until about 1927/28.[17]

Church Life: Decline and Awakening

The immigrants brought their religious culture with them. That meant, among other things, that a number of civil village communities joined together in a Mennonite church congregation. In the Chortitza Colony Cornelius Warkentin, the deputy from Prussia, organized the religious life. Before he left he appointed two elders, Johann Wiebe and David Epp. In the first decades the eighteen villages formed one larger Flemish and one smaller Frisian congregation. In the Molotschna seven congregations were formed in the first two generations, whose elders, preachers and deacons formed the "Mennonite Church Meeting" (*Konvent*). The first elder, Jakob Enns, was elected already in 1805.

Although the Christian settlers, including the Mennonites, usually brought the structures of congregational life with them, this life was not particularly lively, and in the first generation it declined both in ethical/moral and social terms. All the same, there was revival with spiritual power and a missionary calling among the immigrants, as for example in the Gnadenfeld, Molotschna congregation.

Enns was not only "a man of energy and a violent character"; he also could not distinguish between church and civil authority, and was unfit and ungifted for his position. His quarrel with the first Oberschulz Claas Wiens and Klaas Reimer created much bad blood. The latter had been appointed as a minister of the Frisian congregation in Prussia. Their debates seemed always to be about offences—fights, the making of debts, drink, gambling—of the citizens and church members, for which the civil administrator (Wiens) was responsible. Elder Enns would not accept that. The realization that the New Testament church only had the duty of admonition and withdrawal of membership had escaped Enns and the Russian Mennonites, or it was slipping away. The reason for this was, according to Toews, the loss of the biblical and therefore Anabaptist understanding of the Church.

Around the middle of the nineteenth century a revival arose among Catholics, Lutherans and Mennonites. This new spiritual life came about due to increased reading of the Bible and edifying literature (Arndt, Hofacker, Menno Simons) and through powerful preaching and teaching. Special help came to these communities from friends and co-religionists in the homeland.[18] Eduard Wüst, a spirited evangelist from Württemberg brought the fire of revival to the Lutherans (1845), and soon also to the Mennonites in the Molotschna; several congregations gladly invited him to speak at their harvest- and mission-fests. His influence also was felt among the Catholics. The writings of the Baptists of Hamburg and the Moravian Brethren congregation on the Volga also exerted positive influences.

It should not be forgotten that there were pious, capable preachers in their own ranks who on the one hand exposed the sinful, immoral life of their members, while on the other they demonstrated a God-pleasing sanctified life. In doing so they prepared the ground for a spiritual renewal of Mennonite life in Russia. Apart from these there were many who prayed for the grace of God and for renewal in their practical lives in Bible and prayer circles, especially in Gnadenfeld.

The renewal happened quietly in individual families and congregations, but also through the protests of men who did not want to go along with the decay of the Mennonite brotherhood any longer. Out of this renewal movement several new congregations emerged over the next decades, among them, the Kleine Gemeinde, led by Klaas Reimer (1812–1819); the Krimmer Mennonite Brethren Church, 1862, led by Jakob H. Wiebe; and the Alliance congregation (*Evangelische Mennoniten-Brüdergemeinde*), 1905. Gradually, but in a lasting way, the majority of the Mennonite population experienced a spiritual and ethical renewal. The three immigrant church groups, Lutherans, Baptists and Mennonites, remained separated by confession and constitution, but often positively influenced one another.

In 1859 a group of persons in the Molotschna Colony who had experienced conversion and come to a living faith, and who found no hearing with the church leaders, celebrated Holy Communion together without the presence of an elder. This caused a sensation and helped bring about a separation. In January of 1860 eighteen brothers, some of whom held responsible positions in the church, declared their exit from the Mennonite Church, and founded an independent church, which became known as the Mennonite Brethren Church. As in the first days of the Anabaptists, they required a personal confession of faith to be presented to the gathered congregation, which then would decide whether to accept this testimony of personal salvation "as genuine." Only true believers should be accepted. They did not want to baptize anyone on the basis of "a faith learned by rote." Soon after the foundation of the Mennonite Brethren, and partly influenced by the Baptists, immersion baptism was introduced. They also wished to practice foot washing. Before long a Sunday School program and increased choir singing enriched the life of the new church.

The Mennonite Brethren definitely wished to remain Mennonite, and to "reform and return the church to its origins." They soon took steps to be recognized as a Mennonite church in St. Petersburg, a petition which was granted in 1864. From that point on there were "Church Mennonites" (*kirchliche*) and "Mennonite Brethren" in Russia.

The reaction to the new group formations, and especially with regard to the Mennonite Brethren, was mixed—from great surprise and calm to active enmity. But not all the leaders of the Church Mennonites were moved to common contrary measures. They also found revival to be necessary, but not division and founding of new churches. There was a general awakening from the lethargic, formal church practice that had established itself in a majority of the churches. In its place arose an active Christianity. And so, the break within the Mennonite brotherhood had led not only to the establishment of two church groups—Mennonite Brethren and Mennonite Church—but to a renewed faith that was opposed, but not extinguished, even by the massive measures of an atheistic state, or by the bloody experiences during the Second World War and its aftermath. Rather, both kinds of Mennonite congregations became Christian witnesses in the emerging Soviet Union.

Life in Czarist Russia

By the middle of the nineteenth century the majority of the immigrant Mennonites had found their place. Most felt comfortable in their new homeland. But much that belongs to the story of the Russian Mennonites—as well as to other colonists—was yet to come.

The Landless Issue and the Daughter Colonies

Economic success and spiritual renewal did not leave the Mennonite community immune to difficulties. As early as 1840 the growing need for land could no longer be met. In large families only one son, the eldest, could inherit his father's farmstead—which by law could not be divided. The other sons had to earn their living as farm labourers. The crafts and industries could only absorb a few. By the middle of the nineteenth century, two-thirds of all family fathers in the mother colonies were without land. Many became *Anwohner*, living at the edge of the village in a small house on a small parcel of land.

The real problem was religious and social: only land owners had a vote in the village. In practical terms the wealthy few ruled over the poor majority. Unfortunately, they did not always seek the welfare of the needy. Preachers and elders almost all belonged to the well-to-do, and all too often they sided with those of means, who were represented in official church meetings and in the area administrative office, and who blocked attempts by the voiceless for a greater say and for land.

In part due to a directive by the government, the difficult situation was saved by dividing certain parcels of village land, by the purchase of large estates outside the colonies, but most effectively by the founding of so-called daughter colonies. In the end the Christian sense of community won out. Both near and distant lands were purchased with colony funds and groups of villages laid out, in which mainly young families were enabled to establish themselves under favourable conditions. The Mennonite settlements were closed villages, confessionally separated from the many other German settlers. The village

plan and the construction of the houses were copies of the first settlers in Russia.[19] That these measures were crowned with an economic
boom may well be due to the fact that they were accompanied by a
spiritual renewal.

In the course of ninety years, at least forty
new colonies came into being with 330 villages. The first settlement was Bergthal with
five villages, settled by Chortitza. The last un-
forced Mennonite settlement was founded on
the Amur River in 1927, after the beginning
of the Soviet Union. The settlers came from
the European and west-Siberian areas. Unfortunately,
no sooner had the new settlers established themselves
in homes, with fields and gardens, churches and schools, than the
authorities forced them into collective farms.

Farm house in Köppental

Over the space of 137 years the Mennonites founded a total of 440
villages and settled them. In the thirty years following 1917, almost all
that they had built in hope and with much effort was destroyed by the
rough hand of the new political powers.

Missions: Czarist Limits—God's Will of Salvation

"As my father has sent me, so I send you! ... Go into all the world
and proclaim the Gospel to the whole creation" (John 20:21; Mark
16:15). These words of Jesus Christ are part of the foundation of faith
and action, not only of the Early Church, but also of the Anabaptists.
History tells us, however, that after a hundred years most Anabaptist
descendants chose to live a quiet and good life, rather than applying
themselves to help others come to faith in Jesus Christ. Mennonites
arrived in Russia as a "confessional and nationally congruent ethnic
group with its own characteristics."[20] And so there followed, according
to Hans Kasdorf, a "seventy year poverty of missions."[21]

Most scholars do not connect the lack of mission impulse to the
limits placed by the original Manifest of 1763. This document had said:
"Everyone is warned not to convince any person living in Russia who is
a Christian co-religionist, to accept his faith and to join his congregation under any circumstances... ...those of the 'Mohammedan' faith
are exempted from this, and these should be won for the Christian
religion."[22] However, the Mennonites (according to Nikolai Kroeker)
interpreted the passage as an explicit, comprehensive prohibition
of missionary activity. But, as Kroeker notes, there was an "almost

complete omission of a missionary motive among the reasons for the emigration to Russia." Consequently it was not surprising that "the Mennonites refrained in general from any proselytizing activities among the Russian population."[23] Christians from other countries, for example from the Basel Mission, carried on missionary activity in Russia among peoples who were not Orthodox, before the Mennonites became active in their own country.

Hans Kasdorf, in his study *Flammen unauslöschlich* (Unquenchable Flames) has shown that missionary activity among Mennonites in Russia occurred in three stages, until it was forcibly ended in the 1920s: revival as the dawn of mission, to 1860; missionary thinking and action, 1860–1917; the flowering of missions, 1917–1929.

1. The First Period, to 1860

In Chortitza the community was closed to change until well into the nineteenth century, but in the Molotschna a missionary spirit entered with the Moravian Brethren of Brenkenhofswalde. Branches of the Bible Society of St. Petersburg (1813) were formed—an arrangement criticized by many. In other places mission festivals had been held since 1820. Support for the Herrnhut mission grew after 1827. Elder Franz Goerz of Rudnerweide preached evangelical sermons—unusual at that time—and arranged mission meetings. In 1854 a considerable sum of money was sent to Holland to support the mission in Indonesia. Within Russia itself there was a general congregational renewal among Mennonites and German colonists.

2. The Second Period, 1860–1917

Around 1860 a new missionary spirit arose among the Mennonites. Among the Church Mennonites (*kirchliche*) this showed itself in a deep understanding of foreign missions. In the new Mennonite Brethren Church it was the recognition that only converted persons are saved before God, and so their Russian neighbours should be reached with the gospel. In 1869 the Church Mennonites commissioned Heinrich and Agnes Dirks to go to Indonesia as missionaries, in cooperation with the Dutch Mennonite Mission (DZV), as noted in chapter III above. In twelve years they established congregations which still exist today. Several Mennonites from Russia were to follow their example and served in Mandailing, Sumatra or on the Indonesian island of Java, under the auspices of the DZV Board. The Mennonite Brethren Church from the outset felt morally obligated to speak to the Russian labourers on the farms regarding their faith, and soon also their neighbours, including Mennonites, Lutherans and Ukrainians, if not directly then in small familiar circles. A number were converted and some were baptized. Because "propaganda" was forbidden under law all of this happened either in secret or with some tension. There was no lasting success among the Orthodox population.

Without warning, the Mennonite Brethren experienced a puzzling change of heart regarding their understanding of mission. They declined further work among the Russians in 1882 on the grounds that "missionary activity among the Orthodox was against the law."[24] Instead they invested their energy and means in foreign missions over the next twenty-five years. The first Mennonite Brethren missionaries, Abraham and Maria Friesen, were sent to India in 1889 with a North American Baptist mission, but they identified closely with the Mennonite Church in their thinking and action.

Up to the turn of the century, both church groups expressed their missionary consciousness especially by travelling ministries (*Reisepredigt*). According to Jakob Toews it was "the spiritual work among our Mennonites." It consisted of evangelization, deeper life meetings and Bible conferences.

In the early years of the twentieth century there was a second period of work among the Russians. It likely was stimulated by the Edict of Tolerance of the government in St. Petersburg, 1905-1906 (after the

Abraham and Maria Friesen.

end of the unfortunate wars of Russia with Japan and after the revolution of 1905), and it dealt with the right to separate from the Orthodox Church and to form "non-conformist" congregations and societies. In 1906 the conference of the MB Church elected a mission committee for the evangelization of Russia—instead of for foreign mission work. Jakob Kroeker, who at this time was a well-known travelling preacher, wrote at the time: "I dare to hope that the church will open a mission field in Russia, the like of which has not been seen before."[25]

3. The Third Period, 1917–1929

In retrospect, the years between 1917 and 1929 appear as "the golden years of the Free Church Movement in Russia."[26] For the first time witnesses for the gospel could move freely among Russians and Ukrainians. In these years the Russian Mennonites made monumental sacrifices.

Working in unity, the believers of the Church and Brethren congregations did not shrink from material sacrifice, or even martyrdom. The gospel was taken to many Asiatic tribes and peoples of the north, an active tent mission was carried out in the Ukraine, and many people travelled long distances under difficult circumstances. Historically, the missionary activity of the Mennonites began in New Samara (*Neusamara*) and then drew in the other Mennonite congregations. Money was raised and individuals who applied to serve were schooled in several pastoral tasks.

In the school house of Dubrovka the tent mission experienced terror on the night of October 26, 1919. Five missionaries and the congregational preacher, Johann Schellenberg, were shot to death or butchered with sabres by Makhno's anarchist band. The first martyr missionaries were Jakob Dyck, Yuschkevitch, Regina Rosenberg, Golitzin, and Luise Huebert-Sukkau. These witnesses for Christ are harbingers of the martyrs of the Mennonite mission in Soviet Russia.

It is reported that the number of Protestant Christians in this time rose from 100,000 to two million, a sign that there were many witnesses serving Jesus and not only Mennonites. This high point of missionary activity came to an end after 1929, but not the time of suffering. God had ignited a missional fire which in the following years of terror would be dampened but not put out.

Freedom Expanded—Freedom Limited

For hundreds of years the Russian people had lived in servitude, even after Peter I began to make Russia into a great empire. The nineteenth century saw a social reform program, as well as a program designed to russify the German population. If Russia was to find a place among the great western European nations, its own people would have to be unified economically, militarily, and culturally, and brought to a higher standard of living. No longer could Russia tolerate the social discrepancy between the well-off foreign enclaves and the less prosperous native population. To meet these pan-Slavic goals, several measures were taken. The peasants were freed from serfdom (1861); the rights to autonomy of the German settlements were further limited; freedom from military service was cancelled in 1874; education became a matter administered by the state (1891); and the Russian language became the obligatory language of instruction in the schools (1891).

The First Emigration—1874–1880

Reform efforts to improve the status and living conditions of the Russian people resulted in the reduction of special rights for foreign colonists. When their right to freedom from military service ended,

Mennonites began to think seriously about leaving the country. Some aspects of the reform eventually were modified to prevent mass departures, but while negotiations were still in process, serious emigration began. First among these were Mennonites from both colonies and from both denominations. Those who left were usually the more conservative Mennonites; they emigrated to the USA and Canada. Even though the decision to leave was not an easy one, about one-third of the entire Mennonite community left—around 18,000 persons, including children. The rights promised them in the new countries lasted for a short time. Our forebears had not yet understood that there can be no special rights for special groups in a free country.

Other German colonists also grew anxious: the entire community of Hutterites moved to North America in order to rebuild their Bruderhofs there, and 300,000 Catholics and Lutherans had emigrated to North and South America by 1912. Returning to Germany was not yet an option. Of the approximately 45,000 Mennonites and about 440,000–480,000 other Germans who remained in Russia, about 45,000 Germans had moved to Siberia before World War I. Land was easier to purchase there, and perhaps they also expected more political freedoms.

As to limits on freedom and resultant suffering, it is worth pointing out that within the world of the colonists it was generally not known that the non-Orthodox Russians, such as the Old Believers, had always been persecuted, banned and destroyed. This changed, following the Edict of Tolerance of 1905, and more so after the Revolution in 1917.[27] The Revolution also ended the privileged status of the Russian Orthodox Church (which had persecuted the dissenters) and it became a persecuted church until the end of World War II.

Alternative Service: The Proper Expression of the Law of Love of Neighbour

When news of the introduction of general conscription spread in 1871, the Mennonites sent a delegation to St. Petersburg with a petition, requesting that the Mennonites be allowed to retain their privilege of freedom from military service. They were received by the Minister of War. He asked both the leaders of the delegation about their request, and in so doing discovered that they could not speak Russian. That surprised and displeased him: "You have been in Russia for seventy years and still cannot speak Russian? That is a sin!" he exclaimed.[28]

Four long years of negotiations followed involving all the government offices, with the government showing extraordinary understanding for the nonresistant principles of the Mennonites. The court officials were very well-informed about the Mennonites, including the fact that as far as nonresistance and love of neighbour were concerned, these were not being practiced as taught. Still, they promised to "spare the consciences of the Mennonites and not to require military service." The final agreement, which came into force on May 14, 1875, provided for a weapons-free alternative service in the Navy, the Fire Department and especially in the Forestry Service.

In spite of difficulties, this humanitarian alternative service survived the First World War and the first twenty years of the Soviet Union. By this means the promise of the Czarina Catherine II to free the Mennonites from military service was respected. In fact, the four-year service (later three) of conscripts was mainly in the Forestry Service. This service was in the charge of a Russian forester. The congregations were responsible for everything else, including the costs and the provision of a preacher. During the First World War most Mennonite young men reported freely to the Medical Corps. Approximately 10,000 served in this way. There

were fifty trains at the front, which went as close as possible to pick up the wounded from the battlefields. These were staffed with Mennonite medics.

The war did not go well for Russia, which suffered military setbacks and huge losses, giving impetus to revolutionary forces and leading to Russia's withdrawing from the war in 1917. Even greater instability overcame the country when Lenin and the Bolsheviks succeeded in

Mennonites as Sanitäter (medical orderlies) in the army during World War I.

overthrowing the Czarist government. In the following political struggles and military battles the status of Mennonites and other citizens became uncertain. The new possibilities and challenges led to the first General Congress of Mennonites in August, 1917 in Molotschna. For the first time official representatives of the Mennonite churches and the Mennonite Brethren churches met and for the first time in the history of the Russian Mennonites "there was a fundamental discussion about nonresistance."[29] On that occasion many positions, including contradictory ones, were voiced. At the conclusion there was still a strong desire to maintain that the principle of nonresistance was rooted deeply in the spirit of the gospels. This conclusion, however, soon was put to the test by murderous bands which attacked the Mennonite colonies; the Mennonite commitment to nonresistance was irreparably damaged when some people in the colonies formed armed groups for defence or "self-protection" (*Selbstschutz*).

In spite of this the alternative service option remained a possibility, but from the beginning of the 1930s this service became the equivalent of convict labor, and the men were treated like prisoners. "In the light of such incrimination," writes Gerhard Hildebrandt, "the decision of many young Mennonites to do alternative service in the Soviet Union deserves our respect." The

> John Mathies served as a medic (Sanitäter) during the First World War. He travelled thousands of kilometres serving the wounded on Red Cross trains. Here he describes his experience on train 209, which visited the Turkish front in 1914.
>
> *We finally arrived at Sarakamis (today in Turkey), the location of the Russian-Turkish front. There we were at an elevation of ten thousand feet and it was bitterly cold. … We then collected many wounded, mostly of Turkish descent. Many had frozen hands and feet, and the smell from pus was terrible. Many died on the way to Tiflis three hundred kilometers away. We cared mercifully for the wounded and unloaded them at the hospital, where many had their legs amputated. … I carried many a wounded or diseased person on my back. They were all so happy, whether friend or foe. To me they were all friends. I am so thankful to God that I had the opportunity to do this work. I like to believe the Mennonites were called to do this task and that they carried out this task as medical personnel in a trustworthy manner.*

Soviet authorities knew well that the *Selbstschutz* "was not directed against the government, but against the licence of bandits and their murderous actions."[30] In 1925 alternative service was put on a legal footing, but then in 1936 again negated by Stalin's constitution. At this point Mennonite alternative service in the Soviet Union ceased to exist.

Additional Aspects of Mennonite Life in Czarist Russia

The life of the Mennonites during the monarchy was more multifarious than has been described so far. The more economic success the Mennonites had, the more opportunities for education became available. Young people attended not only the *Zentralschule* in the colonies, but also higher schools and universities in Germany, Switzerland, and also the Soviet Union. They became familiar with cities and came to appreciate the urban life. Not all returned to the farm after receiving their education. Due to economic success there was need for trained business persons, and they soon moved to the cities with their families. At the end of the nineteenth century a number of Mennonite families lived in Berdiansk and Ekaterinaslav. Mennonites no longer were an isolated, backward enclave in the country. Although only one percent of the Mennonites lived in the cities around the turn of the century, they influenced not only the life of their colonies but also the social life of their new communities.

In the middle of the nineteenth century a Mennonite literature developed, hardly noticed at first and then confronted by opposition. A few names will be mentioned here. Of Bernhard Harder's more than one thousand occasional poems, one has found a prominent place as a song: "Die Zeit ist kurz, o Mensch sei weise," and the Christmas poetry of Aron G. Sawatzky, "O Fest aller heiligen Feste, o Weihnacht, du lieblicher Schein" has become well-known. In this golden period of the Mennonites in Russia Peter M. Friesen wrote the first history of the Russian Mennonites. Among those who became known as writers in Canada were, among others, Arnold Dyck, Dietrich H. Epp, Hans Friesen (= Fritz Senn), Jakob H. Janzen, Peter J. Klassen, and Dietrich Neufeld.

Publishing houses followed. The Raduga Publishing House was one of the first. It published papers like the *Friedensstimme* as well as calendars and missionary literature. The song books of Isaak Born, *Heimatklänge* and *Liederperlen* (8 volumes), were printed at Raduga. Both song collections were reprinted in Germany after the Second World War by "Brücke zur Heimat." With the collapse of Czarist Russia (1917–1922), however, the beginnings of Mennonite culture were choked off.

There is no agreement on whether there was a "Mennonite architecture" in Russia, but much was built that was beautiful. The first settlers did not live long in their earth huts. By the First World War most of the houses made with clay and wood had disappeared. Artistic buildings took their place, made of bricks and stone: residences, schools, churches, hospitals, schools for the deaf and dumb, windmills, steam mills, factories and much else.

School for deaf and mute in Tiege, Molotschna.

In the Soviet period, the majority of these buildings were first misused and then destroyed. Some buildings are still standing today. Some of the churches, which had been left to ruin have, since Glasnost and Perestroika, been given back to Christians, and have been rebuilt as houses of God. One example of this is the church in Petershagen (Katusovka).

The Mennonites of Prussia had assembled their own song book not long before they emigrated to Russia, and they took their new song book to Russia. With the help of a *Vorsänger* (song leader) these songs were sung in many congregations in the next hundred years. Because there were no instruments and no persons educated in singing and music, their singing was destined to deteriorate.[31] An early renewal came via the Pietist settlers from Brandenburg, who in 1835 founded the village of Gnadenfeld. As awakened believers they brought a happy, lively singing with them to the Molotschna Colony.

Fifteen years later a wider reform of singing and music came about. The beginnings came with the pietistic Lutheran evangelist Eduard Wüst (1818–1859), and were continued in the newly-founded Mennonite Brethren Church, where they were developed and spread. Choir singing and singing in four parts were new, but quickly embraced. Soon the harmonium, guitar, violin and other instruments found a place in the life of the church. Love of singing was fostered, especially through contact with the Christian Music Society (*Sängerbund*) which had begun in Germany in 1879. At this time the Mennonite congregations published their first new songbook, and the way was prepared for the renewal of Russia's Mennonites in music and song. Choir singing became a tradition, and remained so until the 1920s when another wave of emigration began.

In the 1930s the highest authorities in the land brought all public church life to an end, but when church worship was suspended, singing became the personal worship of the believers. Praise, thanks, sorrow and pain, calls for help and complaint—all of this was in the songs. Singing was done in the kitchen, in the fields, at needlework, at the child's bedside. Singing strengthened parents and also formed the child. The youth used every opportunity to gather and sing. Singing protected them from the influence of the atheistic world around them. When persecution and exile receded, and God granted awakening and new congregations, then indeed singing began again in the congregations, and later, when many were able to emigrate to Germany, they brought with them their choir music—and they still sing on.

The period prior to the First World War appeared to be a golden time. Those who fled the country considered that time to be unique, living on both in memory and in written history as an almost perfect time. Today—perhaps somewhat extremely—the question is put as to whether there ever really was such a "Mennonite Paradise." We cannot deal with that question here. What is clear is that the Russian

Mennonites reached astonishing economic and cultural heights. But the story also has its dark sides, some of which have been suppressed heretofore.[32]

The Soviet Union, the Mennonites and the Other Soviet Germans

With the taking of power by the aggressive, militantly atheistic Communist Party in Russia, the living situation for Germans living in the USSR turned desperate over the next seventy years. To some degree it was the same for church people and non-church people. Even those who identified with the goals of the Party often were not safe.

The New Russian State, The Soviet Union (USSR)

The Tolerance Edict of Czar Nicholas II and the October Manifest of the First Russian Revolution of 1905 did not satisfy the Russian population, nor did Russia's entrance into the First World War halt the subversive activity of the workers' movement. Czar Nicholas II was forced to step down on March 15, 1917. Under Lenin's leadership the radical party of Bolsheviks succeeded in taking power by means of an armed rebellion on November 11, 1917 in Petrograd (St. Petersburg), and subsequently to come to power in Moscow as well. After the murder of the Czar's family in 1918 and four years of devastating civil war, the Union of Soviet Socialist Republics (USSR) was proclaimed. When complete it comprised fifteen republics in which some 110 national peoples (minorities) had their home. The Germans had a special place among these minorities. As an ethnic group they had no territory. Their lands, which at the outset were considerable, were gradually taken from them.

The Second Emigration, 1923–1930

After the February Revolution of 1917 the Mennonites attempted to integrate their philosophy of autonomous education into the new Marxist state system. The civil war of 1919, which ravaged the German-Mennonite areas of the Ukraine, nullified their efforts. In many villages (Yasikov, Molotschna, Sagradovka) whole families were literally slaughtered. In the starvation period and typhoid epidemic which followed (1921–22) hundreds died in the Mennonite colonies. Thanks to the help from MCC, which had been created for this purpose, many lives were saved. Still the situation of the Germans in general, and of Mennonites in particular, became increasingly unbearable. Even worse than war and hunger were the pressures the new government placed upon the churches and schools. The authorities sought to control what preachers could say, and what teachers could teach children and youth.

C. F. Klassen, P. F. Froese, and H. F. Dyck.

If at first reluctantly, soon the urge to emigrate took over. Not only individuals, but entire congregations and societies in America and the USSR began organized efforts in Moscow, seeking to find a way to exit the country. Key spokespersons for the organized emigration were B. B. Janz, C. F. Klassen and Peter Froese. On the American side the leaders were P. C. Hiebert, Orie O. Miller and David Toews.

David Toews, Harold Bender, C. F. Klassen.

The emigration of about 20,000 Russian Mennonites began on July 17, 1923 when the Empress of France, a steamship of the Canadian Pacific Railway, with its cargo of 800 refugees landed in Quebec. The migration continued for four years until the Soviet government put an end to it.

Parallel to this wave of emigration occurred the golden years of mission in Russia (1917–1929), as described above. There also was a major revival among Mennonites, 1924–1925, a process that began after 1918. What Reimer described as a missionary evangelistic movement across the country was also present among Mennonites: many conversions, personal evangelism within the colonies, and also among the Russian peasantry. The evangelist Adolph Reimer reported to the Ukrainians, how God used Johann Peters and his wife among the Yakutians and other pagan tribes of northern Siberia.[33]

The first group from Chortitza leaves for Canada.

Mennonites in the Soviet State

The emigration movement was well under way when B. B. Janz, as representative of the Agricultural Union, attempted to negotiate acceptable conditions for Mennonites to remain in Russia. The final and fruitless attempt along those lines was the All-Union Conference of Mennonites held in Moscow in January 1925; it was received negatively and even with hostility by the authorities. Many of the conference participants who did not manage to emigrate were later imprisoned, shot or died in exile. The Moscow conference came to be known as the second Martyr Synod.

A parallel development was the rise to power of Stalin in 1924 and the subsequent collectivization of agriculture. This involved forced migrations, confiscations, and the auctioning off of farms in the Ukraine, in the Volga region and in Siberia. The settlers who had once been invited to Russia concluded that they could no longer accept these conditions, and the pressure to emigrate continued to grow. What followed thereafter has been described in numerous books. The settlers took things into their own hands. Leaving behind house and farm, thousands travelled to Moscow in order to force the authorities to grant exit permission. At its height, between 13,000 to 15,000 people had taken refuge in the southern suburbs of Moscow; most of them were Mennonites, although there were also Lutherans and Catholics among them.

Thanks to intensive intervention from abroad, a few were saved. In addition to the efforts of the German Embassy in Moscow, Benjamin Unruh appealed on behalf of the refugees with the government in Berlin and the German Red Cross. Elder David Toews intervened with the League of Nations in Geneva. Eventually about 5,000 Mennonites (plus 1,000 from other confessions) were allowed to enter Germany. Here they found lodging until they were resettled in

Benjamin Unruh

Brazil and Paraguay. Some 400 remained in Germany and over 1,000 eventually were able to move to Canada.

Those who remained, numbering about 8,000, were forcibly removed from Moscow and sent back, usually not to their homes, but directly to Siberia and Turkestan. Some of the Mennonites did not give up hope. They attempted a secret flight to Manchuria and China. Beginning from Mennonite settlements along the Amur River in far eastern Russia, they fled across the Amur, singly and in groups, in the cold of the 1930 winter. Months and years later, several hundreds managed, with the aid of MCC and European Mennonite relief organizations, to move from Harbin and Shanghai to North and South America. This ended the second immigration wave.

The promises made by Lenin and Stalin in their speeches about equal rights for all and the autonomy of the German minority never materialized. Pinkus names two characteristics that account for the hostility to the Germans in general and the Mennonites in particular: "their clinging to religion on the one hand, and to private property on the other. These made them deadly enemies of the new regime."[34] The terrible fate of the Germans of Soviet Russia in the 1930s—their loss of land and property, dekulakization, forced resettlement, artificially created starvation, repression, arrests, execution—can only be explained not only by German origin, but also their Christian faith witness. This can be seen in the high proportion of preachers, pastors and other believers who were banned and liquidated.

The Russian Germans and their Confession of God and the Bible

Direct persecution of the German religious communities, which was even more severe for the Orthodox, began in 1922 after the end of the civil war. The government had no thought-out plan and the authorities often acted arbitrarily, but they proceeded from a common ideological paradigm that was atheistic-materialistic and Marxist. Religious policy was formed accordingly. The second phase of religious legislation, which openly declared war against religion, began with the edict of April 8, 1929. This ruling was still in force as law in 1990. With this roughly-sketched legislation, the Soviet government had created a weapon it used indiscriminately against believers and churches. The number of victims of Stalinist terror, based upon sources found after the collapse of the Soviet Union, is in the millions.

In the first forty years of the Soviet Union the number of Russian Germans remained almost stable, but the number of Mennonites decreased even though the birth rate increased in spite of the crises. The number of "hidden" Germans and Mennonites who had emigrated does not account for the loss. It is probable that every ten years more than 300,000 Germans died unnatural, violent deaths. An entire German generation was lost in the Worker's Army (*Trud armiia*).

The number of Mennonite victims will never be known precisely, but it could be in the area of 30,000 or more. Dyck observes that following the civil war, 30 percent of Mennonite deaths were due to measures taken by the state.[35] At the same time, not all Mennonites were faithful to the death; some also went over to the Bolsheviki.

> In the years around 1930, thousands of fathers and mothers were carried off and never returned. I reflect about the fact that mostly the quiet ones had to go, who carried no guilt towards communism... We remember the witness of a man, who at the time was 6 or 7 years old. On a certain day he heard his father saying to his mother in a worried voice: "Who will be the victim today? The car is standing again near the village office and they walk around through the whole village..." During the night he was woken up by voices of strangers. He saw how his fragile, slight mother embraced his father, both crying bitterly. The family never saw the father again. And his mother had to wear herself out caring for four children.

Despite the decimation, the fact remains that in 1989, when the emigration of Germans out of the Soviet Union was already in progress, more than two million persons of German nationality still lived in the Soviet Union. Mennonites made up barely 10 percent of that number. We may assume that the Soviet government did not pursue a policy of literally eliminating the Russian Germans, but rather attempted to erase their ethnic and Christian identity, and thus force their conformity. This would explain the taking of the clergy from the churches, and the forbidding of assemblies and open meetings. Before the beginning of the Second World War (1936–38) most of the preachers, priests and pastors had been imprisoned and exiled, or forbidden to preach, and churches, chapels and monasteries had been closed and secularized. From the mid-1930s there was no public church life in the huge Soviet Union with a population of almost 200 million.

The Second World War and the Deportation of the Russian Germans and Mennonites

Germany's attack on the Soviet Union on June 22, 1941, was not only a breach of the Non-Aggression Treaty, it also generated a dangerously tense relationship between Moscow and the German settlements. Supposedly, for the security of the Germans, the authorities began forced resettlement from "dangerous areas" in the path of the quickly-advancing German army, and finally from the whole European part of the USSR. The Volga settlement, including the Mennonite villages lying to the north, was totally relocated. The Orenburg settlement and those Mennonites living in Siberia (and other Germans there) were not involved in this move. But immediately after the war began, all German men between the ages of sixteen (later fifteen) and fifty-five were mobilized. Orenburg and Siberia did not escape this mobilization. After the harvest of 1942 all the women from the age of sixteen (later fifteen) to fifty-five were taken away. Only women with children younger than three years escaped. The captives had to work under the worst conditions in the north (Archangelsk, Vorkuta), and in Siberia to Magadan, with the majority working in the mines and forests of the Urals.[36]

The quickly-moving German army, however, overran the Ukraine, the Crimea and the Caucasian region. It penetrated deeply into European Russia, advancing to Leningrad and conquered the greater part of Stalingrad on the Volga. All of the Germans living in these areas who had not been deported now came under the civil authority of the *Wehrmacht*, the German Army. They were considered *Volksdeutsche* (ethnic Germans) or, for geographic reasons, Black Sea Germans. Together with many Ukrainians they rejoiced at being delivered from the Communists.[37]

Church life could only be reintroduced in a limited form and in some places. Although the men were absent because of the war, Sunday schools and choirs began again. There were revivals here and there, for example in Zagradovka.[38] During the period of occupation some collective farms were dissolved, although not in all regions, e.g., not in the Molotschna, and there was an enthusiastic renewal of agricultural activity. Led by the German Centres (VoMi: *Volksdeutsche Mittelstelle*), teacher training schools (LBA) were organized that promoted German self-consciousness.

Most Germans had not been considered reliable in Stalin's time because they were not trusted, but there were exceptions. At the outbreak of war in 1941 there were several thousand Germans, including 100 Mennonites, in the Red Army. During the German occupation this changed. Many young Mennonites came to serve in the German army. This did not serve them well after the war: on the Allied side they had difficulties emigrating, and on the Red side they were considered traitors, which could often mean death.

The enthusiasm for "the Germans" and for all things German was occasionally dampened, when it became known that the Germans had systematically killed Jews, but in general, the Mennonites who lived through that period have always been grateful to their historic homeland for all help received.

After one-and-a-half years of German occupation the German army was forced to withdraw early in 1943. Not only were cities, settlements and bridges destroyed, but all German civilians were taken along.

An estimated 350,000 persons of German descent from the occupied territories began fleeing westward. Before the war ended, some 200,000 were overtaken by the Red Army and deported back to the Soviet Union. The remaining 150,000 Russian refugees were in the west, but not yet safe. Some 50,000 to 60,000 were brutally taken by Russian commandoes and forcibly repatriated, sentenced to ten or twenty-five years of exile and hard labour for "betrayal of their socialist homeland." More than one-third of the 270,000 men repatriated died en route or upon arrival in the deserts and forests. Many of the survivors later arrived in the Federal Republic of Germany recounting these experiences.

Included in this large group of refugees were some 35,000 to 37,000 Mennonites, of whom more than 20,000 found themselves back in Russia again, together with other "repatriated" Germans. Those who managed to escape, around 15,000, emigrated to South America and Canada through the help of MCC and other European Mennonite and United Nations agencies. Some 1,200 persons remained in Germany. The work of C. F. Klassen and Peter and Elfrieda Dyck on behalf of the refugees must be mentioned in particular. Together with Hans von Niessen, leader of the *Mennonitische Umsiedler Betreuung*, they welcomed Mennonite resettlers from Russia and assisted them in building congregations. The experience of Russian German Baptists was similar to that of the Mennonites.

Before the end of the war something unexpected happened: early in 1944 Stalin allowed the Orthodox churches to open their doors again, and in October 1944, the same permission was granted to the Evangelical Christians, the Baptists and the Pentecostal churches, with certain restrictions. Only the German Baptists and Mennonites were not granted such permission, but remained forbidden religious communities for another fifteen years.[39] For this reason many Mennonites in Russia joined the Baptists and Evangelical Christians, where many were converted to personal faith in Jesus Christ. As members of these churches they today call themselves Baptists. For this reason about half of the Baptist resettlers in the Federal Republic of Germany have a Mennonite background.

After long negotiations between the Allied countries and the Soviet Union and Germany's unconditional surrender of May 8, 1945, the mutual repatriation of Russian and Allied troops and prisoners of war was concluded. But that did not put an end to the dire situation in Europe, especially in the territory of the broken Third Reich. The division of Germany into four zones soon gave way to the partition into

East- and West Germany. More than ten million refugees were living in the West, and they had to be helped and integrated. Looking back, it may be said that by the grace of God, and by the active involvement of Germans and Americans (the Marshall Plan), things soon improved economically.

The First Years after World War II in the Soviet Union

During and after the Second World War more than 800,000 Russian Germans from the southwest of the USSR were forcibly relocated to the north and east of the USSR. Through this relocation all the German settlements in the European Soviet Union, with the exception of Orenburg and Altai, were dissolved. That was Stalin's long-term goal. Of the departed Mennonite population of ca. 62,000 it appears that ca. 20,000–30,000 did not die natural deaths. Some 1.5 million Russian Germans, including the very young and the old, found themselves incarcerated, treated like criminals in concentration camps, losing their legal status, their land, and their freedom of movement.

After Stalin's death (March 3, 1953) temporary improvements took place. In September, 1955, Chancellor Konrad Adenauer of Germany successfully negotiated the freeing of the last German prisoners of war in Soviet camps, some 9000, and of some 20,000 *Altreichsdeutschen* (Germans from former German territories). These negotiations also eased conditions for the Russian Germans. On December 13, 1955 a decree was issued by the Presidium of the Higher Soviet of the USSR "On the cancellation of limitations in the legal status of the Germans and their dependents in special settlements."[40] With this act the special status of the settlements was eliminated and their inhabitants were able to leave their places of confinement—but they were not allowed to return to their previous homes or territories and received no compensation for their confiscated properties. In effect, by 1956 the Germans had regained some rights, but remained refugees within the USSR, a powerful reason why

In 1939 Anna Kröker married Abraham Kröker, a widower with nine children. When he proposed to her, he wanted her to promise that she would be a good mother to his children, in case the secret police would arrest him. She made the promise and tried later to keep her pledge. They only lived together three years; then Abraham and many other men were arrested and never returned. Anna and Abraham also had two sons together. The elder died as an infant, and the younger never got to know his father. Anna cared for her large family alone. One day there was no more food. In order to be able to keep a small reserve of flour, she took six sugar beets, rotting in a puddle on the street. It was a bad mistake. The administration, to whom she was a thorn in the flesh because she always spoke out on behalf of justice, charged her with theft. Six sugar beets cost her five years of hard labour in a prison camp.

many Russian Germans absolutely wished to emigrate. The Russian government finally agreed to a reunification of families for persons who had received German citizenship as refugees during the war.[41] This created the basis for the resettlement of the Russian Germans.[42]

The freedom experienced by Christians after Stalin's death in 1953 was of short duration. When Nikita Khrushchev became the mightiest man in the Communist Party, he changed his early, mild attitude toward Christians. His anti-religious campaign led to an even tighter supervision of church life and to a new closing of churches. This situation lasted until the mid-1980s.

Christians in the Soviet Union were not always unified in their response to the actions of the state. In the Baptist Union, for example, one group said "We must obey the authorities"; the others emphasized "We must obey God rather than man." Thus the Baptists were brought to a separation. Separation into two camps also took place with the Lutherans and Mennonites, and the resettlers in Germany have been marked by this division to this day.

Perhaps because the Russian Germans were willing to emigrate, and because of a more relaxed policy with respect to Germany, the Presidium of the Higher Soviet passed several edicts which favoured the German minority. By the end of the 1960s they had been partially rehabilitated. Nevertheless, they still were denounced as fascists by the population, and were not allowed to return to their former places of residence. More and more German families saw no future in the Soviet Union and applied in increasing numbers for permission to emigrate.

Developments within the Russian-German Minority: Grounds for Emigration

Stalin succeeded in separating the Germans from their land base and dissolving their closed settlements. At the beginning of the Soviet period some five percent of the Germans lived in cities, while the rest lived in the countryside and worked in agriculture. According to census statistics, by 1979, 51 percent lived in cities and followed non-agricultural professions. Well into the 1980s certain paths of education and certain professions were closed to those who openly confessed faith in Jesus Christ.

The fact that the Mennonites developed ethnic, confessional characteristics had much to do with their history of life in closed settlements. Where faith was based exclusively on ethnic-confessional factors, it could not withstand the pressures of the Soviet system, and either gave in to Communism or fled underground. Enmity against German Christians was massive up to at least 1985. In spite of this, Russian Germans after the Second World War time and again found faith and God. Congregations with a very living faith continued to be formed, even though persecution of believers in the free congregations was continuous until the time of Gorbachev (1986).

A spiritual awakening broke out in the difficult years 1945–47 in the places of exile: the work camps, factories and forests. Small "congregations" came into being on the steppes of Khazakhstan and in the forests of the North, far from civilization. The testimony of believing mothers who lived their faith before their children, was exemplary and effective. In the evenings they would read from surviving Bibles to their children; they sang songs and told them of Jesus.

Just at the time of the international thaw, around 1955–57, a second spiritual awakening took place, greater than the one ten years before.[43] This renewal, accompanied by an openness to the conversion of those who were not yet believers, persisted until the third wave of emigration in the 1980s. In a state where all religion was forbidden and the free churches persecuted, it is not surprising to find that there are no exact figures on the number of Mennonites, German Baptists and Baptist Mennonites. Kasdorf estimates 35,000 to 40,000 Mennonites in Baptist churches in 1988, further estimating that there were some thirty Mennonite Brethren congregations and fifteen to twenty Mennonite Conference churches in the 1970s.[44] Sawatsky reports that at the end of the 1970s, some 30,000 mostly MB members belonged to the AUCECB (All Union Council of Evangelical Christian Baptists).[45] When compared to the number of resettled Mennonites and Mennonites in Baptist churches of the Federal Republic of Germany, which number 56,000–60,000, the estimates relating to the former USSR appear realistic.

> There were no longer local congregations, but the whole congregation of Russia was alive! The preachers were absent, but the Holy Spirit was present. The Bibles had been taken away, but not the Word of God in their hearts! Here the sermons heard much earlier found their application. Now they experienced the blessings of earlier work with children and youth, of family devotions. Bereft of their men, the faithful women and mothers took over not only the physical nourishment of their children, but also their spiritual education.

In 1989 the resettlement of Mennonites, Baptists of Mennonite background and other Baptists was at its height when the realization dawned that Russia had been their home for 200 years. The 100 year anniversary had been celebrated! Why should there not be

a celebration now? Congregational leaders agreed that there should
be. Congregations in Omsk, Orenburg and Karaganda took the initiative and made plans that on August 11–14, 1989, thanks should be

given to God under the Great Oak
in Chortitza (now Zaporozh'e)
and His Word be proclaimed
there. Under the leadership of
Gorbachev, freedom was in the
air. Viktor Fast, leader of the enterprise, obtained official permission and some railroad cars were
rented. At its stops along the way
there was singing, testimony,
and the handing out of religious
tracts. More than 100 persons
from the eastern areas arrived,
some by car. On Friday morning

John N. Klassen addresses the participants of the 200-
year celebration under the Great Oak in Chortitza.

several hundred persons had gathered under the oak in bright sun-
shine—most of them local Ukrainians. They witnessed a joyful service of thanksgiving and praise to God including choir music, words
of explanation, and a long, original word of thanks by a Ukrainian
Christian. The author of this chapter was asked to give the celebratory
address.

A number of services were held in local Baptist congregations,
who hosted the visitors. For the final meeting, the visiting Mennonites
were offered the city stadium, and to everyone's surprise it was filled
with more than 10,000 persons. The mayor of Zaporozh'e gave a word
of greeting—only a few years before no one would have thought that
such an event would ever be possible in the USSR. Besides the many
choir numbers, greetings and poems, Gerhard Hamm, a well-known
evangelist in the USSR, preached on the love of God (John 3:16). Several hundred persons testified that they wished to believe what they
had heard, and came forward, where they were given a passage of
Scripture. Guests from overseas were perhaps the most astonished at
the proceedings. There was a group from North America, among them
Peter and Elfrieda Dyck. Seventeen resettled Mennonites and Baptists
came from the Federal Republic of Germany. The most popular topics,
apart from the message from the Word of God, were emigration and
evangelization.[46]

Emigration and Dispersion of the Russian Germans

Until the First World War, Germany imported between 350,000–500,000 foreign-speaking workers to Germany.[47] Nevertheless, by the 1920s, when tens of thousands left the Soviet Union because of its economic and religious policies, the way was not open to the historic homeland in Germany. The fact that small groups of Mennonites later did remain in some parts of Germany made little difference to the general situation: Germany was closed for German people from Russia. At the end of the 1920s, only a few thousand refugees were granted temporary stays before they needed to migrate further.

The Third Russian-German Emigration

Although the earlier migration waves were directed to various countries in South and North America, by the end of the twentieth century re-settlement to Germany finally became possible, thanks to inter-governmental agreements. It became possible for all Soviet Germans to emigrate. The history of this third Mennonite migration must be understood within the framework of developments in Russia and the history of Evangelical Christian Baptists.[48]

At the end of the Second World War, when Germany had literally ceased to be a country, it became the place of refuge for Germans and other nationalities from the east, numbering eight million refugees and deported peoples by 1950. Over the next fifty years, Germany took in a further five million, of which about two million were Russian German immigrants.

In order to receive an exit visa for entry into the Republic of Germany after the Second World War, applicants needed an invitation (*Vyzov*) which, until 1990, had to be sent by relatives of the first rank and done on forms prepared by the German Red Cross. In the early years after 1950 this process could take as long as ten years. It would begin when

Herbert Wiens writes,

Germany was the land of dreams. Everything was put at risk: career, future chances, health, one's entire existence, yes even that little bit of freedom that we had gained within a totalitarian state. Once the wish to emigrate had become public there came job dismissals, harassment at the workplace and in school, prohibition against changing legal residence to another location, confiscation of property and houses, house searches and arrests. It was even worse morally speaking, an atmosphere of general rejection and condemnation, that artificially surrounded the immigration applicants. People were stereotyped as criminals, simply because they wanted to claim their legitimate right to immigrate. Rejections, rejections, rejections ... usually with no reason given. The people were powerless against the authorities, even when they claimed rights on the basis of Soviet law, the Constitution, the agreements etc. The authorities would answer: "We make the decision. If we wish we will let you out, if not, then you'll stay here." Who is related to whom, that the local authorities determined in their own way. To demonstrate against it publicly usually did not help.

the potential emigrant communicated to his relatives in Germany his desire to emigrate. The relative then obtained the *Vyzov* and sent it to the candidate, who would then start the application process in the office of the local police. Before Gorbachev's liberalizations, this was a long and complicated process, and often was unsuccessful. This tragic story of family reunification came to a good end with the Soviet law on entry and exit of 1987.

Since the 1990s the German government has slowed down the application process by requiring a waiting period of four to five years in order to keep the number of applicants manageable. Since 1996 the key means of control has been the language test.

Exit and Entry for Russian-German Resettlers

In August 1950 Friedland was designated a Transit Camp. It became the gateway home for prisoners of war, deportees, and resettlers. Since that time around 6 million persons have been processed through this camp. For all immigrants this little village has taken on an unforgettable positive and life giving significance. The early immigrants in particular retained warm memories of their arrival in Friedland.

The constant need to make personal decisions or choices was problematic for people who had spent their lives under a dictatorship, and caused great difficulties from the outset. In point of fact, everything had been provided for—at least that was the impression the resettlers got. But in the long run German state welfare could not guarantee health and happiness. Here Christians had an advantage, being able to draw strength and hope from the fellowship of believers because of their relationship to God, something non-Christians were unable to do. The Mennonites provided additional assistance, both spiritual and material, not only from America but also from the Netherlands. For example, several times the Dutch churches provided an organ on the occasion of the dedication of a new church building. There have also been mutual exchange visits between newly-

One of the first free church Russian resettlers that became known was the Mennonite family Ewert and Frau Helene Loewen. Peter Ewert from Chortitza was able to make contact with his family in Germany. In 1963, after eighteen years of separation, he was granted an exit visa to Germany to live with his wife Olga. Better-known was Frau Helene Loewen, who managed to be reunited with her husband Wilhelm Loewen living near Neuwied am Rhein, in 1965 after years of effort. Mr. Loewen's persistence in bringing his wife to Germany finally succeeded. It was a newsworthy event, the story of a miracle of God. They lived together for five years until Wilhelm's death. Frau Loewen thereafter lived for many years as a respected member of the congregation in Lage/Lippe. Soon after Frau Loewen's arrival, other Mennonite families came to Karlsruhe. In 1969, there already were several resettler families in the Lage/Lippe congregation.

established congregations and the more established Dutch congregations, which were once the place of origin of many Russian Mennonites. Dutch Mennonites also served on the board of the Mennonite Resettler Services committee (*Mennonitische Umsiedlerbetreuung*).

When Russian Germans, Mennonites in particular, arrived in the German Republic, they usually encountered some unexpected and confusing things that did not correspond to their idealized notion of Germany. They missed strict order in the schools. Mennonite believers missed the respect they had expected for older people. Early immigrants of the 1970s, especially those from free church Baptist and Mennonite orientations who sought out local places of worship, also sensed a lack of personal warmth in the churches, and not only in society. They found it inexplicable and alien that so few people attended worship. They were accustomed—and that in an atheist land—to go to worship at least once on Sunday. In Germany they encountered a widespread lack of interest in religion and secular self satisfaction. It was "Homecoming to a Strange Land," according to one author.

But such disappointments should not be generalized too broadly. Many resettlers, many Mennonite families, and entire congregations remain thankful for their homecoming to the home of their forebears. The option to return to the Russian homeland remains and a few have returned—but only very few. Although the resettlers are still received as full fledged German citizens, the native German population showed more reserve as the stream of immigrants kept growing at the end of the 1980s. Possible reasons for this were the worsening employment situation, the slowing of market competition, rising taxes, and insufficient readiness of the new arrivals to integrate themselves. These factors contributed to the conclusion that the immigrant stream needed to be stopped, or at least drastically curtailed. Over the course of fifty-four years (1951–2004) a total of almost 2.3 million Soviet citizens were received as Russian German resettlers. Of these, about 12 percent had connections to Mennonite or Baptist churches.

> "On August 27, 1974, we arrived... by bus in Friedland, the reception camp at the border. We were taken care of by Red Cross nurses. A feeling beyond description. Finally we had come home in freedom from exile. On German soil. When the bells rang and all were brought into the dining hall where welcoming words were spoken, this was so moving and beautiful that no eye remained dry. Tears of joy. One must have experienced this himself to understand how happy we were, when little by little we received everything which is necessary to live," according to Hilda Driedger.

> Asked about his fatherland, Jakob Bergen writes: "Our fatherland is there, where we spent our youth. For our children this is Germany. For us it is: people, climate and everything to which we were accustomed. And even when now we are in a new fatherland, where the government and the people have received us heartily, where we have been taken care of in everything, nevertheless we won't forget Russia, our real fatherland."

Extent of the Resettlement—How Many Russian Germans Immigrated?

The movement of Mennonites from the Soviet Union came as a surprise to most Christians in the West: they had prayed for relief and religious freedom for believers in the Soviet Union, but very few had imagined a migration of such massive proportions. When family reunification began to become a reality in the late 1960s, it was indeed a miracle of God. In human terms, the MCC, German Mennonites (*Vereinigung*, then also *Verband* after 1975), Dutch Mennonites and other Christians provided extensive help to the immigrants in the process of registering, welcoming and assisting in the integration to Germany.

During the 1980s, Baptists represented 15 percent and the Mennonites 10 percent of the total number of resettlers.[49] After the mid-1990s that proportion declined because most Baptists and Mennonites had emigrated.

The following table shows in abridged form the statistics of registered Resettlers, including congregations and the number of church members		
Total Aussiedler (Resettlers) from the CIS	2,298,938	2,298,938
Total Baptists-Mennonites, Family members	1965–2004	275,000–285,000
Total Baptist-Mennonite Congregations	1972–2004	ca. 418
Total Church Membership	end of 2004	ca. 77,000
Total Membership including those in existing German Church Unions		ca. 86,000

Confessional Traditions of the Russian Germans

The German settlers who immigrated to Russia more than 200 years ago belonged to one of three confessional traditions: Lutheran, Roman Catholic, and Mennonite. Just as 200 years brought many changes into the lives of the German settlers, so also there were shifts in confessional membership. Due to influences from abroad a number of new confessions emerged, of which the Baptists are the largest. The Mennonites, according to research by Pinkus, remained at the 10 percent total of the whole.[50] This number may well be an overestimate, if Mennonites are counted separately from the German Baptists.

Confessional Registration upon Return to Germany

In the official record which the immigrants filled out in Friedland or at other transit camps, there also was an entry for confession or church membership. The answer was optional and often was filled in without indicating personal conviction. On the basis of such information official sources publish lists of immigrants and their religious membership, but the data has gaps. Recent studies have made estimates more precise. Particularly helpful was the demographic data from eight Mennonite villages in the Altai settlement, near Omsk and from Orenburg in Siberia, where almost the entire population emigrated in the late 1980s and early 1990s to Germany. This data revealed first, that 7,913 persons from these Mennonite villages had been registered in Germany, and second, that of these, 1,638 had been members of an MB or Church Mennonite congregation (*Kirchengemeinde*) in the old homeland. When this is extrapolated, it means that about 21 percent of the immigrants from Russia had already been baptized upon confession of faith. Put differently, for every church member in these Mennonite villages in Russia there were an additional four persons, not yet belonging to a congregation as members.

Religion and Faith among Russian German Immigrants

Whereas one's confession is often a cultural aspect of an ethnic group, faith is something personal. "Faith," according to Pöhlman, "is to place one's trust in and to hold fast in God's faithfulness and to believe in God's promises."[51] For the free church persons examined here, it is particularly true that faith is something personal. This was the understanding of the Anabaptists. However, during the following centuries, many Mennonites began to lean toward becoming a family church. According to Toews, the Russian Mennonites had developed into a virtual *Volkskirche* (peoples' church).[52] Through the renewals of the nineteenth century and the testing of the twentieth the Mennonite communities in Russia recovered a New Testament understanding of faith and community. For that reason Mennonite immigrants usually made a conscious distinction between a cultural confessional orientation, and being a believer.

Religion and Faith among Immigrants (Aussiedler), *Mennonites and Baptists*

Some scholars of the history of the Germans in the Soviet Union, such as Pinkus and Fleischhauer, have contrasted believers to confessional adherents. Pinkus has concluded that "in view of all existing estimates and partial data, one can conclude that 20 to 25 percent of the German population in the Soviet Union, that is 400–500 thousand persons, are believers.[53]

Among believers growth usually occurs on two levels—biological and spiritual. Concerning the latter, research suggests that 50,000 to 60,000 believers of Mennonite—Baptist orientation came to Germany since the 1960s. New immigrant believers are added annually. But since these new Christian congregations do also evangelize in various forms, the number of believers has grown, and through their baptism the local churches also grow. For the early years the number of baptisms are estimated; from 1989 onward they are based on research. There have been 30,000 baptisms in the immigrant Mennonite and Baptist churches since the 1960s.[54]

Biological growth has also taken place. Approximately 280,000–290,000 ethno-confessional Mennonites and Baptists immigrated to Germany since the 1960s. This number did not remain static, since the immigrants had large families. Demographic data of immigrants from eight villages reveals an annual increase of 2.4 to 2.9 percent, or an annual biological growth rate of 2.5 percent which, extrapolated, means 55,000 to 65,000 children born in Germany.

In summary, we can assume that as of 2005, between 335,000 and 345,000 persons live in Germany who can be considered as belonging to the Baptist-Mennonite families in ethnic confessional terms; that is, families and church members counted together, including immigrant Christians within the existing German church unions. The remaining question—how many of these consider themselves Mennonite and how many regard themselves as Baptist will be addressed at the end of this discussion.

Immigrant Mennonites and Baptists (*Aussiedler*) Organize their own Congregations

In this section we report on the establishment of 420 free churches from the Baptist and Mennonite traditions and on their relationships to each other. Members coming from the large churches (Lutheran and Roman Catholic), did not establish any congregations in West Germany. On the basis of existing church law, upon their immigration to Germany, resettlers from these denominations automatically become members in a parish of their confession, at their permanent places of residence.

Initial Church Situation of
Mennonite Refugees and Immigrants

As noted above, approximately 15,000 Mennonites and an unknown number of Baptists were among those who escaped the deportation following World War II.[55] Around 1,000 of these Mennonites did not emigrate further, settling in Germany as it was established in 1949. These people provided the point of reference for the subsequent reunification of families from the USSR.[56]

Some MCC workers and preachers remained in Germany, even after the refugee immigration had ended. These included Cornelius C. Wall, Heinrich H. Janzen, and Jakob W. Vogt. Wall and Janzen were among the first teachers at the European Mennonite Bible School founded in 1950 in Basel (later Bienenberg), Switzerland. Janzen also was a widely appreciated speaker at conferences and a radio speaker on *Quelle des Lebens* (Source of life) and *Worte des Lebens* (Word of life).

Through the ministry of these brethren from overseas and their cooperation with fellow believers locally, many young people deeply disillusioned by the war found new hope for the future. Congregations were re-established, and new congregations were also founded. Refugees from Mennonite Brethren communities in the Soviet Union and Poland formed a Mennonite Brethren congregation in Neuwied on the Rhine in July 1950. It was the first MB congregation in western Europe. Participants did not view their action as the founding of a new denomination, since all of them were members in already existing Mennonite Brethren congregations elsewhere. Before the later process of family reunification began, two further congregations of Mennonite Brethren were established in Neustadt/Weinstrasse (1960) and Lage/Lippe (1965). These and several other congregations became connecting points for the *Aussiedler* (immigrants) who soon began to arrive.

The Establishment of the First
Russian-German Umsiedler *Churches*

When the first German immigrants of free church orientation came from the USSR, they already had relatives who had themselves at an earlier time come to Germany as refugees. It was genuine family reunification. The earlier immigrants had first settled in Lage, Bielefeld, Espelkamp and Neuwied/Rhein, and formed Mennonite refugee congregations. The Russian Baptist refugees, who had established themselves in Germany after the Second World War, initially also attempted to establish separate congregations, but were absorbed into the Union of Evangelical Free Churches (German Baptists, not resettlers).

This situation changed after 1970. As more and more immigrants entered the country, there also were numerous ordained preachers and *Älteste* (elders) among them. These groups decided to establish independent congregations modeled on congregations in Russia. The first such Russian German congregation was founded in Paderborn in 1972. It was a Baptist-Brethren congregation.

The military camp of Espelkamp north of Bielefeld was converted into a place for war refugees (Mennonites and others) after May, 1945. With the aid of American alternative service workers, houses and a church were built for the Mennonites of West Prussia. Later, refugees who returned from South America also settled there. A Mennonite Church and a Baptist church consisting of German believers existed in Espelkamp as early as 1952. The Russian Mennonites arrived in the early 1970s. They founded a Mennonite Brethren congregation in 1974. This was the first Mennonite Brethren congregation that the *Aussiedler* (immigrants) organized in Germany.

The history of this church was similar to that of many other new congregations. Its growth was rapid and in 1977 the congregation built its first "prayer house" (*Gebetshaus* or church). In 1980 the 600-member congregation experienced a split. Sixteen years later, in 1996, the majority from both congregations decided to reunite their fellowships. Currently this congregation claims 2,000 members meeting in three church buildings, filled to capacity on Sundays. Two further congregations were added in this city. A bit further north in Rahden there are three additional new congregations. The five congregations just referred to bear no Mennonite designation, but virtually all their members are of "Mennonite origin."

During the early 1970s a small number of Russian German Christians settled in Bielefeld, and some began to meet for worship in June, 1974. They came from various Mennonite and Baptist congregations in the Soviet Union and formed the first Russian German congregation in the city of Bielefeld. Soon the congregation became self-sufficient and now meets in two churches in Bielefeld.

This congregation now considers itself Mennonite Brethren. It initiated a Russian radio program in 1975 and in 1977 sent Fridolin and Eva Janzen as their first missionaries to Brazil. Since 1979 the Bielefeld congregation has regularly conducted evangelization events. Through a Bible school run by the congregation beginning in 1985, more than 200 persons formed by the two-year schooling program are now active in congregational ministries and in mission.

The first *kirchliche* Mennonite congregation was established in Neuwied in 1977, three years after the first MB congregation in Espelkamp. Thirty believers separated themselves from the large Mennonite congregation that had been in existence since 1681. This was historic since Neuwied now became the first locality in Germany to have two Mennonite churches (*kirchlich*). Initially it seemed unthinkable that there could be two congregations bearing the same name in one locality.[57] When the same thing happened some years later in Espelkamp, it was less upsetting. The congregation in Neuwied grew steadily, not only through immigration, but also through conversions and baptisms. This Neuwied Mennonite congregation now has three church buildings in Neuwied and a fourth in Rengsdorf. The total membership in Neuwied in 2004 was 560 persons.

The Gebetshaus (church building) of the Bielefeld congregation.

The first Mennonite Church (*kirchlich*) in Bielefeld should also be mentioned. It was formed in 1980. It existed first as a branch of the Bechterdissen congregation (Leopoldshöhe), and then grew rapidly. By 2005 eight *Bethäuser* (sanctuaries) had been built for about 3,000 believer-members.

In this way, through the new immigration as well as through evangelization, conversion and baptism, more and more congregations emerged. Within two years of the founding of the first congregation in Paderborn (1972), eight other *Aussiedler* congregations had been established in Germany. Within five years the number of new congregations totaled twenty-three; by 1987, about sixty congregations had been established. In the next eleven years through 1998, a further 300 congregations were established through immigration and divisions. Nine of these 360 congregations had already been established before 1972 through Mennonite war refugees. Because these nine now consisted of a high percentage of *Aussiedler*, they are considered part of this group of congregations. In addition ten congregations of similar origin belong to West German church unions (BEFG Baptists, Freie Ev. Gemeinden). By 2004 there was a total of 420 new Free Church congregations.

Unique Aspects of these Church Plantings

The immigrant congregations always began on their own initiative, but were warned and discouraged from establishing their own congregations. Leaders from Canada viewed it as dividing the church of Jesus Christ, and indigenous German congregations expected the immigrant members to join their churches. After the assistance given to the new citizens, these new churches were seen as a sign of thanklessness. The old established Mennonite churches and indigenous German Baptists found it very difficult to accept and understand this trend among the *Aussiedler*. Later, Mennonites from the Netherlands and abroad provided major assistance for church building.

One phenomenon that the established German population rejected decisively was the so-called isolation into ghetto churches. The immigrant congregations, however, did not regard their stance as isolationist, but rather as obedience to the Word of the Lord. "You are not of this world" (John 17:16) therefore they could not cooperate with those who, according to *Aussiedler* understanding, were following the world. Further, they felt their isolation rested on mutuality, and the *Aussiedler* were used to being pushed into isolation.

In specific sections of Germany the proportion of immigrants reached 10 percent of the population, e.g. in Augustdorf. In Espelkamp, immigrants constituted 9,000 out of 27,000 citizens. It is understandable that the natives have felt squeezed. Some cities therefore have declared a halt to accepting more immigrants. At times older immigrant congregations put a hold on new member applications, because they could not promise to meet the expectations of the new and it would lead to unpleasant differences among believers. Therefore some established congregations offered assistance to the newer immigrants to establish their own new congregations.

Since the unification of Germany, the government has attempted to foster the settlement of Germans from the former Soviet Union in the former East Germany. The new immigrants perceive this as a disadvantage and attempt to move to the western provinces as soon as legally possible. About half of them had succeeded by 2000. Those belonging to the free churches are also part of this trend.

Staff members from the ABD (the earlier MUB) under the direction of Hermann Heidebrecht, and volunteers from immigrant congregations in the west provide aid to help the *Aussiedler* get established in eastern Germany. In 2000 approximately 3,000–3,500 families of free church background lived in towns and cities of the former East Germany. Thanks to assistance from the west, about twenty growing congregations, branches and house groups that include 400–500 believers have emerged.

The new congregations have adopted a great variety of names. Little value is placed on the historic names. The words "Baptist" and "Mennonite" get dropped in favour of the word "Free" (Free congregation, Free Church). When a group leaves a congregation in order to form a new one, in most cases the designation of the mother church is not carried over into the new name. Here the immigrant congregations are part of a general trend, since among congregations in the west confessionalism and denominationalism are suspect, whereas the idea of a network seems to be preferred when working together.

Immigrant (Aussiedler) *Churches and their Church Unions*

By 1994 eleven groups of churches had formed, all of whom had a Russian German character, but which also differed from each other. The majority of the congregations belong to a union. Some groups of congregations have been registered as voluntary societies (*Verein*) under a common name. Other groups have a common leadership without organizing as a society or union. One group of churches relate to each other as the "unaffiliated churches." Still other congregations function quite independently. Till now there has been only minimal cooperation among the unions or societies. Membership transfer is rare. Most congregations and unions are active in some form of mission and humanitarian aid. In virtually all of these groups there are Mennonite congregations. Often one senses a degree of congregational patriotism. But this does not depend on the name Baptist or Mennonite, but more on the earnestness and the ethical norms of the congregation.

Distinctives in the Life of Russian Mennonites

Russian immigrant congregations stand out because of their singing in worship: congregational song, choirs and groups. The songs consist less of the heavy chorales or the rather light modern choruses; mostly they are personal gospel songs, often translated American songs, which already were known in Russia. The newer songs are often sung with the aid of an overhead projector; otherwise a songbook is used.

Usually singing is done with instrumental accompaniment. Most congregations try to establish an orchestra. In the early years there were annual choral festivals, consisting of choirs in a union of churches, or organized by a group of congregations. In the 1990s Christmas carol singing in local congregations became a favourite, where the native population is also invited.

The Sunday morning worship service remains the high point in the life of faith. Attendance at worship is usually about one third higher than membership. The two or three additional meetings held during the week have a lower attendance.

Russian German congregations believe and teach that each person must be converted if he/she does not want to perish. This is also the position of the Evangelical Lutheran *Brüdergemeinden.* Not only do the *Aussiedler* churches conduct special evangelization services, but in virtually every sermon there is a call to decision. Most *Aussiedler* reject small circles meeting in homes and know little about friendship evangelism.

Nevertheless these congregations grew in the final years of the 1990s more through conversions in Germany than through immigration. Most of the children from member families (about three quarters) convert and join the church. In addition, over one quarter of those baptized (in the congregations researched) came from families where there has been neither active faith nor close ties to a church. This shows that the immigrant congregations are also reaching families outside their own circle.

Congregations with their own Buildings (Prayer Houses)

The immigrant free church congregations were prepared to meet for worship almost anywhere, but very quickly attempted to buy or build their own "prayer houses" (church buildings). It is through these shared, voluntary and tireless building projects that the *Aussiedler* have gained the most positive notoriety within the native German population. Initially the prayer houses consisted mostly of a large meeting hall and a dining hall for the many festivals. At present additional rooms for children and youth work are included in building plans.

Prayer house Düren

Education, schooling and training are not equally valued among Russian Germans churches. Primary schooling is generally affirmed as good and necessary, but not necessarily the list of courses offered in German primary schools. Sex education is a point of conflict. Practical trades are more strongly endorsed for advanced education, but an increasing number of youth currently choose university education. Many young people also attend Bible Schools, but not all go with the blessing of their congregations.

The Russian Germans, the Baptist-Mennonite free churches included, are an ethnic community with many young people. Of the 340,000 Mennonite-Baptist persons of the free church tradition originally having come from the former USSR, there were at least 100,000 young people between the ages of six and twenty in 2004. They fill up the worship services on Sundays, sing in the choirs, and meet together during the week. They usually participate in many of the service opportunities. That Russian German youth also make up a majority in the juvenile delinquent centers is a common claim, but official state-sponsored research does not substantiate the allegation. There are young people from free church traditions, including from Mennonite homes, serving sentences in prison. Only one is one too many. Nevertheless, those families that maintain ties to faith and church do not usually present candidates for the prisons.[58]

Baptist-Mennonite congregations show an increasing vision for mission. At first they sent humanitarian aid to the former Soviet Union, linking it with the proclamation of the Gospel. But over many years they also have assisted with church planting in eastern Europe. Subsequent to the collapse of the Wall in 1989 and the reunification of Germany in 1990, there have been more and more church planting initiatives in the former East Germany. So far, the "reached" are mostly fellow Russian Germans who settled there. Native Germans are reached by the evangelistic efforts, and there are conversions, but few become members of the Russian German congregations. Native Germans as members in Russian German congregations represented only one to two percent of the total membership in 2004.

Believers from the east are afraid of anything that sounds ecumenical. The knowledge that the Orthodox Church and the Baptist Union in the USSR were part of the World Council of Churches has made them cautious. From that perspective they often view church unions, associations and even mere cooperation between congregations in a locality with skepticism, and even refuse to participate.

Fundamentally the Russian Germans, as good inheritors of Anabaptism, have a high view of Scripture and a high ethical sensibility. In practice, sometimes ethical stances are argued that are not truly biblical in their basis, but are based in tradition. On the other hand, ethics is seen by many not as an issue of holiness or sanctification, but as a means of salvation. As a result, assurance of salvation comes into doubt. Generally speaking, the *Aussiedler* Christians are widely respected as industrious and honest workers. They represent an element of stability in society, in the sense that Jesus called his disciples to be "the salt of the earth and a light unto the world."

The Baptist and Mennonite Wings within the Immigrant Baptist-Mennonite Churches

Because of their common history and theology, Baptist and Mennonite immigrant congregations cannot be understood apart from each other. Yet they can be distinguished, since each group has managed to preserve some of its unique identity.[59]

Baptist resettler congregations are almost three times as numerous as Mennonite congregations, in 1998, 40,000 compared to 22,000 members, 258 congregations over against 98. The average growth of the Baptists during the last five years before 1998 was almost three times as high as compared to the Mennonite immigrant congregations. There is no obvious reason for the more rapid growth of one group over the other. Perhaps a remark by Ross T. Bender, a former president of the MWC can apply also to *Aussiedler* growth: "Baptists do mission wherever they go."[60] Subsequent statistics to 2004 show no change in the Mennonite and Baptist patterns.

When asked about their confessional membership, it is common that MBs and Baptists will answer: "Baptist and Brethren—they are the same." That indicates a certain confessional broad-mindedness that should be honoured. Congregational switching between MB and Baptist churches can be observed. Church (*kirchlich*) Mennonites show a stronger self identity, and there is little switching of membership among them. Within Baptist congregations 56.7 percent have a Mennonite background. Within Mennonite congregations, 19.1 percent are not of Mennonite origin, meaning that 80.9 percent were ethnically Mennonite. The differences between these congregations are minor today. According to Löwen (1989) and Reimer (1996), the differences are so minimal that they could easily form a common union.[61]

The Expansion of the Russian Mennonites: a Global Community?

We can assume that in many countries where Mennonite Christians are found, there will also be some Russian Mennonites. Aside from the first three major immigrations from Russia to various countries, there were also individual families who found their home anywhere in the world. The conservative Russian Mennonites moved from Canada to Mexico (1922) and to Paraguay (1926). Together with others they then moved to Bolivia (1954), Belize (1958) and other countries. Some went from Germany to Australia.

As new immigrants they often made major contributions to the agricultural and industrial development of their new homelands. Mennonites are numbered among anthropologists (P. G. Hiebert), missiologists (G. W. Peters), pedagogues (A. H. Unruh), writers (P. J. Klassen; P. P. Klassen) and among other professions. Above all, God has used them again and again as witnesses in the new place of settlement. They also have been sent as missionaries to non-Christian lands as well as to those already reached by the gospel. Mostly, they have moved from country to country for conscience sake, to *maintain* their faith. But God wanted more from them. Therefore God has re-awakened them, filled them with God's Spirit, and sent them out again to *spread* their faith. Although Russian Mennonites settled in villages and colonies, they never fully isolated themselves. The Mennonites in Russia felt themselves to be a brotherhood of like-minded Christians.

Mennonites in Russia and the Diaspora have always had a keen interest in one another and other Mennonites. Some of the inspiration for Mennonite World Conference developed in Russia already prior to World War I. In spring of 1912 a minister Regier of Mountain Lake, Minnesota, visited Heinrich Pauls, minister of the Lemberg Mennonite church (today Lwiw), Ukraine. The two agreed that it would be good for Mennonites from around the world to meet. Pauls published a proposal for an "Internationale Mennonitenkonferenz" at Lemberg for the week prior to Pentecost, 1913.[62] At the time, the idea bore no fruit, and in two years, World War I shook the nations.

When the first Mennonite World Conference was held in Basel in 1925, two Russian Mennonite delegates travelled to attend, but were not allowed to cross the Swiss-German border. Conference participants met the two on the border at the toll gate. The first Russian Mennonite delegates who were able to attend a MWC Assembly were present in Wichita in 1978, and delegates have participated in all subsequent gatherings. Mennonite "trans-national links" include Mennonites from Russia.

Is this the End of the Russian Mennonites?

If there is a grand total (2005) of 280,000–290,000 Russian German free church immigrants in Germany, of which 170,000–180,000 are Mennonites or of Mennonite origin, are there any Mennonites left in Russia today? "Is the story of 200 years of life and suffering among the people of Russia coming to an end?" asked Gerlach already 15 years ago.[63] It is an old question. Walter Quiring published a picture book about Mennonite life in Russia up to 1940, giving it the title *Als Ihre Zeit Erfüllt War* (When their time was fulfilled). The sub-title was: *150 Jahre Bewährung in Russland* (Tested and Preserved for 150 Years in Russia). Peter J. Klassen spoke of the "disintegration of the Russian Mennonite world"[64] whereby he described the beginning of the end at the time of World War I. And Gerhard Wölk wrote:

> With the celebration of the 200th anniversary of the Russian Mennonites in the Soviet Union (1989) the last chapter of the history of the German Mennonites in Russia was written. In light of the continuing immigration wave and the continuing political situation in the Soviet Union, it is clear that those who want to remain

> German, have no other alternative but to emigrate to
> the Republic of Germany. For the remainder, ethnic
> assimilation can no longer be stopped. The time of
> German Mennonitism in Soviet Russia has reached its
> inescapable end. [65]

Wölk went on to say, however, "to be Mennonite is above all a faith orientation, open to any tribe and nation." That is, it is possible for Mennonite congregations to exist within all the language groups of the USSR, provided mission efforts continue. This was the idea that Walter Sawatsky sensed at the 200th anniversary celebrations in Zaporozh'e: "The Russian/Soviet Mennonites are contemplating religious freedom, emigration and the prospect of the evangelization and moral renewal of the Soviet people. As they do so, their issues once again become the issues for all those of Russian Mennonite origin."[66]

It is a fact that today very few persons remain within the former Soviet Union countries who still call themselves Mennonite or have Mennonite roots. Is that a sad fate? Is the end of the Mennonites in Russia of God? Or has this Dutch-German Mennonite group of Anabaptist origin fulfilled its task there, and may now return to the historic homeland?

Those are questions we cannot answer here. But the question about the task needs more focus in conclusion. What was the task of the Mennonites in Russia? Were the Mennonites called to Russia by God? What was the goal, exactly? Or were the Mennonites carrying out an assignment on behalf of the Russian Empire? As to the latter, we know that this entailed making the land fertile; it included building up model agriculture from which the peasants were to learn how to be good farmers, thus adding to the building of the civilization of the Empire. The original Manifesto also spoke of mission to Muslims. Naturally also, the invitation from Catherine II included the establishment and development of a new standard of living for the immigrants. The immigrants to Russia certainly contributed to fulfilling these multiple expectations. Nevertheless, our deeds, as the Apostle Paul said of his own, are always partial, incomplete. But they remain good deeds nevertheless.

What is the prospect for the Mennonites in Russia today? Very few remain, but a few call themselves Mennonite and have chosen to remain, in order to build the church. For example, there is Andreas Peters in Novosibirsk, and Gerhard Warkentin in Karaganda. Others work closely with Baptists in Omsk, Saran, Bishkek and in other places, playing leading roles in building the church, in mission and Bible school training. Statistically their number is quite small, perhaps less than 1,000.

Most who have immigrated to Germany have not forgotten Russia. Even if all the Dutch-German descendants of the Anabaptists were to immigrate to the West, they could still—as the American Anabaptists go as missionaries to Africa—return to Russia as missionaries and build Mennonite congregations. It has already begun.

Translation: Victor Duerksen and Walter Sawatsky

Mennonite Settlements in the Russian Empire

Mission Efforts in Europe: New Congregations, New Questions

by Neal Blough

Introduction

This chapter tells the surprising story of a twentieth century re-establishment of relationships between European and North American Mennonites and how it affected the churches in Europe. Their history is extremely intertwined. European Mennonites began moving to North America already at the end of the seventeenth century, and continued through the twentieth century.[1] At their origins, North American Mennonites were Europeans who had joined the flow of emigration towards the "new world." As time went on, relationships continued, flourished and waned. Family ties, linguistic and cultural commonalities, correspondence and continuing emigration allowed relationships to be maintained between Mennonites and Amish of Swiss, Alsatian, German or Dutch-Russian origins on both sides of the Atlantic. Later, North American Mennonites became more culturally American than European, their church structures were diverse and sometimes the result of separations, and English became the language used in their contacts with Europeans. The various geographical origins in Europe of North American Mennonites, the different periods of emigration which contributed to differing mentalities, and a fairly "schismatic" nineteenth century, created a surprising variety of Mennonite groups in Canada and the United States.[2]

Our story is one of North American Mennonite service and mission agencies coming to Europe in the twentieth century, one of re-established relationships between "cousins" who had become more and more distant, who no longer really knew each other. It is a story of projects and churches being born, of successes and failures, of cooperation and friendships, of tension and mutual misunderstandings.

233

Outside of continuing family ties, mission was one of the reasons and one of the ways that Mennonites from Europe and North America stayed in touch with each other in the nineteenth century. Dutch Mennonites, soon to be joined by Mennonites from south Russia and Germany, were sending missionaries to Java already in 1851.[3] Mennonites from Germany who settled in Iowa starting in 1839 were quite aware of the mission efforts of German Mennonites and were sending contributions to the Dutch Mennonite Mission already in 1857.[4]

A Mennonite group in Pennsylvania also took an interest in the mission work of Dutch and German Mennonites in the mid-nineteenth century and began sending money to the Dutch Mennonite missionary society. When Russian Mennonites began emigrating to North America in the 1870s, some of them affiliated with these same "General Conference" Mennonites who were supporting the European mission efforts.

World War I and the Russian Revolution created a new urgency and new possibilities for transatlantic Mennonite relationships. In 1917, the "Old" Mennonite church organized the "Relief Commission for War Sufferers."[5] Working under the auspices of the American Friends Service Committee, some sixty North American Mennonite volunteers were able to do relief and service work, mostly in France, but also in Germany, Poland, Austria and Russia.

The extreme difficulties experienced by Russian Mennonites during the revolutionary period became a source of major concern. The Relief Commission sent three workers from France to investigate larger needs in Russia.[6] In 1919, California Mennonites raised money and gathered clothing and supplies for suffering Mennonites in Siberia, and in July of 1920, a commission dispatched by Russian Mennonites arrived in Kansas and reported to an inter-Mennonite group. Apparently, the Russians were aware of the rather splintered nature of North American Mennonite reality, and the commission "asked that the North American response to needs in Russia not be fragmented into separate conference projects but be a strong, united, all-Mennonite effort."

Meeting of the *Deutsche Mennonitenhilfe* in Oberursel, Germany on June 28, 1922. The meeting was called together by the Dutch pastor F. C. Fleischer from the Dutch *Fonds voor Buitenlandsche Nooden*. Present were representatives from Russia, Germany, Switzerland, the USA and the Netherlands.

This crisis of famine among Mennonites in south Russia became the occasion for the creation of the Mennonite Central Committee (MCC) in 1920. Its first meeting in Chicago, on September 27, 1920, brought together representatives from seven different Mennonite conferences and relief organizations to respond to the plea for help from Mennonites in Russia, but also to formulate a common response to the famine from the North American churches.[7] Several Dutch Mennonites also visited Russia or worked there among the needy for some time, in cooperation with MCC.[8]

The situation of Mennonites in the Soviet Union thrust different groups of North American Mennonites into a common project that confronted the harsh realities of the political world.[9] Nevertheless, North American inter-Mennonite cooperation was not easy. MCC was not a marriage born of affection, but a cautious contract born of necessity. Not having anticipated longer-term needs, in 1924 North American Mennonites were talking of disbanding MCC. This did not happen and the situation in Russia kept the different constituencies of the MCC concretely involved in the life of European Mennonites. Canadian Mennonites especially helped in resettling around 20,000 Russian Mennonites by 1927, and after 1930 MCC helped Russian Mennonites resettle in Paraguay.[10] The beginnings of Mennonite World Conference and its European gatherings in the 1920s and 30s also contributed to building bridges across the Atlantic. Political circumstances and a sense of trans-Atlantic solidarity were thus major factors in the first efforts of North American inter-Mennonite collaboration. Nevertheless, mistrust and even suspicion between Mennonite groups in North America was common into the early 1940s and beyond.[11] The real starting point for inter-Mennonite cooperation among North Americans once again found its origin in European events, with the coming of World War II.

> The program in Italy ... consisted of services to displaced people in UNRAA refugee camps. We have had twelve MCC workers loaned to UNRAA who have served as welfare workers in camps. During the past summer, an MCC service has been set up in northern Italy among the Waldensians. We now have a Center at Torre Pellice with a number of our workers stationed there who have charge of material aid distribution consisting of 126 tons of supplies valued at $57,081.11 sent over for this purpose.
>
> – Atlee Beachey, 1947

A Mennonite worker brings food and clothes to a Waldensian orphanage in Torre Pellice on a bicycle, 1947.

MCC in Europe after WWII: Re-established Relationships

The story of Mennonite Central Committee's involvement in Europe prior to, during and immediately after the Second World War has already been told, and only those aspects directly related to our story will be mentioned here.[12] Preceding and after the outbreak of hostilities in Europe in 1939, MCC maintained a presence in several countries (Spain, France, Poland and Germany) as long as possible. Once the war was over, amidst immense destruction and suffering, MCC undertook a major relief effort in many of the countries that had been directly affected by the deadly struggle.

One result of these programs was a renewal and strengthening of relationships between European and North American Mennonites. MCC had offices not only in Frankfurt (Germany) and Basel (Switzerland), but until the late 1960s also in Amsterdam at Koningslaan 48, which also functioned as a channel of contact between North American and Dutch Mennonites, including several seminary students. The post-war MCC experience had allowed many North American Mennonites to have a first-hand experience of the European context and revealed possibilities for continued involvement. As relief efforts tapered off and became less and less necessary, the question was posed of continuing a North American Mennonite presence in Europe. Interest was shown on all sides and MCC, along with its constituent conference members, began to envisage how a more "spiritual" (or church-oriented) and less "material" (or relief-oriented) continuing presence might be possible. Different Mennonite mission agencies began considering the possibility of a European presence.

The question was complicated from the outset. As we have already seen, Mennonite Central Committee was by far the most visible institutional expression of North American Mennonite presence in Europe. Europeans saw and experienced a "common front" which did not accurately represent the divided nature of the North American Mennonite scene.[13] For their part, North Americans began to discover the variegated characteristics of European Mennonites, who were divided into different national bodies with important historical and theological differences among themselves and few, if any, institutional expressions of unity. The diversity on both sides became a major challenge for all concerned.

In the summer of 1950, the Mennonite Central Committee organized a study tour which, along with MCC personnel, included representatives of various North American Mennonite mission agencies.[14] One of the goals was to explore the possibility of these mission agencies doing work in Europe.

Between July 29 and August 14, 1950, the study group visited various MCC project locations in Europe and consulted with European Mennonite church leaders in Germany, the Netherlands, France, Switzerland and Luxembourg. The Europeans expressed gratitude for the assistance provided by MCC

Missions represented on the MCC summer tour of 1950

- General Conference Mission (binational)
- Mennonite Brethren Mission (binational)
- Mennonite Board of Missions (binational)
- Brethren in Christ Mission (binational)
- Conservative Amish-Mennonite Mission (USA)
- Eastern Mennonite Missions (Lancaster Conference, Pennsylvania) (USA)

and recognized that new bridges were being built across the Atlantic. While some concern was raised that the European churches had not always been adequately informed about MCC's intentions and programs, the European Mennonites consulted during the trip expressed interest in the possibility of continuing help from North America in such areas as youth work, Christian education, mission materials, etc.

On the basis of this study tour, the MCC executive committee recommended that further aid be given to the European churches and saw MCC as "the channel through which this help reaches our European brethren," although it was clear that since MCC was not the "mission agency" of the various constituent groups, "some special needs may be referred to individual groups for administration and/or support."

At this point the organizational differences between a unified Inter-Mennonite MCC and the various North American Mennonite denominations began to render the situation more complicated. Already before the study tour, one US Mennonite Mission had begun work in Sicily. The MCC report recognized that "the constituent groups ... should be recognized as having freedom in working in non-Mennonite areas in Europe,"

At least eight Mennonite missions were established in Europe between 1949 and 1953. The first of these was the mission in Sicily, established in 1949 and administered by the Virginia Board of Missions and Charities. In the following year the Elkhart board established a mission in Belgium and the Conservative Mennonites one in Germany. A year later the Conservative and the Eastern Mennonite mission boards opened a work in Luxembourg. The Elkhart board began work in England in 1952, in France in 1953, and in Israel the same year. The Mennonite Brethren established a mission program in Germany and Austria in the same decade, while the Beachy Amish began witnessing in Germany.

but also expressed the desire that "groups contemplating work in such areas should be encouraged to counsel and advise with the MCC for any help and suggestions that the latter agency might be in a position to give." In any case, the period immediately preceding and following 1950 saw a flurry of North American mission interest and involvement in western Europe.

Ten years later, according to an MCC report in January 1961, there were almost fifty North American Mennonite mission personnel representing these different agencies at work in Europe.[15]

New Mission Projects in Europe

The various strands of our story cannot all be told in detail. Some are quite well documented and others not.[16] The stories that follow do not exhaust the history, but aim to provide a picture of how the various mission agencies went about their activities. We have chosen to describe projects that took place in countries where European Mennonites were already present, or projects that developed relationships with European Mennonite churches.

Virginia Mennonite Mission Board

Not all Mennonite mission efforts in Europe were the fruit of direct planning, strategy or experience with MCC relief work. The Virginia Board of Missions and Charities began its work in Sicily as a follow-up to correspondence and ensuing relationships. A Sicilian woman, Franca Ceraulo, had a nephew in Elkhart, Indiana and through him, J. D. Graber of Mennonite Board of Missions and Charities in Elkhart, found out that Franca had requested baptism. He contacted Virginia Mennonites who were planning a visit to Italy. So it was that in 1949, Lewis Martin and Jason Weaver, both Mennonites from Virginia, went to Sicily to look for Franca Ceraulo. Weaver, a deacon in his home congregation, indeed baptized her.[17]

Franca Ceraulo with missionaries Mr. & Mrs. Lewis Martin

Soon after the first baptism, *Centro Agape*, the first Mennonite church in Italy, was born (1949), and a continuing stream of Virginia Mennonites served as missionaries, church planters and pastors.

The first Italian Mennonite Conference was held at Palermo, Sicily, in April of 1960. At the time this chapter was written, the *Chiesa Evangelica Mennonita Italiana* (Italian Evangelical Mennonite Church) is made up of eight congregations (six in Sicily and two in southern Italy) with 258 baptised members.

Mennonite Board of Missions and Charities [18]

Planning for MBMC involvement in Europe began in 1949 with approval of the plans for a Mennonite Gospel Centre in London, as soon as suitable personnel could be found.[19] It would be 1953 before Quintus and Miriam Leatherman arrived to open the London Mennonite Centre at the same place where MCC had earlier established its English headquarters and children's home.[20] The first workers sent to the continent, David and Wilma Shank, arrived in Belgium in 1950. The work in Belgium was to follow up on work done by the Mennonite Relief Committee, which already in 1947 had urged MBMC to "prepare itself for this task at the earliest possible time, so that the mission effort in Belgium may capitalize to the full upon the relief work of that country."[21] Orley and Jane Swartzentruber arrived in Paris in 1952, followed by Robert and Lois Witmer in 1956.

The projects in these countries varied according to the context. In England the London Mennonite Centre welcomed international students and saw the birth of a local congregation, the London Mennonite Fellowship (at present known as the Wood Green Mennonite Church). In 1981 the Centre ended its student ministry and became a teaching centre for the development of Anabaptist theology and the peace witness in the British context.

The London Mennonite Centre had been influenced among others by the community ideas of "Reba Place" and by the publications of the "Sojourners Community" in Washington. However, these high ideals also led to a period of struggle and pain. An unpublished evaluation-paper (1982) says: "Continuing concern in [the] congregation in which many members live in households in Highgate and others live at a distance by themselves: we must be vigilant in working against a two-level congregation of household members and 'outsiders.'" The picture shows members of the present Wood Green Mennonite Church in London, participating at an anti-Iraq war demonstration.

In Belgium, a multi-faceted ministry developed, based on the principle of working with other Protestants while keeping in touch with European Mennonites. The year 1953 saw the opening of the "Foyer Fraternel," with a Mennonite Centre, chapel and library. The same year saw the birth of the "Brussels East" congregation which would later affiliate with the French Mennonite conference. Inter-Protestant projects involved work among Spanish immigrants, who formed a small congregation that worshiped in Spanish, and with the Rixsensart Protestant congregation which was established in 1955. Jules Lambotte, a Belgian who associated himself with the work in Brussels, was involved in a publishing ministry, the founding of a congregation and a "Centre évangélique" in the small town of Flavion. In 1980, the Brussels Mennonite Centre was "re-founded" with ministries focusing on mediation, a peace library, dialogue with NATO, and drama.

The situation in France was somewhat different because of the possibilities of collaborating directly with French Mennonites. MBMC located its ministries in the suburbs of Paris and in 1954 a local organization called the *Mission Mennonite Française* (MMF or French Mennonite Mission) was founded as the institutional means to facilitate cooperation between North American and French Mennonites in Paris. The first Parisian Mennonite congregation was founded in 1954 in the

southern suburb of Châtenay-Malabry. Work among the mentally handicapped children and adults developed as well and led to the establishment of two institutions that functioned on the basis of government funding.[22] The *Foyer Grebel*, a centre for international students, was begun in 1976 in Saint Maurice and a multi-racial congregation that grew out of this ministry was founded in 1981.

A multi-racial church is born in Paris, the *Foyer Grebel* Christian Community in 1980.

From almost the beginning, North American and European Mennonites, via EMEK, jointly sponsored the *Foyer Grebel* project. In 1989 the Paris Mennonite Centre began functioning in Saint Maurice and several years thereafter, as had been the case in London, the ministry among international students ceased its activities. Work was focused more directly on Anabaptist history and theology, teaching, and inter-church relationships. A third Parisian congregation was born in 1997 in the northern Parisian suburb of Lamorlaye and the Saint Maurice congregation moved to Villeneuve le Compte, east of Paris, in 2003. All three congregations have become members of the French Mennonite Conference (AEEMF).

Because of contacts developed in London, peace-making and reconciliation ministries began in Northern Ireland (in conjunction with MCC) in 1978. Spanish immigrants from Belgium moved to Burgos and Barcelona, and together with congregations coming out of Mennonite Brethren and Brethren in Christ mission work, the beginnings of a small Spanish Mennonite conference were born. In order to facilitate communication and contacts between projects and churches, as well as to foster contacts with European Mennonites, MBM workers and their European colleagues and friends began

An example of transatlantic cooperation: Board meeting of the Mission Mennonite Française in Canada. From left to right: Pierre Sommer, Robert Witmer, Pierre Widmer, René Kennel, André Kennel, Albert Klopfenstein, Max Schowalter.

regular meetings (called "Colloquium") in 1975. These meetings bring together people from the various countries already mentioned as well as from the Netherlands, Switzerland, Finland, Sweden and Lithuania, and continue to serve as a means of establishing relationships between European Mennonites and these new projects and congregations.

Eastern Mennonite Board of Missions and Charities

Concern for the situation of European Jews led Isaac Baer, a Mennonite from Maryland, to Hungary with MCC in 1949. His convictions about mission among the Jews of Europe were shared with members of the Eastern Board (Lancaster Pennsylvania Conference). Exploration of this concern led to consultation with Mennonites in France and Luxembourg, and after deciding that such a direction was not the best way to proceed, the Eastern Board decided to begin its mission in Europe in the region of northeast France and the Duchy of Luxembourg. The first missionary couple (Clarence and Lela Fretz) arrived in Luxembourg in September of 1951. They were accompanied by Harvey and Mildred Miller, who were sent by the Conservative Mennonite Conference Mission (later known as Rosedale Mennonite Missions).

From the very beginning, Eastern Board's work was carried on in cooperation with Mennonites in both France (Pierre Widmer) and Luxembourg (Joseph Oesch). Horst Gerlach, a German Mennonite who had studied at Eastern Mennonite College in Virginia, helped formulate the mission's three-pronged ministry in the following terms: witness to the un-churched, witness to the semi-religious (those with a half-way commitment to a religious group), and help for European Mennonites.[23] In order to implement such ministries, a variety of activities were organized first of all in Luxembourg, and later on in France. Language study created contacts and channels for sharing very early on, and the work proceeded with personal contacts, literature distribution and visitation. In June of 1953, a weekend Bible Conference was held in Dudelange, Luxembourg. A summer Bible school began the same year, and the Bible school contacts with children gave way to craft classes with children. A summer Bible camp for children also functioned well for a number of years. In 1956 a winter Bible class began for young people, including European Mennonites. Summer and winter camps were held for many years: a campsite was secured, and a vacation chalet built in 1971 served as a year-round retreat used by Christian groups from Holland, Germany and France.

In 1960 a new chapel was built in Dudelange, and in the following year official responsibility for the mission program was taken on by the Luxembourg Mennonite Association. Unfortunately, the few congregations in Luxembourg eventually dropped their ties with other European Mennonites and now exist as independent evangelical churches.

Eastern Board's work in France began in 1954, and from the beginning was carried out in collaboration with French Mennonites. Glen and Elisabeth Good arrived in 1954 and settled in Thionville, in the region of Lorraine, close to the border with Luxembourg. Work moved quickly toward the establishment of a new congregation in Thionville. Sunday services began in 1961, and a chapel and youth centre were dedicated in April of 1965. In 1967, a French Mennonite couple, Michel and Marlise Klopfenstein moved to Thionville to help with the project; they took on pastoral responsibility in 1970. From that point on, work was done to establish another congregation in the small industrial city of Longwy. The influence of the charismatic movement was important in the beginning and in the continuing life of this congregation, whose meeting hall was dedicated in 1971. Vincent Fernandez, (French, of Spanish origin) became pastor of the Longwy congregation in 1977. Both the Thionville and Longwy congregations affiliated with the French Mennonite Conference.

In 1962, the Associated Mennonite Mission of Lorraine (AMML) became the institutional basis for Eastern Board's cooperative work in France. AMML became the partner agency for the Eastern Board in France, but also developed its own mission projects.

Just as the work in Luxembourg spilled over into France, it also had repercussions in Germany. In 1955 work began in Neumühle as a follow up to previous activity by two young German Mennonite women, Dora and Maria Lichti. In 1957, Jeltje de Jong from the Netherlands also became involved, so cooperation with European Mennonites was a part of the project from the very beginning.

The work in Neumühle was patterned after what had been done in Luxembourg: home visitation, summer Bible school, craft classes and a lending library were the primary activities. In 1977 the work was transferred to the German Mennonite Mission Committee (DMMK), for whom it became the first mission project within Germany. A small congregation was founded and still exists today as part of the German Mennonite conference. A variety of continuing projects were carried out in partnership with a newly-founded German Mennonite Home Mission, begun in 1969 by a group of Mennonites in Bavaria. Together with *Heimatsmission*, Eastern Board began to work in southern Germany, in Munich, Freising, and Dachau.

The staff of the Summer Bible school in Neumühle, ca. 1960, which drew about 120 attendants yearly.

Several congregations were founded together with the *Heimatsmission* but in 1990, along with the newly-founded churches, the organization became independent of the German Mennonite conference. EMM has continued its work in Europe up to the present day and still has partnership relationships—involving either finances or personnel—with the French and the German Mennonites.

Conservative Mennonite Mission Board

The Conservative Mennonite Mission Board (known today as Rosedale Mennonite Missions) was represented on the MCC study tour of 1950 by Elmer G. Swartzendruber.[24] John Gingerich, a young MCC worker from the Conservative Conference arrived in Espelkamp, Germany in 1949 and from that point on, Espelkamp became well-known among members of the conference and their mission board. The Espelkamp project became the focal point for the Conservative Mennonite Mission efforts in Europe, alongside cooperative work with Eastern Mennonite Missions in Luxembourg.[25] The Espelkamp project began as a follow-up partnership with MCC in October of 1950 and continued under the sole responsibility of the Conservative Mennonite Mission beginning in 1952.[26] The program consisted of continued distribution of relief in the early years, then the building of houses, personal evangelism and preaching in German churches.

There already was a local German Mennonite church with whom the missionaries had contact, but for theological reasons, total cooperation did not seem possible during the first several years. In 1958 a voluntary service centre and a new chapel, known as *Mennoniten Heim*, were built close to the local Mennonite church. For many, the *Mennoniten Heim* was seen more as a non-denominational mission effort than as Mennonite, but the mission con-

Bad Pyrmont congregation: Heinrich Boschmann baptizing in the river.

stantly dealt with the question of whether or not to found another local church.[27]

By the year 1976, the mission decided to transfer the program and properties of the *Mennoniten Heim* to another evangelical group, and possibly even the local Mennonite congregation. Willingness to consider the possibility of turning the project over to local Mennonites had to do with the development of the congregation. Immigration of Mennonites from Russia and Paraguay, who were theologically more conservative than many German Mennonites, apparently modified the theological perspective of the Espelkamp Mennonite church enough that the Rosedale Mission now felt comfortable with a transfer of the project. The transfer took place in 1978 when Rosedale

Mennonite Missions left Espelkamp and began work elsewhere in Germany. At this point, time and energy were spent with the planting and pastoring of a congregation in Bad Pyrmont, where Heinrich and Katharina Boschmann had been active beginning in 1975.[28]

Mennonite Brethren Missions

As much as, or perhaps more than for other groups, post-war MCC involvement in Europe was crucial for Mennonite Brethren mission efforts in Europe. The Mennonite Brethren had strong emotional and family ties in Europe. Given the fact that many Mennonite Brethren who lived in Russia were deeply affected by the War, it is not surprising that MB efforts focused on helping their "cousins." Neustadt and Neuwied were points of MCC involvement because of Mennonite (and Mennonite Brethren) refugees from the east who came for help.[29] Vienna was also a city where MCC began work early and helped Mennonite refugees from Poland and Russia.[30] These three cities were to become places of Mennonite Brethren mission involvement.

Much the same as had been the case for other North American Mennonite mission agencies, Mennonite Brethren missionaries followed up on MCC relief work by helping to establish new congregations of believers, many of whom were refugees. One conscious difference with other agencies was the existence of Mennonite Brethren refugees and a strong desire to help them in particular. One of the cities that was decisively helped was Neuwied on the Rhine. In addition to C. F. Klassen, the believers in Neuwied gratefully remember the early ministries of H. H. Janzen, C. C. Wall and H. K. Warkentin. They realized that the Polish and Russian Mennonite Brethren refugees who had not emigrated needed to organize themselves as an autonomous, local congregation. Consequently, on July 23, 1950, under the guidance of Cornelius C. and Anna Wall, the first Mennonite Brethren Church with twenty-three charter members was founded in the county of Neuwied.[31] The second congregation came to birth in Neustadt, where George H. and Marianne Jantzen arrived in 1958.[32]

Between 1950 and 1991, with the help of numerous Canadian and American mission workers, twelve Mennonite Brethren congregations were founded in various German cities, including Neuwied, Neustadt, Lage, and Bielefeld. At present there are fifteen Mennonite Brethren congregations banded together in the *Arbeitsgemeinschaft Mennonitischer Brüdergemeinden in Deutschland* (Conference of Mennonite Brethren Churches in Germany). It is clear that ethnic and family ties, plus a shared knowledge of the German language played an important part in the success of these efforts.

These church-planting efforts were not limited to northwest Germany, but also extended to Austria and from there to Bavaria, where a series of new congregations were planted over the years. Linz saw the birth of the first Mennonite Brethren congregation through contacts among the numerous refugee camps. In 1953, two missionary families (Gossen and Vogt) arrived in Linz, where together with Abe and Irene Neufeld they helped to found the first Mennonite Brethren congregation in Austria in 1955.[33] Similar work produced local churches in Steyr, Weis, Salzburg, Vienna, and in other cities. In 2005, there were six congregations who were a part of the *Mennonitische Freikirche Österreich* (Mennonite Free Churches of Austria).

The Austrians had close relationships in neighbouring Bavaria, which led to the birth of several congregations over the years. The first Bavarian congregation was born in 1970 in Traunreut. Others followed in Traunstein, Bad Reichenhall, Munich and elsewhere. These congregations have joined together to form the *Verband der Evangelischen Freikirchen Mennonitischer Brüdergemeinden in Bayern* (Association of Evangelical Mennonite Free Churches in Bavaria), which currently brings together seven congregations. The three different Mennonite Brethren conferences have united in the *Bund der Europäisch-Mennonitischen Brüdergemeinden* (European Conference of Mennonite Brethren Churches). Recent immigration into Germany has also resulted in the creation of some forty-five independent Mennonite Brethren congregations.

Mennonite Brethren church-planting efforts have extended to European countries with no historical Mennonite presence. In 1976 two couples from North America and one couple from Austria went to Spain to study language, culture and investigate places and possibilities for beginning a new work. Portugal would be next on the list.[34]

Missiological Approaches and Relationships between European and North American Mennonites

The initial motivation for a North American Mennonite presence in Europe was one with which all could agree, due to the vast amount of human need and suffering left in the wake of World War II. As material needs diminished and a more self-conscious missionary approach was adopted by various agencies, they began to reflect missiologically about their involvement. North American Mennonites had been involved in missionary efforts from the end of the nineteenth century onward, but these had all taken place in areas of the world outside of Europe. In 1950, American and Canadian Mennonites were still largely "ethnic" in character and had not yet developed extensive means and strategies for sharing the gospel with their North American neighbours. Secularized, war-torn western Europe would be a special challenge, one for which American missionaries in general, and Mennonites in particular, were probably not really prepared.

How did North American Mennonite missionaries understand Europe in general and European Mennonites in particular? It would probably be safe to say that most Mennonite missionaries in Europe shared a rather negative understanding of the spiritual state of Europe. This was evident when working in pre-Vatican II Catholic countries such as Italy, Spain, or Austria, where harassment of non-Catholics was a common practice. But it was also the case for other countries in which Mennonite churches had been present for many centuries. One can find several examples of pessimistic evaluations of the new "mission field," which basically reflect the Mennonite and/or Evangelical viewpoints of the mission agencies.

In the eyes of most mission agencies, the "Constantinian" state-church heritage of western Europe was a particularly difficult hurdle to overcome. Whether they were Catholic or Protestant, official churches dominated the religious scene and were perceived as either indifferent or self-sufficient. Mennonite missionaries basically saw Europe as a "spiritual wasteland."[35] Such a point of view could perhaps be understood as North American "arrogance," and in some cases it probably was. However, European churches and theology in general were indeed struggling with the violent legacy of two World Wars, the Russian Revolution, and increasing secularization.

> Europe has been shaped by state churches, whether Catholic or Protestant. In a 1968 report J. A. Toews wrote: "To establish free churches in Europe is not an easy task. Perhaps in no other area of our conference outreach do we face such a formidable religious establishment." "The greatest barrier," wrote G. H. Jantzen, missionary to Europe, "was tradition. With a church background they feel they have all that is needed."

Nevertheless, several North American Mennonites were aware of this struggle and of the major currents of European theology in the 1950s. Perhaps the most sophisticated effort to penetrate the European mentality from a missiological point of view came from David A. Shank, missionary in Belgium 1950–1972.[36] Shank was part of a group of young North American Mennonite intellectuals living and studying

...Dechristianized society does not in general recognize 'professional' missionaries, and a large part of it looks with suspicion and scorn at 'agents' of the church.... It is only as an integral part of formal society, as one who is 'in the world'—who has identified himself with society in the modern sense of the word—that a missionary is qualified to bear the message.

– David A. Shank

in Europe, who were influenced by Harold Bender's "recovery of the Anabaptist Vision," attempting to understand how Mennonite theology, ethics and mission could come to terms with twentieth century western culture.[37] It is important to note that especially in these post-war years, North American Mennonite theologians and historians continually came to Europe for doctoral studies. Their studies in Europe and contacts with European Mennonites allowed them to have important roles in the North American churches during the second half of the twentieth century. It also led some Mennonite mission agencies to foster renewal among European non-Mennonite Christians by drawing on the resources of the Anabaptist vision of church and discipleship.

It is also important to note that MCC, and in some cases mission agencies, consciously saw their work as expressing the "Anabaptist Vision" and its practical implications in terms of peace witness.

Theology and teaching were also seen as expressions of the church's mission. One concrete expression of such an approach was the joint founding (European Mennonites and MCC) of the European Mennonite Bible School (Bienenberg) in Liestal, Switzerland in 1950.[38] This school has played an important theological and practical role for congregations in Switzerland, France and Germany.

In many cases, Mennonite missionaries were not just "generic" representatives of North American evangelical missions. Those who came consciously as Mennonites were aware of the fact that their historical and theological roots were in Europe. This played a role in shaping their presence in Europe. Several mission agencies saw their presence in terms of historical continuity, as part of a larger ongoing history of Mennonites. It should also be noted that in the first generation of MCC and mission agency presence, Mennonites from various parts of North America and Europe—including the Dutch and the Alsatians, were able to communicate in the German language. Only quite recently, with the shift of the Alsatian Mennonites to the French language and the increasing use of English as a common means of communication in Europe, has German lost it capacity to function as an "inter-Mennonite" language.

Nevertheless, as has already been intimated, historical and family ties to Europe did not keep North American Mennonites from having a critical evaluation of their "cousins." North Americans sometimes considered themselves as those who had "escaped" and were now in the process of "returning" to those who had remained behind, suffering from the brutality of two world wars and bound in the traditions of a cold, formal church. This simply reflects the fact that a consciousness of historical and ethnic relationships did not do away with cultural and historical differences between North Americans and Europeans. These differences could lead to criticisms and tensions from both sides.

When MCC first began its relief work, it made a special effort to work together with already existing European Mennonite churches and structures. In theory, European Mennonite churches were recognized and were to be treated as partners. After the 1950 study tour in which MCC invited various mission agencies to visit European Mennonite leaders, MCC appears to have envisaged continuing recognition and partnership as the basis of any North American mission ventures in Europe. The first two recommendations of the executive committee report point in this direction.

Pacifist Reformed pastor André Trocmé had mobilized the entire village of Le Chambon-sur-Lignon to become a refuge for Jews fleeing the Nazi occupants of France. After the war Trocmé moved with his wife Magda just outside of Paris to Versailles, where he worked as general secretary of the International Fellowship of Reconciliation.

During a visit to Mennonite Publishing House in Scottdale Pennsylvania in 1953, Trocmé discovered that Mennonite missionaries Orley and Jane Swartzentruber had recently arrived in Paris. He ... contacted the Swartzentrubers, thus beginning a relationship that contributed to the founding of the Mennonite church in Châtenay in 1956. In 1961, along with the Mission Mennonite Française, the congregation created a sheltered workshop for mentally handicapped youth and adults.

Reformed pastors André Trocmé (right) and Edouard Theis (left) at the inauguration of the Châtenay-Malabry church building, October 26, 1958. Both were active in the Fellowship of Reconciliation and strongly encouraged the birth of a "historic peace church" in Paris.

1. Since our European brethren have expressed to the American Mennonites their desire for assistance beyond material aid, we should recognize our obligation to continue to give such assistance as is desired and needed.

2. The MCC, being in the best position to serve as a liaison in such services, should continue to be the channel through which this help reaches our European brethren. It is possible, however, that some special needs may be referred to individual groups for administration and/or support.[39]

The second recommendation anticipated that the "united front" approach would probably not work, because of the diversity of North American Mennonite conferences and rivalry between MCC and mission agencies. The report went on to suggest complete freedom of activity outside of areas where European Mennonites were not present, while at the same time encouraging mission agencies to consult with MCC.

In reality, church-planting efforts would be the work of mission agencies, while MCC remained in Europe as a liaison with European Mennonites, dealing more directly with social issues and the peace witness. In several cases, such as in Ireland or Portugal, MCC and mission agencies collaborated with European Mennonites in attempts to combine mission and peace witness.[40]

As time went on, MCC continued to work as much as possible with European Mennonite churches. Mission agencies sometimes, but not always, linked up with European Mennonites, especially those where there was theological compatibility and some sense of a "family" relationship. This meant that the first several decades saw little contact or partnership between North American Mennonite missionaries and the more "liberal" Mennonites of the Netherlands and northern Germany. As had the French, Swiss and south German Mennonites, North Americans had been much more influenced by Pietism and evangelicalism than by theological liberalism. Even though there often were important differences on the "peace position" with their European counterparts, North American missionaries seemed to be more at home with the more conservative piety and theology of the still largely rural Mennonites of Alsace, Switzerland and southern Germany.

On July 18–21, 1967 a "Europe Mission Study Conference" was held at the Bienenberg, with the participation of representatives of the European Mennonite conferences, MCC and the North American mission agencies. In a study paper given during the conference, John Howard Yoder summarized how North Americans and European Mennonites had been in relationship. According to Yoder, North American Mennonites "have tried almost every possibility which logic could suggest in finding ways to relate to sister churches in Europe." The options ranged from "formal and direct collaboration" to a basic ignoring of the presence of European Mennonites and working on one's own, because it was "assumed that most Mennonite churches of Europe are not exceptions to the general low level of faith and faithfulness which characterizes Christianity in Europe in general."[41] These remarks were made in 1967. Nevertheless, the description of these various kinds of relationships still fits four decades later.

Efforts were made to facilitate relationships and to create common projects. As time went on, institutional efforts were made to remedy the lack of clarification and collaboration between North American and European Mennonites. In North America, gatherings of mission board secretaries and MCC as the Council of International Ministries (CIM), attempted to deal with the variety of agencies and experiences of lack of collaboration and even "competition" in certain parts of the world. The annual meetings of the CIM included a "Europe Task Force" which attempted to discuss and coordinate (when possible) mission efforts in Europe. European Mennonites have been regular participants in these meetings.

In 1987 Alle Hoekema, representing EMEK, reported how European Mennonites had responded to the North American Mennonite presence in Europe. Hoekema recognized that Europeans "often have a certain distrust" of the North American approach.[42] Europeans were not always consulted when new projects were begun, and the large variety of Mennonite mission agencies was often confusing. Nevertheless, Hoekema wrote at that time that there was a "growing understanding and cooperation, not only between European Mennonites themselves, but also between us and you." The report also holds up several of the North American initiatives as positive in helping the European Mennonites to ask an important question: "should mission take place overseas only, or do we have a task in Europe as well?" As for the future, Hoekema stated: "Cooperation will require from our side more courage and vision; from your side a larger prudence and sensitivity."

Results

What conclusions can be drawn from these approximately fifty years of new relationships between European and North American Mennonites? One obvious result is a re-establishment of relationships between distant cousins. These relationships helped in a small way to change the face of the European Mennonite churches.

New Churches and Centres

New churches were initially founded in countries where there already were Mennonites: Germany, France and Luxembourg. In these cases, sometimes the churches became members of national conferences, such as in France or Germany; in other instances new conferences were founded, especially in Germany as in the case of the Mennonite Brethren.

Secondly, churches were founded in countries where there had been no historical Mennonite presence, namely in Austria, Belgium, England, Italy, Portugal and Spain. This phenomenon always posed the question of identity. Were these churches Mennonite? If so, how were they to relate to other European Mennonite churches? Or were the newly-planted churches evangelical, or generic "free" churches, without a specific Anabaptist identity?

In three cases, Mennonite Centres (London, Brussels and Paris) were closely linked to newly-founded congregations. The Centres worked specifically on the question of Mennonite-Anabaptist identity and how it related both to other Mennonites and to other Christians. This often led to the Mennonite theological agenda being developed and presented in surprising new contexts, such as the Anabaptist Network in Britain, where non-Mennonite churches and groups who found the Anabaptist vision useful and helpful in their own traditions, came together in new and creative ways. The Anabaptist Network in Britain now numbers some 1200 active participants from all over Britain, from a wide range of church backgrounds. Although the Network includes some Mennonites and members of a Hutterite Bruderhof, it is comprised mainly of Christians from traditions that do not have direct historical links with Anabaptists. Participants come from Catholic, Anglican, Quaker, Methodist, Baptist, United Reformed, Pentecostal, House Church and other backgrounds. They have found the Network a rallying point and an opportunity for dialogue. New members joining the Network

Dirk Willems arrested me.

I came across the Anabaptists in the context of a history lesson. If it wasn't for Dirk Willems' courageous and merciful action, I don't think I would have been arrested by Anabaptists at all... But Dirk's choice intrigued me, and through the study course Workshop I started thinking about peace-making. I was strongly attracted to these people because they were gentle, and the ideas they explored taught me about the radical ways of nonviolence in Jesus' life and in Anabaptists' lives today.

Up until I met Anabaptists, I hadn't engaged with this Jesus and his followers who were learning to be gentle but firm and creative in the face of conflict and injustice. The impact has rooted my values in hope and prayer.

– Gilly Greenwood, London

have frequently expressed a sense of "coming home" to a tradition that embodies their own convictions and provides a framework that integrates these.[43]

Work from London also spread to Ireland, where Mennonite practices of conflict resolution continue to be used in various settings yet today. Young urban churches in London, Paris, Barcelona, Brussels and elsewhere struggled with what it meant to be "Mennonite" when there was not an "ethnic" base or historical tradition. Could Mennonite theology actually attract secular urban Europeans? In Paris, for example, these congre-

An urban multiracial Mennonite church in a Parisian suburb: Châtenay Malabry.

gations were the first urban expressions of the Mennonite church in France. They struggled to integrate mentally handicapped people and foreigners into their midst and constantly had to come to grips with whether or not it made sense to be "Mennonite."

Mennonite congregations in Spain, originating from the work of three different North American agencies (Mennonite Brethren, Brethren in Christ, MBM-Mission Network), have developed relationships among themselves and are now relating to other European Mennonites.

At present there are six small congregations with a total of 155 baptized members in Barcelona, Burgos, Madrid, Vigo, and Malaga. Because of the presence of teachers and theologians in these congregations, Mennonite theology is beginning to have an impact on the broader Evangelical-Protestant world in Spain. This impact has been helped by the existence of Spanish language literature on Anabaptist history and theology made

Spanish Mennonite theologian Antonio González and his wife Aida (Madrid). González, author of several books, holds PhD degrees in both philosophy and theology and is teaching at the United Evangelical Theological Seminary in Madrid.

available from the Latin American world. The Spanish Mennonite congregations at present have contacts in Uruguay, Argentina and Colombia and a mission project in Benin. After discussion with the Mennonites of Italy, they have set as a goal to grow to 500 baptized believers in order to have a more solid sociological basis to move into the next generation.

Some of these projects developed into interesting models of cooperation between European and North American Mennonites. Church planting efforts in Portugal brought together IMO, EMEK, MCC, and MBM. Before disappearing because of an urban renewal project in the 1990s, the *Foyer Grebel* (an international student centre in Paris) was staffed and financed by Dutch, French, Canadian and American Mennonites.

Of course, there were also problems and failures. Some congregations or projects did not succeed and had to close. Sometimes Europeans and North Americans failed to understand each other. Too many times, North American Mennonites formulated and implemented projects without taking into consideration their European brothers and sisters. Sometimes, Europeans reacted negatively to certain projects only because they originated from the other side of the Atlantic.

Without a doubt this story reveals some of the weaknesses of Mennonite history and ecclesiology. Mennonite divisions in Europe were transplanted to North America and then brought back to the continent. Further divisions in North America created different agencies that sent workers to Europe without consultation or coordination. North American Mennonites were not capable of creating a common front or common projects. The lack of unity among European Mennonites and their own theological differences further complicated how North American agencies proceeded.

Nevertheless, the efforts described in this chapter have produced many good results and important new relationships across the Atlantic. It is hoped that the development of Mennonite World Conference can help these different groups find a more common ecclesiological ground. Whereas previously there was no structural or institutional link between diverse European and North American Mennonites, now most of them are members of Mennonite World Conference. In addition, the projected founding of a European branch of the Global Mission Fellowship can perhaps also contribute to greater solidarity and mutual accountability between Mennonites in relation to mission projects. Historical changes always produce new questions. At present, it is important to correctly understand the theological implications of these questions and to work at formulating and implementing new solutions.

Mennonite Life in Europe: Crossing Borders

by Ed van Straten

The earlier chapters in this book deal with the history of Mennonites in specific countries in Europe, but can we speak collectively of European Mennonites as well? In this chapter we consider Mennonite life and history in Europe as a whole, beyond national borders. The present moment is an interesting one in history, for national borders are rapidly losing their political and economic meaning inside Europe, as the European Union is gaining more and more strength—though Switzerland is still outside that Union. Apart from Swiss, Ukrainian, and Siberian brothers and sisters, most other European Mennonites are now able to travel to Barcelona, Spain, to attend the Mennonite European Regional Conference (MERK) in May 2006 without being stopped at borders for passport control. This is the eighth MERK gathering, and the fact that these meetings are taking place underlines the growing feeling among European Mennonites of belonging together, of having some common history, and sharing a common future. These international meetings themselves are part of our European Mennonite history. The first was held in Switzerland at the Bienenberg Bible school and conference centre in 1975; since then they have been held in Germany, the Netherlands, Switzerland and France.

The Nineteenth Century

Mennonites in Europe have always been aware of each others' existence, even in former times when contacts were rare. To note only two early examples, Dutch Mennonites helped their persecuted Swiss sisters and brothers during the eighteenth century, and for generations Swiss Mennonites maintained contact with the descendants of former Swiss immigrants in Mennonite congregations in Alsace and the Palatinate.

As far as international European contacts were concerned, people travelled at all times, but travel was difficult, time-consuming and tiresome before trains began connecting cities and countries starting in the 1830s. Writing letters was the only other way of communicating. Of course, each community was interested primarily in its own existence. European Mennonite congregations have always cherished their autonomy and independence, a fact that has kept them at a distance even from their own conferences. That was the case around the year 1800, when our story begins. How did European Mennonites live at this time? How did they develop? How did they cope with the changing times, and how did their thinking, their theology, their Christian and congregational lives develop?

Until the French Revolution Mennonites in most European countries had been considered second-rate citizens, to whom many civil rights were denied. In this, Mennonites shared the fate of several other minorities. In Catholic countries, other Protestant denominations could be such minorities; in the Protestant Netherlands, the Roman Catholics had hidden churches just as did the Mennonites and, just as the Mennonites can point out their

Weierhof. View of Adamshof, at the back. A sign on the wall says: Built in 1710 by Jakob Krehbiel, son of the Mennonite immigrant Peter Crayenbühl. The farm was named after Adam Krehbiel, a renowned lay preacher. The Mennonite congregation gathered on the first floor at the right, until the "Lehr" was built in 1770.

Amsterdam Singel Church—invisible from the street—so the Roman Catholics can show you their former church, named "Our Dear Lord in the Attic," which is now a museum.

As the influence of the French Revolution spread throughout Europe, and religious minorities were granted equal rights (on paper, at least), the effects varied. In most countries Mennonites profited by their new status, but the French Mennonites had a hard time adjusting, according to Jean Séguy,[1] who describes the deterioration of Mennonite religious and communal life in this period. It took French Mennonites a century to get back on their feet. In the course of that century, many French and other European Mennonites lost their convictions on nonviolence and non-participation in war. There were others, however, (such as part of the Balk congregation in Friesland in 1853) who left Europe, partly or solely because they did not want to give up these convictions.

Apart from the Dutch and northern German Mennonites most Mennonites in the early nineteenth century lived in villages or small towns, also often on isolated farms, and in Switzerland they lived at elevations above 1000 meters. In the Netherlands and in northern Germany many lived in larger cities, such as Hamburg and Amsterdam, but even in these regions numerous Mennonites lived in villages, working as farmers or (as in some parts of

---

In April 1851 the mayor of Saint-Mihiel, in the French Meuse region, passed on the following request, written by the Mennonites in the region, to the Minister of Religious Affairs in Paris.

Monsieur le Ministre,

The faith of the Anabaptists has been around for centuries, and if it doesn't count a great number of followers in France, it is because its adherents, living in utmost modesty, have always rejected all means of propaganda, and not having been authorized their meetings could lead to judicial prosecution, as has happened several times.

This faith teaches the highest morals and very generally its disciples scrupulously follow the laws of probity and virtue. Nevertheless, this religious denomination has not yet been recognized by the French government in the sense that to this day it has not received any subvention of the State and it finds itself left to its own resources.

Nevertheless this subvention would be an act of real justice. We are French, like the followers of other religious groups; we pay our taxes as they do, and our children, like theirs, follow the banners to defend the honour and integrity of the fatherland.

Thus it would be a clear violation of justice if our religious group would not be subsidized like the others. That subsidy would not be a heavy burden on the budget; the Anabaptist faith counts a very restricted number of disciples in France and consequently has only a few pastors. On the other hand this recognition could not encourage the formation of new religious denominations, since our faith is very old.

Consequently I have the honour, Monsieur le Ministre, to beseech you to be so good as to let the Anabaptist faith be recognized by the Government, so that under the terms of the constitution it can receive the little subsidy to which it is entitled. In the hardly probable case this recognition would meet with difficulties, I have the honour to beg you to be so good as to grant us a little bit of help that would permit us to practice our faith with some dignity.

Be so good, I beg you, Monsieur le Ministre, to receive the assurances of my deepest respect.

St-Mihiel, April 6, 1851
— Christian Oesch

the Netherlands and Germany) as fishermen. Their communities were not large and tended to be rather conservative, not only in belief but also in life style. In the rural areas, children usually did not go to school very long; in the cities the education was better. Here and there children could attend Mennonite schools. It was within the family that children learned the skills they needed to become good farmers or housewives; from their parents and grandparents as well as in church they learned about the faith. Religious instruction was often based on the Dordrecht Confession of Faith; there also were special books for the religious education of the children. Many people made use of pious literature for their personal and family devotions to keep their faith alive, although this was less so with Mennonites living in the big German and Dutch cities. Later religious education became the task of preachers. Often catechetical books were written in the form of question and answer.

Grandparents usually lived on in the homes of their children. Senior people who had no children or who had never married had to look to another relative for lodging, but in the cities there were other solutions. The (now extinct) Danzig (Gdansk) congregation, for instance, founded a home for aged people who had no relatives with whom to stay; it dated back to the seventeenth century. In the Netherlands there are still the so-called courts (*hofjes*)—small houses built around and opening on to a courtyard that could be closed during the night. Each "court" had a governing board that decided who would be accepted as a lodger. Mennonites built such courts just as other churches did. The Mennonite *hofjes* still exist in most places,

One catechetical booklet was written by Leonhard Weydmann in Monsheim in 1852, and revised by his son Ernst Weydmann (1837-1903), pastor in Krefeld who had studied at the Amsterdam seminary. This is what he writes about the way Christians have to realize God's love in their lives (questions 99 to 102):

Q. 99   **In which situations of life should we practice the love towards God and our neighbour?**
A.:   *In all situations, especially as members of the family, citizens and members of the Christian congregation.*

Q. 100 **How about the family situation?**
A.   *Husbands and wives through love and faithfulness, children through gratitude and obedience, brothers and sisters through unity and love, masters through justice and mildness; servants through faithfulness and docility.*

Q. 101 **How as citizens and subjects?**
A.   *Through respect and obedience towards the government, love towards your fatherland, selflessness and intercession. On the other hand, the government owes us protection, justice and gentleness.*

Q. 102 **How as members of the Christian congregation?**
A.   *By sanctifying Sunday and commemorative days, by true participation in the life of the congregation, obedience towards the agreed order and a peaceful attitude towards members of other denominations.*

but are now used most often to offer housing to single young people or students.

The Dutch Mennonites also founded homes for the elderly. The first home for the elderly in Mennonite Russia was in Rückenau on the Molotschna, founded in 1895; the German city of Krefeld opened one in 1906. After 1945 more of those old peoples' homes were built.

In the Netherlands and in Russia, Mennonites also founded orphanages; elsewhere orphans were taken into the families of relatives, friends or neighbours. With the assistance of MCC, two children's homes were opened in France (Mont des Oiseaux, near Wissembourg) in 1945, and Valdoie, which also includes a home for the elderly, in 1950; elsewhere they have been closed due to changing social circumstances. It remains unclear whether the "social consciousness" of the European Mennonites was an outgrowth of their specific faith only, or a following of the social norms of their time. In the Netherlands other denominations had orphanages and old people's homes as well. Mennonites there and in northern Germany felt a special responsibility for the improvement of the social life of the society at large. For that reason they often were found among the "liberal" and later "socialist" political streams.

Urban Mennonites were involved in commerce and in industry as well as in professional jobs (doctors, teachers). As we have seen above, some also got involved in government, while others were board members of important foundations or institutions, which sometimes were secular. This meant that urban Mennonites usually had more contacts with non-Mennonites and were thus more open to the general culture, as the chapter on the Netherlands makes clear.

Dutch *Hofje*. The Haarlem congregation still maintains three *hofjes*. The photograph shows two women in traditional dress at the beginning of the twentieth century in a fourth *hofje* which no longer exists, the *Blokshofje*.

Pietism and Enlightenment

By the nineteenth century, being a Mennonite was nearly always just a matter of belonging to a Mennonite family. Mennonites were encouraged to marry other Mennonites, and they usually did. In their spiritual life the European Mennonites were strongly influenced by Pietism—under several different names, like "Réveil"—which emphasized "a personal, emotionally-experienced conversion resulting in the application of this experience in daily life in doing good works and in certain forms of nonconformity."[2] For the early Anabaptists, by contrast, conversion was not primarily a matter of emotion but an act of the will to leave behind the sinful life and enter the new community under the leadership of the Holy Spirit. But this difference between Pietist emphases and Anabaptist ones was hardly felt. Samuel Gerber from the Swiss Sonnenberg congregation wrote about the theology of his congregation before 1945:

> Our congregations were fashioned by Pietism and Biblicism. [We were shaped by] the necessity of conversion and of being born again, justification through faith and the Mission imperative in the expectation of the Second Coming of Christ to establish His kingdom.[3]

Jean Séguy describes how the idea of a second birth after baptism became pervasive in pietist Mennonite groups in France. Menno Simons would have been surprised about being born again *after* baptism (his point in his treatise on baptism is exactly that conversion and second birth have to come before baptism) and about the teaching of justification through faith alone. It must be said here that the influence of Pietism was less felt by the Mennonites in the Netherlands, though it was by no means absent there. At least, in the Netherlands (and in north Germany as well) a sober form of piety, often Jesus-centred, always has characterized the faith of the Mennonites. As examples we mention a Dutch tear-off calendar with brief daily devotional texts, published over a period of years (until the late 1950s), and many devotional texts in the *Jaarboekjes*.

Nearly everywhere in Europe (also in Lutheran and some Calvinist churches) Pietism is very much alive. A partial re-orientation on the older Anabaptist principles came about after the American Mennonites made their influence felt after 1945. Sjouke Voolstra points to John Howard Yoder's theology as "a contemporary variety of the 'mystical' Anabaptist legacy" and "a modern variation on the theme *Gelassenheit*."

It is not certain, however, that this modern interpretation of yieldedness to God will elicit a response, either inside or outside Anabaptist circles.[4]

The Enlightenment marked another significant intellectual and social influence. Philosophers in France and the Netherlands in the seventeenth and eighteenth centuries emphasized human reason as the means for learning the truth about the world around them. They discussed new ways of discerning reality, of living together in society, new political forms and methods, and new forms of education. Catharine the Great of Russia was strongly influenced by Enlightenment ideas, and the Mennonites and many others she invited to cultivate the empty Ukrainian lands profited as a result.

The influence of the Enlightenment on most Mennonites in the Netherlands and Germany was more direct. Enlightenment thinking tended to emphasize the importance of the individual person, as did Pietism. This was a shift away from the emphasis on the community which had been so important to Menno Simons and the early Anabaptists. During the twentieth century the influence of the Enlightenment became more widespread, contributing to a growing rationalism in religious life and gradual erosion of community life among Mennonites.

> **A simple, yet true story**
>
> *A woman had listened to many sermons by all kind of preachers. Also, she had read the Bible and had become more and more confused and desperate, till on a good day—and certainly it has been a good day to her!—the following truth was revealed to her: with my poor human reason I cannot climb up to God. If God does not descend to me, I will never be able to find Him. And at this very moment she knew who Christ is. God, who lets Himself be found, who enters your house, your heart, the history of this poor humankind, to make it rich.*
>
> *– From a book of meditations, 1955*

Sober Lifestyle

Mennonite congregations in Europe were traditionally led by elders and preachers. In some places, such as in certain regions of France for a brief time, elders were chosen by the whole congregation, including the women. A theological education or any other special training for elders and preachers did not exist around 1800, except in the Netherlands. There were congregations in Germany and the Netherlands who had some preachers who had studied elsewhere. Around 1800 the tradition of lay ministers and congregational leaders was still followed in most places.

Swiss Mennonites near Kampen, Netherlands, eighteenth century. Till 1822 the "Swiss Brethren," who had arrived in 1711, formed their own congregation in Kampen; they differed from the Dutch Mennonites in their sober dress and lifestyle. Engraving by W. de Meulen.

Most Mennonites throughout Europe were known to be hard-working people, living sober lives. A majority of them drank alcohol, in moderation; some also smoked tobacco. Their church buildings or places of worship were very simple. In some places they gathered in farms or other buildings that could not be recognized as churches. Also their clothes were simple and, in some areas such as in France, very traditional. But leading simple lives did not always mean the Mennonites were poor. In Holland, Germany, Poland and the Ukraine, years of hard work resulted in a certain amount of wealth, which would grow even more in the new century.

Although nineteenth-century European Mennonites had been granted equal rights as citizens, Mennonites mostly went on living as they had before, whether as farmers, fishermen, or urban dwellers. But the nineteenth century brought new political realities and the seeds of war and revolution that would deeply influence the lives of Mennonites and all Europeans until the present day. The Franco-Prussian War of 1870–1871 deeply affected Mennonites in Alsace-Lorraine, as we have seen, and the First World War (1914–1918) also deeply affected the lives of many Europeans, including the Mennonites. When Alsace-Lorraine was returned to France at the end of World War I, the Mennonites of that area became French citizens again, but for a long time had their own German-speaking conference, which seldom cooperated with the French-speaking one—there was a difference in language but also in culture. There were revolutionary upheavals in Russia, with terrible consequences for all people living there, as we have seen.

Two world wars were fought in Europe in the twentieth century; however, the seeds of revolution and war were sown during the nineteenth century, which also was the century of technological and industrial development. Steam engines revolutionized factories; trains connected areas and cities and now quickly transported people, newspapers, books, ideas and products. Industrialization saw Mennonites in several places in Europe starting and running factories, which introduced new lifestyles. Some of them became household names in Germany, in Holland and in Russia. No longer were Mennonites in Europe far away from each other; they began to travel and visit each other and reported on their visits on their return home. International networks of theologians existed, and mission efforts expanded these networks from Gnadenfeld to Amsterdam, from Basel to Hamburg.

The European Experience

The first important development in modern Mennonite life as a European experience is the start of Mennonite missionary activity. We have seen above how the British Baptists awakened the Dutch and German Mennonites to the concept of mission in the 1820s. As we have also seen, after the Second World War the German, Swiss and French Mennonites founded their own mission boards and then cooperated, together with the Dutch mission board, in EMEK, the European Mennonite Evangelization Committee, founded in 1951; since 1995 it has been named the EMMK—European Mennonite Mission Conference.

From the middle of the twentieth century the French Mennonites sent missionaries to the African Republic of Chad (from 1963 on under the EMEK umbrella) and to the Pacific island of Guadalcanal, whereas German Mennonites were interested in Latin America. Swiss and Dutch Mennonites worked in Papua Barat (the former New Guinea), the eastern-most part of Indonesia; French and Swiss worked side-by side in Chad. Many Mennonites from European countries also joined missions from other, non-Mennonite, churches and organizations in different parts of the world.

With the end of the Second World War came the gradual dismantling of European-controlled colonies, and a re-visioning of traditional mission enterprises. For example, the leader of the Javanese Mennonites, Suhadiweko Djojodihardjo, at the end of the 1970s, expressed the opinion that being just a "daughter" of a mission board was not fitting for the Javanese Mennonite Church anymore, given that Indonesia had been an independent nation since the seventeenth of August, 1945. Rather his church should have direct church-to-church relations with the board of the Dutch Mennonite Conference (ADS). The Dutch Mennonites agreed and the ADS church board became a direct partner to the GITJ (the Javanese Mennonite Church). Later a leader of the Indonesian Chinese Mennonites, Mesach Krisetya, underlined in a speech to the General Council of the MWC in 1993, in Bulawayo, Zimbabwe, the importance of the equality and interrelatedness of all the Mennonite churches. International mission was changing its focus.

In the present day, mission is finding new forms, and includes missionary projects in the European countries themselves—partly run by North American Mennonite agencies, partly by the European Mennonites themselves. Primarily through North American missionary efforts, new Mennonite communities have come to life in Belgium, France, Germany, Spain, Italy, Portugal, and the Ukraine. The European projects include new Mennonite centres (as in the city of Almere in the Netherlands and until recently, the *Foyer Grebel* in Paris), but also in the exchange of people, for instance between the Netherlands, Germany and African countries.

Mission opened the world to Mennonites in Europe. Former missionaries travelled around and lectured in the congregations; church papers contained stories from the mission fields and members of congregations learned to feel related to far away groups of people and to assume responsibility for what was being done in those exotic places where people ate different food, had different trees and plants, and were surrounded by different animals. Since 1945 that has changed; now European Mennonites are being asked questions about their faith and life-styles by Christians from the (former) mission fields.

Long before the MERK conferences began, EMEK (EMMK) organized conferences where participants from France, Germany, Switzerland and the Netherlands met and learned to know one another. In these encounters, people found out about each others' lives, their respective beliefs, convictions and differences. Sometimes there were conflicts because of strongly-held opinions, both on theological and practical issues, as well as about policy decisions. Usually friendship and brotherly/sisterly feelings prevailed. These conferences brought people out of their safe and cosy home congregations and exposed them to faith convictions far more, or far less strict than what they were used to.

This same experience was shared by people attending other European Mennonite meetings, like assemblies of EMFK (European Mennonite Peace Committee), the "Trainee" (exchange visitor program) committee, and Mennonite Aid Organizations. Most of these organizations started after 1945. Between 1925 and 1936 three Mennonite World Conferences were held in Europe, and being mainly

European affairs, they had an integrating effect on European Mennonites. At the third and last MWC meeting before the Second World War, (in Amsterdam and Elspeet, the Netherlands, 1936) differences were discussed within the framework of a dialogue about faith and culture. As has been seen above, at that time German Mennonites tended to give an unreserved "yes" to their culture, which was then a Nazi culture. Not all German Mennonites present in Elspeet were of the same opinion, however. After the meeting at Elspeet several participants went to Fredeshiem, another Dutch Mennonite retreat centre, where they held a Mennonite Peace Conference and founded the International Mennonite Peace Committee. A copy of a page with their signatures and home-

Photograph of the signatures under the Fredeshiem peace document, 1936.

towns, written down at that conference, demonstrates that several Americans (among them Harold Bender and Orie O. Miller), Canadians and Dutch were among them, but also at least three German Mennonites. This International Peace Committee still exists but is now integrated as the Peace Council within MWC.

As has been noted in various places in the previous chapters, during the nineteenth century the radical issues that had set the Anabaptists of the sixteenth century apart from society at large had mostly been forgotten, as is clear from the letter from St. Mihiel above. Being in the world but not of the world no longer had meaning; the peace position was forgotten by most—though not by all. It would take until after the Second World War before it became a really serious issue. The discussions in Elspeet in 1936 made visible how far most European Mennonites had strayed from the original Anabaptist beliefs.

One of the pioneers in recovering a peace witness was Cor Inja, a young Mennonite man in the Netherlands, who was taken to prison in the early 1920s as a conscientious objector. Interestingly, some fifty years later he was knighted for his many contributions to conscientious objection in the Netherlands. Inja was a member of the Mennonite Task Force Against Military Service (*Arbeidsgroep van Doopsgezinden tegen de Krijgsdienst*), which was founded by conscientious objectors

The renewal movement in the Netherlands crossed national boundaries and apparently got the attention of Mennonites elsewhere in Europe. In *300 Jahre Mennoniten Gemeinde Weierhof* we read:

As a young man in his early twenties Christian Galle took a lively, even enthusiastic part in the youth work that in those days started to flourish rapidly in our southern German Congregations. (...) In recognition of his work for the young, the Youth Committee sent him, with some other representatives, to Holland in 1922 to take part in the so called "Congregations' Day."

in 1922 as a section of the *Gemeentedag Beweging* (Congregations' Day Movement), already described.

At the same time the French and Swiss Mennonites were experiencing a revival and German Mennonites, too, took new initiatives. Congregations and conferences in western Europe, feeling the winds of change, tried to respond to new situations by establishing new ways of organizing groups in the church: youth groups,[5] summer Bible schools, summer camps, Sunday schools, women's groups and special meetings for women, choirs and other organizations that brought people together on issues of faith and Christian practice. Conference and retreat centres were opened, evangelization efforts began, schools opened, homes for the aged were built, and peace issues were addressed.

This spirit of renewal led to the establishment of several retreat centres in the Netherlands. Around this same time (during the 1920s) we see the establishment of a German Mennonite retreat centre near Karlsruhe called "Thomashof," and during this same time Christian Neff succeeded in organizing the first Mennonite World Conference in Basel, Switzerland, in 1925, attended mainly by European Mennonites. Part of the Dutch delegation went there by airplane, a very new means of transport at that time and a symbol of the new times, the new world in which the Mennonites found themselves. The second Mennonite World Conference (in Danzig, 1930) was solely devoted to discussing the problems of the Russian Mennonites living under, and fleeing from, the Soviet regime and exploring the options that were open for helping them. It was oriented to the ways and means of giving aid—but at the same time it was a forum where Europeans (and Americans and Canadians) met each other. Mention has already been made of the third Mennonite World Conference in 1936. All three were organized and presided over by Christian Neff.

As has been stated in chapter IV, Christian Neff (1863–1946) was an influential leader, spiritually as well as in the fields of Mennonite history, hymnology, and education. He eagerly used new technical inventions: he was a very early owner of typewriters, cars, and telephones. His wife Lydia and he were a matchless team in all undertakings, to which has to be added their famous hospitality. Christian Neff served the Weierhof congregation for over fifty years. In the words of Ernst Crous, "Even in the great moment of his life when the theological faculty of the University of Zürich conferred upon him the honorary doctorate in theology in 1925, all he could say in his modesty about his work was that he had endeavoured conscientiously to fill a lack in the service of his brotherhood."[6] In this respect Christian Neff was an exemplary European leader.

War-Time in Europe and Post-War Reconciliation Efforts

The Second World War can be seen as a watershed in European Mennonite life—as in European church life in general. To most European Mennonites, the Second World War was a traumatic experience, often leaving wounds that were hard to heal. The memories still linger with the older people, and sometimes their suffering deeply influenced their children.

During the war itself, Mennonites were confronted with difficult choices. The first question was: Do I go along with the Nazi ideology? Do I support Nazi goals in Europe (in France, the Netherlands, in Germany itself)? Some Mennonites did. They often were seen later as traitors, as people who had sided with a terrible enemy and thereby shared the responsibility, for instance, for the millions of murders committed in the concentration camps. This led to deep divisions between people, and these painful divisions can still be felt today. Some Mennonites in the Netherlands to this day don't want to talk about their parents' or their own war experiences for this reason. German Mennonite families also have their dark memories that no one wants to discuss. Sometimes divisions came into the church itself, as when the secretary of the Dutch Mennonite Church (ADS) board was a known Nazi fellow traveller, and could not always be trusted—or so the other board members felt.

There also were moving examples of reconciliation between Mennonites who might be seen as enemies, even during the war. We will recount one such story here. Herman Keuning was the Mennonite pastor in the small Frisian village of Irnsum during the war. His wife An was deeply involved in the resistance work; often the pastor's house was a hiding place for evacuees and people sought by the German occupiers. Toward the end of the war the stream of refugees stopped, and the young couple hoped that they could again use the front and rear rooms of their house, but suddenly the space was requisitioned as an emergency infirmary by the Germans. A German-speaking medical officer came in with three medics, and they started converting the rooms. The war front was getting closer. An Allied parachute invasion was expected in the area around Leeuwarden, and so the medics were preparing for numerous casualties on the German side. An tells what happened next:

> The first evening at dinner-time after this new use of our home, we were sitting at the table in the crowded dining room, the remaining children [of the many who had found shelter with the couple] at their own separate table, about to share bread. Bread is all we had. There was a knock at the door. The medical officer came in and asked permission to use our stove to fry an egg. With his own frying pan, a chunk of bacon, and two eggs in his hand, he got busy. In no time, the room filled with a delicious, almost forgotten aroma. No one said a word.
>
> The man felt the quiet and looked up to see us all watching him, mesmerized. He stood straight up, pulled out his pistol, and turned a full circle. He saw our surprised and frightened faces, screamed, and dashed out of the room. We heard him crying in the hall. I went out to him. He was crouching in the corner behind the door, crying his eyes out. He looked up at me, distraught and at his wits' end. Before he knew what was happening, I had my arms around him. He was just a boy in his early twenties, barely older than me.
>
> In jerks he managed to tell me what was so wrong. He was a Prussian German, and during a raid he had been given a choice: join the army or get a bullet in his head. It was a hard decision for him and his medics. They were all Mennonites who believed in nonviolence. But with the permission of the Mennonite elders, the young men went with the army to Russia. This officer had just finished studying medicine, so it was his job to work with the medics and care for the ill and the wounded. That initially gave him less of a sense of guilt, because he wasn't expected to participate directly in the violence of war (although he clearly carried a pistol for self-protection). But in the hell that Russia was in those days, he discovered that whenever it got very quiet about him, it was

wise to fear for his life. That was what happened in our room, and when he saw only innocent, frightened faces, something snapped inside him. He saw his home in us, his village. "We are Mennonites and have promised God not to kill," he said. I thought it was safe to tell him he had come to a Mennonite parish. "Unbelievable," was the only word he could utter. Deeply moved, we sat there together. He called over his medics. We went back into the room where the fried eggs were now shrivelled up on the corner of the stove. The children still thought they were a great delicacy though, and each took a bite.

We held a service of gratitude that evening with all the residents, including the medics who participated fully. I can still remember the singing and feel the fellowship and joy surrounding this "coincidence."[7]

Another example of reconciliation across the national borderlines is told by Pierre Widmer. As a French army officer he was imprisoned by the German army during the war. To him it became a time of learning in many ways. He became more open to the nonresistance principle of the early Anabaptists and Mennonites, and eventually he arrived at a position of conscientious objection. Later he became one of the most important leaders of the French Mennonites, and his stance of nonresistance was part of the influence he exerted on his people.

After the war European Mennonites outside Germany were faced with the question of how to deal with their German brothers and sisters. When the Mennonite Church of The Hague, Netherlands, was looking for a new pastor around 1990 and the name of a German Mennonite person was suggested, some older people said: "Oh no, not a German!" They were still afraid that asking a German to become pastor would split the congregation. But in general, one can say that good relations have been restored, not in the least because of the many inter-European Mennonite meetings that have been held.

When the war was coming to a close, Mennonites from West Prussia had to leave their homeland and flee to West Germany where, bereft of nearly everything and often with sad memories of missing family members, they had to build up a new life or go on to Canada or other countries in the Americas. The end of the war also brought many Russian Mennonites to the west, as described in chapter VII above. Some groups reported to Dutch authorities at the Dutch-German border, saying they were descendants of Dutch Mennonites. An inventive pastor came up with the idea to create a special passport for them. With the help of some Dutch authorities and MCC, the 'Mennopas' was created, serving as a semi-official document with which several-hundred refugees were helped.

During the most recent decades, the need for reconciliation has decreased, partly because younger generations are taking over leadership, partly because European Mennonites have stood side-by-side in matters of war and peace elsewhere in the world. Yet, we have to admit that certain things remain covered with a taboo of silence.

Involvement of MCC and North American Mennonites

The towns and cities of western Europe were in a desolate condition after the war. Churches and houses had been destroyed; food was scarce. This is where MCC came in, sending helpers, food and clothing. Young people (the so-called "PAX boys") came to help rebuild houses and churches. In 1951 the first group of 20 conscientious objectors began working in Espelkamp, Germany. From there the reconstruction work spread to Mennonite locations, such as Backnang and Krefeld, and non-Mennonite locations as well. MCC opened offices in different countries and made contact with the local Mennonites, and a wider range of people learned to know one another. Europeans

"PAX boys" sort donated clothing

were confronted with American Mennonite ideas about nonresistance and a congregation-centred spiritual life. American Mennonites were surprised by European life-styles. This sometimes led to misunderstandings but also to a new awareness.

With the Americans came the influence of Harold S. Bender. His influence had already been felt in Europe before the Second World War, but only in limited circles, such as when the International Mennonite Peace Committee was founded in 1936. Bender already was corresponding with Christian Neff about the Mennonite World Conference prior to the first one being held.[8] Harold Bender's biggest impact, however, came with the publication in Europe of his trail-blazing article "The Anabaptist Vision." This address, presented in December 1943, to the American Society of Church History, of which he was then the president, was published in *Mennonite Quarterly Review* in April, 1944. In it he discussed the original principles of early Anabaptist faith and theology as he saw them: as an Anabaptist vision.

> The Anabaptist vision (he wrote) included three major points of emphasis; first, a new concept of the essence of Christianity as discipleship; second, a new concept of the church as brotherhood; and third, a new ethic of love and nonresistance.

About discipleship he wrote:

> The great word of the Anabaptists was not "faith" as it was with the reformers, but "following" (*Nachfolge Christi*). And baptism, the greatest of the Christian symbols, was accordingly to be for them the "covenant of a good conscience toward God" (1 Peter 3:21), the pledge of a complete commitment to obey Christ, and not primarily the symbol of a past experience.

This alone came as an eye-opener to many in Europe who, through pietistic influences, had been shaped by Protestant thinking about faith and grace, and to whom "past experience" was of the utmost importance. A few pages later they could read:

> For Anabaptists, the church was neither an institution (Catholicism), nor the instrument of God for the proclamation of the divine Word (Lutheranism), nor a resource group for individual piety (Pietism). It was a brotherhood of love in which the fullness of the Christian life ideal is to be expressed.

Soon "The Anabaptist Vision" was translated and then studied and talked about by European Mennonites. I remember these discussions in the Dutch Mennonite Peace Group (*Doopsgezinde Vredesgroep*) and how inspiring I found them as a young man. We see the influence of Bender's "Anabaptist Vision" in the growth of nonresistance and conscientious objection among Mennonites in Europe. This did not come about overnight.

When my family and I stopped at the farm of the Swiss Mennonite pastor, Samuel Gerber in 1968, he had just come back from a day of

nnonite Church Canada
Resource Centre
600 Shaftesbury Blvd., Winnipeg, MB R3P 0M4
Toll-free: 1-866-888-6785   *Europe: Testing Faith and Tradition*

272

military training to which each Swiss male citizen was called every year. He had found it a pleasurable experience and, after he had taught Christian teachings to some young people from the Sonnenberg congregation, he sat down with me to discuss, among other things, the ideas of Harold Bender (a pleasurable experience for both of us). At that time, conscientious objection was not yet a thing to be expected among Swiss Mennonites. This changed, however, a few years later when several young Mennonites began to refuse to do military service and were imprisoned in the early 1970s. Since 1996, Swiss citizens can apply for civil instead of military service as conscientious objectors and, to this date, some fifty members of Swiss Mennonite congregations have taken that option.[9]

Until military conscription was abolished in the 1990s, a State Committee existed in the Netherlands to judge the arguments of conscientious objectors. When I became a member of this Committee—appointed by the Queen—I became the second Mennonite on the commission; two more were to follow, all four of us members of the Dutch Mennonite Peace Group. Our membership was to ensure that conscientious objectors were treated fairly. Our motives for participating in this Committee as Mennonites were grounded in "The Anabaptist Vision." We wanted to contribute to the understanding that the idea of nonresistance and pacifism are good and honourable ideas that ought to guide people's lives.

Harold Bender also influenced Mennonites in France in a similar way. Jean Séguy counted 45 articles on nonresistance in the French Mennonite monthly *Christ Seul*[10] between 1946 and 1962. This is not to say that Bender's influence changed everything—the influence of Pietism, of Revivalism, of Enlightenment individualism is still very much alive among European Mennonites.

Another North American who had a great impact in Europe after the Second World War was John Howard Yoder. He had a big influence on Mennonite peace theology as it developed in Europe and North America. In 1949 he came to Europe as director of the MCC relief office in Frankfurt. Later he studied at the University of

Typically, I would just run into Yoder at different times and places. Once I entered a train compartment and found him there, reading a book. Another time we came across each other in the restaurant of the World Council of Churches building in Geneva, Switzerland. Again another time (November 1991) I saw him walking past my office in Amsterdam. That time he was on his way to give an address to the students of the Seminary there. I sat in. After his lecture the students could ask their questions in Dutch; he would answer in English. Although he could both read and understand Dutch reasonably well, he could not speak it. But he was fluent in French and German. He died in December 1997.

– Ed van Straten

Basel, debating with Karl Barth on the latter's position concerning Christian participation in war. Yoder was an influential participant in the so-called Puidoux conferences—so-called because they were first held in the Swiss town of Puidoux in 1949—where representatives of the three historic peace churches met with representatives of other churches to discuss peace theology. The Puidoux conferences were held in response to a request by the World Council of Churches, to which we will return. John Yoder had contacts with many European Mennonites, among them many of their leaders. According to Jean Séguy he supported Pierre Widmer in publishing the articles in *Christ Seul*, mentioned above.[11]

The relationship between European and American Mennonites has been furthered by the many contacts made possible by the modern means of transportation. American Mennonite choirs and tour groups now visit European congregations, just as European Mennonite choirs perform in American and Canadian Mennonite churches. Members of choirs and tour groups stay with Mennonite families and visit important historic sites. For many Americans and Canadians these travels are attractive because they learn to know a little about their European roots.

An international youth group of Inter-menno trainees (ca. 1980) mixing with European visitors in Museum Unterlinden, Colmar, France, attentively studying the famous Isenheim Altar painting by Matthias Grünewald.

A more intensive cultural contact is provided by the exchange programs. The Intermenno Trainee Program, which began in 1963, receives young American and Canadian Mennonites for a year-long stay with European Mennonite families, and the International Visitor Exchange Program (IVEP) does the same for young European Mennonites who live for a year in Canada and the US. Since 1946 MCC had been helping European students and farmers travel to North America for a year-long visit. American and Canadian Intermenno trainees work with Europeans and learn to appreciate European ideas and culture; they

Saturday, August 12, 1961 in Berlin

mennonite voluntary service

Having begun to work not before Wednesday we had to take all our energy this morning, get up at 6 o'clock, and start at 7-7:30 to our jobs. The Grünewald group went with the people of Lichtenfeld putting beds up there for more refugees. We at Tempelhof had to wrap margarine and to cut cold meat again for distribution to the refugees. For lunch we had cold meat, potatoes, and horse radish sauce, so there wasn't too much to prepare and we could quit working at 12 o'clock. We ate lunch there. The other group had to eat here at Berliner Strasse.

In the afternoon it was decided to go to East Berlin. [...] East Berlin looks desolated in comparison to the western part of the city. Many ruins are left. There is not much traffic. Traffic lights are not up anyway, probably just to look at and to show that the Russians aren't behind in their development. The Stalin Allee whereto almost all of us went, shows new houses in Russian architecture. Unexpectedly all of us were back by 10 o'clock or a little later to end the day with our devotions together. (During this weekend of 12/13 August, the Berlin Wall was built).

– From a diary, MVS Camp, West Berlin, 1961.

are instrumental in the exchange of ideas. Intermenno-Holland once tried to involve some Indonesian girls in the program but the Dutch government blocked that effort.

Finally, MCC has been instrumental in organizing international summer work camps on behalf of young people, through Mennonite Voluntary Service (MVS). In 1961 no less than 19 camps were held in many parts of Europe. They provided an excellent chance for young Mennonite people from across Europe and North America to meet one another, and also to get to know many others, including Muslims. MVS helped in rebuilding churches, such as the church in Witmarsum, in renovating children's homes in France and the Bienenberg in Liestal. MVS volunteers assisted in hospital work and refugee camps in Berlin and participated in peace work in Greece and even Morocco.

Berlin, on the day the Berlin wall was constructed.

Russian *Aussiedler* and Recent Refugees

Mennonites living in the former Soviet Union were initially prevented from moving west by the "iron curtain," but since the collapse of the USSR many Mennonite settlers, the so-called *Umsiedler* (resettlers) or *Aussiedler* (immigrants), have settled in western Europe. On the basis of their still speaking German, the *Umsiedler* were welcomed by Germany when they managed to leave the Soviet Union and later Russia, Kazakhstan, etc. Once in Germany, most *Umsiedler* did not mingle with the German Mennonites. There were some contacts, however scarce, with German and also Dutch Mennonites. Dutch Mennonite organizations sent money to help groups start building churches. A busload of *Umsiedler* Mennonites from Bielefeld, Germany, visited the MERK gathering in Elspeet, the Netherlands, in 1996, for example, and a handful of Dutch Mennonites visited an *Umsiedler* meeting in Bielefeld. But in general, there is a deep divide caused by differences in history, theology and culture. The *Umsiedler* are also divided among themselves, as we have seen above, but the sense of distance between them and their western European counterparts is probably even more substantial.

At a meeting in Neuwied, Germany, organized in the 1980s by MCC to see whether more cooperation would be possible in Europe between Mennonites in the fields of aid, mission, and peace work, the representatives of the different *Umsiedler* groups made it clear that the word "peace" reminded them too much of the Soviet propaganda, and so they did not want to have anything to do with the European Mennonite peace movement. But they also had objections to cooperating in relief programs or mission projects. Even so, the meeting itself clearly was a meeting between brothers and sisters, even though agreement was not possible on the items on the agenda.

Unfortunately this meeting did not produce a European version of MCC. There remain many Mennonite relief organizations in Europe, but most of them are national organizations. Cooperation across borders does exist, however, through shared projects within the IMO (International Mennonite Organization), within the *Mennonitisches Hilfswerk* (Mennonite relief) based in Germany, and the Dutch *Bijzondere Noden* (Special Needs). The German organization *Christliche Dienste* (Christian Service) helps to find service placements for people from all over Europe who are willing to do relief work in other parts of the world.

One recent aspect of relief and peace work has been providing a shelter to refugees and to foreign migrants from outside Europe who are called "illegals" or, in the French language, *sans papiers* (without legal documents). In many places Mennonites, like many other Europeans, have worked to help these people. Sometimes they have sheltered people in their church buildings; often they have collected money, protested to the authorities, and visited refugee camps. This activity is still going on, often in cooperation with people from other churches. When war tore the former Yugoslavia apart during the 1990s, Mennonites from Germany, Switzerland and the Netherlands travelled there to take stock of what was needed and to help. They brought back frightful stories of rape and murder, and organized relief efforts for those who were suffering. Some people who were instrumental in this effort met during the 1994 MERK gathering in Colmar, France, to discuss the programs. Jasmina Tosic, a Yugoslav Christian who worked on distributing some of the material aid, presented a workshop during the MERK meetings held in Ludwigshafen, Germany, in 2000.

The work with and for the "illegals" is not so much a concerted European Mennonite thing, perhaps because of the different national rules and laws, but it does affect Mennonites in many European countries. European Mennonites are showing their responsibility for the victims of war, poverty and the sometimes inhuman behaviour of states.

The Role of Women

One reason the *Umsiedler* gave for not wishing to cooperate in the preparations for the 1996 MERK conference was that women were allowed to be active participants during the meetings. The role of women in Mennonite church-life in western Europe is a story in itself. In 1860 a Paris-based non-Mennonite author, Alfred Michiels, published a book about French Mennonites he had visited. He reports how an elder told him, among many other things:

> Each one of us in turn can function as a pastor, if the community judges him to be capable and chooses him to do so. To that end we have yearly elections. Everybody votes there, women as well as men, as we consider the woman to be our equal before God.[12]

In southern Germany women had the same voting rights in congregations, as a letter from 1769 demonstrates,[13] unlike female members in the Netherlands, northern Germany and the eastern countries. In the Netherlands, women in some congregations were allowed to cast a vote in choosing a pastor beginning around 1865. Not long after this some Dutch congregations expanded those voting rights to other cases as well, and by 1900 this was the case in the majority of Mennonite congregations in the Netherlands. In 1905 women became eligible to be elected as church board members in the Middelburg congregation (the Netherlands), and soon after in other Dutch congregations as well. At present, only one congregation in the Netherlands does not allow this. At the end of 1977 Abraham Gerber told me that his Sonnenberg congregation in Switzerland had just decided to give voting rights to sister members.

As has been seen above, there have been female pastors in Mennonite congregations in the Netherlands since 1911, the first one being Annie Mankes-Zernike. In German Mennonite congregations female pastors have been ordained since the last quarter of the twentieth century, but this does not mean that the German Mennonites were not interested in what was happening in the Netherlands. In 1905 the *Mennonitische Blätter* reported that in a 1904 meeting of representatives of the Dutch congregations the hope was expressed that in the future women could enter the seminary.[14] It took some time for the changes to be introduced elsewhere.

Of course, women had been active in Mennonite church life from the start, in other ways. Apart from doing chores and, in some cases, hosting the congregation for the Sunday morning worship service, as happened for instance in many congregations in France during the nineteenth century, women always played a role in the Christian education of the children, first in their own families, later on as Sunday school teachers. Often they visited the elderly and the sick. In the Netherlands and in Germany the institution of deaconess, as mentioned in article 9 of the Dordrecht Confession of Faith, was found in many congregations. In most of these congregations deaconesses disappeared during the nineteenth century. The Amsterdam, Haarlem and Utrecht Mennonite congregations kept the office of deaconess alive, however. Their function was to keep track of the old, sick and poor members and to care for them wherever and whenever needed. They would bring them food, clothes and provide other forms of support.

The deaconess office became the basis later for the German institution of deaconesses, although it took a different form. In Germany the office was tied to the "Deaconess Homes," rather than being an office with a single congregation. The founder of the Deaconess Homes,

Theodor Fliedner (1800–1864), was quite aware of the Dutch Mennonite way, but he thought the institution should fit within a general Protestant system. Thus it happened that in Germany around 1900, Mennonite deaconesses received their training in existing Deaconess Homes, but then served under Mennonite leadership in the south German congregations and in hospitals. One of them, Liesel Hege, served in the Tayu hospital (Java, Indonesia) under EMEK from 1950 to 1968. For some time, a part of the German retreat centre Thomashof, near Karlsruhe, served as a home for retired Mennonite deaconesses.

The MERK meetings have helped to highlight the talents of women. Women are visible as speakers and preachers and as leaders of workshops. And in the contributions of Europe to Mennonite World Conference Assemblies, such as in Calcutta in 1997 and at Bulawayo in 2003, women played an important public role. That was a conscious attempt to tell the world how Mennonite Europe thinks about the place of women in the church.

Interdenominational Relations

Ecumenical contacts among Christians in Europe have been significant and influential since the end of the Second World War. Of course, there were sporadic contacts between Mennonites and non-Mennonite churches before this. Jean Séguy reports on contacts between French Mennonites and the Salvation Army and other groups, for instance; Swiss and French Mennonites met with other Pietists in the Sankt Chrischona Bible School, and Dutch Mennonites met with both liberal and evangelical groups. However, after 1945, contacts were formalized and often became more intense. Soon after the Second World War the Conference of European Churches (CEC) was founded, with one of its goals being the creation of a platform where German Christians could meet again with Christian Churches from other European countries. Not much later it also became a place where Christians from the communist East and the non-communist West could meet, the Cold War notwithstanding. The Dutch and northern German Mennonites became members of the CEC, and in 1948 the Dutch and northern German Mennonites also were among the founding members of the WCC when it was launched in Amsterdam. In the view of many other European Mennonites, however, ecumenism in general, and the WCC in particular, were too liberal or "left wing," and these Mennonites found their inter-church contacts in the World Evangelical Alliance. The headquarters of both movements are geographically close, the one being connected with "Geneva" and the other with "Lausanne." On an optimistic note, both movements are opening up more and more to each other, thereby extending their ecumenical spirit.

An important development took place at the Harare, Zimbabwe, Assembly of the WCC in 1998. Fernando Enns, representing the German Mennonites on the WCC Central Committee, proposed a *Decade to Overcome Violence*. Enns had discussed this proposal earlier in a meeting of Mennonite delegates in Elspeet, the Netherlands, in October 1998. Other member churches of the WCC were well aware of Enns' Mennonite background, and they expressed an interest in Mennonite peace theology and everything connected to it. In the end the proposal was accepted, providing a dramatic example of Mennonite thinking influencing WCC policy. As Enns has pointed out, participating in the WCC offers an opportunity for Mennonites to make their theology better known throughout the WCC and its member churches.

As mentioned above, the WCC had asked the three Historic Peace Churches (Mennonites, Quakers and Church of the Brethren) to initiate discussions about their attitudes to war and peace immediately following the founding of the WCC in 1948—only three years after the Second World War. During that first Assembly WCC adopted a resolution saying "War is contrary to the will of God"; the Historic Peace Churches answered by saying "Peace is the will of God," and from this the Puidoux conferences were initiated in 1949. The committee set up by the peace churches to take part in these ecumenical discussions developed into a still-existing ecumenical organization, known since 1975 as *Church and Peace*. Here Mennonites meet with other Protestant and Roman Catholic groups who adhere to a nonresistance theology. In May 1999 *Church and Peace* celebrated its fiftieth anniversary at the Bienenberg. Keith Clements, general secretary of CEC, delivered the Sunday morning sermon, underlining the importance to the European churches of the peace testimony of "Church and Peace."

Ecumenical contacts on a smaller scale, that is dialogue meetings between churches, have offered similar opportunities for giving testimony to Mennonite peace theology. These meetings have taken place on a national scale in Germany and France between Mennonites and Lutherans, and in the Netherlands between Mennonites and Calvinist/Presbyterians. On a worldwide scale there have been dialogues between

Mennonites and Calvinists, Mennonites and Baptists, Mennonites and Roman Catholics, and most recently Mennonites and Lutherans. However important these meetings are—they do "officially" reconcile people that have lived apart from each other for centuries and also help soothe the pain of old wounds inflicted in the past—unfortunately they have scarcely any effect on the life of Mennonite congregations in Europe. The most positive results are the good and fruitful contacts local Mennonite congregations establish with their Lutheran, Calvinist, Roman Catholic and other neighbour churches. Here is where people recognize each other as Christians across denominational borders. That this is happening is partly a result of Mennonites integrating more and more in national social and cultural life.

As a result of the help European Mennonites give to refugees they also are confronted with Islam and other religions. That makes them ask new questions. Is God only a God of Mennonites? Of Christians? Or also of people from other religions? What in my faith and behaviour is faith and what is, in fact, culture? Thus these ecumenical and interreligious contacts can have a refreshing influence on our communities.

Changing Cultures, Changing Communities

In an article about the Sonnenberg congregation in Switzerland, Samuel Gerber writes about the growing integration of Mennonites into European society:

> We now have only 20% farmers and about 80% have jobs in other fields of work; some are studying. .... Fifty years ago Mennonite cultural life mainly carried the stamp of farming and congregational life. .... Now the circle of cultural engagements is much larger. We visit many events outside the congregation: classes, musical performances, sports events. Mass media found entrance in our families. School instruction has changed. The (German language) private Mennonite schools have disappeared; only one remains. Most of our youngsters now speak French. The more gifted ones go on to secondary schools, some even higher. Most try to learn a trade. This brings new ways of thinking in the families and the congregations, but new problems as well.[15]

This process of acculturation has been going on at different speeds, at different times and at different places in Europe. At the time of this writing, we can say that practically all European Mennonites have become urbanized. Some of the *Umsiedler* families have attempted to escape this reality by emigrating to Canada, hoping that there they will not be overtaken by the process.

As we have seen in previous chapters, in many places Mennonites had their own elementary schools during the nineteenth and twentieth centuries. The Mennonite secondary school at Weierhof, founded in 1867 by Michael Löwenberg,[16] is a good example: the school still exists, but cannot be called a Mennonite school anymore. In its earlier Mennonite phase it did have an influence on European Mennonites: Pierre Sommer, one of the most influential leaders of the French Mennonites in the first half of the twentieth century, studied there in the 1880s and 1890s under Christian Neff for a total of three years.

As we have seen, Mennonite pastors in Europe generally did not receive any special training at all, except in the Netherlands. Neff gave some training to aspiring preachers at the Weierhof school. After the Second World War, the Bienenberg Bible School began offering courses. In 1989, *Umsiedler* united in the *Bund Taufgesinnter Gemeinden* opened a seminary in Bonn (BSB). French theology students now may study in Vaux sur Seine, where some Mennonites are on the teaching faculty. German theological students often study at one of the many (non-Mennonite) German universities; some European students go to the United States for their theological studies, primarily at AMBS in Elkhart, Indiana; Bethel College in Newton, Kansas; the MB seminary at Fresno; and Eastern Mennonite University in Harrisonburg, Virginia. European Mennonites have also taught at these institutions. Since 1997 several Mennonite students from eastern Europe have studied at the International Baptist Theological Seminary in Prague (Czech Republic), which shows great interest in Anabaptism. In recent years, Mennonite theological educators from several European countries have met to exchange views. There is, as yet, no general European approach to Mennonite theological education. Both the institutional, theological and geographical contexts differ too much for there to be a united approach.

Conclusion

Some general observations can be drawn in conclusion. First of all, it is significant that the coming of political equality and citizen's rights in the nineteenth century had different results for Mennonites in different countries. As we have seen, Mennonites in France saw their numbers dwindle, largely through migration. Sixteen French Mennonite congregations disappeared in the nineteenth century,[17] and some Anabaptist principles like nonresistance disappeared. Mennonites in Krefeld and Hamburg experienced similar changes. But in the Netherlands the opposite was the case. There membership numbers had declined dramatically during the eighteenth century, but with the founding of the ADS in 1811, things took a turn for the better, at least as far as numbers are concerned.

There appear to be several reasons for the reversal in the Netherlands. First, the seminary produced educated preachers who were better qualified to preach and lead than were the untrained pastors before them. Second, the newly founded ADS had a fund from which poorer congregations could temporarily be subsidized, so that they could call seminary-trained pastors to their congregations. Third, over the centuries many Dutch Mennonite families had become quite wealthy and during the nineteenth century it became fashionable to become a member of a Mennonite church. Yet another reason for this growth was the more open, liberal atmosphere found in the Mennonite congregations as opposed to the more conservative Dutch churches. That made them attractive to people who wanted to live as Christians without being immobilized (as they felt it) by overly strict dogmatic rules. In the Netherlands this growth continued until about 1950; since that time there has been a sharp decline in numbers.

By contrast, in France the slow decline ended around 1900 and under the leadership of Pierre Sommer, and after him under the leadership of his son-in-law Pierre Widmer, the number of members stabilized. In the Europe of today, we see that all Mennonite groups, with the exception of the *Umsiedler* congregations, are small and, in many cases, getting smaller. These examples show that experiences within Europe can be very different depending on conditions within countries and the responses of the church to those conditions.

Fortunately there are convergences to report as well. Throughout Mennonite Europe there is a growing interest in formulating new statements or confessions of faith. In the Netherlands, the late Sjouke Voolstra[18] was a strong advocate, and though he met with resistance—many Dutch Mennonites were afraid of a "paper pope"[19]—still the recent North American "Confession of Faith in a Mennonite Perspective" (1995) has been translated into German, French and Dutch and widely discussed.

A problem that began to emerge between European Mennonites in the early twentieth century, as international meetings began, is the difference between the southern Mennonites (south Germany, Switzerland, France) and the northern ones (north Germany, the Netherlands). The issues that became visible then are still very much with European Mennonites today, and form an important part of our experience. One might summarize the divide between northern and southern Mennonites by saying that it is a difference between the heart—the seat of emotional life—as opposed to the mind—the seat of reason—being central to faith. Of course, French Mennonites have the gift of reason, just as the Dutch know that their heart must be at the centre of their faith. The difference in religious emphasis is not absolute, but nevertheless, it is present. French Mennonites in particular have had a hard time not condemning the beliefs of other Mennonites as unbelief, whereas others have been tempted to dismiss what they thought of as the backward conservatism of the French.

A positive approach to all this diversity would seem to be to consider the different Mennonite traditions of heart and mind as riches by which all could profit. This would require openness to listening intently to one another, in a willingness to share and learn. There are a good many issues on which European Mennonites disagree, such as abortion, euthanasia, homosexuality, the position of women in the congregation. The challenge is to be able to discuss different opinions without denying the true Christian faith of the other as the source of their opinions. Insofar as this process can take place, it will further the development of European, inter-Mennonite fellowship, strengthen the Mennonite church in all regions, and make European Mennonites better partners in our ecumenical contacts with other churches.

> **The late Charly Ummel, writing in the Swiss church paper *Perspektive*:**
>
> *Remodeling our confession of faith in the beginning of the 21st century should not just lead to a document, for better or worse; we should work on it. Above all, it should open up a dialogue that puts into play our theological differences, seen not as fears one hardly dares to formulate, but as riches and as complementary visions. We discuss feminism, homosexuality, family crisis, church discipline, sometimes without even touching on the subject and the problem itself, because everyone is sure to be right and to know the answers to the questions which are put.*
>
> *Let us not lose sight of the essential, let us have the courage to speak openly and frankly, leaving our prejudices and labels aside, and maybe we'll recover the spirit of the Gospel—given its place so well by Christ in the Sermon on the Mount—rather than the letter that often, in the Pharisee way, injures and paralyzes.*

Intensified ecumenical contacts have led to the question: "What sets us apart from the others? Or, in other words, what justifies our standing apart as Mennonite congregations and conferences? What is our place among the other churches?" Answering these questions undoubtedly will be our task as Mennonites in Europe for the near future. The focus has now fallen on what is essential about us as Mennonites, and what contribution we might be able to make, as Mennonites, to local, national and worldwide interchurch developments. Working out the answers to these questions will have to be done both in relation to "Geneva" and to "Lausanne," both in the context of the more liberal north and the more pietist south. One might say that a new "Anabaptist Vision" needs to be developed that speaks to people living in a world that is radically different from the world of the early Anabaptists. Nevertheless, this new vision must be a continuation of the free and radical way of reading the Bible and looking at the world that the Anabaptists initiated.

Of course, in the new global context, developing a relevant Anabaptist-Mennonite vision is not something that will be done just by European Mennonites—it has become a worldwide effort, reflecting the fact that Europe can no longer think of itself as the centre of the world, and the fact that European Mennonites now form a small minority within the global Mennonite-Anabaptist fellowship. It is to be hoped that European Mennonites will be able to embrace the challenges ahead, within the context of their changing environment, and let themselves be guided by the Spirit of God in openness to the wider community of faith.

Conference centre in Barcelona, site of MERK 2006.

Epilogue: Looking Ahead

by Alle G. Hoekema
and Hanspeter Jecker

The publication of this volume marks the first time a European Mennonite church history has been written by a team of authors from a number of countries and backgrounds. Our aim has been to write this volume on behalf of Mennonite readers and others not only in Europe, but also elsewhere in the world. In an authors' meeting several years ago John Lapp, one of the general editors of the series, emphasized the necessity to write in such a manner, that readers elsewhere in the world receive answers to their questions about this particular European history. Time and again in preparing this volume we had to observe how Europe-centred and focused exclusively on our own church history we as Mennonite church-historians tend to be. Working together on this volume taught all of us involved a valuable global lesson. Did we learn enough? Did we pay sufficient attention to the interaction between European Mennonites and African, Asian and Latin American Mennonites? Has the political, economic and religious context of the European Mennonites from 1800 to the present been taken into account well enough? Since this represents the first common effort to write our Mennonite European history from such a perspective, we have to confess that much could have been improved—especially if we had had another five years to do more research and to discuss methodology, historiography, geographical boundaries and many other such details with each other!

Nevertheless we are glad that this volume is now in the hands of readers. In this epilogue, we want to draw a few conclusions as to the most striking issues presented by this history, and to sketch some projections into the future.

Diversity

Seen from the perspective of Mennonites and others living on other continents, Europe may seem to be one geographical and homogeneous region, and the history of European Mennonites may also look to be a single, undivided history. However, Anabaptists, Mennonites and *Doopsgezinde* in Europe have been, and still are, divided by many basic differences. First of all, there is division by language: German, Dutch, French, Russian, English, Spanish, Italian, not to speak of Frisian, *Plattdeutsch*, *Schwyzerdütsch* and other regional languages! This fact has made communication difficult, both in the past and in the present. Therefore it is surprising to notice how many inter-European contacts existed already during the eighteenth and nineteenth centuries among Mennonite scholars and Mennonite groups.

In the second place, Mennonites have also been divided by national boundaries, many of which were unstable during most of the two-hundred-year span that circumscribes the history described in this volume. Often the countries in which Mennonites lived waged war against each other, and more than once the question whether priority should be given to belonging to the people of God, or belonging to some nation state, became a difficult dilemma in the often bitter realities of life. Thirdly, European Mennonites were, and still are, divided in their social and cultural life-style: some are farmers in Swiss mountain villages, in the south German hilly country, or in the West Prussian or Russian plains; others are urban citizens in, for instance, Hamburg, Danzig, Amsterdam, Bern and more recently, Paris, Barcelona and London. The policies of local and national governments adopted towards religious minorities such as the Mennonites certainly enforced these cultural and social differences.

A fourth factor, and an important one, is related to the different government policies adopted in different countries: some Mennonite groups were allowed to stay where they were born, to settle down and to become a respected (and sometimes affluent) part of society or, if not given all freedoms, at least allowed to become respected *Stille im Lande*, quiet citizens. Other Mennonites have been migrants during most of the two centuries from 1800 on, partly because of religious persecution, partly for economic reasons. Especially the involuntary migrant aspect of many European Mennonites has caused them to be a minority which is basically different from other religious denominations on this continent.

All these factors influenced the theological and ethical interpretations of the spiritual heritage of Mennonites: the radical discipleship which had motivated their fathers and mothers in the faith. So arose the tension between more rationalistic and more ecumenical Mennonites on one side, and more pietistic, sometimes charismatic, and more evangelical Mennonites on the other. Sometimes these differences were obstacles that prevented meeting one other; fortunately, at other moments, a deep fraternal love was able to overcome such barriers.

Political Barriers

Of course, in the nineteenth century there were many instances when wars or nationalistic sentiments did prevent contact or cooperation between Mennonites in Europe. At that time, however, it was still possible to practice one's faith in an isolated way in different territories. This became impossible during the twentieth century.

Two important divisive barriers for Mennonites during the twentieth century were the Communist regime in Russia (and after 1945 in eastern Europe as a whole) and the Second World War. The Communist regime hit the Russian and Ukrainian Mennonites very hard, as it did other German-speaking minorities in those territories as well. For many years contacts between west-European Mennonites and their Russian brothers and sisters were very limited, and in the 1950s and 1960s such contacts as there were aroused serious suspicion on both sides of the iron curtain. When five Russian brothers (Baptists and Mennonites) participated in the Wichita Assembly of the MWC in 1978, there were rumours that at least one of them had to play the role of watchdog. On the other hand, the assistance that west-European Mennonites were able to provide to those who could manage to flee to the West meant a deepening of feelings of fellowship.

As to the Second World War, it is not without reason that the period between 1933 and 1945 has been described extensively in several of the chapters in this volume. Speaking freely with one another about this cruel war may still be one of the last taboos facing our church. Even though individual Mennonite brothers and sisters from several countries have expressed their feelings of guilt, sorrow, pain and forgiveness to each other, the years of the Nazi regime still form a serious barrier between Dutch and German Mennonites. The feelings and opinions of Russian and Ukrainian Mennonites, and German, Dutch and also French Mennonites often differ deeply here. Although heroes, fellow-travellers, traitors, foes and cowards could be found on all sides, it remains very difficult to discuss these things openly with each other. Yet, we will not truly become a European Mennonite family until such taboos are broken down. Oral history can play a role here, but it is only recently that efforts have been initiated to collect oral testimonies about this time of war. We do not have much time left to speak with such witnesses!

Cooperation

On a more positive note, the work of mission and relief organizations after 1945 was a blessing, in that it forced Mennonites from Germany, Switzerland, France and the Netherlands to cooperate. Certainly, this cooperation (starting with EMEK, the European Mennonite Evangelization Committee in 1951, only six years after the war), has been very important for the European Mennonite church of today. The role of MCC should not be underestimated here. As has been indicated in several chapters in this volume, inter-Mennonite collaboration in missionary work did start in the nineteenth century already, but whereas missionary organizations mainly cooperated on behalf of mission fields in Asia, Africa and South America, the relief organizations started projects on behalf of *Umsiedler* and *Aussiedler*, both in West Germany and in countries like Paraguay and Brazil. In both cases, missions and relief helped to bring global perspectives to bear: European Mennonites came out of their cocoons. The peace witness, especially in Europe itself, became a third aspect of this growing globalisation. Of course, the MWC assemblies, especially the ones held in Europe, and the gatherings of the European Mennonite Regional Conference (MERK) formed an important stimulus as well.

Identity and Unity

To date, the recent mission and relief integrating efforts have been supported by the established (and numerically shrinking) west-European Mennonites only. Seen from an historical point of view, one can understand fully why *Aussiedler* and *Umsiedler*, who settled down in Germany have hesitated in joining such efforts. Their lines of reflection are still marked by the dilemmas of a fatherland which is both lost and the source of cruel experiences, and not yet by the challenges a new, united western Europe can offer. However, from the perspective of the unity of all Mennonites in Europe, the self-isolation of this large group of Mennonites makes the others feel concerned. In the near future European Mennonites will need to define or redefine their identity in the midst of many other Christian denominations, both evangelical and ecumenical in orientation, within a European society which is secularised, multi-cultural and multi-religious. Such a redefinition presupposes the possibility of open discussions between all groups involved.

From the chapter on the *Aussiedler* above it can be concluded that the many groups of *Aussiedler* in present-day Germany still wrestle with their identity. Are they Mennonites? A branch of the Baptists? Are they Evangelicals? Whereas other west-European Mennonites have begun meeting together more frequently, and seem to understand and appreciate each others' contexts little-by-little, the *Aussiedler* are still too occupied with their internal affairs, partly looking backwards to the unfortunate end of their history in Russia, partly trying to cope with their new, and in some respects threatening, cultural situation. In numbers, however, the *Aussiedler* far exceed the older, established Mennonites in Germany, the Netherlands, France and Switzerland. This imposes a certain obligation on both sides, it seems, as they set out on the quest for a new Anabaptist identity in Europe.

Without pronouncing any judgment, we also have to admit that for many *Aussiedler*, most other European Mennonites have become too "worldly." This presents a challenge to both sides.

The history of the *Ausssiedler* has been, and in part continues to be, a history of *migrants*, even in the New Testament sense of being "strangers and aliens" (Ephesians 2:19). What does this mean to other Mennonites in Europe, and to other Christians in general, who face the arrival of many other groups of such migrants, as for instance, Armenians, Pakistani Christians, Ethiopians and Eritreans, Congolese refugees and others? What are the lessons we can draw from this Mennonite migration history?

Old and New Congregations

A number of Mennonite congregations have died out over the past two centuries. Sometimes this was due to economic reasons, such as changing trade patterns or depopulation of rural areas, as in northern Germany and the Netherlands, sometimes it was due to government limitations or to a lack of innovative faith. The total disappearance of Mennonite congregations in Prussia and (the present) Poland, and the near-extinction of Mennonites in Russia and the Ukraine form a hurtful category on its own. Here the effects of war become visible in its cruelest form, similar to what is experienced in our time by the large numbers of refugees who are on the move in Asia and Africa.

On the other hand, new urban congregations have emerged as a result of migration or the work of active students' groups. A new, post-war phenomenon in Europe is church-planting by missionary organizations. The slogan "mission on six continents" has been taken up by Mennonites as well! In the necessary quest for identity—of which the writing of a global Mennonite history forms a part—we may be stimulated enormously by the members of the new missionary congregations in Europe which have been described above. These new congregations are based upon solid biblical Anabaptist convictions instead of upon family traditions or the carrying of typically Mennonite names. Will it be too heavy a burden for these small missionary communities to take the lead in this quest for identity? Will they be strong enough to survive, once the North American midwives who assisted at their birth, withdraw in the future? The assets these new, young communities bring to the older Mennonite family are a strong sense of peace and reconciliation (London, Belfast); a convincingly evangelical attitude (Italy), and a desire to serve the needy in society (Barcelona). We have to confess that only a few of the established Mennonite communities are really ready for multi-cultural openness; the missionary congregation in Paris provides a good example in this respect, and points the way to an important task that lies ahead for all European Mennonites.

It is the hope of the editors that this volume will contribute to a reflection on our past, on behalf of our future. Looking back over two centuries of history of European Mennonites, it is evident that often (yet certainly not always!) their fate was determined by events totally outside the control of the churches or the members themselves. Of course, we can draw lessons from history, at least when we sincerely try to record this history in a fair and, as far as possible, "objective" way. Nevertheless, it remains difficult to make predictions concerning the future. The present geographic map is completely different from the one two hundred years ago. Numerically and socially, the influence of Mennonites in western Europe has decreased. Nobody, however, can measure the strength of faith; that lies beyond the competence of historians, no matter how carefully the congregational life in the past and present has been described. In the end, it is this factor of faithfulness and trust which will decide the future presence and role of Mennonites in Europe.

Appendix A

List of Anabaptist-Mennonite Conferences in Europe (2006)[1]

Organization name	MWC Membership	Year Established[2]	Country	Number of Congregations	Number Baptized
Mennonitische Freikirche Österreich	Non	1970	Austria	6	416
Broederschap der Amish Mennonieten	Non		Belgium	1	13
Centre Mennonite de Bruxelles	Non	1972	Belgium	2	35
Members in Russia, Ukraine, Kazakhstan, Kyrgyzstan, Siberia	Non		CIS		4000
Association des Eglises Evangéliques Mennonites de France	Full	1925	France	32	2100
AGAPE-Gemeindewerk - Mennonitische Heimatmission e. V.	Non	1969	Germany	6[3]	180[3]
Arbeitsgemeinschaft Mennonitischer Brüdergemeinden in Deutschland	Non	1966	Germany	15	1519
Arbeitsgemeinschaft Mennonitischer Gemeinden in Deutschland	Full	1990	Germany	54	5900
Arbeitsgemeinschaft zur geistlichen Unterstützung in Mennonitengemeinden e.v.	Non	1978	Germany	24	5573
Bund Taufgesinnter Gemeinden	Non	1989	Germany	9	3500
Evangelische Freikirche Missionsgemeinde Bad Pyrmont	Non		Germany	1	43
Mennonitenbrudergemeinden (Independent Mennonite Brethren congregations)	Non		Germany	46	13970
Mennonitenkirchgemeinden (Independent Mennonite congregations)	Non		Germany	7	1800
Verband der Evangelischen Freikirchen Mennonitischer Brüdergemeinden in Bayern (VMBB)	Non		Germany	5	291
Beachy Amish Mennonite Fellowships (Ireland)	Non	1992	Ireland	1	22
Chiesa Evangelica Mennonita Italiana	Full	1981	Italy	8	258
Association Mennonite Luxembourgeoise	Non	1953	Luxembourg		
Algemene Doopsgezinde Sociëteit	Full	1811	Netherlands	121	10200
Associação dos Irmãos Menonitas de Portugal	Non	1989	Portugal	5	100
Nathaniel Mennonite Church (Beachy Amish Mennonite)	Non		Romania	1	43
Asociación de Menonitas y Hermanos en Cristo en España	Assoc.	1989	Spain	7	153
Konferenz der Mennoniten der Schweiz (Alttäufer), Conférence Mennonite Suisse (Anabaptiste)	Full	1983	Switzerland	14	2300
Christian Union of Mennonite Churches in Ukraine	Non	2004	Ukraine	4	180
Evangelical Mennonite Church (Beachy Amish Mennonite)	Non		Ukraine	2	74
Brethren in Christ Church, UK	Non		UK	5	215
British Conference of Mennonites	Assoc.	1987	UK	1	25

[1] Data from Mennonite World Conference (2006).
[2] The origins of some preceding organizations are considerably older.
[3] Information from 2003.

Appendix B

Chronological Chart of Anabaptist-Mennonite History

	General History	Church History	Anabaptist History (Switz., So. Ger, Alsace, Moravia)	Anabaptist History (No. Ger, Netherlands, Prussia, Russia)
1500–1525	1500ff Growing unrest in general population 1521 Imperial Diet of Worms: Luther outlawed	1516 Erasmus Greek NT 1517 Luther's Theses 1520ff Radical Reformation movement (Karlstadt, Müntzer) 1522 September Bible (NT)	1519 Zwingli in Zürich 1523 Establishment of Reformation in Zürich 1523f Separation between Zwingli and radical circle (Grebel, Mantz, Blaurock, Reublin, Stumpf, Brötli etc.); attempts to contact Karlstadt and Müntzer	1500ff Sacramentarian movement in the Netherlands
1525–1550	1525 Peasants' War: Defeat of the Peasants 1548 Augsburg Interim	1528 Imperial edict against Anabaptists 1529 Comp. Zürich Bible 1529 Marburg: no consensus between Luther and Zwingli in Q.of Supper 1530 Augsburg Confession 1534 Comp.Luther Bible 1536ff/41ff Calvin in Geneva 1545ff Catholic Reform (Council of Trent)	1525 First Believers' Baptism in Zürich 1525ff Persecution and spread (Switz., Alsace, so. Ger., Moravia, Austria). 1527 Schleitheim Articles (M.Sattler, Swiss Brethren) 1528ff Marpeck circle (Alsace/Switz./so. Ger.) 1533 J.Hutter community leader in Moravia: Hutterites 1540ff Differences with Spiritualism (Schwenckfeld)	1530ff Melchior Hoffman's extensive Anabaptist mission activity (Neth., no. Ger.) 1534f Anabaptist kingdom, Münster 1536 Menno becomes Anabap. (Mennonites) 1540ff Conflict with Spiritualism (Joris and others) 16th century emigration (Neth. to Prussia)
1550–1600	1598 Edict of Nantes; end of Huguenot War	1550-1650/1700 Orthodoxy 1555 Peace of Augsburg 1566 Second Helvetic Confession	1554ff Strasbourg Conferences (Swiss Br., Hutt., Mennonites) 1570ff Massive emigration Swiss Br./so. Ger. to Moravia 1571 Frankenthal Disputation betw. Anabaptists and Reformed 1585 Protestant Swiss Cantons unite against Anabaptists	1554ff Mennonites ban Swiss Br./ Hutterites 1561 Death of Menno Simons 1562 Martyrology: *Het Offer des Heeren* 1579 Union of Utrecht: Religious freedom – End to persecution and discrimination
1600–1650	1618ff Thirty Years' War 1648 Peace of Westphalia	1606ff Johannes Arndt's "True Christianity"	1614 Execution of H.Landis (Zürich) 1618-48 War brings end to most communities in Alsace, Palatinate, Moravia 1630-50 End of almost all communities in Zürich through expulsion and emigration (to Alsace and the Palatinate 1648ff.)	1608 Contact of English separatists with Dutch Mennonites – Foundation of the Baptists (1609) 1632 Dordrecht Confession
1650–1700	1672-79 Dutch War 1685 Revocation of the Edict of Nantes 1688-97 Palatine War	1675 Programmatic writing for Pietism: Spener's *Pia Desideria* 1699f Arnold's "Unpartheyische Kirchen- und Ketzerhistorie"	1660 Alsatian communities accept "Dordrecht Confession" 1664 Legal toleration in the Palatinate 1671ff/1690ff Intensive persecution in Bern: expulsion and emigration to Alsace und the Palatinate – Diplomatic und financial help from Dutch Mennonites. 1693ff Amish	1660 First edition, *Martyrs Mirror* 1683 Emigration of Krefeld Mennonites and Quakers to Pennsylvania
1700–1750	1701-14 War of Spanish Succession	1700ff Mandates vs Pietists, esp. against separatist radical wing 1708 Founding of the Schwarzenauer Baptists (Church of the Brethren) 1730ff Infl. Herrnhuter	1711ff Further expulsions from Bern 1712 Eviction from Alsace, emigration to the Jura, Palatinate, Montbéliard, Netherlands, North America 1743 End persecution in Bern	1735 Theol. Seminary in Amsterdam

General History	Church History	Anabaptist History (Switz., So. Ger, Alsace, Moravia)	Anabaptist History (No. Ger, Netherlands, Prussia, Russia)	
1788 Constitution, USA **1789ff** French Revolution **1799** Napoleon crowned Emperor	**1750ff** Growing influence of the Enlightenment and Rationalism	**1750ff** General acceptance of Mennonites and their integration into society. **1773** First gathering place in the Palatinate: Weierhof **1780ff** Emigration from Alsace, the Palatinate (and Prussia) to Volhynia und Galicia	**1789ff** Mennonites from Prussia to the Ukraine: Chortitza (colony est.)	1750–1800
1815 Defeat of Napoleon; Congress of Vienna **1830** Belgium secedes from Holland **1830/48** European Revolutions **1848** Communist Manifesto	**1815ff** Movements of Spiritual Awakening **1834ff** "German Baptism": Baptist free churches	**1803/05** Ibersheim Resolutions **1815ff** Further emigration to NA (to the end of the 19.century, for economic reasons and debate about military service) **1832ff** "New Anabaptists": S. H. Fröhlich – Expand to Switz./Alsace/so. Ger., then to east Europe, NA **1835** Division in the Emmental "Old- and New Anabaptists" **1847** First church building in Switzerland: Basel-Holee	**1803:** Molotschna (colony est.) **1811** Union of Dutch Mennonites in the Algemene Doopsgezinde Societeit (ADS) **1847** DZV (Mennonite Mission Society)	1800–1850
Est. of general military conscription in Europe **1870** Franco-Prussian War **1885** Berlin Conference of colonial powers	**1875ff** Holiness Movement	**1854** Founding of the "Verband" **1860ff** Development of the "Neutäufer" into a closed community **1868** Standing Order: Ger. Mennonites allowed CO status **1886** Founding of the "Vereinigung" **1887** South German Conference **1880ff** Marked influence of the Holiness Movement	**1851** P.Jansz (Neth.) first Missionary (Java) **1860** Est. of MB churches in Russia **1871** Heinrich Dirks – first Russian Menn. missionary (Sumatra) **1873ff** Emigration Russian Menn. to NA **1889** Abraham and Mary Frieren to India	1850–1900
1914-1918 World War I **1918ff** Communism, Russia **1929** World Economic Crisis **1933** Nazis come to power **1939-1945** World War II	**1900ff** Religious Socialism **1905ff** Pentecostal Movement **1920ff** Bruderhof movement (E.Arnold) **1920ff** Dialectical Theology (K.Barth and others) **1948** Founding of WCC	**1913ff** *Mennonitisches Lexikon* **1920** Founding MCC and MWC **1925** MWC I, Basel; 1930 MWC II, Danzig; 1936 MWC III, Netherlands **1944** "Anabaptist Vision" – Question of self-identity **1949** First Mennonite communities in Italy	**1917ff** Renewal Movement in Neth. **1923ff** Emigration of Russian/Prussian Menn. to NA/SA/Ger **1936** Intl. Mennonite Peace Committee **1941** Flight/deportation of Russian Mennonites **1945** End of the West Prussian communities	1900–1950
1957 Eur. Common Market **1966-1973** Vietnam War **1967** European Union **1968ff** Student unrest **1970ff** Oil crisis; "Limits to growth" **1989** Fall of Berlin Wall **1991** End of USSR **1991** First Iraq War **2003ff** Second Iraq War	**1960ff** Growth of Evangelicalism **1973** WCC World mission conference in Bangkok: Moratorium for Mission **1974** World Evangelization Congress in Lausanne **1975** Dialogue Mennonites/Baptists with Calvinists, Neth. **1989-1992** Luth.-Menn. Dialogue, Ger.	**1950** European Mennonite Bible School (Theol. Seminary Bienenberg) **1951** Foundation EMEK **1952** MWC V, Switzerland; **1957** MWC VI , Germany **1953/54** Mennonites in England, Belgium, and Paris **1984** MWC X, Strasbourg **1974** Regular consultations, Mennonites and the ETG in Switzerland **1975** MERK I, Switz.; **1981** MERK III, Ger.; **1988** MERK IV, Switz.; **1993** MERK V, Fr.; **2000** MERK VII, Germany **2006** Growth of mission churches: 1.3 million Mennonites worldwide **2006** MERK VIII, Spain	**1967** MWC VIII, Netherlands **1973ff** Return of German Russians to Ger. **1973** Founding of IMO **1977** MERK II, Neth.; **1989** Founding of BTG **1990** Founding of AMG **1996** MERK VI, Neth.	1950–

Abbreviations

ABD	*Aussiedler Betreuungsdienst* (Immigrants' Assistance Service)
ADS	*Algemene Doopsgezinde Sociëteit* (General Mennonite Conference, Netherlands)
AEEMF	*Association des Eglises Evangéliques Mennonites de France* (Conference of Evangelical Mennonite Churches in France)
AFHAM	*Association Francaise D'Histoire Anabaptiste-Mennonite* (French Association for Anabaptist-Mennonite History)
AMBS	*Associated Mennonite Biblical Seminary* (Elkhart, Indiana, USA)
AMG	*Arbeitsgemeinschaft Mennonitischer Gemeinden in Deutschland* (Association of Mennonite Congregations in Germany)
AMML	*Association Missionnaire Mennonite de Lorraine* (Associated Mennonite Mission of Lorraine, France)
ASM	*Arbeitsgemeinschaft Südwestdeutscher Mennonitengemeinden* (Association of Mennonite Congregations in Southwest Germany)
BEFG	*Bund Evangelisch-Freikirchlicher Gemeinden* (Union of Evangelical Free Church Congregations)
BMS	Baptist Missionary Society
BN	*Bijzondere Noden* (Foundation for Special Needs, Netherlands)
BSB	*Bibelseminar Bonn* (Bible Seminary Bonn)
CD	*Christliche Dienste* (Christian Service, Germany)
CEC	Conference of European Churches
CIM	Council of International Anabaptist Ministries (North American)
CIS	Commonwealth of Independent States (former Soviet Union)
DMFK	*Deutsches Mennonitisches Friedens-Komitee* (German Mennonite Peace Committee)
DMMK	*Deutsches Mennonitisches Missions Komitee* (German Mennonite Mission Committee)
DVG	*Doopsgezinde Vredes Groep* (Mennonite Peace Group, Netherlands)
DZR	*Doopsgezinde Zendingsraad* (Mennonite Mission Board, Netherlands)
DZV	*Doopsgezinde Zendings Vereeniging* (Mennonite Mission Society, Netherlands)
EMEK	*Europäisches Mennonitisches Evangelisations-Komitee* (European Mennonite Evangelization Committee)
EMM	Eastern Mennonite Missions
EMMK	*Europäisches Mennonitisches Missions-Komitee* (European Mennonite Mission Committee)
ETG	*Evangelische Täufer-Gemeinden* (Evangelical Anabaptist Congregations; in North America known as *Apostolic Christian Church* [Nazarene])
GDB	*Gemeenschap voor Doopsgezind Broederschapswerk* (Mennonite Association of Congregational Renewal, Netherlands)
GITJ	*Gereja Injili di Tanah Jawa* (Evangelical Church on Java, Indonesia; also called Javanese Mennonite Church)

HVDM	*Hilfswerk der Vereinigung Deutscher Mennonitengemeinden* (Relief Organization of the Association of Mennonite Congregations in Germany)
IBB	*Indianer-Beratungs-Behörde* (Inter-Mennonite Advisory Board for ministries with Paraguayan Indians)
IMO	*Internationale Mennonitische Organisation* (International Mennonite Relief Organization)
IVEP	International Visitor Exchange Program
JSM or JuWe	*Jugendwerk Süddeutscher Mennonitengemeinden* (Youth Work of South German Mennonite Congregations)
KMS / CMS	*Konferenz der Mennoniten der Schweiz (Alttäufer) / Conférence mennonite suisse (Anabaptistes)* (Conference of Mennonites of Switzerland)
KSM	*Konferenz Süddeutscher Mennonitengemeinde* (Conference of South German Mennonite Churches)
KZ	*Konzentrationslager* (concentration camp)
MB	*Mennoniten-Brüdergemeinden* (Mennonite Brethren Congregations)
MBM	Mennonite Board of Missions
MBMC	Mennonite Board of Missions and Charities
MCC	Mennonite Central Committee
MEDA	Mennonite Economic Development Agency
MERK	*Mennonitische Europäische Regional-Konferenz* (Mennonite European Regional Conference)
MH	*Mennonitisches Hilfswerk* (Mennonite Relief Agency, Germany)
MHC	*Mennonitisches Hilfswerk Christenpflicht* (Mennonite Relief Agency Christenpflicht)
MHV	*Mennonitischer Heimeverein* (Association of Mennonite Old People's Homes)
MJN	*Mennonitische Jugend Norddeutschlands* (Mennonite Youth, North Germany)
MMF	*Mission Mennonite Française (MMF)* (French Mennonite Mission)
MUB	*Mennonitische Umsiedlerbetreuung* (Mennonite Resettlers' Assistance)
MVS	Mennonite Voluntary Service
MWC	Mennonite World Conference
NATO	North Atlantic Treaty Organization
SMEK	*Schweizerisches Mennonitisches Evangelisations-Komitee* (Swiss Mennonite Evangelization Committee)
SMM	*Schweizerische Mennonitische Mission* (Swiss Mennonite Mission)
SMO	*Schweizerische Mennonitische Organisation* (Swiss Mennonite Relief Organization)
SOH	*Stichting Oecumenische Hulp* (Foundation for Ecumenical Aid)
VELKD	*Vereinigung Evangelisch-Lutherische Kirche Deutschlands* (Union of Evangelical Lutheran Churches in Germany)
WCC	World Council of Churches

End Notes

Chapter I

1 The term "Anabaptist(e/a)" is used neutrally in English, French or Spanish. Only in the German language is it connected to the old term used for heresy (*Wieder-Täufer*).

2 The Swiss Mennonites have named their conference in this way for only a few years—earlier they called themselves "Old Evangelical Baptist-Minded Congregations" (*Altevangelisch Taufgesinnte Gemeinden*) or "Old Baptists" (*Alttäufer*) in contrast to the "New Baptists" (*Neutäufer*) of Samuel Fröhlich. Among the members of the Mennonite World Conference, there are several groups who do not use the term "Mennonite" in their name.

3 The excessive good works of the saints were sold in portions in the letters of indulgences; they were to reduce the expected punishments in purgatory for one's own sins.

4 The term "Free Church" was used first in the nineteenth century in Scotland to emphasize the independence of a Scottish church from the Church of England.

5 J. P. Jacobszoon, "Johannes Deknatel, een amsterdamse mennist in het gezelschap van Zinzendorf," (MA ["doctoraal"] Thesis, University of Amsterdam, n.d.).

Chapter II

1 According to the dictionary *Le Petit Robert*, Paris, 2002, nationalism is a doctrine founded on the exaltation of national sentiment, subordinating all internal politics to the development of national power and claiming the right to assert this power externally without limitations of sovereignty, the opposite being internationalism.

2 The word "ecumenical" was first used in connection with evangelical groups by the evangelical, Adolphe Monod in 1846. He spoke of an "ecumenical spirit." Already in 1795, the London Missionary Society belonged to all of the denominations.

3 Danièle Hervieu-Leger, *Vers un nouveau christianisme?* (Cerf, 1986).

4 Max Weber, ed. by Stephen Kalberg, *The Protestant Ethic and the Spirit of Capitalism*, 3rd edition (Los Angeles: Roxbury Publishing Company, 2001).

5 Pierre Gerbet, *La Construction de l'Europe*, Coll. Notre siècle, (Paris : Imprimerie nationale, 1983), 12.

6 John A. Lapp & C. Arnold Snyder (eds.), *A Global Mennonite History: Africa* (Kitchener: Pandora Press, 2003).

7 Jean-François Zorn, *Encyclopédie du Protestantisme*, (Paris: Editions Cerf et Genève: Labor et Fides, 1995), 221.

Chapter III

1 After the fall of Emperor Napoleon, the countries which had defeated France came together in Vienna to define the new borders of European countries. At the Congress of Vienna, the Netherlands got Belgium and the Grand-Duchy of Luxembourg. In 1830, the Belgians began a war of secession. Since Belgium was Catholic and also did not contribute much to the economic growth of the total country, the Dutch were not unhappy to let the Belgians go.

2 For example: Zonist Mennonites (father and son Van Nieuwenhuijzen) founded and headed the soon influential *Maatschappij tot Nut van 't Algemeen*, a society to promote the welfare for all people. With good public schools, libraries, children's school books etc.

they hoped to enlighten society and to educate the lower classes in natural and Christian virtues.

3   Quoted in Annelies Verbeek, *"Menniste Paus." Samuel Muller (1785-1875) en zijn netwerken* (Hilversum: Verloren 2005), 49.

4   Jan de Liefde, *Gevaar, Gevaar! En geene vrede! Een woord tot de slapenden en de in slaap gewiegden* (Zutphen 1844).

5   Pieter Post, "God! ontzaglijk Albestuurder! Een 'voortreffelijk' lied van Arend Hendrik van Gelder (1756-1819)," in *Doopsgezinde Bijdragen NR* 28 (2002): 115-126.

6   J. J. Schiere, "De architectuur van doopsgezinde kerken," in *Doopsgezinde Bijdragen NR* 3 (1977): 71-100.

7   J. M. Welcker, "Een Eeuw Doopsgezinde Kweekschool, 1811-1914," *Doopsgezinde Bijdragen NR* 11 (1985): 44-86; see also J. M. Welcker, "De Doopsgezinde Kweekschool tot 1940," *Doopsgezinde Bijdragen NR* 15 (1988): 11-54.

8   E. I. T. Brussee-van der zee, "Broederschap en nationaal-socialisme," *Doopsgezinde Bijdragen NR* 11 (1985): 118-129.

9   See Jeanet van Woerden-Surink, *Hollandsch Doopsgezind Emigranten Bureau 1924-1940* (n.p., Seminary Paper, 1999).

10 E. I. T. Brussee-van der Zee, "Broederschap en nationaal-socialisme," 121-122.

11 Anton van der Lem, "Men of principles and men of learning: The Mennonite backgrounds of some Dutch historians, with special reference to Johan Huizinga and Jan Romein," in Alistair Hamilton e.a. (eds), *From Martyr to Muppy. A historical introduction to cultural assimilation processes of a religious minority in the Netherlands: the Mennonites* (Amsterdam: Amsterdam University Press 1994), 203-221. Jan Romein was another noted historian, baptized as a Mennonite in 1913, but later turning to socialism. A well-known poet, Herman Gorter, followed a similar track.

12 Quoted by E. I. T. Brussee-van der Zee, 119. See for this paragraph also Gerlof Homan, "Nederlandse doopsgezinden in de Tweede Wereldoorlog," *Doopsgezinde Bijdragen NR* 21 (1995): 165-197 which is a revised version of his article in *MQR* 69 (1995): 7-36.

13 No major study has been written about the Dutch Mennonites during WW II. At present a task force is collecting oral history reports. The diaries and reports of a Mennonite-Quaker task force in Zaandam/Amsterdam, initiated by Cor Inja to assist Jews during World War II, are awaiting publication. Besides referring to Elisabeth Brussee's article and Gerlof Homan's essay in note 12, we can mention Nine Treffers-Mesdag, "De pastorie in Sneek onder de bezetting. Eenige persoonlijke indrukken van de positie en de houding van doopsgezinden in de Tweede Wereldoorlog," *Doopsgezinde Bijdragen NR* 24 (1998): 273-280. Pastor Mesdag and his wife posthumously received "the medal of the Righteous among the nations" of Yad Vashem, Jerusalem. A few other Dutch Mennonites received the same honour. See also André J. du Croix, "Weerloos weerbaar; het verzet van dominee André du Croix, (1910-1945)" and Gerlof Homan "Een doopsgezinde gemeente in oorlogstijd: Zuid-Limburg, Heerlen," both in *Doopsgezinde Bijdragen NR* 31 (2005): 223-262 and 263-276.

14 Information on this section in R. de Zeeuw, "De vlucht van Bijzondere Noden," *Doopsgezind Jaarboekje* 81, (1987): 22-32; J. E. Klanderman, *Hulplijnen. Het Hulpwerk van de Doopsgezinde Broederschap in Nederland in de periode 1947-1980* (n.p., Seminary Paper, 1991).

15 A brief overview of the mission work of European Mennonites, including a list of all mission workers from 1851 till 1972, can be found in Leo Laurense, *125 Jahre Zusammenarbeit in der mennonitischen Mission* (s.l.: EMEK, 1972).

Chapter IV

[1] Christoph Wiebe, "'… daß und warum sie im Aussterben begriffen seien.' 21 Reflexionen zu Gegenwart und Zukunft der deutschen Mennoniten," in *Mennonitische Geschichtsblätter*, 61 (2004): 97-108.

[2] Diether Götz Lichdi, *Mennoniten im Dritten Reich, Dokumentation und Deutung* (Weierhof: Mennonitischer Geschichtsverein, 1977), 47.

[3] Lichdi, *Mennoniten im Dritten Reich*, 145-46.

[4] Dirk Cattepoel, "The History of Mennonites in Germany, 1936-1948, and the Present Outlook" *Proceedings of the Fourth Mennonite World Conference, Goshen, IN. and North Newton, KS. Aug. 3-10, 1948* (Akron, PA: Mennonite Central Committee, 1950), 14-15.

[5] Lichdi, *Mennoniten in Geschichte und Gegenwart*, 199.

Chapter V

[1] *Mennonitische Blätter* 2 (1858): 19.

[2] *Gemeindeblatt* 3 (1879): 20.

[3] Markus Nägeli, "Die Evangelische Gesellschaft des Kantons Bern in der Auseinandersetzung mit der Heiligungsbewegung," in Rudolf Dellsperger, Markus Nägeli, Hansueli Ramser (Eds.), *Auf dein Wort. Beiträge zur Geschichte und Theologie der Evangelischen Gesellschaft des Kantons Bern im 19. Jahrhundert*, (Bern: Berchtold-Haller-Verlag, 1981), 223-496. (Quotation on page 380).

[4] *Kurzgefasstes Glaubensbekenntnis der Altevangelischen Taufgesinnten-Gemeinde im Emmental. Mit Belegen aus der Heiligen Schrift* (Langnau: Christliche Schriftenniederlage Johann Kipfer, Kehr, 1937). Cf. Hanspeter Jecker, "Die Militärfrage. Die Haltung der schweizerischen Täufer zur Entwicklung der Allgemeine Wehrpflicht," Basel: (mimeographed manuscipt) 1976, 15f.

[5] These minutes are kept in the Conference Archives at Jeanguisboden near Corgémont.

Chapter VI

[1] Marc Lienhard / Pierre Widmer (Ed.), "Les entretiens Luthéro-Mennonites (1981-1984)" in *Cahiers de Christ-Seul*, Montbéliard, N·16, July 1984.

Chapter VII

[1] Horst Gerlach, *Die Russlandmennoniten: Ein Volk unterwegs* (Kirchheimbolanden: Selbstverlag des Verfassers, 1992), 13-18.

[2] George K. Epp, *Geschichte der Mennoniten in Russland*, I, "Deutsche Täufer in Russland" (Lage: Logos Verlag, 1997), 55-80.

[3] Hans-Christian Diedrich and Gerd Stricker (eds), *Das Gute behaltet: Kirchen und religiöse Gemeinschaften in der Sovjetunion und ihre Nachfolgestaaten* (Erlangen: Martin Luther Verlag, 1985), 15; Reinhard Schott, "Integration von Aussiedlern" in *Gnadauer Kongress "Schritte zueinander" Gunzenhausen 1993* (Dillenburg: Gnadauer Verlag, 1993), 212.

[4] Diedrich and Stricker (eds), *Das Gute behaltet*, 17.

[5] John Friesen, "Russia 1789-1850" in *Mennonites in Russia* (Altona: Friesen Printers, 1989), 28.

[6] Diedrich and Stricker, 17.

[7] George K. Epp, *Geschichte der Mennoniten*, 143.

[8] Epp, 177; Gerlach, *Die Russlandmennoniten*, 25; John A. Toews, *A History of the Mennonite Brethren Church* (Fresno: Board of Christian Literature, 1975), 28, 29.

[9] Epp, 149; Friesen, "Russia 1789-1850," 34.

[10] Gerlach, 27.

[11] In Friesen, 1989, 130.

[12] Gerlach, 21.

[13] Gerlach, 54.

[14] Gerlach, 32.

[15] Gerlach, 32.

[16] Gerlach, 33

[17] Gerhard Hildebrandt, "Das Bildungswesen der Mennoniten in Russland von der Zeit ihrer Einwanderung bis 1930," in 200 Jahre Mennoniten in Russland (Bolanden-Weierhof: Verlag des MGVs, 2000), 63.

[18] Hans Kasdorf, Flammen unauslöschlich (1991), 15-112.

[19] Wiens, in Hildebrandt, 200, 153-169.

[20] Diedrich, (1985), 16.

[21] Kasdorf, (1991), 54.

[22] Karl Stumpp, Die Auswanderung aus Deutschland nach Russland in den Jahren 1763 bis 1862 (Stuttgart: Landsmannschaft der Deutschen aus Russland, 1985), 16.

[23] In Gerlach, 58.

[24] Kasdorf, 82.

[25] Kasdorf, 84.

[26] In Kasdorf, 114.

[27] Sawatsky (1981), 35.

[28] In Hildebrandt, 169.

[29] Hildebrandt, 179.

[30] Hildebrandt, 188, 187.

[31] According to Wesley Berg, cited in Friesen, 203.

[32] See Friesen, 347, 349, and also James Urry, None but Saints: The Transformation of Mennonite Life in Russia 1789-1889 (Winnipeg: Hyperion Press, 1989).

[33] John A. Toews, A History of the Mennonite Brethren Church, 117.

[34] Benjamin Pinkus and Ingeborg Fleischhauer, in Die Deutschen in der Sowjetunion (Baden-Baden: Nomos Verlagsgesellschaft), 56-57, 84.

[35] Johannes Dyck in Sawatsky (2005), 78.

[36] Gerlach, 103-107.

[37] Meir Buchsweiler, Volksdeutsche in der Ukraine am Vorabend und Begin des Zweiten Weltkrieges. "Ein Fall doppelter Loyalität"? (Tel Aviv: Bleicher Verlag, 1984), 306-307.

[38] Klein in Klassen 2001: 89a, Interviews, private archives.

[39] Loewen 1995, 143-145; Walter Sawatsky, Soviet Evangelicals Since World War II, (Scottdale, PA: Herald Press, 1981), 84-97.

[40] Pinkus/Fleischhauer, (1987), 358.

[41] Alfred Eisfeldt, "Die Deutschen in Russland – gestern und heute" in Bernd G. Längin (ed), Globus Spezial. Die Deutschen in der UdSSR – einst und jetzt (Bonn: VDA-Verlag und Vertrieb, 1989), 38-57.

[42] In earlier official documents the terms "Umsiedler" and "Aussiedler" are used interchangeably. By definition "Aussiedler" are persons who themselves, or their ancestors, in 1937 lived outside Germany, and now, since 1951, in accordance with a contractual agreement, immigrate into the Federal Republic of Germany.

[43] Walter Sawatsky, Soviet Evangelicals Since World War II, 64.

[44] Kasdorf, 166.

[45] Sawatsky, 281.

[46] Sawatsky in Friesen, (1989), 328-332.

[47] Klaus J. Bade, ed., *Deutsche im Ausland – Fremde in Deutschland* (Güterloh: Bertelsmann Club, 1992), 312.

[48] John N. Klassen, *Church Planting and Church Growth Among Evangelical Russian German Christians in Germany in the Tension Between Immigration and Integration*, unpublished Dissertation, University of South Africa, Pretoria SA, 2003, 194.

[49] See Hans von Niessen's article in *Mennonitisches Jahrbuch*, 1990.

[50] Pinkus/Fleischhauer, "Die Deutschen in der Sowjetunion," 44.

[51] Pöhlmann, (1993), 768.

[52] John A. Toews, *A History of the Mennonite Brethren Church* (Fresno: Board of Christian Literature, 1978), 20-21.

[53] Pinkus/Fleischhauer, 465. See also John N. Klassen, 2003 (cf. note 48 above), 113-120.

[54] Statistics of the *Bund Evangelische Freie Gemeinden* were not available. Our assumption is that 3000-4000 baptisms took place during these years.

[55] Peter and Elfriede Dyck, *Auferstanden aus Ruinen* (Weierhof, 1994), 59-72.

[56] Alfred Eisfeld, *Die Russlanddeutschen*, vol. 2, (München: Langen Müller, 1992), 125-129.

[57] Interviews by the author.

[58] See Rainer Strohl, "Young Immigrants between Assimilation and Marginalization," University of Bielefeld study, 1999.

[59] See Walter Sawatsky, in Paul Toews ed. *Mennonites & Baptists* (Winnipeg: Kindred Press, 1993), 113.

[60] Ross T. Bender, "Learning from the Baptists", *Courier,* Volume 16 nr. 2 (2001), 7.

[61] Heinrich Löwen Jr. *In Vergessenheit geratene Beziehungen: Frühe Begegnungen der Mennoniten-Brüdergemeinden mit dem Baptismus in Russland. Überblick,* Band I (Bielefeld: Logos, 1989), and Johannes Reimer, *Auf der Suche nach Identität: Russlanddeutsche zwischen Baptisten und Mennoniten nach dem zweiten Weltkrieg* (Bielefeld: Logos, 1996).

[62] See D. G. Lichdi, *Mennonitisches Jahrbuch* (2003): 9.

[63] Horst Gerlach, *Die Russlandmennoniten*, 117.

[64] In John Friesen, *Mennonites in Russia*, 346.

[65] In Gerhard Hildebrandt, *200 Jahre Mennoniten in Russland*, 240.

[66] In John Friesen, *Mennonites in Russia*, 332.

Chapter VIII

[1] Richard K. MacMaster, *Land, Piety, Peoplehood. The Establishment of Mennonite Communities in America* (Scottdale: Herald Press, 1985); Frank H. Epp. *Mennonites*, Vol. 1, *1786-1920, The History of a Separate People*, (Toronto: MacMillan, 1974). The adjective "North American" will be used to include Mennonites from both Canada and the United States. Until very recently, the largest Mennonite conferences were bi-national and the mission efforts described in this chapter were usually undertaken jointly by Canadian and US mission agencies and missionaries.

[2] Paul Toews, *Mennonites in American Society, 1930-1970. Modernity and the Persistence of Religious Community* (Scottdale: Herald Press, 1996), 268.

[3] Alle Hoekema, *Dutch Mennonite Mission in Indonesia.* (Elkhart IN: IMS, 1991).

[4] Melvin Gingerich, "North American Mennonite Overseas Outreach in Perspective 1890-1966," *Mennonite Quarterly Review*, 39/4 (month/year):262.

[5] Robert S. Kreider, Rachel Waltner Goossen, *Hungry, Thirsty, a Stranger. The MCC Experience* (Scottdale: Herald Press, 1988), 26.

[6] *Ibid.*

[7] See Gingerich, op. cit.; Kreider-Goossen, 31; John D. Unruh, *In the Name of Christ. A History of the Mennonite Central Committee and Its Service 1920-1951*, (Scottdale: Herald Press, 1952), 16.

[8] Jeanet van Woerden-Surink, *Hollandsch Doopsgezind Emigranten Bureau 1924-1940*, n.p. Seminary paper, Gouda, 1999, 8.

[9] In an eighteen month period from March 1922 to August 1923, MCC fed seventy-five thousand people including sixty thousand Mennonites. Nine thousand Mennonites are said to have been saved from starvation. (Kreider/Goossen, 24).

[10] Gingerich, 269-270.

[11] Toews, 267.

[12] John D. Unruh, *op.cit.,* ; Cornelius J. Dyck (ed.), *Responding to Worldwide Needs, The Mennonite Central Committee Story, Volume 2.*(Scottdale: Herald Press, 1980);Kreider/Goossen, *op.cit.*; Peter & Elfrieda Dyck, *Up from the Rubble*, (Scottdale: Herald Press, 1991); Michel Paret, *L'Action sociale mennonite en France au XXᵉ siecle, approches diachronique et analytique*, 3 volumes (Paris, Ecole Pratique des Hautes Etudes, Vᵉ Section, novembre 1997).

[13] Sixteen North American Mennonite groups were members of MCC in 1944. Cf. J. Robert Charles, "North American Mennonite Agencies in Europe since World War II," *Mission Focus*, (September 1998): 49.

[14] The information concerning this study visit is taken from a 1950 MCC executive committee report made available to me by Robert Charles.

[15] C. J. Dyck (ed.), *The Mennonite Central Committee Story, Vol. 2, Responding to Worldwide Needs*, (Scottdale: Herald Press, 1980), 51.

[16] Most of our documentation comes from North American sources, for reasons of accessibility. Much of this story is still waiting to be told, and would be based on a close reading of various European Mennonite church periodicals, committee archives and interviews with European Mennonites who were or still are involved in these stories.

[17] Francesco Picone, Tony & Marilena Ceraulo, *New Awakenings in an Ancient Land,* (Palermo Italy: Centro Agape, 1999), 5. Harry Anthony Brunk, *History of Mennonites in Virginia 1900-1960*, vol. II (Verona Virginia: McClure Printing Company), 409.

[18] Originally the bi-national mission agency of the "Old" Mennonite Church, its name was changed to "Mennonite Board of Missions," but in 2002 it began carrying on its work in Canada through the auspices of Witness and in the USA as Mennonite Mission Network. The bi-national Commission on Overseas Mission of the General Conference Mennonite Church also became a part of Witness and Mennonite Mission Network. Two bi-national mission agencies thus became national entities.

[19] Guy F. Hershberger, *The Mennonite Church in the Second World War*, (Scottdale: Herald Press, 1951), 168. A timeline of MBM's involvement in Europe can be found in Alan Kreider, *Anabaptist Christian: Revived and Relevant*, 10-12. This pamphlet is number 16 in the *Mission Insight* series edited by James Krabill and published by Mennonite Board of Missions (2001).

[20] Peter J. Dyck, *Up from the Rubble*, 15.

[21] Hershberger, op. cit., 167.

[22] "Les Amis de l'Atelier" in 1960 and "Le Domaine Emmanuel" in 1965.

[23] Information taken from an unpublished manuscript on the history of Eastern Mennonite Missions by A. Grace Wenger.

[24] Ivan J. Miller, *History of the Conservative Mennonite Conference 1910-1985*, (Grantsville Maryland, Ivan J. and Della Miller, n.d.), 255.

302   *Notes for pages 244–253*

25 Ivan Miller, *op.cit.*, 259, 260.

26 Emily Brunk, *Espelkamp, The Mennonite Central Committee shares in community building in a new settlement for German refugees,* (Karlsruhe: Mennonite Central Committee, 1951), 41; Ivan Miller, 258.

27 Ivan Miller, 264.

28 According to the Rosedale Mennonite Missions website, the *Missionsgemeinde Bad Pyrmont* currently has a membership of 45. As far as we know, it does not have any official Mennonite affiliation, although it does appear on the Mennonite World Conference listings of Mennonites in Europe.

29 J. A. Toews, *A History of the Mennonite Brethren Church,* ed. by A. J. Klassen, (Fresno CA: M.B. Churches, 1975), 434.; Phyllis Martens, *The Mustard Tree.* (Fresno, CA: M.B. Board of Christian Education in cooperation with Board Missions/Services, 1971), 124.

30 J. A. Toews, 436. See also Franz Rathmair, "Die Mennoniten-Brüdergemeinden in Mitteleuropa," (unpublished paper, 1991), 6.

31 John N. Klassen, "The Mennonite Brethren Churches in Central Europe," (unpublished paper, 1991).

32 John N. Klassen, "The Mennonite Brethren Churches in Central Europe," 2; J. A. Toews, 434.

33 J. A. Toews, 435.

34 *YEARBOOK 54th Session General Conference of Mennonite Brethren Churches,* Buhler Kansas, August 3-6, 1978, M.B. Publishing House, Hillsboro, Kansas, 86; *Yearbook 56th* Session General Conference of Mennonite Brethren Churches, Reedley California, 1984, 66.

35 "Europe is the seedbed in which the Anabaptists, our spiritual fathers, had their origin. Over much of Europe the Gospel spread rapidly. But a great change has come over Europe in the centuries that have elapsed. Most of her people ignore the church. Communism shows its ugly face in many places. Much of Europe has literally forgotten God." *Missionary Messenger,* Annual Meeting Supplement, May, 1959 (Eastern Board), 2.

36 David A. Shank, "A Missionary Approach to a Dechristianized Society," *Mennonite Quarterly Review,* (January 1954): 39-55.

37 This group came to be known as the "Concern Group," named after a series of theological pamphlets with the title *Concern.* "The Concern Group" was affected by theological post-war developments by virtue of the fact that several of its initiating participants studied under Karl Barth, Emil Brunner and Oscar Cullman. Others participated in ecumenical discussions about church renewal. Thus within the European theological context, Mennonite students were led to ask fundamental questions about Mennonite theology, questions having to do with the nature of the church, its mission, its polity and its relation to Christendom at large." J. Lawrence Burkholder, "Concern Group," in *Mennonite Encyclopedia* V, 177-180.

38 Samuel Gerber, *Vous puiserez aux sources du salut, Ecole biblique mennonite européenne 1950-1990,* (Liestal Switzerland : Ecole Biblique Mennonite Européenne Bienenberg, 1990).

39 MCC Executive Committee, October 6, 1950.

40 Cf. Reynold Sawatsky, "Portugal," *Mennonite Encyclopedia,* volume 5, 717.

41 John Howard Yoder, "Historical Perspectives and Current Issues," from the Proceedings of the Europe Mission Study Conference, July 18-21, 1967, Bienenberg Bible School, Liestal, Switzerland.

42 Alle Hoekema, "Lessons and Hopes from Mennonite Cooperation in Europe," paper given at the European Task force meeting, CIM, 1987.

43 Taken from http://www.anabaptistnetwork.com/ See also Alan Kreider and Stuart Murray, *Coming Home: Stories of Anabaptists in Britain and Ireland* (Kitchener: Pandora Press, 2000).

Chapter IX

1 Jean Séguy, *Les Assemblées Anabaptistes-Mennonites de France* (The Hague - Paris, 1977).

2 *The Mennonite Encyclopedia* (ME) IV, 176-179.

3 In *Informations Blätter* (IB) Heft 9, (1986).

4 Sjouke Voolstra, *Beeldenstormer uit bewogenheid. Verzamelde opstellen*, (Hilversum: Verloren, 2005), 198.

5 *Mennonitisches Lexikon* II, 442. The Mennonite youth movement was located primarily in Germany and the Netherlands.

6 Ernst Crous, " Christian Hege and Christian Neff as Historians," in *Mennonite Quarterly Review* Vol. XXXIV, (July 1960): 171.

7 An Keuning Tichelaar and Lynn Kaplanian-Buller, *Passing on the Comfort. The War, the Quilts, and the Women Who Made a Difference* (Intercourse, PA: Good Books, 2005), 102-103. When she gave me permission to include this passage, An Keuning told me that this episode was very important to her, because it went to the heart of her being a Mennonite.

8 Lapp and van Straten, "Mennonite World Conference," 14.

9 See *Perspektive*, May 4, 2005, 5.

10 Séguy, *Assemblées-Anabaptistes-Mennonites de France*, 675.

11 Ibid.

12 Alfred Michiels, *Les Anabaptistes des Vosges*, nouvelle edition (1980), 75.

13 Waltner, *300 Jahre Mennonitengemeinde Weierhof*, 22. However, in the same book we read (50-51) that in 1889 only men over 21 years old had the right to vote about the bylaws that were drawn up in the Weierhof congregation.

14 In *Mennonitische Blätter* (1905), 4.

15 *Informations Blätter*, Heft 9, (1986), 94.

16 Waltner, *300 Jahre Mennonitengemeinde Weierhof*, 39.

17 According to P. Sommer, *Un Almanach Mennonite 1901-1951*, 1951.

18 Sjouke Voolstra was a seminary professor and, until his untimely death in 2004, an important spiritual leader.

19 In the Netherlands, as elsewhere, one writes his or her own confession of faith, in one's own words, and reads it to the church board or the congregation before being baptized in a Mennonite congregation.

Sidebar Credits

Chapter II

35 Parliamentary Decree, 1792. J.-B. Duvergier, *Collection complète des lois, décrets, ordonnances, règlements et avis du conseil d'Etat*, Vol. 5. (Paris: Guyot et Scribes, 1834), 105-107. Translated by Neal Blough.
46 Lausanne Covenant found at: www.lausanne.org
47 Population statistics: unattributed.
50 August Bebel, in A. Bebel *Ausgewählte Schriften und Reden*, vol. 1. ([East] Berlin: Dietz, 1970), 299.
51 Leonhard Ragaz, in Markus Mattmüller, *Leonhard Ragaz und der religiöse Sozialismus. Eine Biographie*. Vol. 1, (Zollikon: Evangelischer Verlag, 1957), 209f.
53 European emigration, F. Delouche, *Illustrated History of Europe*, 297.

Chapter III

64 Samuel Muller, *Feestrede gehouden door Samuel Muller ter viering van zijne vijfentwintigjarige ambtsbediening* (Amsterdam 1852), 22.
65 S. Hoekstra, quoted by W. F. Golterman, *De Godsdienstwijsbegeerte van S. Hoekstra Bzn* (Assen: Van Gorcum 1942), 25.
66 Joost Hiddes Halbertsma, *Doopsgezinden en hunne Herkomst benevens eenige Kerkredenen* (Deventer 1843), 378.
67 Jan de Liefde, *Gevaar, Gevaar! En geene vrede! Een woord tot de slapenden en de in slaap gewiegden* (Zutphen 1844), 5.
71 Albert van Delden, from B. Rademaker-Helfferich, *Een wit vaantje op de Brink. De geschiedenis van de Doopsgezinde gemeente te Deventer* (Deventer: Arko Boeken 1988), 150.
77 G. Knuttel, on Schoorl, in *Op weg van gisteren naar morgen. 1917-1992. Van Gemeente Dag beweging naar gemeenschap Doopsgezind Broederschapswerk* (1993), 11.
78 Cor Inja, *Geen cel ketent deze dromen. Een dagboek over ideaal en werkelijkheid van de doopsgezinde dienstweigeraar en socialist Cor Inja uit Zaandam, geschreven in gevangenschap van 25 maart tot en met 19 november 1925* (Hilversum: Verloren 2001), 142.
82 Abram Bärg, in Jeanet van Woerden-Surink, *Hollandsch Doopsgezind Emigranten Bureau 1924-1940.*
83 Cornelis Lely, from K. Jansma, *Lely, bedwinger der Zuiderzee* (Amsterdam: Paris, 1954).
85 Story of Jaap van der Meer, in *Indien ik u vergete. Vijftig jaar na dato* (Amsterdam: VDGA, 1995).

Chapter IV

105 Peter van der Herberg, in *Sie kamen als Fremde. Die Mennoniten in Krefeld von den Anfängen bis zur Gegenwart*, ed. by Wolfgang Froese. (Krefeld [Stadt Krefeld], 1995), 125.
106 Johann Donner, in *Orlofferfelde Chronik* transcribed by Werner Janzen, 1996: www.bethelks.edu/jthiesen/prussian/orlofferfeldechronik.html
110 The *Vereinigung*, 1933, cited in Lichdi, *Die Mennoniten im Dritten Reich*, 118-119.
115 Christian Neff, in Gary J. Waltner (ed.), *300 Jahre Mennonitengemeinde* (Weierhof) , 51.
116 *Ibersheimer Beschlüsse*, courtesy Agape Verlag (Lichdi, *MGG*, 176).
126 Emden church members, 1933, in Lichdi, *Mennoniten im Dritten Reich*, 43.
128 Gerhard Thiessen, cited in Lichdi, *Mennoniten im Dritten Reich*, 106.
133 Driedger family story, unattributed.
135 Hans Hübert, "Auf Umwegen nach Bechterdissen," in *25 Jahre Mennonitengemeinde Bechterdissen 1956-1981*, 21.

136 Thomashof Declaration, in *Gemeindeblatt der Mennoniten*, (September 15, 1949); see Lichdi, *Mennoniten in Geschichte und Gegenwart*, 205.
139 Fernando Enns, unattributed.

Chapter V

161 Zaire refugees, see "Asylbewerber Musey wurde von Mennoniten versteckt gehalten," in *IDEA-Magazin* 3 (1988), (February 8): 8.
165 Conscientious objector imprisoned, told by Hanspeter Jecker.

Chapter VII

182 Von Trappe pamphlet, available at: www.russlanddeutschegeschirchte.de/deutsch/mennoniten_trappe.htm
186 Claas Epp, Jr., from *Mennonite Encyclopedia*, II: 234.
191 Johann Cornies, from *Mennonite Encyclopedia* I: 718; Gerlach, 1992, 29.
192 Jakob Enns, in Toews, 1975, 20.
198 Dubrovna tent mission, in Hans Kasdorf, *Flammen unauslöschlich*, 131.
201 John Mathies diary, in L. Klippenstein and Jacob Dick, eds., *Mennonite Alternative Service in Russia* (Kitchener, ON: Pandora Press, 2002), 78-81.
208 1930 recollections, from Jakob Friesen, *Schönhorst - Heimat einmal* (Abbotsford: Selbstverlag, 2005), 178.
211 Anna Kroker, in *Mennonitische Rundschau*, November 2005; Erica Jantzen, *Six Sugar Beets, Five Bitter Years* (Kitchener, ON: Pandora Press, 2003).
213 Gerhard Wölk, "Frömmigkeit", in *200 Jahre Mennoniten in Russland* (Bolanden-Weierhof: Mennonitische Geschichtsverein, 2000), 233.
215 Herbert Wiens, *Volk auf dem Weg - Deutsche in Russland* (Stuttgart: Landsmannschaft, 1997), 22.
216 Loewen family, from Gerlach, *Die Russlandmennoniten*, (Kirchheimbolanden: Selbstverlag, 2002), 171.
217 Hilde Driediger, *Überlebenschronik* (Hagen: Elvira Driediger, 1997), 141.
218 Resettler congregations, John N. Klassen.
226 *Aussiedler* church, Merle Good, "The Aussiedler: A Growing Church" in *Courier* vol. 17 nr. 1, (2002): 10.

Chapter VIII

235 MCC report: "Report of Relief Projects in Europe," by Atlee Beechy, January 23, 1947, in *The Mennonite Central Committee Story*, vol. 2, 46.
237 Mennonite missions, in Melvin Gingerich, *Mennonite Quarterly Review*, 39/4 (1965): 262-269.
239 London Mennonite Centre, quoted from Jacob H. Kikkert, *Radicale christelijke gemeenschappen missiologisch bezien*. N.p. Seminary paper, Amsterdam, 39.
247 State churches: citation from Phyllis Martens, *The Mustard Tree, The Story of Mennonite Brethren Missions* (Fresno CA: Mennonite Brethren Board of Christian Education in cooperation with Board Missions/Services, 1971), 129-130.
248 Dechristianized Society, David A. Shank, "A Missionary Approach to a Dechristianized Society," *MQR* (January 1954): 39-55.
249 André Trocmé, from Robert Witmer.
252 Gilly Greenwood, told in Alan Kreider and Stuart Murray, *Coming Home: Stories of Anabaptists in Britain and Ireland* (Kitchener: Pandora Press, 2000), 62.

Chapter IX

257   Christian Oesch, in Jean Séguy, *Les Assemblées Anabaptistes-Mennonites de France* (The Hague - Paris, 1977), 434.
258   Catechism, Leonhard Weydmann, in *Katechismus zum gebrauch der Taufgesinnten. Aufs neue bearteitet und herausgegeben von E. Weydmann, Pfarrer in Crefeld* (Crefeld, 1888), 39-41.
261   Meditation, by Oepke Trinus Hylkema (1902-1988), Dutch Mennonite pastor, in a booklet with meditations, *Wat hemel en aarde verbindt* (The Hague, 1955), 55. Reprinted in Pieter Post (ed), *Laat ik toch maar knielen. Spirituele teksten uit de Nederlandse doopsgezinde traditie* (Gorinchem: Narratio, 2005), 31.
266   Christian Galle, in Gary J. Waltner (ed.), *300 Jahre Mennonitengemeinde Weierhof 1682-1982* (Weierhof: MGW, 1982), 67.
274   Berlin diary, excerpt from an unpublished diary of the MVS Camp which worked among refugees in West Berlin, August 7- September 2, 1961.
283   Charly Ummel, in *Perspektive* nr. 15, August 10, 2005.

Bibliography

General

Dyck, C. J. (Ed.). *Introduction to Mennonite History.* Scottdale, PA: Herald Press, 1993.
Dyck, C. J. *Spiritual Life in Anabaptism.* Scottdale, PA: Herald Press, 1995.
Friedmann, Robert. *Mennonite Piety Through the Centuries.* Goshen: Mennonite Historical Society, 1949.
Gastaldi, Ugo. *Storia dell' Anabaptismo.* 2 vols. Torino: Claudiana, 1972-1981.
Gerlach, Horst. *Bildband zur Geschichte der Mennoniten.* Uelzen: Verlag Günther Preuschoff, 1982.
Goertz, Hans-Jürgen (Ed.). *Die Mennoniten.* Stuttgart: Evangelisches Verlagswerk, 1971.
Hershberger, Guy F. (Ed.). *The Recovery of the Anabaptist Vision.* Scottdale, PA: Herald Press, 1957. (German Translation: *Das Täufertum - Erbe und Verpflichtung.* Stuttgart: Evangelisches Verlagswerk, 1963).
Klaassen, Walter. *Anabaptism: Neither Catholic nor Protestant.* Kitchener, Ont.: Pandora Press, 2001[3].
Lichdi, Dieter Götz. *Die Mennoniten in Geschichte und Gegenwart. Von der Täuferbewegung zur weltweiten Freikirche.* Weisenheim am Berg: Agape-Verlag, 2004.
Loewen, Harry, and Nolt, Steven. *Through Fire and Water.* Scottdale, PA: Herald Press, 1996.
Loewen, Harry. *No Permanent City: Stories from Mennonite History and Life.* Scottdale, PA: Herald Press, 1993. (German Translation: *Keine bleibende Stadt - Mennonitische Geschichten aus fünf Jahrhunderten.* Hamburg: Kümpers, 1993.)
_____. *Why I Am a Mennonite: Essays on Mennonite Identity.* Scottdale, PA: Harold Press, 1988. (German Translation: *Warum ich mennonitisch bin.* Hamburg: Kümpers, 1996.)
Mennonite World Handbook. Carol Stream: Mennonite World Conference, 1990.
Ott, Bernhard. *Missionarische Gemeinden werden.* Uster: Verlag ETG, 1996.
Penner, Horst / Gerlach, Horst / Quiring, Horst. *Weltweite Bruderschaft.* Weierhof: Mennonitischer Geschichtsverein, 1995[3].
Smith, C. Henry. *The Story of the Mennonites.* 5th ed. Newton, KS: Faith and Life Press, 1981.

Encyclopedias, Bibliographies and Periodicals

Bauman, Chad Mullet, and Krabill, James R., *Anabaptism and Mission. A Bibliography 1859-2000*. Elkhart IN: Mennonite Mission Network, 2002.

Hillerbrand, Hans J. *Anabaptist Bibliography 1520-1630*. St. Louis, MO: Center for Reformation Research, 1991.

Mennonitisches Lexikon. 4 Bde. Weierhof 1913-1967.

Mennonite Encyclopedia. 5 vols. Scottdale 1955-1990.

Mennonite Quarterly Review. Goshen: Mennonite Historical Society, 1927ff.

Springer, N. P. & A.J. Klassen. *Mennonite Bibliography 1631-1961*. 2 vols. Scottdale, PA: Herald Press, 1977.

Chapter References – for further reading

I Overview of Anabaptist-Mennonite History, 1525 to 1800

Blanke, Fritz. *Brothers in Christ*, trans. by Nordenhang, J. Scottdale, PA: Herald Press, 1961. (German Original: *Brüder in Christo. Die Geschichte der ältesten Täufergemeinde*. Zürich: TVZ, 1975 / Winterthur: Schleife-Verlag, 2003).

Clasen, Claus-Peter. *Anabaptism. A Social History, 1525-1618*. Ithaca: Cornell Univ. Press, 1972.

Goertz, Hans Jürgen (Ed.). *The Anabaptists*. London: Routledge, 1996. (German Original: *Die Täufer. Geschichte und Deutung*. München, 1980).

_____. *Konrad Grebel - Kritiker des frommen Scheins 1498-1526. Eine biographische Skizze*. Hamburg: Kümpers, 1998.

_____. *Profiles of radical reformers : biographical sketches from Thomas Müntzer to Paracelsus*. Scottdale, PA.: Herald Press, 1982. (German Original: *Radikale Reformatoren. 21 biographische Skizzen von Thomas Müntzer bis Paracelsus*. München: C.H. Beck, 1978.)

_____. *Religiöse Bewegungen in der Frühen Neuzeit*. München: R. Oldenbourg, 1993.

Horst, Irvin B. *The Radical Brethren: Anabaptism and the English Reformation to 1558*. Nieuwkoop: De Graaf, 1972.

Jecker, Hanspeter. *Ketzer-Rebellen-Heilige. Das Basler Täufertum von 1580 bis 1700*. Liestal: Verlag des Kantons Basel-Landschaft, 1998.

Kobelt-Groch, Marion. *Aufsässige Töchter Gottes*. Frankfurt: Campus-Verlag, 1993.

Krahn, Cornelius. *Dutch Anabaptism*. The Hague: Nijhoff, 1968.

Association Française d'Histoire Anabaptiste-Mennonite (Ed.). *LES AMISH: Origine et particularismes 1693-1993*. Ingersheim : AFHAM, 1996.

Meihuizen, H.W. *Van Mantz tot Menno*. Amsterdam, 1975.

Mellink, A.F. *De Wederdopers in de Noordelijke Nederlanden 1531-1544*. Groningen/Djakarta, 1954.

Packull, Werner O. *Hutterite Beginnings*. Baltimore: The John Hopkins Univ. Press, 1995.

Schäufele, Fritz. *Das missionarische Bewusstsein und Wirken der Täufer*. Neukirchen-Vluyn: Neukirchner, 1966.

Snyder, C. Arnold. *Anabaptist History and Theology*. Kitchener, ON: Pandora Press, 1995.

_____ & Huebert Hecht, Linda (Eds.). *Profiles of Anabaptist Women. Sixteenth-Century Reforming Pioneers*. Waterloo, ON: Wilfrid Laurier University Press, 1996.

Stayer, James and Goertz, Hans-Jürgen. *Art. "Täufer,"* in: TRE (Theologische Realenzyklopädie), Vol. 32, Berlin: de Gruyter, 2001, 597-623 (With important bibliographical indications).

Strübind, Andrea. *Eifriger als Zwingli*. Berlin: Duncker & Humblot, 2003.

Wenger, John C. *Even Unto Death*. Richmond, VA: John Knox Press, 1961. (German Translation: *Die Täuferbewegung*. Wuppertal/Kassel: Oncken, 1995³).
Williams, George H. *The Radical Reformation*. Kirksville: Truman State Univ. Press, 1992³.
Yoder, John H. *Anabaptism & Reformation in Switzerland*. Kitchener, ON: Pandora Press, 2004 (German Original: *Täufertum und Reformation im Gespräch*. 2 Vol., Karlsruhe: Schneider, 1962 / Zürich: TVZ, 1968).

Sources

Bangs, Jeremy Dupertuis (Transl. & Ed.). *Letters on Toleration. Dutch Aid to persecuted Swiss and Palatine Mennonites 1615-1699*. Rockport, ME: Picton Press, 2004.
Braght, Thieleman Jansz van. *Het Bloedigh Tooneel, of Martelaers Spiegel der Doops-gesinde of Weereloose Christenen* (1985; facsimile of the 2ⁿᵈ, illustrated Amsterdam 1685 edition, introd. by Verheus, S.L. & Alberda-van der Zijpp, T.), (English Translation: *The Bloody Theater or Martyrs Mirror of the Defenseless Christians* (transl. of the Dutch 1660/1685 edition by Joseph F. Sohm), Scottdale, PA: Herald Press, 1950 ff.)
Cramer, S. and F. Pijper (Eds.). *Bibliotheca Reformatorica Neerlandica. Geschriften uit den tijd der Hervorming in de Nederlanden.* 's-Gravenhage 1903-1914. (Multiple volumes)
DOCUMENTA ANABAPTISTICA NEERLANDICA, Leiden: E. J. Brill 1975 ff. (Multiple volumes)
DOPERSE STEMMEN. Series of 7 volumes of sources with introductions, 1: 1974 – 7:1994, Amsterdam: Doopsgezinde Historische Kring.
Fast, Heinold. *Der linke Flügel der Reformation*. Bremen: Schünemann, 1962.
Meihuizen, H.W. (Ed.). *Menno Simons, Dat Fundament des Christelycken Leers*. Den Haag, 1967.
CLASSICS OF THE RADICAL REFORMATION. Scottdale. PA: Herald Press, 1973 ff. (Multiple volumes)
QUELLEN ZUR GESCHICHTE DER TÄUFER IN DER SCHWEIZ . Zürich: TVZ, 1952ff. (Multiple volumes)
QUELLEN ZUR GESCHICHTE DER (WIEDER)TÄUFER. Leipzig: Heinsius, 1930ff. & Gütersloh: Bertelsmann, 1951ff. (Multiple volumes)
Simons, Menno. *Opera Omnia Theologica, of alle de Godtgeleerde Wercken*. Amsterdam: De Bataafsche Leeuw, 1989 [facsimile of the Amsterdam 1681 edition, introd. by Verheus, S.L. and Alberda-van der Zijpp, T.] (English Translation: *The Complete Writings of Menno Simons.* Transl. of the Dutch 1681 edition by L. Verduin and J.C. Wenger. Scottdale, PA: Herald Press, 1956).
Snyder, C. Arnold (Ed.). *Anabaptist texts in translation*. Kitchener, ON: Pandora Press, 1999 ff. (Multiple volumes)
Wolkan, Rudolf (Ed.). *Das große Geschichtbuch der hutterischen Brüder,* Macmillan Colony, 1982.

II The Political, Economic, Social and Religious Context in Europe, 1789–2000

Bruun, Geoffret. *Nineteeth Century European Civilization, 1815-1914*. New York/Oxford: University Press, 1960.
Caron, Jean-Claude and Vernus, Michel. *L'Europe au XIXᵉ siècle : des nations aux nationalismes, 1815-1914*. Paris: Armand Colin, 1999.
Delouche, Frédéric, ed. *Illustrated History Of Europe*. New-York: Barnes & Noble, 2001.
Gerbet, Pierre. *La Construction de l'Europe*. Paris: Imprimerie nationale, 1983.
Girault, René. *Peuples et nations d'Europe au XIXᵉ siècle*. Paris: Hachette, 1996.
Gisel, Pierre (Ed.). *Encyclopédie du protestantisme*. Paris: Cerf et Genève: Labor et Fides, 1995.
Golo, Mann. *The History of Germany since 1789*. London: Chatto & Windus/GB, 1968. (German Original: *Deutsche Geschichte des 19. und 20. Jahrhunderts*, Frankfurt am Main: Büchergilde Gutenberg, 1958.)

Greeley, Andrew M. *A Sociological Profile, Religion in Europe at the End of the Second Millenium.* Brunswick (USA) and London (UK): Transaction Publishers, 2003.

Jenkins, Philip. *The Next Christendom.* Oxford: University Press, 2002.

Kaiser, David. *Politics & War.* Cambridge, MA: Harvard University Press, 1990.

Lamaison, Pierre. *Généalogie de l'Europe.* Paris: France Loisirs, 1994.

Mayeur, J.-M. / Pietri, C. / Vauchez, A. / Venard, M. *Histoire du Christianisme des origines à nos jours. Guerres mondiales et totalitatismes (1914-1958),* T. XII. Paris: Desclée-Fayard, 1990.

Remond, René. *Religion et société en Europe. La sécularisation aux XIXe et XXe siècles, 1789-2000.* Paris : Seuil, 2001.

Rioux, Jean-Pierre. *La révolution industrielle, 1780-1880,* coll. Points Histoire. Paris : Seuil, 1971.

Sirel, François (et al.). *Les fondements du monde contemporain, manuel d'Histoire de 2e.* Paris: Magnard, 1996.

Tiersky, Ronald. *Europe Today.* Oxford: Rowan & Littlefield Publishers, 1999.

Weber, Max. *L'éthique protestante et l'esprit du capitalisme.* Paris : Plon, 1994 (German Original: *Die protestantische Ethik und der Geist des Kapitalismus,* in: Archiv für Sozialwissenschaft und Sozialpolitik, XX./XXI. Band 1905, 1-54 and 1-110. English translation: *The Protestant Ethic and the Spirit of Capitalism.* Los Angeles: Roxbury Publishing Company, 2002).

Wegs, R. J. & Ladrech, R. *Europe since 1945.* 4th ed. New York: St-Martin's Press, 1996.

III Mennonites in the Netherlands

Bornhäuser, Christoph. *Leben und Lehre Menno Simons'.* Neukirchen: Neukirchner 1973.

Deppermann, Klaus. *Melchior Hoffman.* Edinburgh: T. & T. Clark, 1987 (German Original: *Soziale Unruhen und apokalyptische Visionen im Zeitalter der Reformation.* Göttingen: Vandenhoek & Ruprecht, 1979).

Eijnatten, Joris van. *Mutua Christianorum Tolerantia. Irenicism and toleration in the Netherlands. The Stinstra affair 1740-1745.* Firenze: Leo S. Olschki, 1998.

Fix, Andrew C. *The Dutch Collegiants in the Early Enlightenment.* Princeton, NJ: University Press, 1991.

Groenveld, S. et al. (Eds), *Wederdopers, menisten, doopsgezinden in Nederland 1530-1980.* Zutphen: Walburg Pers, 1980 (and later reprints).

Hamilton, Alastair. *The Family of Love.* Baden-Baden: Ed. Valentin Koerner, 2003.

Hamilton, A. / Voolstra, S. / Visser, P. (eds). *From Martyr to Muppy.* Amsterdam: Amsterdam University Press, 1994.

Hoekema, Alle. *Dutch Mennonite Mission in Indonesia.* Elkhart IN: IMS, 2001.

Horst, Irvin B (Ed.). *The Dutch Dissenters.* Leiden: E. J. Brill, 1972.

Israel, Jonathan I. *Radical Enlightenment.* Oxford: Oxford University Press, 2001.

Joldersma, H. and Grijp, L. (eds.). *"Elizabeth's Manly Courage."* Marquette: Univ. Press, 2001.

Koolman, Jacobus ten Doornkaat. *Dirk Philips. Friend and colleaugue of Menno Simons, 1504-1568.* Kitchener, Ont.: Herald Press, 1998 (Dutch Original: *Dirk Philips, vriend en medewerker van Menno Simons, 1504-1568.* Haarlem : Tjeenk Willink & Zoon, 1964).

Koop, Karl. *Anabaptist-Mennonite Confessions of Faith.* Kitchener, ON: Pandora Press, 2004.

Kühler, W.J. *Geschiedenis der Nederlandsche Doopsgezinden in de zestiende eeuw.* Haarlem: Tjeenk Willink, 1964^2.

_____. *Geschiedenis van de Doopsgezinden in Nederland II, 1600-1735* (first part). Haarlem: Tjeenk Willink, 1940.

_____. *Geschiedenis van de Doopsgezinden in Nederland. Gemeentelijk leven 1650-1735.* Haarlem: Tjeenk Willink, 1950.

_____. *Het Socinianisme in Nederland.* Leeuwarden: De Tille, 1980².
Mellink, A.F. *De Wederdopers in de Noordelijke Nederlanden 1531-1544,* Leeuwarden: De Tille, 1981²
Van der Meulen, P. *De wording der Algemeen Doopsgezinde Societeit,* Wormerveer: Meijer, 1947.
Van der Zijpp, N. *Geschiedenis der Doopsgezinden in Nederland,* Arnhem: Van Loghum
    Slaterus, 1952 (reprint 1980).
Verbeek, Annelies. *"Menniste Paus".* *Samuel Muller (1785-1875) en zijn netwerken,*
    Hilversum: Verloren, 2005.
Visser, Piet and Sprunger, Mary. *Menno Simons.* Altona, MB: Friesens, 1996.
Voolstra, Anna / Hoekema, Alle / Visser, Piet (Eds.). *Sjouke Voolstra, Beeldenstormer uit
    bewogenheid. Verzamelde opstellen,* Hilversum: Verloren, 2005.
Voolstra, Sjouke. *Het Woord is vlees geworden.* Kampen: Kok, 1982.
_____. *Menno Simons.* North Newton, Kansas: Bethel College, 1997.
Waite, Gary K. *David Joris and Dutch Anabaptism 1524-1543.* Waterloo: Wilfried Laurier
    University Press, 1990.
Zijlstra, Samme. *Om de ware gemeente en de oude gronden. Geschiedenis van de dopersen in
    de Nederlanden 1531-1675.* Hilversum: Verloren, 2000.

Periodicals

De Zondagsbode 1-55 (1887-1942).
Algemeen Doopsgezind Weekblad (ADW) 1-60 (1945-2005; successor of *Zondagsbode*).
Doopsgezind NL, 1 (2006) ff. (bi-weekly successor of *Algemeen Doopsgezind Weekblad*).
Doopsgezind Jaarboekje, 1 (1905) ff.
Stemmen uit de Doopsgezinde Broederschap, 1-12 (1952-1963).
Doopsgezinde Bijdragen 1-56 (1861-1919); *Doopsgezinde Bijdragen, Nieuwe Reeks,* 1 (1975)
    ff. (both series fully indexed by: Rademaker-Helferich, B. *Registers op de Doopsgezinde
    Bijdragen oude en nieuwe reeks.* Hilversum 2002).

IV Mennonites in Germany

Baum, Markus. *Against the Wind.* Farmington, Pa.: Plough Publishing House, 1998 (German
    Original: *Stein des Anstoßes. Eberhard Arnold 1883-1935.* Moers: Brendow, 1996).
Brons, Antje. *Ursprung, Entwickelung und Schicksale der Taufgesinnten oder Mennoniten / in
    kurzen Zügen übersichtlich dargestellt von Frauenhand.* Norden: Soltau, 1884.
Driedger, Michael D. *Obedient Heretics.* Aldershot: Ashgate, 2002.
Dyck, Peter and Elfrieda. *Up from the Rubble,* Scottdale PA: Herald Press, 1991. (German
    Translation: *Auferstanden aus Ruinen.* Kirchheimbolanden: Verlag Horst Gerlach, 1994).
Goertz, Hans-Jürgen. *Das schwierige Erbe der Mennoniten. Aufsätze und Reden.* Leipzig:
    Evangelische Verlagsanstalt, 2002.
Froese, Wolfgang. *Sie kamen als Fremde.* Krefeld: Verlag des Stadtarchivs Krefeld, 1995.
Hübert, Klaus. *Die Mennoniten in Deutschland heute,* in: Wort und Tat, Heft 11, 18.
    Jahrgang, Nov. 1964.
Keller, Ludwig. *Ein Apostel der Wiedertäufer : [Hans Denck].* Leipzig: S. Hirzel, 1882.
Keller, Ludwig. *Die Reformation und die älteren Reformparteien.* Leipzig: G. Hirzel, 1885.
Klassen, Peter J. *A Homeland for Strangers.* Fresno, CA: Center for M.B. Studies, 1989.
Klassen, Peter P. *Die schwarzen Reiter.* Uchte: Sonnentau, 1999.
Klassen, Peter P. *Und ob ich schon wanderte...* Bolanden-Weierhof: Mennonitischer
    Geschichtsverein, 1997.
Lichdi, Diether Götz. *Mennoniten im Dritten Reich.* Weierhof: Mennonitischer
    Geschichtsverein, 1977.

Mannhardt, Wilhelm. *Die Wehrfreiheit der Altpreussischen Mennoniten: Eine geschichtliche Erörterung.* Marienburg: Komm Helmpels, 1863.

Neff, Christian, ed. *Gedenkschrift zum 400jährigen Jubiläum der Mennoniten oder Taufgesinnten 1525 - 1925.* Ludwigshafen: Konferenz der Süddeutschen Mennoniten, 1925.

Penner, Horst. *Die ost- und westpreußischen Mennoniten.* 2 Vol., Weierhof: Mennonitischer Geschichtsverein, 1987ff.

Schäfer, Gudrun (Ed.). *Die Speisung der Hunderttausend.* Landau: Knecht, 1997.

Unruh, Benjamin H. *Die niederländisch-niederdeutschen Hintergründe der mennonitischen Ostwanderungen im 16., 18. und 19. Jahrhundert.* Karlsruhe: Schneider, 1955.

Waltner, Gary (Ed.). *300 Jahre Mennonitengemeinde Weierhof 1682-1982.* Kirchheim-Bolanden: Mennonitengemeinde Weierhof, 1982.

Periodicals

Der Mennonit 1948-1973.

Die Brücke 1986ff.

Gemeinde Unterwegs 1974-1985.

Gemeindeblatt der Mennoniten 1870-1941; 1947-1973.

Mennonitische Blätter 1854-1941; 1974-1985.

Mennonitische Geschichtsblätter, ed. Mennonitischen Geschichtsverein, 1936ff.

Mennonitisches Jahrbuch (before *Christlicher Gemeindekalender* 1891-1941, then *Mennonitischer Gemeindekalender* 1951-1970), ed. Konf. Süddt. Mennonitengemeinden e.V. 1971ff.

V Mennonites in Switzerland

Bienenberg-Studienheft 1/1993. *"Alt- und Neutäufer",* Bienenberg: Selbstverlag, 1993.

Geiser, Samuel H. *Die Taufgesinnten Gemeinden im Rahmen der allg. Kirchengeschichte.* Courgenay: Selbstverlag, 1971.

Gerber, Samuel. *Mit Freuden Wasser schöpfen. Europäische Mennonitische Bibelschule 1950 1990.* Liestal: EMB Bienenberg, 1990 (French Version: *Vous puiserez aux sources du salut. Ecole biblique mennonite européenne 1950-1990.* Liestal: Ecole Biblique Mennonite Européenne Bienenberg, 1990.)

Gratz, Delbert L. *Bernese Anabaptists and Their American Descendants.* Elverson: Mennonite Historical Society, 1994[2].

Jecker, Hanspeter. *Von Pietisten, Separatisten und Wiedertäufern.* Basel: Job Factory, 2003.

_____. "Swiss Mennonites: Conscientious Objection to Military Service," in: Peachey, Urbane (ed.). *The Role of the Church in Society. An International Perspective.* Carol Stream: Mennonite World Conference, 1988, 17-32.

Miller, J. Virgil. *Both Sides of the Ocean.* Morgantown, Pa.: Masthof Press, 2002.

Mueller, Ernst. *Die Berner Täufer.* Frauenfeld: J.Huber, 1895.

Zürcher, Isaac. "Die Alttäufer im Fürstbistum Basel 1700-1890," in: *Mennonitica Helvetica* 15/16 (1994).

Periodicals

Mennonitica Helvetica (former *Informationsblätter*), ed. Schweiz. Verein für Täufergeschichte, 1977ff.

Perspektive / Perspective (former *"Zionspilger"*) 1882ff.

VI Mennonites in France

Baecher, Claude. *Bibliographie anabaptiste francophone* (cf. http://www.bienenberg. ch/biblioanab/index.html).

Fath, Sébastien. *Du ghetto au réseau : Le protestantisme évangélique en France (1800-2005).* Geneva : Labor & Fides, 2005.

Klopfenstein, Yves. *Attitudes mennonites face à la guerre: Histoire et analyse des prises de position concernant la non-résistance et l'objection de conscience en France. 1946-1962.* (Master's thesis) Faculté de Théologie Protestante de Strasbourg, 1992-1993.

Nussbaumer André / Wolff Michèle. *Histoire des Assemblées Mennonites françaises à la veille de l'an 2000.* Herborn: Sepher, 2003.

Seguy, Jean. *Les Assemblées Anabaptistes-Mennonites de France.* Paris : Mouton, 1977.

Servir la vie ! 50 ans d'action sociale (Commémoration des 50 ans de l'Association Fraternelle Mennonite). Collection « Les Dossiers de CHRIST SEUL », N° 2-3/2000, Editions Mennonites.

Sommer, Pierre. "The present situation of the French-speaking Mennonites," in: *Mennonite Quarterly Review,* October 1928, 268-274.

Widmer, Pierre. "From military service to Christian nonresistance," in: *Mennonite Quarterly Review,* October 1949, 246-256.

Periodicals

Christ Seul, 1907ff.

Les Cahiers de Christ Seul, 1980ff.

Les Dossiers de Christ Seul, 2000ff.

Souvenances Anabaptistes - Mennonitisches Gedächtnis, Bulletin Annuel de l'Association d'Histoire Anabaptiste-Mennonite, 1981ff.

VII Mennonites in Russia

Buchsweiler, Meir. *Volksdeutsche in der Ukraine am Vorabend und Beginn des Zweiten Weltkrieges. Ein Fall doppelter Loyalität?* Tel Aviv: Bleicher Verlag, 1984.

Diedrich, H.-C. and Stricker, G. (eds.). *Das Gute behaltet: Kirchen und religiöse Gemeinschaften in der Sowjetunion und ihre Nachfolgestaaten.* Erlangen: Martin Luther-Verlag, 1996.

Dietz, B. and Hilkes, P. *Rußlanddeutsche.* 2 Aufl., München: Olzog, 1992.

Dyck, Arnold. *Lost in the Steppe.* Steinbach, Man.: Derksen Printers, 1974.

Eisfeld, Alfred. *Die Deutschen in Russland – gestern,* in: Bernd G. Längin (Ed.). *Globus Spezial:Die Deutschen in der UdSSR – einst und jetzt.* Bonn: VDA, 1989, 38-57.

Enns, Adolf. "Mennonite Education in Russia," in: John Friesen. *Mennonites in Russia.* Altona: Friesen Printers, 1989, 75-98.

Epp, Frank H. *Mennonite Exodus.* Altona, Manitoba: D. W. Friesen and Sons, 1962.

Epp, George K. *Geschichte der Mennoniten in Russland,* vol. I. Lage: Logos Verlag, 1997.

Epp, George K. *Geschichte der Mennoniten in Rußland.* 3 Vol., Lage, 1997-2001.

Friesen, John. "Russia 1789-1850," in: John Friesen. *Mennonites in Russia,* 1989, 43-74.

Friesen, John (Ed.). *Mennonites in Russia : 1788 - 1988; Essays in honour of Gerhard Lohrenz.* Winnipeg, Man.: CMBC Publications, 1989.

Friesen, Peter M. *The Mennonite Brotherhood in Russia 1789-1910.* Fresno, Calif.: Board of Christian Literature, General Conference of M.B. Churches, 1980^2 (German Original: *Die Alt-Evangelische Mennonitische Bruderschaft in Russland 1789-1910.* Halbstadt, 1911).

Gerlach, Horst. *Die Russlandmennoniten.* Kirchheimbolanden: Selbstverlag, 1992.

Heinen, Ute. "Die Situation in der Gemeinschaft unabhängiger Staaten (GUS)," in: *Informationen zur politischen Bildung.* Bonn: Bundeszentrale f. pol. Bildung (Hrsg.), 2000.

Hildebrandt, Gerhard. "Das Bildungswesen der Mennoniten in Russland von der Zeit ihrer Einwanderung bis 1930," in: *2000 Jahre Mennoniten in Russland*, Bolanden- Weiherhof: Verlag des Mennonitischen Geschichtsvereins e.V., 2000, 47-69.

Hörmann, Artur. *Aber die Heimat winkte in der Ferne - Eine russlanddeutsche Trilogie*. Siegen: Im Selbstverlag der J.G. Herder-Bibliothek, 1999.

Kahle, Wilhelm. *Evangelische Christen in Russland und der Sowjetunion*. Wuppertal und Kassel: Oncken Verlag, 1978.

Kasdorf, Hans. *Gemeindewachstum als missionarisches Ziel*. Bad Liebenzell: Verlag der Liebenzeller Mission, 1976.

Klassen, Heinrich. *Mission als Auftrag. Zur missionarischen Existenz in der Sowjetunion nach dem Zweiten Weltkrieg*. Lage: Logos, 2001.

Klassen, John N. *Migrationen der Mennoniten. Beweggründe und Ziele der Wanderungen der Mennoniten von Preußen nach Russland und die heutige Aussiedlung zurück nach Deutschland*, in: *Freikirchen Forschung 1995*. Verein zur Förderung der Forschung freikirchlicher Geschichte und Theologie an der Universität Münster e.V. (Hg.). Münster: Selbstverlag des Herausgebers, 109-141.

Klassen, John N. *Church Planting and Church Growth Among Evangelical Russian German Christians in Germany in the Tension Between Immigration and Integration*. Pretoria, S.A.: Dissertation University of South Africa, 2003 (Unpublished).

Klassen, Peter P. *Die Mennoniten in Paraguay*. 2 Vol. Bolanden: Mennonitischer Geschichtsverein, 1988.

_____. *Die rußlanddeutschen Mennoniten in Brasilien*. Bolanden: Mennonitischer Geschichtsverein, 1995-1998.

Lachauer, Ulla. *Ritas Leute, Eine deutsch-russische Familiengeschichte*. Reinbek bei Hamburg: Rowohlt, 2002.

Legiehn, Hans. *Unser Glaube ist der Sieg: Biblische Glaubenslehre*. Borken: Atempause, 1995.

Loewen, Harry. "A House Divided: Russian Mennonite Nonresistance and Emigration in the 1870s," in Friesen, *Mennonites in Russia*, 127-140.

Löwen, Heinrich jun. *In Vergessenheit geratene Beziehungen*. Bielefeld: Logos, 1989.

Niessen, Hans von. "Die Mennonitische Umsiedlerbetreuung," in *Mennonitisches Jahrbuch 1996*. Lahr: St.- Johannis- Druckerei, 1996, 101-104.

Pinkus, Benjamin / Fleischhauer, Ingeborg. *Die Deutschen in der Sowjetunion. Geschichte einer nationalen Minderheit im 20. Jahrhundert.*Baden-Baden: Nomos, 1989.

Pritzkau, J. *Geschichte der Baptisten in Südrussland*. Lage: Logos, 1999.

Reimer, Al. *My Harp is Turned to Mourning*. Winnipeg, Manitoba: Hyperion Press, 1985.

Reimer, Johannes (Ed.). *Auf der Suche nach Identität*. 1. Aufl. Lage: Logos, 1996.

Sawatsky,Walter W. / Penner, Peter F. (eds). *Mission in the Former Soviet Union* Schwarzenfeld, Germany: Neufeld Verlag, 2006.

Sawatsky; Walter. *Soviet Evangelicals Since World War II*. Scottdale, PA: Herald Press, 1981.

Stumpp, Karl. *Die Auswanderung aus Deutschland nach Russland in den Jahren 1763 bis 1862*. 7. Aufl. Stuttgart: Landsmannschaft der Deutschen aus Russland, 1991.

Toews, J. B. *A Pilgrimage of Faith*. Winnipeg: Kindred Press, 1993.

Toews, John B. *Czars, Soviets, and Mennonites*. Newton, KS: Faith and Life Press, 1982.

Unruh, A. H. *Die Geschichte der Mennoniten- Brüdergemeinde*. Winnipeg: Christian Press, 1954.

Urry, James. *None But Saints*. Winnipeg: Hyperion Press, 1988. (German Translation: *Nur Heilige. Mennoniten in Russland, 1789-1889*. Steinbach, MB: Crossway, 2005.)

Wiebe, Rudy. *The Blue Mountains of China*. Toronto: McClelland and Stewart, 1970.

Wisotzki, Elisabeth. *Die Überlebensstrategien der rußlanddeutschen Mennoniten*. Unveröffentlichte Dissertation, Bonn 1992.

Wölk, Gerhard. "Wehrlos durch Christus," in: *Mennonitisches Jahrbuch 1988*. Karlsruhe: Heinrich Schneider Offset- und Buchdruck, 1988, 85-88.

VIII Mission Efforts in Europe

Blough, Neal. "The Anabaptist Vision and its Impact among French Mennonites," in: *Mennonite Quarterly Review*, July 1995, 369-388.

Brunk, Emily. *Espelkamp - The Mennonite Central Committee shares in community building in a new settlement for German refugees*. Karlsruhe: Mennonite Central Committee, 1951.

Charles, J. Robert. "North American Mennonite Agencies in Europe since World War II," in *Mission Focus*, September 1998, 48-51.

Dyck, Cornelius J. (ed.). *Responding to Worldwide Needs - The Mennonite Central Committee Story, Volume 2*. Scottdale, PA: Herald Press, 1980.

Gingerich, Melvin. "North American Mennonite Overseas Outreach in Perspective 1890-1966," in *Mennonite Quarterly Review*, October 1965, 262-279.

Hershberger, Guy Franklin. *The Mennonite Church in the Second World War*. Scottdale, PA: Herald Press, 1951.

Keim, Albert N. *Harold S. Bender 1897-1962*. Scottdale, PA: Herald Press, 1998.

Klassen, John. *The Mennonite Brethren Churches in Central Europe*. Unpublished paper, 1991.

Kreider, Alan and Murray, Stuart. *Coming Home. Stories of Anabaptists in Britain and Ireland*. Kitchener, ON: Pandora Press, 2000.

Kreider, Alan. "West Europe in Missional Perspective: Themes from Mennonite Mission 1950-2004," in J. R. Krabill, W. Sawatsky & C. E. Van Engen (eds.). *Evangelical, Ecumenical and Anabaptist Missiologies in Conversation*. Mary Knoll: Orbis Books, 2006.

Kreider, Robert S. and Goossen, Rachel Waltner. *Hungry, Thirsty, a Stranger. The MCC Experience*. Scottdale, PA: Herald Press, 1988.

Martens, Phyllis. *The Mustard Tree, The Story of Mennonite Brethren Mission*. Fresno CA: Mennonite Brethren Board of Christian Education in cooperation with Board Missions/Services, 1971.

Mennonite Central Committee. "Report of the Study and Co-ordinating Mission in Europe, July 29-August 14, 1950," in MCC Executive Committee minutes, October 6, 1950.

Miller, Ivan J. *History of the Conservative Mennonite Conference 1910-1985*. Grantsville, Maryland: Miller, 1985.

Paret, Michel. *L'Action sociale mennonite en France au XXᵉ siecle, approches diachronique et analytique*. Dissertation, 3 volumes. Paris: Ecole Pratique des Hautes Etudes, Vᵉ Section, November 1997.

Picone, F. / Ceraulo, T. / Ceraulo M. *New Awakenings in an Ancient Land*. Palermo Italy: Centro Agape, 1999.

Rathmair, Franz. *Die Mennoniten-Brüdergemeinden in Mitteleuropa*. Unpublished paper, 1991.

Shank, David A. "A Missionary Approach to a Dechristianized Society," in *Mennonite Quarterly Review*, January 1954, 39-55.

Toews, John A. *A History of the Mennonite Brethren Church: Pilgrims and Pioneers*, edited by A. J. Klassen. Fresno CA: General Conference of Mennonite Brethren Churches, 1975.

Unruh, John D. *In the Name of Christ. A History of the Mennonite Central Committee and Its Service 1920-1951*. Scottdale, PA: Herald Press, 1952.

Wenger, A. Grace. *History of Eastern Mennonite Board of Missions and Charities Work in Europe*. Unpublished manuscript, n.d.

Yoder, James. *European Project*. Sponsored by the Beachy Amish Churches of America. Sugar Creek OH: Schlabach Printers, 1982.

Index

Authors and Editors for *Europe: Testing Faith and Tradition*

Claude Baecher (1955), *Hégenheim, France*, academic dean of the French speaking department at the Bienenberg Theological Seminary in Liestal (Switzerland) and pastor of the French Mennonite congregation of La Ruche in St. Louis.

Neal Blough (1950), *Paris, France*, director of the Paris Mennonite Center, professor of church history at the "Faculté Libre de Theology Evangélique," member of the Châtenay-Malabry Mennonite congregation near Paris.

James Jakob Fehr (1958), *Monsheim, Germany*, pastor of the Mennonite congregations in Monsheim and Obersülzen and occasional lecturer in philosophy at the University of Mainz.

Alle G. Hoekema (1941), *Haarlem, Netherlands*, missionary in Indonesia (1969-1977), pastor in Alkmaar and Haarlem, and since 1989 lecturer at the Mennonite Seminary (missiology and practical theology); now part time assistant professor at the Vrije Universiteit, Amsterdam.

Hanspeter Jecker (1954), *Muttenz, Switzerland*, teaching assignment with MCC in Congo (1980-1982), professor of church history at the Bienenberg Theological Seminary in Liestal (Switzerland), president of the "Schweizerischer Verein für Täufergeschichte."

John N. Klassen (1929), *Meckenheim, Germany*, former pastor in three Mennonite Brethren Churches in Germany; since 1987 teacher of ministry at the "Freie Hochschule für Mission," the "Bibelseminar Bonn" and in various churches.

John A. Lapp (1933), *Akron, Pennsylvania*, Executive Secretary Emeritus, Mennonite Central Committee; former professor of history and Dean, Goshen College, and coordinator of the Global Mennonite History Project for Mennonite World Conference.

Diether Götz Lichdi (1935), *Heilbronn, Germany*, businessman, pastor of the Mennonite congregation Stuttgart, editor of the *Mennonitisches Jahrbuch* from 1982 to 2003, editor of the *Mennonite World Handbook*, 1990.

C. Arnold Snyder (1946), *Kitchener, Ontario*, professor of history, Conrad Grebel University College, Waterloo, Ontario (Canada); managing editor, Pandora Press, general editor of the Global Mennonite History project.

Ed van Straten (1931), *Leidschendam, Netherlands*, former teacher at the Mennonite theological Seminary in Pati, Indonesia and former Executive Secretary of the Algemene Doopsgezinde Societeit (ADS); he has volunteered for Mennonite World Conference in various capacities.

Annelies Verbeek (1972), *Haarlem, Netherlands*, pastor of the Mennonite congregation of Haarlem, member of the editorial Board of *Doopsgezinde Bijdragen*.